D0064793

CUSTOM AND GOVERNMENT
IN THE
LOWER CONGO

Custom and Government in the Lower Congo

Wyatt MacGaffey

UNIVERSITY OF CALIFORNIA PRESS

BERKELEY, LOS ANGELES, LONDON

1970

University of California Press
Berkeley and Los Angeles, California
University of California Press, Ltd.
London, England
© 1970 by The Regents of the University of California
ISBN: 0-520-01614-9
Library of Congress Catalog Card Number: 70-85451
Printed in the United States of America

To the memory of
HENRY RICHARDS
ngwankazi

PREFACE

In the spring of 1969 I attended an African Studies conference in Philadelphia; on the napkins provided at lunch during the conference was printed a map of Africa, and among the few place-names that could be included in so small a map was that of Mbanza Manteke, a village in the Lower Congo. The map is a curious example of a cultural survival, a relic of the 1890's when Mbanza Manteke was famous to thousands of Americans and Britons interested in West Africa. Since then attention has moved elsewhere, and now Mbanza Manteke shares the common obscurity of innumerable African villages.

I lived in Mbanza Manteke throughout 1965 and made two return visits in 1966. From January to July 1966 I lived in Kasangulu, a town southwest of Kinshasa from which Kasangulu Territory takes its name. Throughout this period, and during two months preceding it in 1964, I visited other parts of the province of Kongo Central. Most of my travels were confined to the part of the province which lies north of the railroad and south of the Congo River, an area roughly corresponding to the south-bank extension of the Nsundi Province of the former kingdom of Kongo. I also, however, visited Manianga and Mayombe.

In Manteke I made a detailed study of the village, visiting other villages of the commune as opportunity allowed. A brief account of methods is given in my article "Field Research in Kongo Central" (1966a). I had received instruction in KiKongo before I left the United States, and my research was conducted almost entirely in that language from February 1965 onward, except in dealings with those town dwellers, particularly government officials, who consider it beneath their dignity to speak their own language and insist on being addressed in French.

My stay in Kasangulu was intended to give me new perspectives on Mbanza Manteke, arising from the contrasts between urban and rural life, Catholic and Protestant predominance, proximity to the metropolis of Kinshasa and relative isolation. Although I did not make a community study of Kasangulu, I used it as a base from which to visit

vii

Lemfu villages and Kinshasa. In Kasangulu itself I attended weddings, funerals, and parties, and frequented churches and territorial government headquarters. The population includes not only BaNtandu, BaLemfu, and BaHumbu (from the outskirts of Kinshasa), but representatives of most areas of Kongo Central. In this respect it is typical of the towns the length of the railroad. Most of my near neighbors and associates, as it happened, were natives of Luozi Territory (*bisi Manianga*). The most striking difference between Manteke and Kasangulu has to do with the supernatural. In Kasangulu Territory, whether in town or village, the more exotic side of custom frequently meets the eye: leaders wear insignia of office, witchcraft is mentioned more frequently in conversation, charms abound, and there are healers, diviners, and priests of curious religions. The heterogeneity of the population may partly explain this condition; Kasangulu people, moreover, are wealthier than those of Manteke, and can better afford the services of specialists.

The methods used at Kasangulu and in my travels elsewhere would have been virtually useless for the study of social structure had it not been for the intensive work done at Mbanza Manteke. The kind of information to be gathered in the course of continuous residence from participant observation, combined with a population register, genealogical analysis, and multiple cross-checking of statements and observations, is quite different from information obtained from the best-qualified and best-intentioned informants or from casual observation. For this reason, there are certain differences between the findings reported here and those reported by some other observers.

I went to Kongo to study the present position of "customary law," the term used in Belgian literature on Congo to refer to much of what anthropologists call social structure. I was particularly interested in the relation between indigenous or traditional forms and processes of government and those that might have evolved during the colonial regime and since national independence in 1960. I wanted to discover the nature and the function of custom, to which a specific role had been assigned by *la politique indigène*, particularly after the innovations of 1920; the extensive ethnography for the area is deficient and ambiguous in this regard. In Congo I continued to say that what interested me was customary law, or *la coutume*, because this is a respectable and relatively innocuous thing to be interested in.

Much of the ethnography of the area is written in terms of the anthropological concepts of the 1920's, according to which matrilineal organization, for example, tends to be referred to a pure type called *le matriarcat*. Domont (1957) provides a crudely explicit example of this technique, whereby observed facts in conflict with the matriarchal model are treated as anomalies. From time to time in this study I find it necessary to refer to some of these outdated concepts and show their inadequacy. From the point of view of anthropological theory, this procedure is unnecessary, and may seem ungracious; there is no point, as an African friend once remarked, in flogging a dead ancestor. The inadequacy of the pure matrilineal model as applied to the BaKongo, whose principal corporations are matrilineal descent groups but whose social relations employ other organizational principles besides matriliny, has been pointed out by A. I. Richards (1950), and would be taken for granted by any modern anthropologist. My researches soon revealed, however, that published accounts of Kongo society have become a cultural influence in their own right.

In addition to what may be called the enthnographic model of Kongo society, which has been conditioned by the work of Wilhelm Schmidt, but also by that of Maine, Durkheim, and others, and which has modified the notion of themselves entertained by the Kongo elite, there is also a folk model, not entirely dissimilar to the first. The common features of the two concern, in particular, the institution of chiefship. In brief, the BaKongo are said to have, or to have had, chiefs, and chiefship is everywhere said to be closely bound up with customary law. Yet references to chiefship always describe it as it used to exist in the ill-documented past, with the assertion, common to ethnographers and to the folk, that custom, as it exists now when there are no chiefs, is in some way degenerate. The anthropologist, confronted by uncertainty regarding the time and place of so important an institution as chiefship is held to be, at once suspects he is dealing with a myth; at least, there is a mystery to inquire into.

This study is intended to do several things. First, it is a description of the social organization of Mbanza Manteke. As far as possible, material on the organization of the household and on marriage has been omitted. Manteke was chosen, almost at random, as a village that was the seat both of a traditional chiefship (as I was told) and of a modern communal government, located in a region both geographically and historically central to the BaKongo which had not been the subject of any serious ethnographic inquiry. Second, the study is a kind of extended test of *la coutume*, the received idea of traditional government, whether in the ethnographic or in the folk version, and an account of the relations between the rural society and the national administration, from the beginning of colonial rule to the present. I refer as extensively as possible to material from other villages in the region, and from other regions in the province; some of it is my own, some comes from published ethnography. I also use court records to give broader coverage and historical depth. The present tense, as used here, refers to the period of research, November 1964 to July 1966.

To present the material I use the method of the case study, hoping thus to allow the data to speak for themselves. Such a hope is of course illusory, since the mere order in which the data are presented depends upon a selection made by the observer. Yet here the method may serve the related purpose of showing how structure emerges from process, and what the relation is between process and various structures or models, contradictory in themselves, which refer to it. The work is organized in three parts, as follows. The first section deals with the units of analysis, that is, with the corporate groups found in Mbanza Manteke, and with the ideology that bears upon them. The second section dwells on characteristic processes, to show how the corporate groups are defined and related in practice. The third considers the relations between custom thus analyzed and government, including chiefship. As in any case study, however, material cited at any point may be relevant to issues discussed before and after it. The reader is therefore warned that the three parts are not mutually exclusive.

The following conventions have been adopted. All names of descent groups are written in capitals: the clan NSUNDI, the house KYANGALA NA NSUNDI. To reduce the number of names, and to keep my informants anonymous, I refer to an individual who may be quoted by the name of his descent group, written in capitals, whenever he is speaking representatively and when no inconvenience results. This convention is consistent with local practice; a speaker refers to himself, in appropriate context, as "mono, NSUNDI." The use of KiKongo terms has been kept to a minimum, despite the distortions created by English substitutes. Two terms only have been retained in the vernacular form: *nkazi*, meaning representative head of a descent group; *mbungu*, referring to a formal communication or presentation.

I am grateful to the Foreign Area Fellowship Program for supporting my field research, and to Haverford College for a grant toward the cost of preparing the manuscript. Neither of these bodies is responsible for any statements made or any views expressed in this study.

In writing the book I have done little more than coordinate the efforts of a large number of generous and hardworking people, to all of whom I express my thanks. Among them are Professor William E. Welmers and M. Noé Diawaku, who made it possible for me to learn KiKongo; the personnel of the American Baptist Foreign Missionary Society, especially Dr. and Mrs. Charles Stuart, who provided valued friendship, welcome hospitality, and indispensable logistical support; Mr. and Mrs. A. G. MacArthur, whose home became our home on our visits to Kinshasa; Professor Benoît Verhaegen and M. Laurent Monnier, who made available the resources of the Institut de Recherches Economiques et Sociales at Lovanium University and their own wide knowledge of Congolese affairs; Dr. John M. Janzen, a congenial colleague whose work on the north bank of the Congo complements mine and whose close cooperation has been a great advantage to me; Professor M. G. Smith, who deserves the credit for any analytical merit discernible in this study; and Janet, Neil, Andrew, and Margret, who have had to put up with many trials.

The people of Mbanza Manteke regarded with polite and friendly tolerance my endeavors to find out about matters that they had good reason to keep obscure. My wife and I remember them and our neighbors of Rue Baudouin, Kasangulu, with great affection, and feel privileged to have been welcomed among them.

The elders of Mbanza Manteke frequently suggest that so great a man as Henry Richards, "the first white man," deserves a permanent memorial; their respect for him is unbounded, and to this day he is the only man to whom they refer as *ngwankazi*, "uncle," without any additional epithet. They feel that his Children and Grandchildren should put up a stone or bronze bust of Richards to replace the photograph that hangs in the church and is already damaged by mold. I am only partly sympathetic to the missionary enterprise, and my research shows that many of the profound changes wrought in Manteke by Richards and his successors were not intended or even understood by them. My respect for Richards is based not so much on what he did as on what he was; like many of the pioneer missionaries in Congo he was a man of profound religious faith, great courage, and remarkable physical endurance. His colleagues found that he was a stubborn individualist, sensitive to slights and often difficult to work with; his flock in Manteke adored him. Among the many stories told about Richards is one that describes his indecision over the verse "Give to everyone that asketh thee" when he was translating the Gospel according to Luke into KiKongo. After hesitating for a fortnight over the possible consequences, he translated the verse literally and taught it to the people. When they heard the text, the villagers began to help themselves to Richards' belongings, but when they found that he abided by his preaching they brought back all they had taken.

Henry Richards was born in 1851 in the county of Somerset in the West of England, and was brought up, I believe, in Bridgwater. As a young man he joined a fundamentalist sect with headquarters in South

Wales. He was sent out to Congo by the Livingstone Inland Mission in 1879. Subsequently the station he founded at Mbanza Manteke was taken over by the American Baptist Foreign Missionary Society, and when Richards retired in 1919 he went to live in the United States with his wife and his two daughters. He died in 1928, and was buried in Hyattsville, Maryland.

Haverford College   W. M.
22 September 1969

CONTENTS

Part III: CHIEFSHIP

MAPS

FIGURES

1

INTRODUCTION: MANTEKE IN KONGO

We went back about ten miles from the river
to a place called Banza Manteke,
and as there were a number of villages about
and the people looked rather friendly, I thought it a good place
to establish a station.
—HENRY RICHARDS

The port of Matadi, the Congo's chief commercial link with the Atlantic and the rest of the world, is full of people from Mbanza Manteke. They work on the ships, on the docks, and in the customs offices. Among them are career bureaucrats — courteous, gray-haired, responsible men — as well as truck drivers, cabin boys, watchmen, machinists, clerks. In the town there are also civil servants, barkeepers, cashiers, schoolteachers, prostitutes. Many of these people have not been back to Manteke for years.

From Matadi to Kinshasa, the national capital, goods and people travel by rail, or by the highway that parallels the railroad. About an hour and a half to the east is the railroad station of Lufu, from which another road, unmetaled, runs north for 52 kilometers through a long shallow valley to Kinganga, a small trading center on the Congo River. This valley is the region of Manteke, known to the administration as the rural commune of the BaMboma (see map 1).

Upon leaving Lufu one passes through a large sisal plantation with headquarters at Kitomesa. This plantation is the only substantial commercial operation in the region; most of its workers are Angolan refugees. The road from Lufu is treacherously greasy during the rains, bumpy and dusty in the dry season. It takes an uncomfortable three-quarters of an hour to reach the mission of the American Baptist Foreign Missionary Society (ABFMS) at Nsona Mpangu, whose schools have helped to channel Manteke men into office jobs from Matadi to

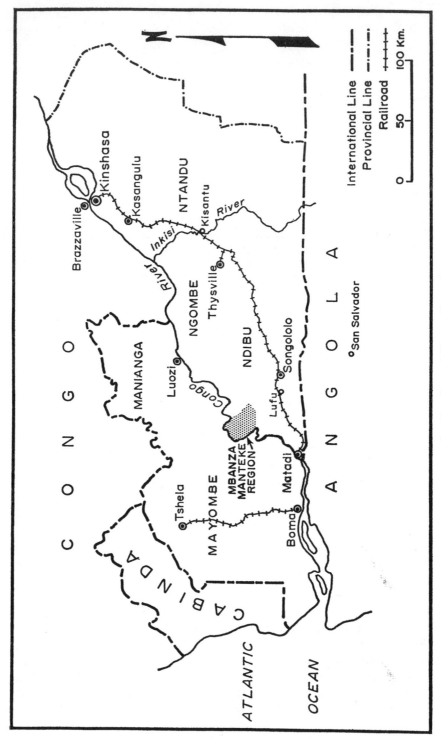

MAP 1. Province of Kongo Central

Kinshasa. Farther up the valley, at Konzo, is a Catholic teachers' college. It is a relatively recent establishment; Manteke has always been Protestant. At Kinganga the river can be crossed in a canoe, sometimes in a motorboat. This settlement used to be a busy place, but the Portuguese who ran it have left since 1960.

All these places in the valley — Kitomesa, Nsona Mpangu, Konzo, Kinganga — are known locally as "company villages," foreign in origin, purpose, and organization. Indigenous villages are found mostly in the hills, where in precolonial times they were safer from attack, or near the river, where the money to be made nowadays from fishing compensates for the isolation. The most important villages lie along the ridge that bounds the valley on the west: Ndemba, Mbanza Manteke, Mbanza Nkazi, Kinkanza. At this height, about 1,500 feet, the air is cooler than in the valley, and there are fewer mosquitoes. On a clear day there is a splendid view of the vast, mountainous, and almost empty landscape (see map 2).

In the thirteenth or fourteenth century Ntinu Wene came through this region from across the Congo River. Tradition says he built his first settlement here before going on to found Mbanza Kongo, the capital of the kingdom of Kongo which stretched from Kinshasa to the sea.[1] Manteke, in those days called Mpemba Nkazi, was subsequently incorporated into the Nsundi Province of the kingdom, whose capital lay far to the northeast and whose governor ruled on both sides of the river. In 1485 the Portuguese sailor Diogo Cão brought the first Europeans to Kongo; in 1491 the king and most of the nobility were baptized as Christians by Portuguese missionaries. The Portuguese alliance at first strengthened the king against insubordinate subjects, but it also introduced traffic in slaves. By the beginning of the seventeenth century, according to Vansina's analysis, the slave trade and related conditions had transformed the organization of Kongo from a kingdom to a scattering of small chiefdoms. In the eighteenth century each chiefdom comprised a capital (*mbanza*) of some two hundred huts and a few villages of about fifty huts each.[2]

Missionaries continued to come sporadically to Kongo, where some of them traveled widely. Among those who have left accounts of their journeyings is Father Jérôme de Montesarchio, who around 1650 twice visited Mpemba Nkazi. There he found (probably at Mbanza Nkazi) a

[1] Cuvelier, 1946, chap. 1; Vansina, 1966, chap. 2. Mbanza Kongo is now San Salvador in Angola.

[2] Vansina, 1966, p. 194. *Vata* (pl., *ma-*), "village," refers to any settlement, including Kinshasa. It also has the sense of "hometown." *Mbanza* means a seat of government and also refers to the ancestral cemetery.

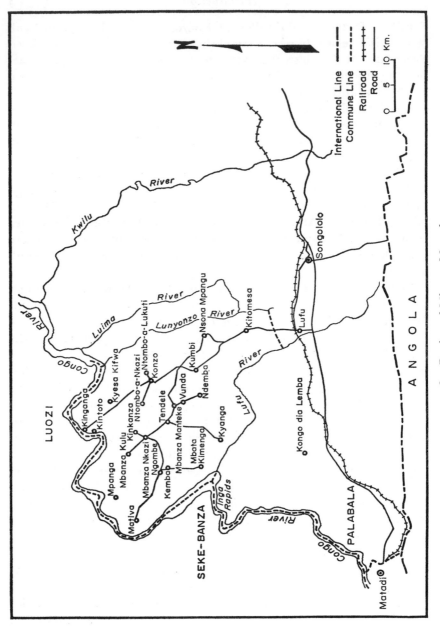

MAP 2. Region of Mbanza Manteke

female chief "having authority over several villages and bearing the title 'Mother of the King of Kongo,' " (De Bouveignes and Cuvelier, 1951, pp. 70–71). The only place Father Jérôme names is Lukuti, which exists today as Ntombo a Lukuti, on a new site not far from the old. In the 1950's the head of this village gave the land for the college at Konzo.

The next European visitor of record was Henry Richards of the Livingstone Inland Mission. Its first station had been established at Palabala, on the mountain just east of Matadi, in 1878, and in 1879 Richards arrived in Manteke to found the second station. In 1884 the mission ceded these and other stations to the ABFMS. H. M. Stanley, who had passed by on the north bank on his way to the coast from the interior of Africa, did not visit Manteke until this same year, 1884, and so is known locally merely as "the second white man."

Richards built himself a wattle-and-daub house on a piece of land called Nkondo, across a muddy stream bed from the hamlet of Mbanza Suki. So plentiful was the mud Richards had to cross to get to the hamlet that he named it Mbanza Manteke, "Mudville." At first his teachings had little effect on his neighbors, and it was a struggle merely to stay alive. "It is difficult to discover the religious notions of the people," he wrote. "They are very superstitious and wicked. . . . They will steal from anybody, and cheat anybody, and they have not the slightest idea that lying or deceiving is wrong." In 1885, however, he won his first converts, and the following year came a sudden mass conversion of the populace, the first Protestant success in the country, known as "the Pentecost of the Congo." "Banza Manteka," reported Richards to the *Baptist Missionary Magazine* of Boston, "is no longer a heathen country."

By this time the people from nearby villages and hamlets had begun to settle on the top of a hill, the present site of Mbanza Manteke, where in the course of the next twenty-five years the mission operated schools, a large hospital, and a printing press. Manteke children went to school and learned to read and write in KiKongo; they also picked up a good deal of English, some of which has remained in the vocabulary. Other BaKongo say *mbumba*, meaning "cat," but "in the real old KiManteke that our elders spoke, it is *puusi*." [3] Most of the men who are now elders worked in mission households as boys. They learned carpentry, tailoring, and nursing. On Sundays the church was full to overflowing. In the 1920's, when the space available was no longer

---

[3] Personal class prefixes: sing., *mu-* or *n'-*; pl., *ba-*. Items of associated culture, such as language, take the *ki-* prefix, pl., *bi-*; e.g., KiManteke, the language spoken in Manteke.

sufficient, the mission began to move to its present site in the valley, at Nsona Mpangu.

In 1882–83 Stanley's agents opened a government caravan route extending from Matadi toward Kinshasa, supplementing the north-bank route opened some time before. Establishing the route meant concluding agreements with local chiefs, building government rest houses, and arranging with the chiefs to recruit porters. Passing through Palabala, Kongo dya Lemba, Manteke (Ndembolo), and Ntombo a Lukuti, the new route followed an old one that linked the interior with the coast for the export of ivory, peanuts, and other products. In 1887 porters carried 60,000 loads from Matadi to Stanley Pool by this route. In 1898 "la mise en service du chemin de fer mettait fin à la plaie du portage dans la région des Cataractes où sa persistance n'eût pas manqué de provoquer un véritable désastre social" (Devroey and Vanderlinden, 1938, p. 180).

The makeshift policy of local administration followed by Stanley and the Congo Free State gave way, after 1908, to the progressively better-integrated *politique indigène* of the Belgian Congo. By the decree of 10 May 1910 the native population was divided into chiefdoms whose boundaries were established by the government in conformity with "custom." By this time Mboko of Mbanza Suki in Manteke, Lutete Mbonzo of Mbanza Nkazi, and another elder in Ngombe, a village to the west, had been given insignia of office and certain responsibilities, mostly regarding the provision of porters. On the basis of these assignments, an area corresponding approximately to the modern commune of the BaMboma was organized into two chiefdoms, Mbanza Manteke and Mbanza Nkazi, and a subchiefdom, Ngombe. Investigation of the relations between these government-sanctioned chiefs and customary or traditional social organization is one of the principal themes of this study.

The decree of 1910 was an attempt to correct evils resulting from the badly organized and poorly supervised recruitment of forced labor and to check the prevalent epidemics of sleeping sickness and other diseases. A number of reforms instituted in 1920 embodied a more positive policy of local development based on indirect rule. This policy enjoined an inquiry into the structure of traditional society in order to identify those whom the natives regarded as chiefs, because the colonial government wanted to make the best use of existing institutions.

Experience showed, however, that customary institutions often failed to serve the government's needs adequately. In 1933 new legislation on native areas (*les circonscriptions indigènes*) prescribed that chiefdoms too small to be administratively self-sufficient might be grouped into sectors, each headed by an official appointed by the government after consultation with the people. This change took effect in Manteke in 1944, when a man from the village of Mbanza Manteke became chief of a sector comprising the three former chiefdoms. The chiefdoms retained a ghostly existence as *groupements*, to which certain administrative functions were delegated.

Until that time Mbanza Manteke and Mbanza Nkazi had had their own courts, instituted by the government, presided over by the chief, and keeping written records. Afterward, they were replaced by a single sector court (*tribunal de secteur*), organized in much the same way. The courts dealt with cases under customary law and with offenses against the chief's ordinances within the field of responsibility allocated to him by the government, such as matters of public order, public hygiene, and compulsory cultivation instructions. Appeal was possible to the territorial court, associated with territorial headquarters, the lowest level of the administrative service. In 1958 the territorial headquarters, having been situated in different towns at different periods, was established in Songololo, some 15 kilometers east of Lufu.

The governmental structure based on the 1933 legislation, though transformed in name, maintained much the same form and functions under legislation enacted in 1957, in 1959, and after independence. The sector is now called a commune, and it has a mayor at its head. The territories (*arrondissements*[4]) are subdivisions of the Province of Kongo Central, created in 1962 (Monnier, 1964).

Songololo Territory has the lowest population density in Kongo Central, except for the plateau region south of Kinshasa. In 1958, the last year for which reliable estimates are available, the figure was 5.65 per square kilometer, including the population of such small towns as Lufu and Songololo, while the average rural density in the whole province was 14.71 (De Smet, 1966, p. 10). The relatively low density in Songololo Territory is apparently related to its lack of economic opportunities; the Manteke region, officially described as arid and rocky, has attracted little commercial investment. Population density (based on figures for 1958) is 6.68 in the commune of the BaMboma, and 4.65 in the *groupement* of Manteke.

The territory is broken up by a series of parallel ridges running roughly northwest–southeast. In one of the valleys formed by the ridges flows the Lufu River, which forms part of the southern boundary of the commune. To the east, the next sizable stream is the Lunyonzo,

---

[4] The word "territory," though not entirely equivalent, is used as the English translation of *arrondissement*.

which forms the northeast boundary. (Until a few years ago, the Luima River formed the commune boundary, but the inhabitants of this eastern segment decided to join the adjacent commune.) To the north and west the boundary is the Congo.

The climate of the area is tropical, with a hot, rainy season extending from mid-October to mid-May, broken for several weeks in February. The dry season is somewhat cooler, the sky being overcast much of the time. Temperatures also vary considerably with altitude. The vegetation is savannah grassland with gallery forests along stream beds; forests of somewhat different composition, located on hilltops, mark the sites of former villages.

The modern commune of the BaMboma comprises, according to the official census for 1965, thirty-one villages ranging in size from Kinkanza (population 840) to Masonso (population 25). These figures do not include the company villages mentioned above, nor the 1,108 Angolan refugees. The total indigenous population in 1965 was 9,111, distributed by age and sex as follows: adult men (over 18), 1,724; adult women, 2,519; boys, 2,597; girls, 2,271. The excess of women and of older people results from an urban drift which caused the colonial government much concern and has accelerated since independence. It has been estimated that the population of such towns as Thysville and Matadi has tripled since 1960. For BaMboma the census showed a drop of 879 from 1960 to 1961. It is mainly the working-age population that has left.

The indigenous population of the village of Mbanza Manteke in 1965 was 582, distributed as follows: adult men, 95; adult women, 170; boys, 137; girls, 180.[5] (There were also 46 Angolans.) The total of 265 adults includes two groups of households whose members live there only because of the men's employment: the teachers at the primary school and the personnel of the communal government — the mayor, clerks, policemen, and others. Also counted in the population are a dozen households of people who, though registered as inhabitants of Manteke, actually live in little hamlets and scattered houses out in the bush. Excluding these three categories, I found 164 adults normally resident in the village itself, 60 of whom were men. It is with this group,

[5] Population totals, indigenous (given first) and Angolan, in selected other villages are as follows:

Kyanga	271	55	Mbanza Nkazi	670	0
Vunda	236	44	Kinkanza	840	0
Ndemba	511	209	Tendele	286	111
Ntombo a Lukuti	159	18	Kyesa Kifwa	136	0
Ngombe	502	0	Ntombo a Nkazi	109	7

Not all the separate villages in existence are recognized by the government.

and in particular with some 25 of the men who may be regarded as elders (*mbuta*; pl., *ba-*), that this study is chiefly concerned.

The people may be described as peasants, in the sense of Kroeber's definition (1948, p. 284). They cultivate the soil with hand tools, and consume most of the produce — manioc, beans, peanuts — themselves. A little food is sold; rather more brings in cash indirectly by being given to relatives in town. Through relatives or from merchants the villagers obtain such goods as salt, certain kinds of dried fish, housewares, tools, cloth, and clothes. There is a good deal of visiting back and forth between Manteke and the towns, by both men and women, which helps to ease economic stresses for the inhabitants of both communities.[6] The difference between village and town is indicated by the price of bananas: in Manteke, 5 francs buys ten bananas; in Kinshasa, one. In Manteke, 100 francs a day would be regarded as a good wage for semiskilled work, but hardly anyone is employed at wage labor; some Angolan refugees work by the day, earning 35–45 francs for a full day of five or six hours clearing bush or hoeing. In Kinshasa semiskilled workers may earn more than 3,500 francs a month.

In addition to income realized from produce, the men make money by engaging locally in part-time specialties. One cuts and binds thatching materials; another grows sugarcane from which, in partnership with another, he makes a liquor (*lungwila*) for local consumption. A third buys kerosene by the bottle, and profits by selling it in small quantities when the stores are closed. A fourth owns an extra house he rents out at 40 francs a month to a policeman. The most important source of extra cash, however, is pensions, payable to the older men who have worked for the missions, for the transportation concern OTRACO, or as sailors out of Matadi. A pension of 200 francs or so per month makes the difference between poverty and a decent though not affluent subsistence.

The village population, therefore, is not simply a residue of rustics left behind when everyone else moved to town. Most of the men have lived and worked in town for varying periods of times, and at least four of them have visited Europe. Some of the women also know Matadi, Kinshasa, and other towns. Although perhaps half a dozen men are completely illiterate, most male villagers can read and write, after a fashion, in both French and KiKongo. On the other hand, nobody speaks French fluently. Most of the women were taught to read at one time, but only a minority are literate now. An occasional newspaper

6 In 1965 the official exchange rates were 150 and 180 francs to the dollar. The unofficial rate, corresponding fairly accurately to the prices of manufactured goods in the shops, rose during the year from about 300 to about 450 francs to the dollar.

reaches the village, and there are several transistor and other radios; when the latest American satellite passed overhead, the village boys knew about it.

Mbanza Manteke is approached by a dirt road extending for some 15 kilometers from its junction with the Lufu–Kinganga road. As the road reaches the top of the ridge it enters the government compound, which contains houses for official personnel. On the right are the remains of the old mission, now occupied by the school, consisting of several decaying plank houses raised on steel legs. The main street stretches toward Vunda on the left. The houses rising from the bare clay range from the poorest, which have wooden frames, reed or wattle-and-daub walls, and thatched roofs, to those built of locally made burned bricks and roofed with corrugated iron. The best houses are plastered and painted and have glass windows and mosquito screens. Under a government mortgage plan a small estate with this type of house was built behind the government compound and next to the mission in the late 1950's. Generally speaking, there are no fences around the houses and, except for the irregular streets, no obvious signs of social organization. Most houses have a kitchen in a separate building, and all are required by law to have latrines, usually located at the edge of the surrounding forest. Chickens, innumerable dogs, and occasional goats and sheep roam about. The only public buildings, besides those of the government and the school, are the Protestant and Kimbanguist churches.[7] There is nothing very exotic in the dress and behavior of the people to catch the visitor's eye.

THE ETHNOGRAPHIC SETTING

The people of the commune of the BaMboma call themselves *bisi Manteke,* even if they come from a village other than Mbanza Manteke.[8] They accept, but rarely use, the designation "BaMboma," which they suggest may have been given them by people living farther east, to whom *bisi Manteke* and all the inhabitants of Palabala, the neighboring commune to the southwest, were "those who live down toward (M)Boma." Boma is a commercial and administrative center much older than Matadi, and formerly of greater importance. As is shown

[7] The Protestant congregation is Baptist, affiliated with the American Baptist Foreign Mission Society. The Kimbanguists belong to the Eglise de Jésus Christ sur la Terre par le Prophète Simon Kimbangu, an indigenous church similar to the Baptist church in organization and forms of worship (Raymaekers, 1959). No other churches or sects are formally organized in Mbanza Manteke, but there are a few individual Catholics.

[8] *Bisi* or *'esi,* sing., *mwisi,* means people of a particular place or group. *Esi* kiNSUNDI means members of the NSUNDI clan.

later, some Manteke clans trace their origin to migrations from the direction of Boma. The principal cultural feature identifying Manteke with Boma is the Nkimba initiation cult (so-called secret society), which flourished on the north bank of the Congo River and reached its most easterly extension in the vicinity of Manteke (Bittremieux, 1936). This cult disappeared from Manteke at the end of the nineteenth century.

It is possible that the Mboma cultural zone owed its identity to a relationship with the Soyo Province of the former kingdom, or to some other political factor of the same period, but in general the divisions of the kingdom provide no guide to modern cultural divisions.[9] In any event, Manteke belonged to the Nsundi Province, as already indicated. The events of the nineteenth century, particularly the slave trade, the commercial orientation toward European factories on the coast, and the building of the railroad, seem to predominate in the background of the present situation (Ngoma, 1963, p. 18; Monnier, 1964, pp. 213–219). More recently, cultural identifications have tended to conform to the administrative boundaries established in the past forty-five years.

Except for some BaTeke and a few others on the eastern margin, the inhabitants of Kongo Central, numbering nearly a million on the eve of independence, are all BaKongo.[10] Other Bakongo inhabit the adjacent countries of Congo (Brazzaville) to the north and Angola to the south; hence the name, Kongo Central. Throughout this area KiKongo is spoken, although the dialects vary widely; some of them are hardly intelligible to the speakers of others. There is a corresponding institutional community, although formal variations sometimes disguise it. This community extends even beyond the frontiers of the former kingdom, so that striking parallels exist between Manteke, for example, and Loango, which lies to the north on the Atlantic Coast (Dennett, 1906).

Ethnographers distinguish several ethnic groups within the population of Mayombe, the western portion of the province, but from the point of view of Manteke residents the people across the Congo River to the west are all BaYombe.[11] To the east, across the Luima River, are

9 This point deserves some emphasis, since ethnography frequently implies that the former provinces persist in some way; sometimes ancient and modern units appear on the same map.

10 Other people refer to them by this name, but mostly they call themselves *bisi Kongo*. Again, ethnography can be confusing. Minor cultural variations, and the particular experiences of individual authors, have produced what appear to be separate "tribes," e.g., Yombe, Kongo, Nsundi.

11 The principal ethnographic studies of Mayombe are Bittremieux, 1920, 1922–1927, 1934, 1936; Van Reeth, 1935; Doutreloux, 1967; De Cleene, 1935, 1936, 1937a, b.

the BaNdibu. This supposed boundary between the two peoples was in fact the boundary of the Manteke chiefdom as drawn by the colonial government; there is no corresponding cultural or social discontinuity, but in Mbanza Manteke people are positive that they are BaMboma and not BaNdibu.

The BaNdibu are conventionally separated from their neighbors to the east, the BaNtandu ("easterners"), by the Inkisi River. At the principal crossing is the large Catholic mission complex of Kisantu, which with the neighboring center of Kintanu constitutes "the cultural and commercial nucleus of the BaNtandu" (Monnier, 1964, p. 219 and map). From the Manteke point of view, the inhabitants of both territories, Madimba and Kasangulu, which lie between the Inkisi River and Kinshasa, are all BaNtandu. Kasangulu Territory, however, is inhabited chiefly by people who call themselves BaLemfu. Both BaLemfu and BaNtandu are heterogeneous groups, and many subgroups such as the BaMbinza and BaMbata can be distinguished among them (see introduction to J. Mertens, 1942), though the criteria for discrimination are obscure and inconsistent. The tendency now is to identify the BaLemfu and the inhabitants of Kasangulu Territory, the BaNtandu (in the strict sense), with those of Madimba.[12] Both groups are heavily Catholic, despite the long-established presence of an ABFMS mission between the two at Nsona Mbata.

In the Ndibu area a plateau (*bangu*) north and east of Kimpese partly isolates a region called Ngombe, historically dominated by the station of the British Baptist Missionary Society (BMS) at Ngombe Lutete. This area is now best known as the birthplace and stronghold of the Eglise de Jésus Christ sur la Terre par le Prophète Simon Kimbangu. In the southwestern part of the region are those who, denying they belong to Ngombe, call their area the Bangu. The division, which has received administrative recognition, seems to be related to a zone-of-influence agreement between the BMS at Ngombe Lutete and the ABFMS at Mbanza Manteke.

This plateau region, however, is subject to another classification, according to which the northern or riverine part of it, including Ngombe Lutete, belongs to Manianga. Ngombe Lutete is situated on the ancient trade route connecting Palabala and Kinshasa. Just to the west is an

[12] During 1964 the former territories of Kasangulu and Madimba were divided to create the new territories of Bombo, comprising the Teke plateau south of Kinshasa, and Haute-Inkisi, comprising the southern half of the original Madimba Territory. My discussion refers to Kasangulu and Madimba territories as they existed in 1965. There are no texts dealing specifically with the BaLemfu; the east in general has been well covered by Van Wing (1959) and J. Mertens (1942). The BaNtandu described by Van Wing called themselves BaMpangu.

area in which several such routes intersected, some of them leading across the river to the north, and in it a number of very large markets flourished in precolonial times. At the turn of the century this area, on both sides of the river, was called Manianga. Since then the term "Manianga" has tended to become identified with Luozi Territory, which occupies all of Kongo Central lying north of the river and east of Mayombe.[13]

To *bisi Manteke*, Manianga means a south-bank zone extending from the plateau all the way west to Kinganga. From the markets in this zone slaves came west to Manteke; in Manteke village there are still those who trace a specific and personal link to "Manianga" villages.[14] The "BaManianga" in this sense are regarded with some friendliness, whereas the inhabitants of Luozi Territory, with whom Manteke people have little contact, are called *bisi Luozi*, and on occasion are described as "enemies." Excepted from this category and this attitude are those inhabitants of Luozi Territory who live just across the river to the north, who are included as brethren under the name *bisi Manteke*. This community is based on the historical comings and goings of migrants across the river at this point, and on common use of the Kinganga–Lufu road, which brings people and produce from across the river to the railroad at Lufu.

[13] The inhabitants of Luozi Territory are therefore called BaManianga. (The form "Nyanga" seen on some maps is erroneous.) The Sundi or Nsundi culture area, to which Laman's three ethnographic volumes (1953, 1957, 1962) refer, includes this territory and adjacent areas in the Congo Republic (Brazzaville). The predominant missionary influence has been that of the Protestant Svenska Missionsforbundet. In my study Manianga means Luozi Territory.

[14] In the middle of this "Manianga" is the Catholic mission of Kasi, to which the evangelization of Mbanza Manteke was at one time entrusted. The articles of Decapmaker (1943, 1949, 1951, 1959) refer primarily to the vicinity of Kasi.

Part I
STRUCTURES

2

THE STRUCTURE OF TRADITION

Native conscious representations, important
as they are, may be just as remote from the unconscious
reality as any other.
—C. LEVI-STRAUSS

The word *kinkulu*, "tradition," means any story of past events, but
more specifically it means the story of the origin and adventures of
each descent group. In this specific sense the connotations of the word
are strongly magical and political. A man without tradition is a
stranger or, worse, an abhorred barbarian. According to a newspaper
article written in KiKongo, Europeans tried to obliterate tradition in
Kongo, believing that a people without tradition could never again
recall where they had come from. If tradition is forgotten, culture is
forgotten. Without culture people cannot know who they are; they
have no respect among nations. The source of tradition is the clan.[1]

A clan's traditions reveal a structure corresponding to that of the
clan itself. In Manteke the words *mvila* (or *luvila*) and *kanda*, meaning "clan," are regarded by the people as interchangeable, but it is convenient to distinguish them here as denoting two kinds of corporation.
The clan (*mvila*) is a category, lacking internal structure, whereas the
local clan section (*kanda*) is a "perfect" corporation, a corporate group
(Smith, 1966). The BaKongo say there are twelve original clans. Earlier
in the century Bittremieux and Van Wing reported nine, but there
is no real contradiction since both numbers have religious meanings.
Nine is connected with such ninefold processes as the one by which,
according to legend, the BaKongo arrived in their present habitat from
the mythical Mbanza Kongo (Van Wing, 1959, pp. 44 ff.; Bittremieux,

[1] *Kongo Dieto*, first issue (n.d. [1959]), p. 5: "Kondua Kinkulu, Kiadi." A stranger
is one who does not speak KiKongo, who has no *luvila* ("clan") (*Kongo dia Wene*,
20 Feb. 1961, p. 3).

1922–1927: *s.v.* "divua"). Twelve has superseded nine probably because of its prominence in the Bible, but it also has traditional religious significance.

The first king in Kongo, Ndo Fonso, created the clans so that the people would not fight among themselves — in other words, so that there might be order (cf. Cuvelier, 1946, pp. 11–12). The clans are therefore the primary categories of Kongo society, and that is in fact what *mvila* means.[2] All who have the same *mvila* (i.e., recognize the same categorical name) are held to be descended matrilineally from the same mother, and thus can claim kinship with one another; but no genealogical links exist at this level. It is probable that in the first phase of the kingdom, before 1700 (Vansina, 1966, pp. 152–154), the *mvila* performed a political function in the organization of regions or provinces, but now it has no organization or common interests. It is not exogamous, though the people sometimes seem to think it ought to be.

The principle of descent is combined with that of locality in the clan sections (*kanda*; pl., *makanda*), which are now the most extensive customary corporate groups. Each clan section is domiciled in a village, or in several villages in the same area, and is divided into houses.[3] Each is exogamous, and in principle acknowledges a common tradition.

In the classical form, the first part of a tradition (*kinkulu*) is a praise name (*ndumbululu*) consisting of the clan name with a number of explanatory phrases and allusions to appropriate insignia of authority. The tradition is the certificate of the clan's spiritual integrity and social legitimacy. Belonging to an *mvila* (rather than the local *kanda*) implies the right to this kind of certificate, even though a man may not know the details of his clan's praise name. Although in principle the *ndumbululu*, with its specific ritual references, is the same throughout a clan, in fact it is not the same, nor is it possible to allocate the local clan sections unambiguously to clans in such a way as to define a list of twelve (or nine) clans into which, in theory, the BaKongo are divided.

The praise name concludes with a statement of the clan's origin in Mbanza Kongo and its departure thence. Numerous examples are available in Van Wing (1959, chap. 2), Laman (1953, chap. 2), and Cuvelier (1934). These statements are extremely difficult to translate, partly because the allusions were always esoteric and are nowadays often lost entirely, even to the owners of the praise name, and partly

[2] Bittremieux, 1922–1927: *s.v.* "mvila." The word means a category or kind; it refers also to formulas recited as invocations and known as *zik'umbu zi zingolo*, "powerful names." See n. 29, below.

[3] *Nzo*, "house"; the more usual term is *vumu* ("belly"), which applies to any level of segmentation.

because the phrases are deliberately ambiguous and have alternative meanings. The *ndumbululu* of MPANGU provides an example (Van Wing, 1959, p. 47):

> A Kongo du roi
> le premier après le roi c'est un homme entier.
> C'est moi Mpangu.
> C'est l'aïeule Nkumbu-Nkumbu (= l'admirable)
>   qui nous donna le jour à tous.
> Lors de notre départ du Kongo
> il y avait neuf caravanes
> neuf bâtons de chefs.
> La corbeille des ancêtres
> nous l'avons apportée, celle qui sert à sacrer les chefs,
> et les anneaux d'herbe aussi.
> Les chemins étaient sûrs
> les villages où nous nous installions étaient tranquilles.
> Nous arrivâmes au gué de Nsimba.
> Nous nous tenions ensemble,
> nous ne nous séparions pas.
> Nous sommes arrivés devant de nombreuses rivières,
> devant les eaux de toute sorte.
> Il est resté une femme, souche de clan, au gué de la Mfidi.

From this and similar traditions, and Van Wing's commentary on them, the following model may be derived. All the clans lived together in Mbanza Kongo until a shortage of food forced them to emigrate. After crossing a vast, featureless expanse, they came to a named ford in a river. Both the trackless waste and the river may be called Kalunga, an expanse that "the eyes can traverse but not the feet" (*ibid.*, pp. 50, 57). It is possible to cross the river only after the chief has demonstrated his magical power, deploying certain devices that are also insignia of chiefship: the chief's staff, sword, or knife, a raphia-fiber mat, or certain trees. The river, also called Nzadi, is analogous to Lethe and similar waters, but in particular traditions it is identified with actual streams in Kongo, usually the Congo River, whose name is Nzadi, or the Inkisi River which Van Wing's Mpangu clans crossed and which is also called Nzadi, or some smaller stream. A tradition stating that "we crossed Nzadi" does not necessarily mean that "we crossed the Congo River."

The circumstances of the crossing divided the clans. One of the well-known ford names is Nsimba (*simba*, "to hold"), which implies (as in the example above, from Van Wing) that until that point the clans held together; it also recalls the Janus figure of the twins (*nsimba*) which pervades Kongo ritual. The ford Nsanda Nzondo, although said

to be near Matadi, is purely legendary; on the other hand, the fords of
the Inkisi are said to be still the property of particular clans. Once
again, ideal concept and the historical reality that may appear to coincide with it must be kept analytically distinct. In traditions that have
nothing to do with the clans, such as those of the modern prophetic
sects, the mythical Nzadi reappears and is similarly identified with
local streams. It is recognizable as a mythical water by the context and
by the magical events associated with the crossing.

Part of the praise name of MBAMBA KALUNGA in the Matadi area, as
recorded by Cuvelier (1934), runs as follows:

> Mbamba Lunga guarded [*walungila*] the gates of the King's enclosure in
> Kongo. . . . We came from Kwingibiti, traveling in thrice nine canoes [*ma-
> lungu*]. We crossed at Nsanda Nzondo [the fig tree of Nzondo] and came to
> Nkumba a Ungudi [the navel of origin], which is the old name of Mbanza
> Kongo. We divided into twelve lineages. Then we fell out among ourselves,
> on account of the war over the cabbage patch. The women began to fight in
> the fields, but brought the quarrel up to the village. After bitter struggles, we
> dispersed.

Across the stream is the secular world of the divided clan sections
(*makanda*), each of which takes up the story of its own *nzila*, the road
it traveled to reach its present territory. Usually the land was unoccupied at the time the clan sections took possession of it, although it
had been inhabited, traditions say, by a race of iron-working dwarfs.
Along the road a succession of villages were built and later abandoned.
The story of these events is no longer the praise name but the tradition proper, the charter of each independent, local clan section. The
most important elements are the list of villages built, the names of the
chiefs who built them, the names of any branches that remained behind, and the details of outstanding incidents. In theory, such a tradition can be corroborated by the groups now living along the route, or
by those that participated in the events. The leading figures in the
story, besides the chiefs, are their sisters, mothers of the children who
founded the houses into which the clan section split. Tradition records
the names and clans of their husbands, and the names of the children.

The story ends with the occupation of the lands now held by the
clan section. Here the essential elements are the circumstances of the
occupation — whether the land was conquered or acquired by other
means — the names of neighboring clan sections that are witnesses to
the boundaries, the landmarks, the details of marriages contracted by
the chief, and the location of his grave. Similar details are required
concerning strangers who arrived after the original foundation and

were given land to settle on, or "to eat from," as the phrase has it. Later chiefs and their graves, right down to the incumbent, are also recorded, but genealogical and other materials showing how living individuals fit into a structure established by the tradition of origin are no longer tradition proper (*kinkulu*), but pedigree (*lusansu*, lit., "upbringing") (discussed in a later chapter).

The structure of tradition may be represented schematically:

Recitation	*Place*	*Social unit*
1. Praise name (*ndumbululu*)	Mbanza Kongo, ordered unity	Clan (*mvila*)
2.	Nzadi or Kalunga, the barrier	
3. Tradition proper (*kinkulu*)	Dispersal in the real world	Clan section (*kanda*)
4.	Present site (*mbanza*)	House (*nzo*)
5. Pedigree (*lusansu*)		Lineage (*futa*) and individual

Van Wing emphasizes the historical importance of these stories as records of actual events.[4] Although historical content undoubtedly exists, I am concerned here with the religious and political significance of tradition. In the traditions of the clans, as in other kinds of Kongo tradition, the content is significant on two levels, the literal (or historical) and the religious; in general, and in praise names in particular, the structure of the story derives primarily from religious logic. The BaKongo characteristically show a weak understanding of the principles of historical structure of sequences of events in time and space. What appears to happen in tradition is that accounts of real or supposed events are organized in terms of a preexisting model that is religious in origin.

The historical Mbanza Kongo, now San Salvador, was the capital of the kingdom discovered by the Portuguese in 1485. The people in general retain no recollection of the historical capital, although a number have been told about it in school. *Bisi Manteke* do not know that the country was once divided into six provinces, and NSUNDI has never heard of a province of that name, incorporating Manteke, ruled by the Mwe Nsundi. Titles and other details mentioned in praise names, such as Ne Mfutila Na Wembo, the tax collector, undoubtedly had their

[4] To illuminate the history of the Kongo kingdom, Cuvelier (1930–31, 1946) correlates a selection of clan traditions from the Matadi region with historical documents.

counterparts at San Salvador, but the Mbanza Kongo of tradition is
primarily a religious idea (MacGaffey, 1968). It is the perfect kingdom
to which the BaKongo hope to return, a place of peace and prosperity
where each clan, and therefore each individual, has its honored role,
and where a benevolent king protects his subjects from all evil and
settles all disputes. The intellectuals, who have read Cuvelier and other
historians or such redactions as De Munck's *Kinkulu kia nsi eto* (1956),
know that San Salvador is not the original, ideal Mbanza Kongo, and
they seek to identify the remote and fabulous Zimbabwe, or an imaginary city in Egypt, as Mbanza Kongo.[5]

TRADITION IN MANTEKE

Superficial ancestral beliefs and practices have not survived very well
in Manteke. The absence of special insignia and traditional costumes,
the colorlessness of religious and political life, and the paucity of musical and artistic creativity are partly attributable to the repressive influence of the Protestant mission. These features are less marked in
the interior villages, even in one as close as Mbanza Nkazi, but even
there the difference from Kasangulu is evident. I encountered only one
praise name, that of NTAMBU, and then only because I was asking for
such information; the word *ndumbululu* itself is unknown, and I was
unable to find an equivalent.[6] Traditions are very plain, colored only
by references to old battles fought by chiefs with splendidly resonant
titles, to half-forgotten customs, and to the material artifacts of an
ancient world. In Manteke village only MBENZA delights in telling the
magical exploits of his forebears; his eyes light up with a naïve excitement, and his stories have a fairy-tale quality:

In Mbanza Wene [which is Mbanza Kongo, or Kongo dya Ngunga, but it is
typical of this man to use the more exotic and ritualistic name] MBENZA lived
with NKAZI A KONGO. At one time MBENZA borrowed money from NKAZI A KONGO
which he could not repay, and had to hand over two of his children, a man
and a woman. Later on MBENZA had many more children; later still, there was
a plague of locusts,[7] and famine arrived. So the clans dispersed and crossed

[5] For example, see *Kongo Dieto*, 27 Nov. 1959, p. 4, for an article devoted to the
origin of the BaKongo.
[6] For NANGA, an inquiry made in 1931 reported three fragmentary praise names,
none of which is now in circulation. The best is "Kinanga kia Malongo Malongo Na
Kunda Mbimbi kafwani mu lungu. Les Nanga conduits par leur chef Na Kunda
Mbimbi étaient si nombreux que pour passer l'eau il leur fallut plusieurs pirogues"
(cf. Laman, 1953, p. 26).
[7] *Makonko*, "grasshoppers" or "locusts." It is typical of the ambiguity of these
stories that the word implies the presence of witchcraft (Laman, 1936: *s.v.* "konko").
"Na Nkazi" refers to famine (Laman, 1953, p. 26).

the Nzadi. Some went on to Kyonzo, across the Congo River; others came to Kongo dya Lemba, southwest of Manteke.

There were three houses of MBENZA: SUBI WA NTANTU, WANGA WA NTANTU, NKENGE WA NTANTU. Their father was NSAKU A MALELE. I, SUBI, was the leader. We found a wonderful land with abundant food, but after a while a war broke out over a patch of cabbage,[8] and SUBI expelled WANGA and NKENGE, who went to Kinti, near Kyanga, on the east bank of the Lufu River, southwest of Mbanza Manteke. Na Nkazi Makonko, chief of SUBI (and hence of all MBENZA), kicked a sort of rubber ball called *kindibi kya ndoki* three times into the air and then to a great distance. It flew over rivers and hills, and where it landed there was no one, but there was good land to settle on. Na Nkazi Makonko told his people to follow the ball, and when they had found a place, to fire a shot, so that he would know where they were. But only I [confides the narrator] know where they crossed the river![9]

A number of traditions speak of a point of dispersal in such a context that there is little doubt they refer to a lesser Mbanza Kongo. Two houses of NANGA, DISA and NSAKA, whose traditions are entirely different, list a sequence of nine villages; the first is said to be near San Salvador, and the last is, in one account, Kulukulu (near Kongo dya Lemba) and, in the other, Nkulukusu (near Songololo). The names have strong magical connotations. In these places there were "twelve clans," which dispersed after a drought or a war. The narrators were very positive about the number nine, mentioning it beforehand; similar lists of nine occur in other examples. The tenth village on both lists is a geographical location specifically known to the owners of the tradition; thereafter the route pursues a readily recognizable path, and the villages are associated with the acts of particular chiefs. According to a tradition told by NANGA KYA DISA,

[8] *Nkovya*, "cabbage" or "manioc leaves." The cabbage war is a recurrent motif in tradition; dispersal follows from a conflict over food. The tradition of MBENZA in Kongo dya Lemba (i.e., the same *mvila* but a different *kanda*, with possibly some historical connection) speaks of a dispersal following a nine-day (or nine-year) war occasioned by a quarrel at a ball game (Matadi 677, 1949).

[9] In speaking of this crossing of the Nzadi, MBENZA said, "Not *this* Congo, of course; the other one, over there," pointing toward San Salvador. I found out about this other river one day when standing on a hill overlooking the Congo River that appears on the maps; two local youths who were with me remarked that people believed that the river, after flowing from Kinshasa to Matadi, returned to Kinshasa, passing south of Manteke and thus isolating it. Yet they know the land and know very well that there is no major stream between them and San Salvador; they are unable to resolve the discrepancy. I mentioned this situation to an educated young man who has a responsible bureaucratic post in Matadi but who regularly returns, unlike most such people, to visit his kinfolk in Manteke. He had never heard of any such belief, and doubted its existence, but the first three people who happened to come down the path confirmed it. The example illustrates the cultural gap between village folk and the urban elite, most of whom rarely, if ever, return to their natal villages.

The elders built Sumpimanga [10] near Kongo dya Ngunga; then Kongo, where a war broke out which led to the dispersal of the clans. On their travels the elders rested at Saala, Zulu, Nzonzala, Kiyakalakani, Mpungu Ndongo, and Nkumba Wungudi, in none of which they built, but passed through only, until they came to Kulukulu, where there were twelve clans who lived together. But one year there came a drought, and because of this calamity they dispersed to find land and water. So NANGA came to Ndemba, south of Mbanza Manteke; the first chief to see this land was Na Ntala mya Masinda, who built Mpompi.

Thereafter was built a series of villages, successively abandoned, which as lands now constitute the DISA patrimony. Among them: Ntumpa, built by the second chief, Na Ntala mya Manene mya Ngo; Nsweka, Mbata Kayi, and Mbata Ngunda, all built by Na Ntala mya Mazwele; Ntandu a Sala, by Na Ntala mya Myenga, who also, having become a great chief, was able to establish a market nearby, called Nsona Myenga; Mongo a Mbangu, built by Na Ntala mya Na Vunda near the modern village of Vunda. Eventually, the two houses of NANGA who had been traveling together all this time, DISA and NKUTI, divided; DISA, the elder, represented at the time by Na Ntala mya Mbazi, built Mbanza Ntala, and allowed his brother Na Ntala mya Ngila of NKUTI to build in Ntombo.

These last two villages, near the modern Mbanza Manteke, are the scene of its bitterest political disputes. Not far away, according to this tradition, Na Ngila also built Makasakasa, KiNtala-Ntala, and a village called Matu ma Na Ntala, "the ears of Na Ntala," because, explained the narrator, Na Ntala was a very tall man; as he strode before his people, scanning the way ahead for a suitable site, his ears turned this way and that. The complete list, beginning with Mpompi, shows eighteen principal villages built on different sites by a total of thirteen chiefs over about eight generations.

The foregoing stories are transcribed from my notes, which inevitably captured only the essentials. Each informant, as he gave me his tradition, referred from time to time to a notebook he carried with him. Every elder should have a book, says NTAMBU, in which to write his traditions and other matters of importance, so that when he dies his heirs will have the facts. NTAMBU's own book is small and rather unimpressive; it is his younger brother who is the clan's political expert. Besides, NTAMBU's position in Manteke is marginal, and their tradition a thing of shreds and patches, improvised shamelessly to suit the opportunities of the moment. Probably for this reason I was able to read and copy from the book. A good book is a massive, bound volume, stuffed with genealogical details and the histories of pieces of land; it is itself a valuable property, carefully guarded.

NTAMBU's book begins with a crude, sketchy, inconsistent account

10 This village, which still exists, appears to have had some special ritual relationship to San Salvador (see account by J. de Munck in "Ngonge," 1960, no. 3).

of NTAMBU origins in Mbanza Kongo, where the original ancestor was fathered by MVIKA NTUMBA. Among the other names by which the NTAMBU clan is known, it says, are MAVENDA, LAWU, NLAZA, and VUZI, the last being none other than Ntotila, the king in Mbanza Kongo.

In the Manteke region, not these names but NGIMBI and NDUMBU are generally recognized as belonging with NTAMBU in the same *mvila*. VUZI and MAVENDA are not represented, and LAWU is a house of NLAZA, which belongs with NTUMBA. This circumstance suggests that the informant has borrowed a praise name he picked up somewhere else. There is a fragmentary praise name in NTAMBU's book, but the political expert later gave me a better version which with much hesitation I venture to translate:

1.	Ntambu a Tana	Ntambu a Tana
2.	Vuzi dya Nkuwu	Vuzi dya Nkuwu
3.	kavuzwa lusala	did not lose his plumes.
4.	Yaya Nkenge	Our forefather Nkenge
5.	wayekama va ntandu a tadi, mukondwa dya nkazi	was inaugurated upon a rock, without knowing hunger.
6.	Yandi i Mavenda	He is Mavenda
7.	wavenda ntangua ye ngonda;	who licked the sun and the moon;
8.	i kimenga kya nene,	a mighty creature,
9.	i sikulu dya nene,	a mighty noise,
10.	dyakulumukina Na Nzambi a Mpungu	which caused God to descend.

The division into ten parts allows the reciter to tell them off on his fingers; I encountered this device on the Bangu, and Bittremieux reports that it was once used for a variety of incantations (1922–1927: *s.v.* "tanga"). Some comments on each part may compensate for the inadequacies of the translation and indicate the many levels of meaning which such formulas carry:

1. The clan section's full name.
2. The more general name of the clan (*mvila*). *Nkuwu* is a mat on which chiefs sat, hence an emblem of authority.
3. *Vuza*, "to root up, pluck." *Lusala*, "a feather." The phrase is a metaphor meaning "in fine fettle," but at the same time it calls to mind such birds as the fishing eagle which are emblems of chiefship and which in turn convey the idea that authority is a spiritual gift. Feathers also imply the power of continued growth and represent the chief's numerous kinfolk and dependents.
4-5. The founding ancestor obtained his authority while reposing on a rock symbolizing his domain and the universe, in a time or place where it was not necessary to eat *nkazi* (a root synonymous with famine).
6-7. In the sense "to lick," *venda* recalls a procedure that formed part of

many traditional oaths, ordeals, and initiations. Like *vuza*, it can also mean to reply to questions, and thus these two phrases recapitulate the sense of the preceding two: that Nkenge, founder of NTAMBU, can withstand all challenges. The phrase *wavenda ntangua ye ngonda* puzzled all my informants. The most confident suggestion was that it implied the possession of special knowledge by Nkenge.

8. *Kimenga*, a living creature, especially in ritual contexts.

9–10. *Sika*, "to sound." A loud noise, musical or otherwise, is essential to a Kongo religious occasion; it is considered at once an invocation and a manifestation of spiritual powers.

The NTAMBU book also contained a list of lands and the names of neighbors who could bear witness to the boundaries, an account of expenses for a house built in 1952, lists of contributions to funerals, and fragmentary stories, the most substantial of which deals with the Nsimbila War. NTAMBU's origins are shady, to put it mildly, and their position in Manteke depends on their ownership of Nsimbila, in the eastern foothills, where most of them live and work. After I had copied the story I heard it retold with added theatrical details by the political expert, and was able to have some points clarified.

The chief who left Mbanza Kongo, says the book, was Na Kimpenzi, whose title was Mayala ma Kongo. When he died, Mfumu Ndongala Zenga Tala took his place. On leaving KiMakanda,[11] which is near Zuku-zuku,[12] NTAMBU built Kilwengidika. The most important of the clans that traveled the same road together were NTAMBU, MVIKA NTUMBA, NKAZI A KONGO, NA NSIMBILA, NANGA KYA DISA, and NA LUKUTI. (This is a real politico-social configuration.) Nkazi Na Mpanzu, (sister's) son to Mfumu Ndongala, ruled at Mbanza Kati in Manteke. When he died, Mfumu Na Nkangu a Mbamba took over the chiefship; he condemned men, and burned them or sold them.[13] At his death a son took his place to safeguard the prerogatives[14] of his father; he was Nsyama Luyambu of MFULAMA NKANGA. When the son died, a woman who "was born with" Ne Nkangu took charge; her name was Lesama Dilweki. At this time NTAMBU scattered everywhere, having no male to be their chief.

The Nsimbila War. — We obtained the land at Mbanza Nsimbila[15] by fight-

11 "Place of the clans."

12 *Zuku-zuku dya Nza*, "the edge of the world," recurs in tradition as the name of a mythical ford.

13 *Yandi wazengisanga bantu, ovo yoka, yevo teka.*

14 *Wene* means dignity, authority, public office.

15 Nsimbila lies in the valley east of Mbanza Manteke. NTAMBU always calls it "Mbanza," implying that it is an independent territory, but other clans hoot at this conceit. For an account of a similar one-day war, see J. Mertens, 1944–1952, XVIII, 285–287.

ing a war. The quarrel arose over a sale marriage.[16] We NTAMBU sold a girl to NA NSIMBILA. Her name was Madede Nkembi, and she was sold to Nsyama Nsemo. When he had arranged the purchase from our *nkazi*, Ne Nkangu, he went to the marriage house and slept with her. Later she came down with leprosy. So Nsyama Nsemo prepared an *mbungu* and went back to Ne Nkangu saying, "Exchange this woman for another; see, your niece is rotten." When he heard this, Mfumu Ne Nkangu said, "From the beginning it is unheard of that a woman once transferred should be exchanged for another. Go back with your wife; if she dies, then come, and I will replace her. Understand?"

Nsyama Nsemo went back to his house with his wife Madede Nkembi, furious indeed that she had not been exchanged. Now the wife had a younger kinsman, a palm-wine drawer whose name was Nyanga Nsyoni and who had a sister called Lusobo. This girl had been given tobacco by a youth, but her *nkazi* didn't know about it. One day when Nyanga Nsyoni had drawn wine he called his sister and went to sell it in the market Nsona Maveve.[17] When she had picked up the wine she called her boyfriend, Nzyuki Kavundi of NANGA KYA MFUTU, who was later the chief Na Makokila. So he went with Lusobo of NTAMBU to Nsona Maveve.

When they got to the market they put down the wine. Nsyama Nsemo of NA NSIMBILA, he who had bought the woman from NTAMBU, asked, "Is this wine for sale?" The girl Lusobo said, "Yes, it's for sale." The man tasted the wine and found it good. "Who drew it?" he asked. Lusobo said, "Elder brother Nyanga Nsyoni." Nsyama Nsemo was truly a cunning fellow. He gave a string of beads [18] as down payment so that the wine should not be sold to anyone else. When the market had dispersed, Lusobo said, "Pour off your wine into your own jug; we're leaving." But Nsyama Nsemo said, "Carry my wine over there. Here is no place to decant it; therefore take it to Mbanza Nsimbila where we shall find something to put it in." Lusobo saw no guile in this; truly he was a cunning fellow.

In Mbanza Nsimbila, Nsyama Nsemo called Lusobo over to a house, telling her to bring the wine. She went in. He said, "Pour the seller's *nsubu*." She poured it, and they drank. Na Makokila didn't go into the house, but sat outside. Then Nsyama Nsemo said, "You, Lusobo, are not going to leave. You're going to take the place of your kinswoman Madede Nkembi. You stay put." Na Makokila protested, "We were sent by her brother!" Replied Nsyama Nsemo: "You shut up; any more nonsense and you'll be tied up. Her brother is a bad lot." But Makokila said, "She's *my* girl!" So Nsyama Nsema told his men to tie them up. They were tied with cord and put in the same house.

When everybody was asleep — "kang, koong; kang, koong" — the girl called to Na Makokila: "Wriggle over here to me!" He wriggled over to Lusobo so that he could put his hands to her mouth. She gnawed and gnawed at the cords until they parted. He freed her, and together they got away and went to tell Ne Nkangu.

16 *Longo lwa nkita. Kita* usually means "to sell," but the narrator insisted that in this instance the marriage was a share marriage, a form of pawnship.

17 Naturally, he would not carry the wine himself.

18 *Kulazi,* a packet of ten chains of a hundred blue beads each, is worth 10 cents (Laman, 1953, p. 153). This currency was still in use in the interior villages in 1912, although it had been abandoned in Mbanza Manteke years before (Richards, Correspondence).

Mfumu Ne Nkangu was angry, and immediately summoned Kinkela Makumbu (Ne Nkangu was the chief who ruled the land; Kinkela Makumbu was his servant [19] and Nsyama Luyambu's). Ne Nkangu called Mabonga of NTUMBA and Na Sangala of NANGA KYA NSAKA (who were his children and grandchildren), went into a house, and took out a box [20] of gunpowder. He told Kinkela Makumbu to sound the war gong: [21] "Send word to Mavambu Ntamba of MFULAMA NKANGA in Matenta, and say that anyone who fails to come will suffer for it when the war is over. You, Na Sangala, take charge of the battle."

With Na Sangala at their head, the warriors went to fight with NA NSIMBILA, who fled, giving up their land. Nsyama Nsemo was killed. Then NSAKU A MALELE was frightened, and fled from Ntumpa. Kinkela Luzwadi was NSAKU; he didn't fight, he ran away, and his land was taken. Ntumpa, Ntava Nkamba, Dyadya, Kidikidi, Kyatola — these are the names of the lands that were taken from NSAKU A MALELE.

. . . So they took the land. (Afterward, Mavambu Ntamba arrived with his band to fight, because word of the war had reached Matenta. . . . MFULAMA NKANGA fired alarm shots and prepared for war, but turned back on the road and did not actually fight.) When the warriors reported back to the chief he rewarded them with a pig. Then NTAMBU and NANGA sat down to discuss the affair. NANGA demanded compensation, so NTAMBU took a pig and gave it to Na Vwaza of NANGA KYA MFUTU, who owned Na Makokila and also Kinkela Makumbu. Then as quittance [22] he paid over a woman, Tembo Mayumba, and a man, whose name was Mavuzi. These two were paid over to MFUTU, now represented by Joshua Kingalu, and all the land was retained by NTAMBU.

Now the Word of God arrived, and Ngwankazi the white man who had come from Mputu said, "Quit settling affairs by handing over people; man may no longer be sold." So Mavuzi whom we had paid over returned to his clan and died in the hands of NTAMBU. Whereupon NANGA said, "Now we are entitled to share in Nsimbila, because the man you paid us has died in your hands." NTAMBU said, "If you want to share, pay us an animal and return part of our ammunition (two boxes of white powder); also return the pig of the agreement.[23] So they returned a part of the powder, but the pig was still owing to NTAMBU.

19 *Mwan'a ngana*, "someone else's child," is usually a euphemism for slave, but it is indicated in the story and elsewhere that Makumbu may have been simply a client. Nsyama Luyambu was mentioned in the list of NTAMBU chiefs.

20 *Kyasa*, worth four pieces of cloth, or 4 francs (Laman, 1936).

21 *Mondo*, a wooden slit gong made from a tree trunk. It no longer exists in Manteke; in fact, the narrator showed himself unfamiliar with it and with other antique instruments he mentioned. In Kasangulu, *mondo* is the common word for a land case, in court or elsewhere, in which this gong plays a prominent part.

22 *Lusuki. Sukula*, lit., "to wash," means to compensate someone, or to redeem an obligation.

23 *Ngulu ya kuswa luvemba*, "pig of rubbing with chalk." Rubbing on chalk signifies quittance from obligations. The nature of MFUTU's claim is not quite clear, but the narrator said that this pig, or another, signified an apology to NANGA because Makokila had been dragged into trouble on account of NTAMBU's Lusobo, although Makokila's kinsmen "had not known of" the link between him and Lusobo.

Until the pig is paid back and the descendants of Tembo Mayumba are accounted for, NANGA has no claim on Nsimbila, according to this argument by NTAMBU.

THE VIRTUES OF TRADITION

The foregoing stories, chosen to show what tradition is, are also basic political documents in Mbanza Manteke. They tell little about Mbanza Kongo itself, its founding, its kings, or its government. When such tradition occurs, it is of recent origin. One "expert" consulted a folder of typescript, on the dingy exterior of which could be deciphered the words "Imprimerie Mission Catholique, Tumba"; the traditions he offered were apparently taken from Father de Munck's *Kinkulu kia nsi eto,* a school text. Another expert, though he consulted no script and asserted that he had been specially selected for instruction by the elders at San Salvador, recounted tradition recognizable as that originally handed down by Father van Bulck, Monsignor Cuvelier, and others. This process has been going on for some time. In 1936 a Manteke witch doctor admitted in court that he prepared his "médicaments indigènes suivant formules contenues dans un petit receuil *Makaya ma nsi* ["Local Herbs"] vendu par les Pères" (Mbanza Manteke 77, 1936). Further afield, the notorious prophet Simon Mpadi declares that when the elders commissioned him in 1927 to prepare the definitive tradition of his clan, VITI NIMI NA MPANZU ZI KONGO, they gave him, as a start, copies of *Ku Kiele Kakusidi Mpimpa Ko,* the Matadi pastoral bulletin, to which Cuvelier contributed many articles whose substance was later incorporated in his *L'Ancien Royaume.* Most of the traditional culture brandished by the Kongo political movement Abako at the time of independence was acquired in Catholic schools and seminaries, principally Kisantu (Lemarchand, 1961).

The relatively better survival of legends of Mbanza Kongo and of a variety of traditional practices in Catholic-dominated areas such as Madimba may be partly due to unrelated historical and sociological factors, but the effects of education are obvious. In Protestant schools — and Manteke is one of the most exclusively Protestant areas in Kongo — the instruction is different. Protestant missionaries, at least since the pioneer days of W. Holman Bentley and his British Baptist colleagues, have not been so diligent in pursuit of custom as the Catholics, and have probably been more eager to suppress it than to assimilate it in the process of civilizing the Congo. Still more important, however, the major achievements of Protestant ethnographers are written in English and are consequently unavailable to most Congolese. Moreover, the teaching method at the secondary level is apparently different; Catholic teachers tend to tell their classes what Kongo culture was like, basing their statements on the work of Van Wing and others, whereas Protestants conduct class research intended to find out what it is or was like. The difference may be more national than religious; most Catholic missionaries are Belgian, whereas most Protestant ones are British or American.

None of these external influences has had much effect on the main body of tradition, which is relevant to the real world and constitutes the charter of the clan sections. The implication that the present society results historically from a process of migration into an unoccupied land has been accepted by most writers on the BaKongo,[24] although it can be disproved from the traditions themselves, which show that the region of Manteke (Mpemba Nkazi) in particular was inhabited before the founding of San Salvador. It can further be shown that statements about dwarfs supposed to have preceded the present population may or may not refer to pygmies, but certainly they represent a religious concept that has nothing to do with any historical dwarfs or pygmies.

Mbanza Kongo is thought of as a densely populated area, a city ruled by a king at the apex of a hierarchy. At the end of the story, according to tradition, there is a small *mbanza*, a mere village, one of many in a relatively lightly populated countryside. The hierarchical form persists within each *mbanza*, but between neighbors the question of ordination or ranking is, at best, in doubt; it existed "originally" (*tuuka Kongo*) but is now a survival, a precedent for something else constructed on the spot. The ethnographers have accepted the same idea, believing that relations between and within descent groups as they now exist have sprung from the decay of something that once existed. The functioning of Kongo society is likened to that of a superannuated automobile: missionaries and natives alike believe that with such a vehicle progress is impossible, and all are eager to repair it, that is, to reconstruct it "as it was in the beginning." Beliefs of this kind are commonly myths serving political functions.

Further exploration of the landscape described in tradition reveals that it was covered by a checkerboard of chiefdoms, each a sovereign entity created by an original immigrant. People discussing the principles of land tenure draw this sort of diagram:

---

[24] E.g., De Cleene, 1936; Malengreau, 1939; Van Wing, 1959; Soret, 1963. The assumptions about migration are briefly discussed by Vansina (1966, pp. 17–18).

NKAZI A KONGO

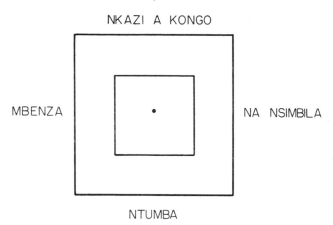

MBENZA   NA NSIMBILA

NTUMBA

In the midst of the domain (*nsi*) is the central settlement, the *mbanza*, and within the *mbanza* is the chief's enclosure (*luumbu*), from which he usually never emerges. Around the enclosure sleep his dependents, including his children, grandchildren, and slaves. When the founding ancestor (of NANGA, say) arrived, the land was unoccupied, but he met, let us suppose, NKAZI A KONGO to the north, whom he recognized as his Father "from the beginning in Mbanza Kongo" (*tuuka Kongo*) and who gave him a wife and conferred upon him the insignia of authority. Later there came NTUMBA, his Child, to whom he stood in the inverse relationship. The three neighboring clan sections thus constitute a patrifilial hierarchy: NKAZI A KONGO–NANGA–NTUMBA; the right to rule in a particular domain is obtained by the Child (*mwana*) from the Father (*se*), and the link is renewed in each generation at the inauguration of the new chief, on whom the chief of the patronal group confers the insignia of office. This model has been elaborated by Doutreloux for eastern Mayombe (1967, chap. v). It does not correspond to modern social morphology, but lies behind most modern political arguments referring to a state of affairs which ought to exist.

To continue the legend: by a different road came NA NSIMBILA and MBENZA; to the former NANGA gave a female dependent in marriage, from the latter he received one. These groups therefore stood to him in the relation of *kinkwezi* ("affinity"), which may be associated with the patrifilial relationship but does not by itself imply any ranking; on the contrary, it epitomizes friendly equality between autonomous neighbors.

Thus is established the original, sovereign estate of a *fondateur*, whose action is described most often by the verb *fonda*, borrowed from

French, or more traditionally by *sema*, which means to create, as in Genesis, I, 1. The land itself, as we shall see, is more valuable as an expression of a position in the community than as a piece of earth.

Within an original foundation, strangers may be received in any of the following categories (examined in more detail in chap. 10): bought slaves, pawns, and the like; members of the same clan (*mvila*) in search of a place to live; children and grandchildren; wandering strangers. To such people land may be made available under any of the following titles: [25]

1) Loan. Slaves and others may be given land "to eat off," with the assumption that what they are not cultivating is not theirs.
2) Gift. Typically, from Father to Son. While the recipient is independent in the use of his land, he may not give it away or otherwise dispose of it to anyone else.
3) Pawn. Temporary pledge to a neighboring chief for a debt of "money," slaves, or goods.
4) Sale. The transfer is complete; no obligations or restrictions bear upon the buyer. A complete territory may not be sold, since to do so would destroy the status and existence of the founding clan section. In some opinions, *nzanza* ("grassland") may not be sold because it lies along the boundary of the original foundation and the sale would obscure the outlines and compromise the title to it. Some "immigrants" have bought for themselves as an independent territory a part of a large territory founded earlier. It is often argued that anyone who bought land must have been a stranger, since the founder of an original territory would have had all he needed.

An entire territory may also be captured in war, or occupied after having been deserted by the original founder. It is said that Mbanza Nkazi was founded by MBENZA, who later moved north across the river; not liking what he saw, he came back, and found his brother NKAZI A KONGO in possession of Mbanza Nkazi. His brother welcomed him back and gave him land to live on, but did not relinquish the chiefship.

All these types of transfer apply also to persons. The traditions show that persons (particularly pairs, a man and a woman) were interchangeable with and hence to some extent equivalent to land, as in the story given above of the Nsimbila War. Each land title implies a particular political relationship between the parties, ranging from neighborly equality (sale) to complete dependence (loan). The title to land is legitimated by an accepted tradition.

Nobody doubts the virtues of good tradition. "All this trouble we

25 I.e., titles recognized in Manteke. In other parts of Kongo it is stated that land cannot be sold and that it never was sold. The difference beween Manteke and other areas in regard to the sale of land is discussed in chapter 9.

have over succession is due to the intrusion of slaves who corrupt the traditions of a land that is not theirs; now true tradition will not return until the dead arise, and every man returns to his own *mbanza*." [26] In spite of their insistence on the abundance of liars in Manteke, the villagers of this region, as of every other region in Kongo, do not doubt that on the whole their tradition is superior to everyone else's, because it alone came direct from Mbanza Kongo.[27] By this they mean that their culture is superior, and their lives are more civilized. "Because we know the straight roads from Kongo,[28] our KiManteke is the purest and most difficult to learn of the Kongo dialects; in contrast, anyone can learn KiNtandu. Because of this superiority the white man of God came first of all to Mbanza Manteke; but the first convert," continues DISA, a Ndemba man himself who is far from sure that the roads leading to the village of Manteke are all that straight, "was a woman from Ndemba!" (as indeed she was).

Real tradition cannot, of course, be picked up just anywhere. The ideal describes a chief wearing bracelets, or at least a wise old elder somewhere in each clan, who knows the secrets. He does not tell them even to members of his own clan, but only to selected nephews who have demonstrated their discretion. Some say tradition is not communicated to any but the chief's heir, or at least only to members of the senior house. Under such practices all other houses of the clan are not better than clients of the aristocracy, dependent on them for the charter of their status. This view is therefore only held by such as DISA, who assert along with it that they are the aristocracy. In reply to which NZUZI snorts, "I own land in Ndemba; DISA says it's mine only because I'm his younger brother [*nleeke*]. He claims everything, just because he's the oldest in the family. It may be all one family, but every man's shirt is his own."

A newspaper article, written when the enthusiasm for custom aroused by independence had not yet declined, asserted that though Kongo lacked mineral wealth it had tradition; it was the only country to have clans, which began in Mbanza Kongo with government (*luyalu*). The whites, continued the writer, had never met real chiefs wearing bracelets; whence, then, came this book, *Nkutama za* [sic] *mvila za makanda* (Cuvelier, 1934)? Nothing but lies. Because many people did not

[26] "As it says in the Bible," added the informant, probably referring to Ezekiel, XXXVI, 24.

[27] The ethnographers of Kongo have usually adopted the parochialism of the informants closest to them, and speak of the culture they know as the true and original culture of the BaKongo.

[28] A road that, as described in a given tradition, is not the direct route from San Salvador is a priori suspect. Compare the notion of the trackless waste, discussed above.

know the fords they crossed or their route from Kongo, the Europeans erroneously supposed that the clans were dying out, but "no government could cause a man to forget his clan [*mvuila*]; [29] it is something that is called in the language of the whites *droit propriété*; as our elders said, *Mvua kiani mbuta, munkolomona mbombo nleki.*[30] From the beginning until now the whites have never found out who are the real owners of the land [*mfumu za ntoto*]" (*Kongo dia Ntotila*, 30 June 1961).

This is a very appealing mystification which a number of Belgian writers have taken seriously, incorporating it in apologetics for the unsatisfactory results of *la politique indigène*; the above remarks could have been paraphrased from De Cleene (1937*b*), for example. It is merely another version of a recurrent motif of Kongo folklore, the treasure in the locked box, lying hidden under a stone somewhere, which is nonetheless real though no one has seen it. One is not surprised to find that the article's promise to reveal all in subsequent installments was not fulfilled.

Despite the ideology, which declares that each territorial foundation is a sovereign entity, the fact is that the relations between foundations are readily transformable. Affines (*bankwezi*) can be subordinated by a shift of genealogical emphasis; the wife-giving Father (*se*) can be reduced in the next generation to the status of Child (*mwana*), and the Child "from the beginning" can be converted into a simple client. In other words, the charter of the *mbanza* does not preclude the establishment of hegemony over a wider area, nor does it define the limits of the domain as precisely as might at first appear. No land title, none of the parallel series of personal statuses on the scale ranging from chief to slave, can be unequivocally distinguished from the one next to it in the series. All is disputable, and tradition is the language of dispute.

Nobody has a good answer to the rhetorical question one hears from time to time across a fire in the evening: "If it's true, why are they so anxious to hide it?" But nobody is prepared to make good his boast that he fearlessly speaks the truth. The idea of secrecy, and the credentials supposedly to be demanded of purveyors of tradition, belong to the mythology and technique of politics. In theory, the enemy could use his knowledge of another's tradition as a demonstration that it is his own birthright, or he could pervert it. Thus DISA, before expounding

---

[29] *Mvuila = mvila*, here implying the *ndumbululu*. In English "clan" and "clan praise name," or motto, are two different things, but not in KiKongo. The word *kanda* means "clan" (or "people," "race") without the connotation of a particular spiritual identity; it could not here be substituted for *mvuila*.

[30] Van Roy and Daeleman, 1963, no. 671: "Celui qui possède est l'ancien, celui qui baisse le nez est le jeune."

the tradition quoted above, removed the meeting from my house to his brother NKUTI's lest my NTUMBA servant overhear the recital. Yet this same tradition is familiar to all the local politicians, who have heard DISA using it in his long-standing dispute with MFULAMA NKANGA; moreover, it is reasonably accessible in the records of the communal court. (The only differences between the two versions correspond to differences in the political situation faced by DISA in 1956 and 1965.)

In reality, secrecy serves to protect the source rather than the information. Na Kingani does not want Na Mpumbulu Tela to be told that he is repeating traditions that challenge Na Mpumbulu's prerogatives, at least not just now, because "the time is not ripe" (*ntangu kayifwene ko*). The principle of the ripeness of time explicitly governs the use of tradition, and labels it at the same time as a politician's weapon. As one wise old elder said, "You put up with the insubordination of slaves for a while, and their appropriation of things they are not entitled to; if they go too far, then when the time is ripe you stand up in the middle of the assembly, reveal to each one whence he came, and send him packing." The corollary of this principle is that tradition, like an American campaign speech, varies each time it is told to suit the audience. "If you want to know the straight roads," advised DISA, "sit in a gathering of only two or three, because when more than two or three are gathered together the road starts winding."

The truth of this advice was made plain after a meeting of NSUNDI elders in Kyesa Kifwa, called especially for my benefit. We discussed the origin of this section of the clan "from the beginning" (*tuuka Kongo*). As the story approached the point at which it should have differentiated and ranked the houses and lineages represented by those present, the pauses grew longer, the compromises less satisfactory, the shuffling of feet more evident. This situation is the kind that should not exist; the conventions of etiquette are intended to circumvent it as far as possible. Thereafter I largely gave up trying to record traditions other than those I found in spontaneous circulation, that is, those that were being used.

3

THE CLANS

Their inward thought is, that their houses shall
continue for ever, and their dwelling places to all
generations; they call their lands after their own
names.

— PSALM 49:11

Mbanza Manteke occupies the Yongo plateau, a widening of the ridge
that runs northwest from Ndemba to Mbanza Nkazi (see map 3). To
the east lies what is here called the Manteke valley, bounded on the
opposite side by the Nsonso ridge which marks the boundary with
Vunda, the next village south. Between Yongo and Nsonso, in "the
sickly hollow of Banza Manteka" (Stanley, 1885, II, 301), lies the
original site of the mission built by Henry Richards, "the first white
man," on land allotted to him by NANGA. Stanley drew the world's
attention to the site as an example of a foolishly chosen one. By 1887 it
had been moved to the top of Yongo, but not before the death of
Richards' first companions, including his first wife.

On the plateau were assembled the inhabitants of the hamlets that
had formerly ringed the valley. By the 1920's the expanding mission,
with its hospital, schools, staff, and clients, had outgrown the building
space available, and the decision was made to transfer it to the east,
to Nsona Mpangu near the Lunyonzo River. After removal of the
mission the continued presence of local government headquarters could
not confer on the community the same appearance of substance.
Mbanza Manteke is a village of pensioners, wrangling over the relics
of defunct prerogatives. On Sundays, in the huge, dusty church built
at the expense of the Clarendon Street Baptist Church, Boston, a
dwindling congregation gathers to hear Joshua Kingalu expound his
depressing view of the destiny of man.

Probably all the villages in the region are similarly synthetic, created

36

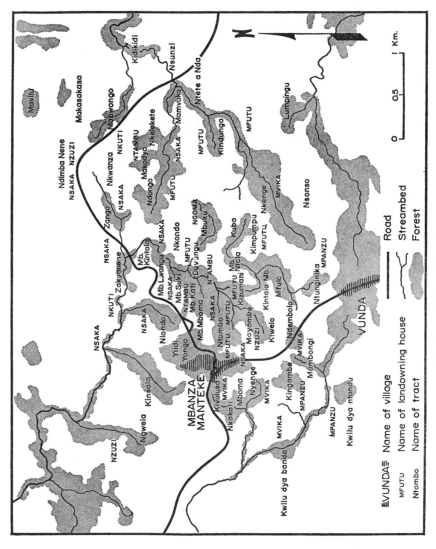

MAP 3. Landholdings in Mbanza Manteke

by the mission and the government in the interests of health and easier administration. A few villages, such as Kyanga and Ntombo a Lukuti, are backed by the typical mixed forest, dominated by giant baobab trees, which marks the site of a very old settlement. In the forest are the graves of the founding ancestors, chiefs with resonant names, memorialized by old gun barrels and a hundred empty gin bottles or, on a very few ancient and honorable tombs, by engraved stones and the remains of elephant tusks. The absence of a forest of this kind near Mbanza Manteke is one of the reasons for thinking that the village, instead of being the seat of the regional paramount chief, as the colonial government chose to suppose, was perhaps something of a refuge area, socially interstitial, an outlier to Mbanza Nkazi.

Shortly after his arrival in 1879 Richards wrote (Guinness, 1882[?], p. 66):

> There are three towns within a quarter mile of our station, and very near each other. I counted thirty huts in one, and about twenty in the other two. The king is named Makokila, and he lives at a town of about the same size half a mile off. Each family has its own hut. They have no plan in building their towns. The houses stand neither in blocks or ranks, but are placed about here and there just as they like. They know that the hills are more healthy than the valleys, and never build in the latter, though the land is so much better and watered more plentifully; but where there is a clump of trees on the top of a hill (and there are plenty of such, mostly palms) one is sure to find a town. The women have to descend into the valley to fetch water. Perhaps this fact accounts in measure for the prevailing dirtiness.

The three towns may well have been those belonging to the house NANGA KYA NSAKA: Mbanza Mboma, Mbanza Suki, and Mbanza Kintala. Makokila's town was Ntombo, belonging to his house, NANGA KYA MFUTU. Farther west was Mayombe, owned by NANGA KYA NZUZI; to the east was NANGA KYA NKUTI. The north edge of the valley was thus occupied by the houses of the NANGA clan section in the order of their seniority, from east to west: NKUTI, NSAKA, MFUTU, NZUZI. Only the first house, DISA, was missing: "DISA had no land, because his trade was weaving sacks."

The south edge of the valley was held by NTUMBA, whose house MVIKA NTUMBA lived in Ndembolo. On a rise in the middle of the valley is Mbanza Ntala, by all accounts the original settlement in Manteke; it was occupied in Richards' time by NGOMA LUBOTA of NTUMBA. Here agreement ends, and the most violent political argument in Manteke life begins: Who owns Mbanza Ntala? The parties to the dispute are NANGA and NTUMBA, with their allies and clients, but the situation is not simply an opposition of two factions, for many lesser disputes are interwoven. Some of these are analyzed later; here we are concerned with the internal structure of the clan sections domiciled in Manteke by tradition.

Seven different clans (*mvila*) are represented in the population normally resident in Manteke village, which excludes people living there only because of temporary employment. The seven clans include about fourteen different clan sections (*makanda*; see fig. 1); an exact count is impossible because of political disagreements. Five of the clan sections (NANGA, NTUMBA, NTAMBU, MBENZA, and MPANZU) assert that Manteke is their domicile, meaning that they have land nearby; however, only the first two are clearly important in the village, the rest being in varying degrees their clients. The remaining nine clan sections are represented by groups and individuals who are also clients in the context of village affairs but who claim no land locally; in several instances these individuals are women whose own clan sections are domiciled elsewhere.

Each clan section is a corporation divided into houses, which in turn are divided into lineages, each with its own name. The name specifies a group occupying a specific position with regard to the affairs of the community, but the relations between groups are expressed genea-

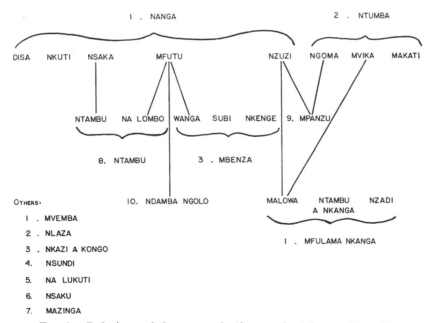

Fig. 1. Relations of descent and clientage in Mbanza Manteke. Braces link houses of the same clan section (*kanda*); straight lines link patrons and clients; sections of the same clan have the same number.

logically; that is, the eponymous founding ancestress of the clan section is said to have given birth to the ancestresses of the houses. The organization of a clan section into houses and lineages is universal in the region and relatively unambiguous. The relationship between the exogamous, corporate clan section, however, and the wider, unorganized clan to which it belongs is often in doubt.

We may begin with NTUMBA, a relatively simple case. When this group arrived from Mbanza Kongo, its original settlement was Kumbi, between Mbanza Manteke and Nsona Mpangu. According to tradition, the three houses — NGOMA LUBOTA, MVIKA NTUMBA, and MAKATI MA NTUMBA — later quarreled over the distribution of a length of cloth which had been divided into four pieces, and they scattered. MVIKA went to Ndembolo, MAKATI to Vunda. But some of MAKATI remained in the valley and are found at Kumbi and Bete. NGOMA LUBOTA, the senior member, went east, but later, having run into trouble, sought refuge with his younger brother MVIKA, and was given land near him. These three houses constitute a single exogamous clan section (*kanda*).

The names of these houses recur all over Kongo as part of a series of names associated with the NTUMBA clan (*mvila*). The association is not exclusive; some of the names occur in other clans, and even when these three occur together their relationship need not be the same. Even though the same thing is true of all the clans, for the individual the original title-holding chief of his clan left Mbanza Kongo; he or his successors eventually arrived at the place where the individual's clan section is now domiciled. (What domiciles a clan section or a house is not the village in which members are found, since both men and women are dispersed, but the land indicated by tradition as its property.) All other BaKongo of the same clan were left behind in the course of this one journey, or set off afterward on further migrations of their own. Tradition specifies the relationship of the houses as descendants of a primordial group of sisters, and therefore all members of the clan, wherever they live, should organize their relationships in the same way.

Thus, within a particular horizon, the tendency is to identify *mvila* and *kanda*. Only analytically can the clan as descent category and the clan section as local group be distinguished. The nearest a villager ordinarily gets to making this distinction is to say that NTAMBU and NGIMBI, for example, which belong to the same *mvila*, once lived in a singe localized exogamous group, but decided to split up on account of quarrels, or to permit themselves to intermarry. For him the primary fact is his own tradition; to deny or question the truth of this tradition is to question his own position in his society and the very fabric of his existence. This view can be maintained only within the limited local horizon, a boundary marked in tradition by the mythical Nzadi and in practice by the range of interaction in local affairs. The latter limit is much less precise than the former, and discrepancies arise between the theory and the political facts embodied in the assertions of other houses.

NLAZA and NTUMBA belong to the same clan,[1] but NLAZA is domiciled in Kinkanza, at so great a distance that the two normally have little to do with each other and never have occasion to argue about land or tradition. On my first visit to Kinkanza I asked NLAZA for the route he had followed from Mbanza Kongo. He and his advisers retired, but soon came back to say that they could not agree on the correct tradition (meaning probably that they could not decide on a plausible story to tell me); then they asked me to return when they had had a chance to think about it. On my second visit I took with me a respected member of MVIKA NTUMBA. It turned out, from the story we were given, that NLAZA had never passed through Kumbi at all; from Songololo they had traveled down the Luima River to Ngombe Luima, whence they had crossed over to Kinkanza.

MVIKA, most disturbed by this account, felt that "somebody is not telling the truth." From his point of view NTUMBA had crossed the horizon by a particular route and established its principal settlement (*mbanza*) at Kumbi; NLAZA of Kinkanza could only be an offshoot of this migration. Subsequently, an MVIKA political expert explained to me that the original foundation at Kinkanza had indeed been made by refugees from Kumbi, but that their house had died out.[2] The position was taken over by members of the same clan who, arriving later by a different route, had originally been accepted at Kinkanza as brothers but at the same time as clients. As such, the members of this group could not possibly know the true tradition and had cobbled a faked substitute, in the process changing the name of the clan section to NLAZA.

This explanation, which would of course be indignantly denied at Kinkanza, points indirectly to a fundamental ambiguity of clan structure, the ambiguity of tradition and of the political-historical model. In the pragmatic local context, are the clan sections to be related to one another as they were "in the beginning," and if so, according to whose tradition? Or are they to be ranked according to the order and

[1] This identification is made in Manteke, but, as already indicated, it would not necessarily be made elsewhere.

[2] An informant gives the houses of NLAZA as LAWU, MALUWA, VASI, and MAKATI, but I did not verify this statement in Kinkanza.

the circumstances of their arrival in the area, and again, according to whose tradition? Each clan section says that its own original chief held the title appropriated to its clan in Mbanza Kongo and that the route it followed in the dispersal was the route of the main body of the clan, and that, in consequence, all other representatives of the clan are dependent on its chief. In regard to NTUMBA-NLAZA the explanation has no practical effect, in the circumstances, other than to comfort members of NTUMBA who happen to turn their minds to their relationship with NLAZA. Where a live dispute exists between neighboring groups, such as the perennial quarrel between DISA and MFULAMA NKANGA in Ndemba, it commonly turns on the rule of succession and its application.

The same situation arises between houses as between clan sections, but the unusual absence of live internal disputes in NTUMBA means that the structure of the clan section is not publicly known in any detail. NTUMBA tradition, too, seemingly lacks a clear shape. An elder of MVIKA NTUMBA, stimulated by my work to collect the genealogy and traditions of his own house, encountered so many contradictions in the responses to his private inquiries among informed relatives that he gave up the attempt. Nor would he show me, as he had promised, such fragments as he had been able to put together; a scrupulously honest man, he refused, rather bitterly, to associate himself with the handing down to posterity of stories, some of which he thought must be false. Neither he nor any member of his house doubts that there is a genuine tradition entitling them to their estate, and no one else can doubt that in time of need MVIKA NTUMBA could put together a tradition as plausible as that of any other house.

Quite different is NANGA,[3] whose most intimate conflicts are the gossip of the marketplace. The five houses are DISA, NKUTI, NSAKA, MFUTU, and NZUZI. DISA's tradition, already cited at some length, indicates that DISA and NKUTI, the former being the elder brother, came to Manteke by the Lunyonzo valley route from Songololo. According to this tradition, NSAKA (or some of them; see chap. 4) came later by the route from Kongo dya Lemba under the leadership of Na Kiba kwa Fuku, who was

[3] In the vicinity of Mbanza Manteke the *mvila* of NANGA NE KONGO includes three *makanda*: (1) NANGA KYA NA NSAMBA (the clan whose affairs are examined in most detail), domiciled in Manteke village and referred to as NANGA; (2) NANGA KYA MFULAMA NKANGA, domiciled in Vunda and Ndemba, where it is in conflict with the DISA house of NANGA, and referred to as MFULAMA NKANGA; (3) NANGA KYA NA MVEMBA (a small clan about which I know virtually nothing), domiciled in Vunda and referred to as NA MVEMBA. Some of the other representatives of NANGA NE KONGO throughout the region are related to NANGA KYA NA NSAMBA in Manteke, but this tradition has now no practical effect in the village. Others, like NANGA KYA NA NGOMBE in Ngombe, are quite independent.

hospitably welcomed by DISA as a fellow clansman. MFUTU is not a true descent group at all, the story continues, but a collection of slaves settled in Ntombo by the owners of Mbanza Ntala; after all, *n'tombo* is the place where a chief hides away his guns, slaves, and other property. One of these slaves, not being a gentleman, seduced a DISA girl; her offspring had to be placed in a separate house, called NZUZI. Thus DISA's tradition historically and politically locates all the houses.

NKUTI agrees with this tradition, except that he says DISA is the younger brother. Despite the minor difference, the two houses are so close that people frequently speak of them as though they were the same, and a junior member of DISA even asserts that the name NKUTI is simply an MFUTU invention, an effort to split the DISA ranks. (Neither has an elder resident in Manteke. DISA is domiciled in Ndemba, where it claims land, and NKUTI is few in number.)

NSAKA's tradition is quite different from DISA's:

In Mbanza Kongo there were four brothers, Ne Kunda Mbimbi, Na Ntala mya Mbazi, Na Ntala mya Masinda, and Na Nkambu. [The second and third of these names appear in DISA's tradition.] They traveled with MBENZA, who married their sister. Together they built nine villages, the last of them Nkulukusu near Kongo dya Lemba. Here they parted from MBENZA, who went on to build near Kyanga and in Paaza. His daughter Na Nsamba married Nimi of NSUNDI and gave birth in Mbanza Ntala to Disa, Nkuti, Nsaka, Mfutu, and Nzuzi, the founding ancestors [4] of the houses of NANGA. They all worked and held land except DISA, who preferred to weave sacks. NKUTI worked, but lacked eloquence. So NSAKA and MFUTU shared the chiefship, and gave land to MFULAMA NKANGA when he arrived. DISA was annoyed at this and left in a huff for Ndemba. We were glad to hear [concludes NSAKA smoothly] that he had obtained some land over there, but of course we don't know the details of his title to it.

Thus NSAKA deposes DISA and establishes an alliance with DISA's prime opponent in Ndemba, MFULAMA NKANGA. MFUTU agrees with this account; in fact, the elders of MFUTU profess so little knowledge of the earlier phases of their tradition that they usually, even in court, rely on NSAKA to recite it for them.

NZUZI's story is another variant; he says he arrived after all the others, by way of Kongo dya Lemba and Kyanga.

At first we lived in Ndemba, but then many people died of smallpox, so our ancestors came to Mbanza Kati in Manteke, where they were received, not by NANGA, but by Na Nkambu [5] of NTAMBU; from the beginning NTAMBU is

[4] Although the ancestors were presumably female, the story continues, as usual, to speak of the acts of the male leaders, the *bankazi*.
[5] Na Nkambu is the name of one of Ne Kunda Mbimbi's brothers, according to

the father of all NANGA. Now, our ancestor Na Kwede was a magician,[6] and other members of NANGA accused him of witchcraft. He was rescued from their threats by his father NKAZI A KONGO, from Mbanza Nkazi, who established him on Yongo and gave him all the land from Mayombe to Yongo.

Torday was very impressed by Van Wing's discovery of tradition and urged the collection of such legends as documents of ethnic history. He himself took a phonograph and recorded a chief's story of his clan. A few days later he was introduced to another man, reputedly the clan's oldest member, to whom he played the recording. The old man's rage and indignation at what he heard were so great that he attempted to smash the machine. Torday then had him record his own version, and went away convinced, it would seem, that he had taken down the true tradition in place of the "corrupt" one (Torday, 1925, pp. 96 ff).

If this incident had occurred in modern Manteke, one could safely guess that Torday had heard the traditions of two different houses. The examples from NTUMBA and NANGA show that there is in fact no such thing as the tradition of the clan or even of the clan section. Tradition is owned by the house; by means of it, each house describes to its own satisfaction the interrelationships of all the houses that make up the section. All the NANGA traditions together, however, agree formally that there are five houses in the section, and that the land is divided among them under one title or another. This accord may not seem to be very much of an agreement, but at the next lower level of segmentation there is not even that much.

THE CLIENTS: NTAMBU, MBENZA, MPANZU

In 1931, when the government inquired into the structure of the clans, NANGA was organized differently from the way it is now. The "genealogy of the chiefs" shows Na Nsamba (i.e., NANGA) and Na Ntambu (NTAMBU) as the sisters of Na Ntala mya Mbazi, and all of them as sister's children to Ne Kunda Mbimbi. Na Nsamba's children are given as Disa, Nkuti, and so on, and Na Ntambu's offspring include two women called Dwingi Mundele and Lusobo. (The adventures of the latter, as recorded in NTAMBU's book, are given in chapter 2.) In other words, in 1931 NTAMBU did not exist in Manteke as the representative

---

NSAKA. In another version of NZUZI's story, it was Ne Nkangu who received him; Ne Nkangu is given as chief of NTAMBU in the story of the Nsimbila War. A challenge on such a point can always be met by saying that the same name belonged to two different men, or that one man had two names. In a pinch, the narrator can deny that he ever used the name "Na Nkambu."

6 *Ngang'a nkisi*, usually translated "witch doctor."

of its own clan, but only as a section of NANGA in the process of differentiation from it.

The official report [7] goes on to describe NANGA KYA NA NSAMBA as the senior branch of NANGA NE KONGO, whose other sections include MFULAMA NKANGA, NA MVEMBA, NANGA KYA NA LOMBO, and MPANZU A NANGA. All these branches, it says, intermarry. The positions of the last two need some discussion.

NA LOMBO or NTAMBU?

The praise name of NTAMBU (translated in chapter 2) gives their clan as VUZI DYA NKUWU. The origin of the local section is described by their patron NSAKA as follows:

Na Maveki of Mbanza Suki in Manteke married Kimpenzi, an NTAMBU girl from over near the Luima. Later, her *nkazi*, Na Mfwila, came to his brother-in-law and borrowed *funda dimosi* ["one thousand"]. Not having the money to repay, he handed over Kimpenzi's kinswoman Dwingi Mundele. When her descendants multiplied we gave them Mbanza Kati. Eventually, NSAKA held a meeting of all the houses of NANGA and the newcomers were admitted to the clan under the name NA LOMBO. After the missionaries came and slavery was abolished, the word got around that they were really NTAMBU, so in 1935 Chief Manyonza took a pig and held a meeting at which he expounded the true tradition in this matter and restored them to the *mvila* of NTAMBU.

In the NTAMBU book Na Kimpenzi is a man, the first great chief who led the clan from Mbanza Kongo. In an unguarded moment NTAMBU himself told me that Kimpenzi was the *sister* of Na Mbila Nzita, the first great chief who had led the clan from Mbanza Kongo, whose successors he listed, right down to himself. At the same time he did not deny that NTAMBU had been enslaved to NSAKA, but implied that the period of enslavement was simply an interlude. Risky though it is to embark on historical reconstructions from tradition, one may accept the majority view in Manteke that NTAMBU are of slave origin, and have patched together this parody of a tradition since their emancipation. And yet there are "experts" in the region, if not in the village itself, who declare that NTAMBU is indeed a legitimate freeman and landowner (*mfumu*) in his own right, a *fondateur*. In other words, NTAMBU is not without political support.

These NTAMBU are the descendants of Dwingi Mundele. The descend-

[7] The *enquête de chefferie* (1931) was a preliminary, required by law, to the investiture of Samuel Manyonza as customary chief. The report is in the political file on Mbanza Manteke located in the archives of the Cataracts District at Thysville.

ants of Lusobo, however, refuse the name NTAMBU and insist that they are NA LOMBO, from the beginning a branch of NANGA which obtained its share of land in Manteke and later split off so that intermarriage would be possible; and that those who call themselves NTAMBU are to this day in slavery — to NA LOMBO or NSAKA, I am not sure which. "But now we have no elder to be our *nkazi* and speak for us, so these outcasts defraud us of our land!"

The woman who is now head of the house, Lusobo's granddaughter, took the case to court in 1957. She apparently had no tradition of her own to offer, but relied on witnesses who, in the event, supported NTAMBU's contention, pronounced more in sorrow than in anger, that she was his own (classificatory) sister of not only the same clan section, but the same house. He cited the following story as proof: [8]

NTAMBU built Mbanza Kati, where they recognize a boundary with NGOMA LUBOTA.[9] Here a girl called Dwingi Mundele grew up.[10] One day Nsakala Joseph, who was a pedlar of MWE NSUNDI from across the Congo River, came to Mbanza Kati. The elders, seeing that he was a strong man, said, "You'd better sleep in Dwingi's house." Subsequently she became pregnant, and they, taking a liking to each other, went off to his village across the river, where she had many children, *mbembe nkunda*.[11]

Later on, many of that family died of smallpox, and Dwingi's sister Lesama Dilweki came to Na Sangala [12] of NSAKA in Mbanza Mboma and said, "Somebody should go after my clansmen who are married away to MWE NSUNDI, but see, we have no *nkazi* to look after us." She gave him two boxes of gunpowder and six lengths of cloth to take over the river as funeral gifts. When Na Sangala arrived, MWE NSUNDI said, "You ought also to pay us a pig, since you have failed to visit your people." [13] So Na Sangala paid a pig out of his own pocket, lending it to Lesama Dilweki to spare her shame. When Dilweki got home she was pleased and said she would give Na Sangala four chickens by way of thanks, but she never did, nor did she repay the pig either. So when Dwingi died her descendants, twelve of them, were brought back to Manteke as bondsmen of NSAKA, and were eventually entered in NANGA [*bakotuswa mu kiNANGA*] under the name NA LOMBO, because they were "such a crowd of strangers."

8 Mbanza Manteke 108, 1957. The text, in Kituba, contains obscurities which I asked the NTAMBU political expert to clarify. Details come from NSAKA's supporting testimony in the same case.

9 This mention of a boundary reveals the wider political context. NA LOMBO are allies of MFUTU, who are at odds with NGOMA over Mbanza Ntala, which adjoins Mbanza Kati (see map 3 and fig. 1).

10 In the NSAKA version, Dwingi Mundele was already a slave or a pawn to NSAKA.

11 This expression refers to the numerous following of a wealthy chief.

12 In NTAMBU's book (quoted in chap. 2) Dilweki was Ne Nkangu's sister and successor, and Na Sangala was his ally in the Nsimbila War.

13 By failing to visit his people, Na Sangala relinquished authority over them, and a "pig" would be required to restore it. NSAKA's version goes on to say that Lesama Dilweki did not repay the pig; this statement is an explicit assertion that NTAMBU are still slaves, or at least pawns, to NSAKA.

Now one day the elders went into the forest Ndongo. There the palm-wine drawer Nyanga Nsyoni drew wine for our elder Ndombe, but afterward they had an argument about which patch of forest to clear. Nyanga Nsyoni hit Ndombe on the head with a piece of wood, and he died. Lesama Dilweki's husband Na Mbibi a Myenge of NKAZI A KONGO brought the body to her; she was angry and said to Na Sangala, "It would be a good thing to send these people back across the river." But he said, "The one who died and his killer are both your people." Which proves [concludes NTAMBU] that we are one house, because they killed a man and we made no fuss about it.

The court decided that NTAMBU was right, but the verdict has had no practical effect except to keep NA LOMBO out of Mbanza Kati, at least for the time being. NA LOMBO insists that the judges were conspiring with NSAKA and NTAMBU, and continues to reject the NTAMBU name and tradition, thus in effect setting itself up as an independent clan section in the *mvila* of NANGA. This situation is very confusing for everybody else; as NZUZI put it, "Manyonza the chief told one lot that they were NTAMBU, and the other lot that they were NA LOMBO. Now when there's a funeral, nobody knows what to do."

The testimonies of NSAKA and NTAMBU in this particular case agree on the point at issue, which is the present status of NTAMBU–NA LOMBO. They disagree on the history of the relationship between NTAMBU and NSAKA. Such disagreement would be critical if there were a dispute between the traditions. The judges are well aware of this possibility; however, it is an important premise of the game that traditions are never compared generally, but only as they bear upon a particular conflict. What has happened in this case is that NTAMBU has obtained the support of NSAKA. Tradition, which is not infinitely malleable, indicates that NSAKA is a qualified witness in the particular dispute, but nothing compels NSAKA to testify, or in testifying to recite his tradition in such a way that it convincingly supports NTAMBU. If NTAMBU requests such support the reply might be, "Get ready a pig," or, as it so often is, *Kizeyi ko*, "I really wouldn't know."

Both the evidence and the circumstances of the case tend to define NTAMBU's status as that of client [14] to NSAKA. The mother of the present NTAMBU was married, like Kimpenzi, to NSAKA, so that he is a child of that house (*mwan'a* NSAKA); the woman who is now NA LOMBO is married, as Lusobo was, to an MFUTU elder. The status of client is not immutable. In all probability, NGOMA was at one time client to MFUTU, or the other way around, but they are on an approximately equal footing in their current dispute. NTAMBU has on several occasions attempted

[14] The term "client" describes a political dependent; it does not translate any KiKongo term. On the other hand, "slave" is used by the people and is not used analytically in this study.

to assert in public, as he still does in private, that he is the one true and original chief in Manteke. In the future, especially if the NANGA houses of NSAKA and NKUTI, weakly represented at present, die out altogether, the political situation might enable him to get away with it.

MBENZA AND OTHERS

Not all the representatives of MBENZA in Manteke can be said to be there as clients. The *nkazi* belongs to the house SUBI, whose tradition domiciles it in Paza, an area lying between Kyanga, Mbanza Manteke, Mbanza Nkazi, and the riverine villages. The former MBENZA village was destroyed by MVIKA NTUMBA in a war that began as follows:

Makonda Nkisi of MVIKA went to the market Nkandu a Nkazi, which was owned by NKAZI A KONGO and was held where the village of Tendele now stands, to sell palm wine. The *esi ki*MBENZA to whom he sold it didn't want to pay on the spot. A quarrel broke out, and Makonda Nkisi was stoned to death. When Na Vwa dya Nkama, chief of MVIKA NTUMBA, heard about it, he was angry and sent warriors who chased MBENZA out of Paaza and took their land. Na Nkazi Makonko [15] of MBENZA retreated to the forest where he built himself a temporary shelter. When he had recuperated he took the name *Na Nkandi* [16] *ngina tombila n'kila ku andwa,* "I've lost my tail but I'll soon get a new one." This name, being not only a name but a powerful spell, was too much for Na Vwa dya Nkama to ignore, so he sent out his warriors again to kill Na Nkazi. Na Nkazi, who was no mean magician, changed his appearance to that of a woman, breasts and all; when the men came up, asking "Where's your husband?" Na Nkazi would reply, "He went that way." This went on until Na Vwa dya Nkama himself, who as a chief had the power to see through the devices that misled ordinary men, came down, found Na Nkazi Makonko hiding at the top of a palm tree, and shot him. [17]

Thus MBENZA lost their land, but in the 1920's the government negotiated its return in exchange for 1,000 francs and the pig of the agreement. This story is MBENZA's own, but NTUMBA agrees with it, although the two are now arguing about the boundary between their properties. (This is the only example of such corroboration I encountered.) Because there is no village at Paza, SUBI lives in Manteke, where the other clans recognize him as MBENZA. Members of the other MBENZA houses,

---

[15] Presumably the name "Na Nkazi Makonko" was assumed by each successive chief of MBENZA, so that the one here mentioned was not the original Na Nkazi who crossed the Lufu River.

[16] *Nkandi* = "a sole survivor"; it is also the name of an almost tailless fish. *Nkila* = "tail" or "following."

[17] The figure of a magical creature in the top of a tree occurs again and again in Kongo folklore.

WANGA and NKENGE, especially the former, can be very scornful of SUBI's pretensions, but they have no elder to challenge him.

NKENGE is represented in Manteke by women who have married in. WANGA say that they have land on the south edge of Paza, near Kyanga, but they are permanent residents of Manteke, possibly because the political climate in Kyanga is too hot for them. They are clients of MFUTU. An ancestor took refuge with his brother-in-law MFUTU after arousing the anger of NLAZA across the Lufu River by mistaking their cow for a buffalo and shooting it dead. In subsequent wars in that direction, MFUTU lost men and took these MBENZA as pawns pending the payment of compensation. One of the pawns, Na Mwinza, grew rich and had slaves of his own. He is mentioned in mission records as a man who befriended Richards when most of the people were uncooperative. The pawns were redeemed, reportedly in the 1920's. Their descendants are heavily intermarried with MFUTU and support them politically; they tend to cultivate land belonging to MFUTU and NA LOMBO.

Many of the so-called MPANZU in the village are known to be descended from MPANZU slaves and themselves accept the fact. The MPANZU proper, according to the generally accepted view, were originally owned jointly by NZUZI and NGOMA LUBOTA. In the last generation they seem to have been clients of NZUZI, but in fairly recent years the clan's male spokesman has been asserting, like NTAMBU, that his land title traces back to an original foundation. At the same time he has been attaching himself to MFUTU, supporting them in land cases against both NZUZI and NGOMA. In the course of his court appearances he has been fined at least twice for giving false witness, a conviction most tradition owners are smart enough to avoid.

The credibility of MPANZU's story is cast still further in doubt by the fact that his sister, his full sibling, a woman who is sometimes spoken of as the group's *nkazi* because her brother is a notorious wastrel, tells a different story. According to her, MPANZU is really MPANZU A NANGA (he says "MPANZU A NIMI," which sounds much more distinguished), with a history and a status much like those of NA LOMBO. In other words, what she says is that MPANZU was formed by fission from NANGA; what he says is that MPANZU is a sovereign estate beholden to no one; and what everyone else says is that the ancestors of MPANZU were bought by NANGA from MPANZU of Nkama, on the other side of Ngombe, near the river. This also is what they say in Nkama.

One house of MFULAMA NKANGA resides permanently in Manteke; they say they prefer to live with their fathers, but their "brethren" domiciled in neighboring Vunda speak scornfully of their descent. Their "fathers" were apparently NZUZI, but the indications are that with a shift in marriage patterns in later generations, and a decline in NZUZI's ability to guarantee land-use privileges and other benefits of patronage, the role is being taken over by MVIKA NTUMBA.

A line of NDAMBA NGOLO women are former pawns of MFUTU, recently redeemed. Although they belong, technically, to the same clan as NTAMBU, nobody ever mentions this fact. Since they are insignificant in village affairs, the point scarcely matters.

In addition to the groups whose traditions and interests involve them in the history and politics of the village, there are some members of the NSUNDI, NKAZI A KONGO, and other clans whose reasons for living in Manteke are individual. It is never suggested in Manteke that they are other than entirely respectable people although, in the villages where their own traditions domicile them, predictably scandalous legends circulate with the palm wine.

THE HEARTH OF NE KONGO

Considered analytically and in context, such traditions show that two groups disputing title to the same estate do so in terms of *kikota*, seniority within the same matrilineal descent group. Dispute between neighbors whose estate are distinct is carried on in terms of *kitaata*, patrilateral filiation. The relationship of cooperating neighbors who are not disputing is summarized as *kinkwezi*, marital alliance. The significance of these kinship terms is examined in chapter 5. Here we are concerned with the political virtues of certain features of the traditions as told, and with general patterns.

Each tradition describes the migration of two houses who are specifically legitimated. All others tend to be lumped together as clients. In theory, if the first house (*nzo ya kota, ngudi ya kota*) was unable to furnish a qualified chief, the second might, but the third could not except with the understanding that he was not a real chief but a substitute. This traditional pattern may be observed again in the everyday attitudes of most members of NTUMBA in Manteke village, for whom anyone not MVIKA or NGOMA is MAKATI, a riffraff. These so-called MAKATI constitute a diverse group whose members have various reasons for being in Manteke. They come from NTUMBA sections domiciled near Bete and elsewhere, whose own traditions give the houses a different order and from whose point of view MVIKA may be the riff-raff. "After all, doesn't *mvik'a* NTUMBA mean 'slave of NTUMBA'?" [18]

18 Etymological abuse of this kind is a commonplace of political gossip. For DISA, MFUTU's slave status is proved, if proof is needed, by the root of the name in *futa*, "to pay."

In other parts of Kongo the pattern implicit here is formally recognized, and people say that a clan should have only three houses. East of the Inkisi River this view tends to become official policy, for it is often held by administrators concerned with land affairs and the semi-professional experts on custom whom they co-opt. If a clan has more than three houses, those in excess are ipso facto of slave origin, unprovided for in the true and original tradition. Any house advancing a tradition that provides for more than three houses in a clan must overcome a prejudice against it.

The official prejudice has a double origin. Many Ntandu clans have only three houses and assert that only three are possible. It appears that the three houses are associated with three offices, those of chief, female chief (*ndona n'kento*), and *sangila*. The last is guardian of the secrets and factotum, a magician (*ngang'a n'kisi*) who may be more active in government than the chief but can never be chief himself. These details vary somewhat according to the informant; the titles, for example, are not always the same, although the relationship among the roles apparently is. Not all the clans that say there can be only three houses know of three associated offices, although even in these instances the informants seemed to insist on the current importance of the chief in a way that nobody in Manteke does. The information has not been checked by observation, but it is doubtful that there is a functioning set of three officers surviving anywhere.

The association of three houses with three offices is not made spontaneously. If asked why there should be only three (houses, or anything else that comes in threes), people quote the proverb, *makukwa matatu malambidi Kongo*, which refers to the three stones supporting the pot in which the eponymous Ne Kongo prepared his magical brew. "Kongo is the name of an object like an earthenware pot which belonged to Ne Kongo, in reference to which our elders spoke this proverb."

The other source of the prejudice is the work of Van Wing, which if superficially studied, or perhaps as summarized for classroom use, gives the impression that having three houses is the rule (Van Wing, 1959, pp. 85–88; for *ndona n'kento*, see p. 111). BaKongo civil servants who have enough education to reach territorial or higher rank have often learned about their own customs in the classroom rather than in the village, and if they are Catholics they have been taught largely from Van Wing's text. As the best, indeed the only, general text on Kongo sociology, religion, and magic, it has been widely regarded as an authoritative description of what all Kongo society is or ought to be, not simply that of the BaMpangu. Many manuscripts lie moldering in the desk drawers of Congolese who feel that the present status of custom in Congo is ambiguous and unsatisfactory, and who are sufficiently educated to try to write down a summary of the problem. Too often the results begin: "La notion de clan dans la société indigène a été bien resumée par le R. P. Van Wing en ces quelques mots . . ."

The relationship between the first and second houses, as between DISA and NKUTI, for example, appears in more general form as the statement that "every chief has to have his *n'tadi.*" The *n'tadi* is the chief's deputy, guardian, potential successor, and rival. The relationship appears frequently between descent groups in the same locality, and I have found a version of it in a prophetic church. As an idea it is related to a profound Kongo distrust of the unique, as of odd numbers; "whole" things occur in pairs, each with its mirror image confronting it. As a practical matter it is related to the tendency toward polarity in political systems: the ins and the outs, the left and the right. Where the political means available do not allow one group to monopolize a particular office, an alternation is sometimes instituted. Usually, however, the two groups live together, quarreling furiously down through the generations, each blaming the other for the destruction of the kind of social order described in tradition.

Dialectics of this sort, in which the rivalry of two constitutes a unit from which a third is excluded, pervade Kongo culture and frequently are recognized by explicit symbols. According to J. Mertens (1942, p. 69), Ntandu chiefs wore three bracelets, one for each lineage of the descent group. Sometimes the first two were called by the names for twins, *nsimba* and *nzuzi*, and might be worn on the left, or female, arm (*koko di kikento*); the third was called "the guardian" (*ndesi*) and might be worn on the right arm. All lineages junior to the initial twins constitute a following (*nlandu* or *n'songi*) excluded from authority; they also, in appropriate context, include a paired opposition, and thus the configuration of all social situations appears variously as dyad, triad, and tetrad.[19]

FATHERS AND SONS

The theory of authority (*kimfumu*) says that a chief is endowed by his Father with the spiritual qualities enabling him to rule. When a clan section inaugurates a new chief, the insignia of office, which are also the devices by which chiefly power is obtained, transmitted, and exer-

[19] An interesting comparison can be made with the system of counting described by Dennett for Loango (1906, p. 62). Each unit is represented by two beads, and each pair of units is marked off by an additional bead, so that five beads are counted as two, ten beads as four, and so on. Even today, children in Kasangulu reckon four peanut shells as ten.

cised, are conferred by a representative of the clan that stands in the relationship of Father to the chief and his clan. There have been no chiefs in Manteke for a long time, and recollections of the ritual expressing the paternal role can be uncovered only, if at all, by persistent questioning. Nevertheless, the idea of patrifiliation (*kitaata* or *kise*) is important in tradition, in which a claim to authority must include a statement of the *kitaata*, the spiritual source of authority. Each clan must know who its Father was. Thus NTAMBU asserts that in the beginning (*tuuka Kongo*) his Father was NTUMBA.

Such a statement does not in itself compromise a local clan section's claim to complete and independent authority over its members and its land, but it can be used to strengthen claims that involve an immediate and secular *kitaata*, in which a particular clan section bestows land and authority on another in the real world, that is, in Manteke. Thus NTUMBA asserts that in Mbanza Kongo he fathered NANGA, a statement that may be interpreted as follows: "In the beginning, NANGA owed his existence to NTUMBA. When the clans left Mbanza Kongo, NANGA came to Manteke where he chose to settle because his father and protector had already arrived there before him and was able to give him a place of his own. In the ordinary way, we would be prepared to recognize NANGA as our friend and equal, but since he's been trying to steal Mbanza Ntala, instead of remaining content with the estate that is his, we are forced to mention the *kitaata*. If you really get right down to it [*ku nsi a nkulu*], NANGA is here only on sufferance anyway."

NZUZI, whose problem is to defend his land against his brethren NSAKA and MFUTU, demonstrates similar forensic use of the *kitaata* principle. According to him, NANGA's father in the beginning was NTAMBU (see fig. 1), a claim suggesting that NSAKA and MFUTU houses of NANGA in Manteke have only a limited say in local affairs, and enabling NZUZI to link himself with NTAMBU rather than with them. NZUZI's land, however, is a gift from NKAZI A KONGO, a powerful neighbor to the north, father of Ne Kwede who was head of NZUZI at a particular time; this immediate and local patrification benefits NZUZI alone.

DISA says that NANGA's father was MBENZA, by which he means MBENZA in Mbanza Kongo, not any particular local MBENZA. He is not closely connected with MBENZA in Manteke, and on other occasions he allots the role of Father to NE VUZI, a still more remote group. MBENZA himself, of Manteke-Paza, says that he is indeed the father of NANGA, meaning that he is the original chief in the Manteke area who bestowed upon NSAKA and MFUTU in Mbanza Manteke whatever estate they have. This statement, however, is made only in private; publicly, as he told me, he recognizes NSAKA and MFUTU as neighbors, and will continue to do so as long as he is on good terms with them. His view of NTUMBA is that MVIKA NTUMBA are usurpers, the real NTUMBA being his own wife's house, MAKATI MA NTUMBA, but this claim he also makes only in private. The question is: On whose side will he testify in the dispute over Mbanza Ntala? He does not say, not even privately.

MBENZA of Kyanga, whose supposed relationship with MBENZA of Paza is not clear to me, have as their *n'tadi* NA MAZINGA, who "traveled the same road" from Mbanza Kongo. Clans that travel the same road are supposed to be able to witness to the truth of one another's traditions, and indeed often do. They also tend to intermarry more often with one another than with other clans. And indeed the groups listed in NTAMBU's book — NTAMBU, NKAZI A KONGO, DISA, MVIKA, and NA LUKUTI — have done so. But in Kyanga the amicable affinal relationship (*kinkwezi*) does not obtain between MBENZA and NA MAZINGA, each of whom says that he arrived first, thereby asserting that he is Father and patron of the other.

These two groups have partly resolved the dispute by a compromise over the headmanship of the village, an office invented by the colonial government and supposed to go to the chief of the clan designated by tradition as the owners of the village, the firstcomers. In Kyanga the office alternates between MBENZA and NA MAZINGA. That is how the people describe the principle; further inquiry reveals that the office, alternating between the clans, has also passed from father to son, the two clans being heavily intermarried, thus fulfilling the adage *kimfumu kya se, kimfumu kya mwana*, "the authority of the child is the authority of the father." This principle, fundamental to the Kongo idea of what authority is, is now most obvious in the ideology of certain prophetic churches.

It was in Kyanga, apparently, that the late government chief, Manyonza, discovered that the father of NANGA was NSUNDI. Using the prestige of his office to aid his inquiries, he made an effort to become what his appointment to office presupposed him to be, namely, an authority on tradition, and at the same time to justify his house, NSAKA, in its disputes with various opponents.

In search of information relevant to Manteke politics I too went to Kyanga, where I found that Manyonza had preceded me. In Kyanga, through which NSAKA says NANGA passed, he found a reputed expert on tradition who confirmed the NSAKA story, and added that since his own clan, NSUNDI, was "the first" to arrive in that area, it "must be" NANGA's father. This detail is now part of NSAKA's tradition, although as Manyonza's heir admits, "many people have never heard of it." Since no

NSUNDI group is domiciled in or near Mbanza Manteke, the assertion is very convenient for NSAKA. NSUNDI in Kyanga, however, makes the assertion simply as a deduction from his own tradition, which relates primarily to his status in that area. In the course of casual discussions, one can watch such deductions being made, although they appear in formal public argument only when the tactical situation calls for them.

Tradition, traced from Mbanza Kongo down to the present, defines an estate, comprising the lands of a given clan section, and the pattern of relationships among the houses and between the section and its neighbors. The particular traditions of the houses disagree in their descriptions of the estate, but agree, for example, that there is such a thing as NSAKA land, under one title or another. Another house could take possession of this land if all the members of NSAKA died out, and in fact DISA-NKUTI allege that this has already happened. Since all houses have reversionary rights in one another's holdings, it is possible to speak categorically of NANGA land, although not of the combined lands of NANGA and NTUMBA. NTUMBA has no share in the NANGA estate, though an NTUMBA house may dispute ownership of a particular tract of land with a NANGA house, as is true of Mbanza Ntala.

The house, not the clan section, is the landowning group; the indications of tradition in this respect are confirmed by the record of land transactions, including the reception of client strangers. Property in land corresponds to property in persons; the houses also own the persons of their members. The NTAMBU argument against NA LOMBO, cited above, shows that compensation for homicide is payable between houses but not within them. Confirmation of this principle is found in stories relating to pawns and slaves, in which the authority who decides whether such persons are incorporated in the descent group, freed, sold, or otherwise disposed of is represented as the head (*nkazi*) of the house.

An estate of a clan section or a house by definition results from the unique intersection of a particular *kitaata*, "patrifiliation," and *kingudi*, "matrifiliation." The members of a clan section or a house are, like the sibling group, children of the same mother and father (*ngudi mosi, se dimosi*). They occupy one "place" or status (*fulu kimosi*). The estate they enjoy, conferred on them by their Father, is at once a tract of land and *kimfumu*, which is social personality, independence, authority, self-respect, and the expectation of prosperity; analogous benefits are conferred upon any child by his father, who protects him from witchcraft and must be consulted in all crises.

4

LINEAGES

I said in my haste, All men are liars.
— PSALM 116:11

The houses of a clan section are divided into lineages, called *mafuta*, a mysterious name for a mysterious subject.[1] Younger men in Manteke are often unaware that the *mafuta* exist. KYANGALA NA NSUNDI, when asked how many *mafuta* there were in his house, first expressed astonishment, then embarrassment, saying he did not know; when pressed, he admitted there were three but refused to divulge their names. Because NANGA has been torn apart by political strife, its inner structure is relatively well known; it is with this clan that we shall be mostly concerned. The word *futa* is also used to refer to the house, just as *vumu* refers to the lineage as well as the house; the distinction made here reflects a tendency, not a rule of usage. The lineage can also be called, with reference to its principal function, the inheritance group. Members of a *futa* inherit one another's belongings (*bavingasananga mafwa*) and share the proceeds from marriages and funerals (*badiisananga mafundu*). A man has no public recourse, in customary law, if a member of his lineage steals from him.

The land belonging to a house is divided up among the lineages, but only in an approximate and provisional way "for the purposes of cultivation." The lineage has the first say in matters relating to the land allotted to it, but it does not have a distinct territorial estate as a house does. Correspondingly, the lineage is not identified by exclusive patrifiliation; no lineage claims a different paternity from the others, and there can be no discrepancies in their statements about the founding fathers of their houses. The divisions that appear on this level are not

1 The suggestion that *mafuta* refers to menstruation (*mfuta*), and carries on the metaphor that makes *vumu* (lit., "belly, womb") mean "descent group," was rejected by informants. *Futa*, "to pay," is another possible root.

a continuation or a repetition of the same kind of opposition as exists among the houses, the corporate levels being distinguished not only by the range of the constituent groups but by the particular affairs that concern them and the criteria that govern their relationships. In other words, the BaKongo do not have the segmentary lineage system that prevails among the Tiv of Nigeria, for example.

Upon inspection, the corporate character of a lineage often turns out to be transitory and elusive. My first example, from the MFUTU house of Nanga, is one of the most difficult.

MFUTU AND THE SIBLING GROUP

There is no question who belongs to MFUTU. With twenty-four resident adult members, half of them women, it is the largest house in NANGA and probably the largest in the village. The most important people, around whom all the controversy swirls, are seven elders. The most widely accepted view is that these men and their followers are divided into five lineages, as shown in table 1. In 1931 the names of the individuals mentioned in table 1, though in a different order and with a different allocation to lineages, were recorded by the government in a so-called genealogy of the chiefs. The 1931 version is the one given out then, and now, by NSAKA, who according to local theory is not a qualified source. The NSAKA version, in combination with others, does give some idea of changes in the political configuration since 1931, but here we are concerned only with current MFUTU versions.

TABLE 1
LINEAGES OF MFUTU

Lineage	Deceased members		Present elders
1. SWETE KYA TONA [1]	Na Bikadyo		Hezekaya
	Thomas		Nkomo
2. LEMBE KYA TONA	Lambi Vanana		Kingalu
	Na Makokila		
3. NDYENGO MYA TONA	*a.*	Na Mpyoso	None
		Lambi Kaya	
		Nsakala Nangudi	
		Nsiku Nsesi	
	b.	?	Maleso
	c.	?	Lusala
4. NZIMBU A TONA		?	Mbwaku
5. YANGA DYA TONA		?	Kinkela

[1] See figure 2.

The names SWETE, LEMBE, and so on, are the names of groups; they refer to magical concepts which the people no longer understand. They are not the names of eponymous ancestresses. The same is true of the names of houses, NSAKA, MFUTU, and the like, but the latter are sometimes personified in such expressions as *Na Nsamba wawuta Nsaka ye Mfutu*, "Na Nsamba gave birth to Nsaka and Mfutu," whereas the names of lineages apparently are not. I heard no statement such as *Mfutu wawuta Swete kya Tona*.

A linked series of names commonly identifies lineages; rarely do the names of houses form a similar series. Thus, the lineages of MFUTU are presented as magical attributes of Tona, which is a title of chiefship; at one time the attributes would have been embodied in charms constituting emblems and sources of chiefly power. When people wish to prove the slave status, or at least the alien origin and inferior pedigree, of all of MFUTU, they point out that "Tona" occurs in the praise name of MAZINGA; however, this kind of argument can be used to prove anything at all.

Identification is made by reference to the name of the lineage, or more often to a well-known male member of it: *mu fulu kya Kingalu*, "the same group as Kingalu"; or, *mu fulu kya Na Makokila. Fulu*, here variously translated "position," "status," "place," or "group," is the ordinary word for place or position; it is not a technical sociological term. The relationship may be expressed by the verb *vwa*, "to own," which is reciprocal and implies "to represent," "to speak for." Kingalu owns Na Makokila; Makokila in his lifetime owned Kingalu, his SiDaSo. The expression refers to matrilineal kinship only; it is not restricted to the lineage, any clansman being potentially the owner of any other.

Identification can be justified, when necessary, by tracing a descent line back to a recognized ancestress, even as far as the original mother of the lineage. Recital of this *lusansu*, "pedigree" (lit., "upbringing"), establishes an individual's link with his house and its tradition (*kinkulu*); the word *lusansu* itself has the same magical implications as *kinkulu*; it is one's personal charter. Traditions tend to be vague at the point in the story which corresponds to the genealogical link between house and lineage; some examples are given below (cf. J. Mertens, 1942, p. 16).

Both inside and outside MFUTU it is usually agreed that the senior lineage is SWETE KYA TONA. The implication is that the founding ancestress was the eldest of a group of sisters, though I did not hear it explicitly stated. The lineage is represented by three elderly people,

Hezekaya, Nkomo, and Mary Ntete, whose relationships are shown in figure 2.

Different accounts of the more remote relationships in this lineage variously identify Lambi Sumbu[2] as Na Bikadyo, as Na Bikadyo's daughter, or as a member of the generation of Ndona Nzinga. It is related that Na Bikadyo, the earliest ruler in Manteke to whom a genealogical link can purportedly be traced, wished to be formally inaugurated after she had become chief, but on the day when Children and Grandchildren had assembled for the event she had an issue of blood, and was deemed unfit. The chiefship then passed to Na Mpyoso of NDYENGO. It is also said that Na Bikadyo was a child of NGOMA LUBOTA, by whom she was given or from whom she bought Kimpumpu, adjacent to Mbanza Ntala; she was buried in this land, which means (according to some) that she had no foundation (*mbanza*) of her own.

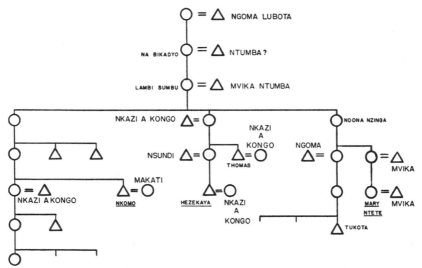

FIG. 2.   Genealogy of SWETE KYA TONA. Names underlined are those of persons now resident in the village.

In 1905 Mfumu Thomas of SWETE became government chief, wearing the medal until his death in 1914. In the interregnum that followed, his nephew Hezekaya was considered as a possible successor but was ruled out because of his youth and his unwillingness to serve. He subsequently had a long and distinguished career as a medical assistant in American Baptist Foreign Missionary Society hospitals. Upon re-

[2] "Lambi" (Nlambi, Ndambi-ndambi) is not a name but an Nkimba title meaning "cook."

turning to the village in the late 1950's Hezekaya built an enormous house, twice the size of any other in Manteke, in the enclosure of poplar trees which formerly sheltered his uncle the chief. The cost of this enterprise exceeded not only his resources but those of several of his nephews who cooperated with him, although they work in Kinshasa and are relatively prosperous; the house is still unpainted and unfurnished.

Referring to this incident, Nkomo corrected himself and said, *"my* nephews"; Hezekaya has no nephews of his own. As Kingalu, who is in a similar or still more distressing situation, remarked, a man without nephews is nobody, he has no authority *(kinkazi ve)*. Hezekaya's history indicates that he is an ambitious man; his ambition may have helped to make him the leading MFUTU politican, the principal opponent of NGOMA LUBOTA in the struggle for Mbanza Ntala.

As his recruiting of the nephews suggests, Hezekaya is effectively the *nkazi* of the lineage. He is nearly seventy, perhaps fifteen years older than Nkomo and thus his senior *(n'kuluntu)*. On the other hand Nkomo, who represents the senior line, is said by everybody to be "the real *nkazi*." He could properly be called Hezekaya's *n'kuluntu*. If both men were public speakers, the difference in principles might produce open conflict; as it is, neither of them speaks well in public, but Hezekaya speaks very forcefully behind the scenes *(ku nenga)* and in the affair with NGOMA LUBOTA has made himself spokesman for all of MFUTU. Nkomo, in contrast, likes a quiet life. Asked why he had built his house at the south end of the village, he said, "Well, when I retired, my brethren asked me to build up there with them, but in those days there were a lot of drinkers in that neighborhood who had some offensive habits, such as urinating against the walls of the house in the evening, so my sister Mary Ntete suggested I build near her." He lives, in fact, almost surrounded by MVIKA NTUMBA, and in connection with the controversy over Mbanza Ntala he sees the force of some NTUMBA arguments, such as those that turn on the story of Na Bikadyo. "So I mentioned this to Hezekaya and Mbwaku; since then they have excluded me from their meetings." Ironically, when these two men failed to appear in court one day against NTUMBA it was Nkomo who was summoned, as their owner, to explain where they were.

Hezekaya, Nkomo, and Mary Ntete share the produce of certain fruit trees left by their forebears. They may exchange gifts of such produce with other members of MFUTU, but not regularly. The pedigree, or respectability, of the members of this lineage is unchallenged even by NTAMBU and DISA, who declare, on another level of argument, that "all MFUTU are slaves."

Lambi Vanana, to whom the members of the second lineage, LEMBE

KYA TONA, trace their descent, had children by several men. One of her children was Na Makokila, whose relations with NTAMBU are recounted in the story of the Nsimbila War. He was "king" in Manteke when Richards arrived; that is, he was then *nkazi* of NANGA. By another man Lambi Vanana had Madede Dyambu, maternal grandmother of Joshua Kingalu, the present *nkazi* of NANGA. Kingalu has children and grand-children but no sister's children; he is thus the last of his line, and a lame duck. It is perhaps for this reason that he was chosen *nkazi* of NANGA; his being the heir of Na Makokila was not mentioned to me as a factor. (Kingalu was also the government chief in Manteke from 1917 to 1921.)

One factor in the choice of Kingalu as *nkazi* was certainly his speaking ability, his style being such as to make him an excellent chairman. He is chosen to express the consensus even on village occasions where his role as *nkazi* is irrelevant. In public and in private he emphasizes the unity of the brethren and never says anything controversial, although he can deliver a stern sermon when occasion demands. He is, in fact, the village's Protestant catechist; the job requires him to conduct services on Sunday mornings and at funerals, and pays him a treasured 200 francs or so a month. As head of the clan section, he should be an expert on tradition, but in all that relates to tradition (*kinkulu*) rather than pedigree (*lusansu*) he relies on NSAKA. In any event, it is not he but Hezekaya who takes the lead in land affairs, which are the corporate concern of the houses, not of the clan section.

Kingalu is not, however, devoid of political instincts. They are revealed in his diligent seeking-out of possible patrons, and in his view of the relation between his lineage and NDYENGO MYA TONA (see table 1). Lusala of NDYENGO says that LEMBE is the third and not the second lineage. If so, then LEMBE is not the heir apparent to NDYENGO, in accordance with the rule of matrilineal seniority, but NDYENGO is the heir apparent to LEMBE. The question is complex because there are three sublineages[3] associated with the NDYENGO position, two of them represented by live inhabitants of Manteke, the third by certain very active ghosts.

The story of the three components of NDYENGO is as follows. According to tradition, when Na Bikadyo of SWETE was unable to go through with her inauguration, she said that her "brother" Na Mpyoso of NDYENGO, whose name implies that "he was a great chief, and when he saw a stranger would have him kidnaped,"[4] should be chief in her

---

[3] There is no specific Kongo equivalent for "sublineage," although *ngudi*, "mother," which applies to segments of any order, could be used.

[4] *Mfumu don Manuele Mpiozo dia Bazika, nzenza kavangwa nkuta, wanwana vita*

place, so that all the money she had spent need not be wasted. Na Mpyoso was the last real chief; having buried his predecessor with two live slaves to hold him, one at the head and one at the foot, he had power his squeamish successors lacked. The earliest named ancestress of NDYENGO MYA TONA is Lambi Kaya, who may or may not have been fathered by Na Mbuku a Wala of NGOMA LUBOTA. Also associated with NDYENGO and Na Mpyoso are the ghosts mentioned above, including Na Vwaza, who was perhaps of the same generation as Lambi Kaya, and the latter's descendants, Nsiku Nsesi, Nsakala Nangudi, and Mampuya. Nsiku Nsesi was given land in the forest Mfula, adjacent to Mbanza Ntala, by his Fathers, NGOMA LUBOTA. The other two were involved in a dispute over the government chiefship with NSAKA and the rest of MFUTU, a dispute so sulfurous that Manteke still reeks of it forty years later (see chap. 10). All of this line died out. The succession is disputed by Lusala and Maleso, whose stories follow.

Lusala's maternal grandmother, stolen as a young girl by NKAZI A KONGO when she was gleaning peanuts, was sold away to Ngombe, west of Mbanza Nkazi; it would have been dangerous to keep her close to Manteke. Her daughter and her grandson, Lusala, were identified and redeemed, after the coming of the missionaries, by a member of SWETE who went to Ngombe as a catechist. The price was a pig and two cooking pots. Lusala has no doubt that he is heir to the NDYENGO position; in his view only he and Kingalu and the SWETE lineage are hereditary freemen and landholders in MFUTU. Others admit that Lusala belongs in MFUTU, "but we are waiting for Kingalu, as *nkazi*, to reveal Lusala's pedigree" so that his status can be properly determined. One opinion is that although Lusala is descended from MFUTU, yet his own and his mother's sojourn in Ngombe have given them "the blood of slavery"; this statement is a version of the rule that a redeemed slave is dependent on the lineage whose members paid for the redemption (Mbanza Manteke 97, 1956; Pool 2, 1953; 33, 1954).

Lusala's line is in the process of extinction. Its principal competitor, the line of Maleso, is expanding. Maleso was the first sector chief in Manteke, the predecessor of the present mayor. After his election to the post in 1944 his initial popularity among his MFUTU brethren waned because, it is said, he put his kinsmen in jail as readily as anyone else. There were doubtless other reasons, but about 1951 a showdown occurred between Maleso and Lusala at which the following story, now common knowledge, was revealed (this version is a composite):

("Le Chef M. ne veut pas que l'on nourrisse les étrangers, il veut qu'on leur fasse la guerre"). Given as a praise name of NANGA (De Roeck, 1958, p. 12), it is, rather, the personal praise name of the chief.

Na Vwaza [5] of NDYENGO went to the Nkenge market at Kongo dya Lemba where a woman gave him her infant to hold while she went to buy some rattles. Seeing that it was a good baby, he put it in his *nkutu* bag and made off with it, bringing it to the MFUTU village of Ntombo in the Manteke valley. Here the infant was given to a palm-wine drawer to raise. When she grew up, Na Makokila married her to Na Mfyengenene of MVIKA. Then when Na Vwaza's line died out, we the Children and Grandchildren put her descendant Maleso in the place; as the proverb says, *Dyala dya lufukunya, ngembo uvingilanga dyo* ["The *ngembo* inherits the nest of the *lufukunya*"].[6] But a lot of people are unhappy about it.

The practice of adoption was regularly resorted to by lineages faced with extinction, but no rule of succession in Kongo is likely to go unchallenged. Maleso himself never suggests that he is anything but NDYENGO, although it is universally known that his matrilineal ancestors were NGIMBI from across the Lufu River. The question of who accepts his legitimacy as NDYENGO and who does not serves as a guide to the political factions in the village.

Two lines, therefore, are competing for recognition as the rightful heirs of Na Mpyoso as NDYENGO. There is also the possibility that neither is entitled to the place, that both must acknowledge the prior claim of the next lineage in order of seniority to succeed to the estate, the real NDYENGO having died out (*fuukidi*). Kingalu of LEMBE, in discussions with me, consistently sought to give me the impression that he was the heir to NDYENGO, or rather, that he *was* NDYENGO, even going so far as to say that Lambi Vanana and Lambi Kaya occupy "one place" (*fulu kimosi*), although genealogical plotting makes it obvious that they do not. If the role of NDYENGO has accrued to LEMBE, then NDYENGO was indeed the third lineage in order of seniority. But if, as Lusala says, NDYENGO was second, then the heir is SWETE, the first lineage. Since LEMBE also is about to be extinct, the best thing for Lusala to do, given the uncertainty of his own status, is to stick close to SWETE. And in fact he does just that, although he has not indicated to anyone what his motives are.

The foregoing discussion, referring only to the first three lineages of MFUTU, reveals two lines of argument, both having to do with succession. In the first, the principle of seniority by descent, that is, birth order of the initial sibling group, is not at issue; the difficulty is to determine what the order was. The second line of argument is a matter of contradictory principles: (1) once an original descent group is extinct, its place is taken by the next-senior descent group; (2) a lineage

---

5 *Vwaza*, "to scramble."

6 *Lufukunya* and *ngembo* are two kinds of bat (cf. Van Roy and Daeleman, 1963, no. 120).

may assure its perpetuation by incorporating strangers, according to approved public procedures. On the difference between the two principles hang half the arguments in Manteke.

So far it has been taken for granted that the membership of the initial sibling group — the list of lineages jostling for position — is fixed. Consideration of the last two MFUTU lineages, NZIMBU and YANGA, shows that the number of lineages is not necessarily fixed, and that the list, in this instance, is probably in the process of complete reorganization. Most outsiders agree that SWETE, LEMBE, and NDYENGO are the only true freemen (*mfumu za kanda*) entitled to share in the MFUTU estate. The following widely known story attributes the origins of NZIMBU and YANGA to slavery and pawnship. The version told by NTAMBU takes off from the story of the Nsimbila War, at the beginning of which Madede Nkembi is married to Nsyama Nsemo. Before that she had been married to Na Tawula of NKAZI A KONGO, and it was her own daughter by this marriage, Tembo Mayumba, whom NTAMBU handed over to NANGA-MFUTU as quittance for their part in the war. The girl was then sold by MFUTU to VUZI DYA NKUWU near Palabala, on the other side of Kongo dya Lemba.

Na Tawula's successor, of the same name, traded down in that direction; he passed through Lukangu, slept in Wolo, and came to the forest Mvwadu. There he hid some food upon which a daughter of Tembo Mayumba happened to come while she was out looking for firewood. Na Tawula caught her eating the food, and enslaved [7] her for theft. After bringing her back to Ntombo a Nkazi he sold a share in her to Na Mafinda of NTUMBA in Ndemba. There she gave birth to two daughters. When one of these was a small girl, the other still at the breast, Na Tawula ran short of money and came to Na Mafinda to try to sell him the woman outright for a hundred *nzimbu*-shells and a box of gunpowder. Na Mafinda, having no money either, preferred to return the woman, regaining his investment. The elder daughter remained in Ndemba to be brought up, but Na Tawula sold the woman and her daughter to Na Vwaza of MFUTU in Ntombo, who scrambled them into MFUTU under the name NZIMBU A TONA.

The elder daughter married in Ndemba and had children. Later on, Na Makokila of MFUTU-LEMBE, who besides marrying Lusobo of NTAMBU had also married into NKAZI A KONGO, suggested to his son Kingalu Musesa, after whom Joshua Kingalu is named, that he redeem his kinsmen in Ndemba; Na Makokila even gave him the pig that Kingalu paid to Na Mafinda for the trouble he had taken in looking after his erstwhile slaves. So Kingalu Musesa of NKAZI A KONGO made his father a present of the daughter, and all her offspring were entered into MFUTU as YANGA DYA TONA. But in reality, they are NTAMBU!

[7] This slave-gathering technique was also used by Europeans (Johnston, 1884, p. 26).

This story is as full of holes as anything else told by NTAMBU, whose interest in it is to discredit the patrons of NTAMBU's rival, NA LOMBO. The transition from tradition to pedigree is marked by the unusual anonymity of the female characters, in spite of the critical importance attached to their identity. The anonymity is associated with the awkward doubling of Na Tawula. The stretching-out of the generations seems both unlikely and unnecessary. The narrator, patently misunderstanding the obsolete institution of partnership (*kimbundi*) as applied to slaves, has Na Tawula redeem Na Mafinda's share in the woman; but the story immediately indicates that Na Mafinda kept his share in Ndemba in the form of the elder daughter. It was probably much the same sort of transaction in which Na Makokila was involved with Kingalu Musesa. Anyway, the story appealed to NZUZI, who used it in court in an attempt to show that his MFUTU opponent, as a slave, could not possibly be the owner of the forest Mayombe; in the words of the court transcript, he said to him, "Si tu veux connaître ton clan, arrêter un cochon." [8] Even NZUZI, however, admitted that the version recited to me was not the same as he had heard before.

Kinkela, whom I have listed (in table 1) as the representative of YANGA, volunteered YANGA as his lineage, but he was not at all sure about it. He takes part in politics only as a follower of Mbwaku of NDYENGO, and it is to this house that the best-informed opinions assign him; in this view, YANGA is extinct. Mbwaku, when asked to list the lineages of MFUTU, revealed that he knew the five names but insisted that all were brethren together, divided if at all into only two lineages: Hezekaya's, which he called NZIMBU, and everyone else's, which he called SWETE. It is possible that he was making a spur-of-the-moment effort to find something to say in response to an awkward question. He was unable, or unwilling, to trace any matrilineal genealogical link between himself and Kinkela and Hezekaya. Hezekaya himself, insisting on unity, refuses to talk about the lineages.

Given the inferior status assigned to his lineage by tradition (i.e., by prevailing public opinion), Mbwaku has no choice but to attach himself as closely as possible to the name of SWETE KYA TONA and the personal leadership of Hezekaya, if he and his followers (NZIMBU and YANGA) are to play a political role commensurate with their numbers. [9]

---

[8] Appeal, Matadi 134, 1958. The phrase "arrêter un cochon" attempts to translate literally *kanga ngulu*, "get ready a pig," a phrase implying rejection.

[9] The demographic factor and the problem of evaluating it quantitatively are mentioned again in chapter 9 (see pp. 198–201). In spite of all the reservations that might be made, the figures for the resident adult membership of the lineages are still instructive. Among the resident adults is one elder who lives sufficiently

But there is another factor. The physical resemblance of the three men alerted me to the fact that their patrilateral relationship is very close. Each is a child or a grandchild of the same lineage of NSUNDI in Vunda, probably a group of brothers (fig. 3).

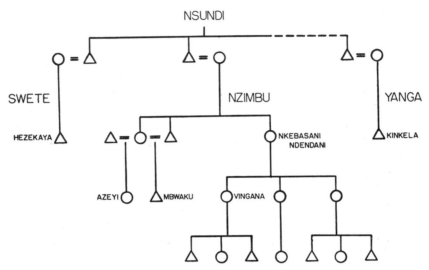

FIG. 3. Patrilateral links of some members of MFUTU.

The NSUNDI in question are a particular house, KYANGALA NA NSUNDI, of a clan section that owns the village of Kyesa Kifwa, near Kinganga, almost beyond the normal range of Manteke social intercourse. KYAN-GALA has many members living in Mbanza Manteke, Vunda, and Ndemba, where they have apparently served for at least three genera-tions as a kind of clearinghouse for patrilateral relations between NTUMBA and NANGA. Although the houses presently dominating Kyesa Kifwa have the usual reservations about the pedigree of the Manteke branch, they are on good speaking terms and participate normally in one another's affairs. NSUNDI owns no land in Manteke, though they may have been given some in Vunda; they are never spoken of dis-paragingly, but merely as landowners from Kyesa Kifwa resident else-where for family reasons. They are strongly intermarried with DISA and MFUTU of NANGA, and with MVIKA NTUMBA and MFULAMA NKANGA. That

close to Manteke, though not in the village proper, to appear frequently in its affairs. The number of adult residents in each lineage (see table 1) is as follows:

1. SWETE: 3	3. NDYENGO *a*: 0	4. NZIMBU: 11
2. LEMBE: 1	*b*: 2	5. YANGA: 4
	c: 3	

much is clear, although I was prevented from obtaining all the relevant genealogical material by the jealousies operating among the three NSUNDI lineages, and by the late date of my own discovery of the importance of this network.

The focus of tradition and scandal is matrilineal succession because matrikinsmen compete for a given estate. Patrilateral links do not attract the same attention; they are ideally suited to cooperative arrangements through which individuals recruit support in opposition to their matrikinsmen, or against other competitors. A brother on the father's side (*mu kise*) makes a good go-between in marriage arrangements, for example. NANGA and NTUMBA are much intermarried, but the value of NTUMBA support in the internecine relations of NANGA houses is reduced by the simultaneous hostility prevailing between NANGA and NTUMBA as a whole. Hence the value of a neutral clearing-house such as NSUNDI.

Another example, much more important in the past generation than in the present one, is provided by NA LUKUTI, whose lands lie toward the Lunyonzo River and adjacent to Kyesa Kifwa. NA LUKUTI was represented in Manteke by the celebrated arbitrator and polygynist Willy "Commissaire" Dyamvimba, whose elaborate tomb crumbles from neglect in the so-called cemetery of the chiefs. This cemetery, which also contains the unmonumented graves of Mboko a Nkosi, Na Makokila, and Thomas, to whom Willy was aide and adviser, is close to the now deserted suburb of Kyese over which he presided and whence, so they say, the assembled voices of NTAMBU, NSAKA, NA LUKUTI, and their ad-

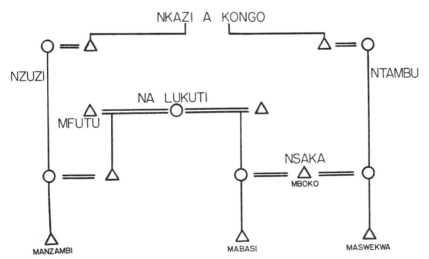

FIG. 4. Selected kinship links of NZUZI, NSAKA, and NTAMBU.

herents echoed across the valleys. Genealogies show the high relative degree of intermarriage among these groups; figure 4 illustrates a fraction of the relevant kinship links resulting from intermarriage. The three men in the most junior generation form one of the best-organized political factions in Manteke.

NSAKA AND THE SIGNIFICANCE OF GENEALOGY

The role of NA LUKUTI introduces the subject of the interrelationships of the lineages of the NSAKA house of NANGA (fig. 5). These lineages probably inhabited the three towns that confronted Richards' first settlement. Since I did not discover the names of these lineages, they are identified by the names of the three towns: Mbanza Mboma, Mbanza Suki, and Mbanza Kintala.

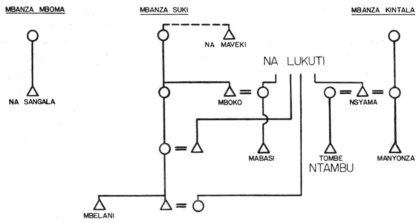

FIG. 5. Lineages of NSAKA.

Na Sangala of Mbanza Mboma is said to have been *nkazi* of NANGA after Na Mpyoso, but he lacked the special powers that flow from the sacrifice of slaves. "Na Sangala," says the current NSAKA, "didn't care for that sort of thing." His role in the Nsimbila War has been described. This line is extinct, everyone agrees.

The last of the lineage of Mbanza Kintala was the late government chief, Samuel Manyonza. The man presently recognized by the government as customary chief of Manteke is Mbelani, *nkazi* of NSAKA, whose definition of his own social status is bitterly resented by many elders in the region, particularly DISA and NKUTI. According to Mbelani, he represents the Mbanza Suki line to which Na Makokila's successor, the government chief Mboko a Nkosi, belonged. Before that the *nkazi* of this lineage was Na Maveki, whose pedigree is unknown, even to Mbelani. It is admitted that Na Maveki bought a large forest from NKAZI A KONGO, which shows, according to NSAKA's opponents, that he must have been a landless stranger; what other reason could there be?

The reason for dwelling on this squabble is that unusually abundant documentation is available for the genealogy of NSAKA, including four compilations made by outside investigators over the period 1922–1965. These documents contain many omissions and contradictions, and there are sometimes vagaries of spelling which make identification difficult. The temptation is to dismiss all or most of the versions as corruptions of an original genealogy no longer available in its entirety. If, on the other hand, one assumes that the informant in each instance was saying exactly what he wanted to say, a pattern emerges. This pattern corresponds to the way in which genealogical information is actually recited and used in real life, and it forces the investigator to recognize that the written genealogy he constructs is quite different, and that the basic principles of genealogy — the distinctions of sex and generation — are only marginally relevant.

The BaKongo are not genealogically minded (cf. L. Bohannan, 1952). Explaining what a *futa* was, Kingalu used the phrase *nkayi mosi*, "descendants of a single grandparent or ancestor." But this dogmatic expression is used by people who are admittedly unable to demonstrate the relationship. Between the founding ancestress of the lineage and the most remote one to whom links can be specifically traced backward from the present, an unspecifiable but large number of generations is believed to intervene. It is pointed out that the ancestors often inherited their names, which came to serve as appropriated titles of lineage and house. Even if the ancestors did not make such identifications, people now do it for them, and use names like Na Sangala and Na Nkazi Makonko to mean "whoever was the leader of that group at that time." Informants' statements from which a genealogy can be constructed include stories about people who married and begot children, and also pedigrees by which individuals link themselves to the estate in which they claim shares. An *nkazi*'s pedigree may list fourteen or fifteen previous holders of the office.

Some informants have a more comprehensive view than others, and some descent groups are more explicitly organized than others, but nobody presumes to offer a complete genealogical record. There are examples of confusion regarding generation and sex; discrepancies begin at the level of the senior informants' grandparental generation, and people are often unsure of a grandmother's name. What they are sure of, or believe themselves sure of, is the status or position (*fulu*) to which the grandmother belonged. "All these people," says the interlocutor, tearing off an incantation of names, "are *fulu kimosi*" ("belong in the same place"). The anthropologist, who has heard the same individual described in the space of ten minutes as the mother, sister, and namesake of another individual, voices doubts that are met with an expression of impatience and yet another version, at top speed: "Kinwani Kyatana Nzingu, Nkunkuta Mbende, Sofi Mandwezi, Lambi Kongo Nangudi . . ."

The real significance of genealogical information, in Manteke thought, may be summarized as follows: The structure of groups, that is, the social morphology, is set out in tradition which establishes positions (*bifulu*), each associated with an estate composed of rights and obligations. At the highest level the clan section (*kanda*) owns rights to marry off its female members to other sections; that is, it is exogamous. Its internal affairs consist mainly of the relations among its component houses, each of which has reversionary rights to the landholdings of the others according to an order of precedence and succession which is itself, in most instances, highly controversial. This estate is represented by an *nkazi*, who ought to be the senior member of the senior house; in practice, he is chosen from the available elders, sometimes with regard to a principle of alternation between the most influential houses. In regulating the internal and external affairs of the clan section, a committee consisting of the senior children (*baana ba mbuta*) of the clan section and other patrilateral and affinal relatives commonly exceeds in importance the elders of the group, including the *nkazi*.

Each house (*nzo, vumu, ngudi*) owns an aggregation of lands and the tradition that is its title. Its internal affairs consist primarily of the relations among its component lineages, which are also regulated to an important degree, at least formally, by a committee of kin. (The operation of these committees is illustrated in the chapters forming Part II of this volume.) Each house also has, or should have, its *nkazi*.

Apart from their common interest in the affairs of the house, expressed in arguments over precedence, the lineages (sing., *futa, ngudi, vumu*) have no external affairs; correspondingly, a lineage has no committee and no public role. The lineage estate consists of movable wealth, including the produce of fruit trees left by the ancestors, the standing crops and private goods and valuables left by deceased members, and a large share of the receipts from funerals and weddings of members. These events are administered primarily by the *nkazi* of the lineage, who is responsible (in theory) for the debts and social obligations of the other members. A lineage's internal contributions and distributions are made in private.

Lusansu, including genealogy, is the kind of argument deployed by groups of matrikinsmen in order to fit themselves into the structure of corporations defined by tradition (*kinkulu*). Applying the concept of a *fulu* to the various NSAKA genealogies, and ignoring the discrepancies regarding generation in particular, we perceive a pattern that makes sociological sense and also permits us to venture some historical speculations. Throughout the documents in question certain names, mostly of men such as Mboko and Na Sangala, are associated in clusters. When these clusters are identified, it can be seen that the remainder of the genealogy consists of a relatively small number of women related to one another and to the clusters of men by sibling ties or matrifiliation. These ties reveal a considerable number of discrepancies until they are read as statements about precedence rather than as genealogical statements. As statements about precedence they correlate very well with relevant political rumors and with the positions of the informants, each of whom presents the structure to his own apparent advantage.

Collectively the documents show four groups of matrikinsmen in NSAKA competing for three *bifulu.* The four are associated with the names Na Sangala, Mboko a Nkosi, Samuel Manyonza, and Mbelani; the last of these lines, that of Na Maveki, has been grafted onto the line of Mboko (see fig. 5). The origins of Na Sangala and Mboko are too remote to be worth pursuing. The Mbanza Kintala line (Manyonza), according to DISA tradition, originated in a migration from Kongo dya Lembe;[10] others say that it came from the east. The forebears of the present NSAKA, including Na Maveki, the man who married Kimpenze of NTAMBU, are said to have come from the east, near Kimpese. (My own cursory inquiries among NANGA of Kimpese confirmed the story of a migration to Manteke, but according to my informants *all* the Manteke NANGA were offshoots of the "original" or Kimpese stem.)

This reconstruction essentially agrees with the stories put forward, though with no coherent justification, by NSAKA's detractors. If it is correct, it tends to explain two puzzles of village political history. The first greatly exercised the government's investigator in 1932: Why did the government chiefship pass, in 1905, from Mboko of NSAKA to Thomas of MFUTU? The second is the animosity that apparently existed between Manyonza, who died in 1962, and his successor, Mbelani. Each

10 From the location of Manteke's Nkimba site just behind Mbanza Kintala, it would seem that the Nkimba rite, which originated in the west, was introduced by the Manyonza branch of NSAKA, probably in the middle of the nineteenth century.

chief may well have regarded himself as the last legitimate member of his house. The reconstruction is no more than plausible, however, and I must emphasize that it is based on reasoning quite different from that usually employed in Manteke to grapple with such questions.

The government chiefship, which returned to NSAKA in the person of Manyonza, was replaced in 1944 by a sector organization with an elected head. Despite the change the office of government chief persisted in a most curious way. After Manyonza's death his sister's son Mbelani became government chief (*chef coutumier*) by displacing his less aggressive and less capable elder brother. Among the many things held against Mbelani is his inheritance, or, as his jealous opponents say, his theft of Manyonza's book of tradition. Be that as it may, Mbelani is the only real technician of *kinkulu* in Manteke, a village very much underprivileged in this regard. Whereas the self-declared experts chant strings of names, thrust their stories upon others while declaiming the importance of secrecy, and contradict themselves with every breath, Mbelani speaks only when he can be effective and collects information in an organized way. He picks up what fits, what is "true" because it fits.

NSAKA is a house that has only one lineage; as the *nkazi* put it, three *bivumu* but now only one *futa*. Its future existence depends on the continuing health of the children of a niece, the only woman of child-bearing age, who is a prostitute in Lufu. Another risk is that of disenfranchisement, should all the current rumors be translated into litigation. Mbelani's prime opponent is the *nkazi* of NKUTI, a house that also has only one lineage of two adult males. Whereas NKUTI believes, with DISA, that Mbelani is an interloper with no right to the NSAKA heritage, and that NSAKA is only a younger brother and client anyway, Mbelani tells the following story, without insisting tactlessly on the inference to be drawn, which is that NKUTI are pawns of NSAKA:

After NGOMA LUBOTA had acquired Mbanza Ntala from Mfutu, Na Kalundi Nkwangu sold a piece of it, a tract of forest on the north slope called Kingangu, to Na Mwandembo of NKUTI. Because the latter had no money, he borrowed *funda dimosi* ["a thousand"] from Mboko of NSAKA. When he failed to repay the loan, Mboko took the land in pawn. Then all of NKUTI died out except for a small girl whom Mboko brought up and whose marriage money he later ate.

There are two curious things about NKUTI. One is that some of its members, those who reside in Manteke village, described themselves as DISA in reply to my census questions, and a number of informants queried the existence of two separate houses. The other is the paucity of legendary or genealogical material on the antecedents of this line and the number of its ancestors who also appear in NSAKA genealogies. Applying the technique described above, it can be shown that the genealogy of NUKUTI is merely a statement that its earliest named ancestress was attached to the lineage of Mboko a Nkosi of NSAKA; the story of Na Mwandembo's loan says the same thing. A plausible historical reconstruction is that the original NKUTI died out and that the present NKUTI were originally a DISA group who became attached to NSAKA in the 1880's and subsequently asserted their independence.

It is no wonder, then, that NKUTI lives in the Lunyonzo valley, on the Kinganga road, where he runs a trading establishment. The ruins of his house are to be seen beside the store he operates in Manteke, which he keeps supplied by means of a truck so beset by mechanical troubles that it is known to passengers as *Nata Vunga*, "Bring a blanket." Says Kingalu, "We urged him to stay here with his brethren, but for some reason he wouldn't." The burden of NKUTI's view of Manteke is that he is the only real traditional chief, and that one of these days he is going to call a meeting and tell each one of "these foreigners," beginning with Mbelani and Kingalu, just what his pedigree is. I looked forward to this occasion, to which I was to be invited, until I realized that it is simply a dream; there is not even any sign that NKUTI commands a battery of suitable traditions which would enable him to mount such an assault.

Further exploration in the debris scattered around Mbanza Mboma, the NSAKA capital, suggests that in the late nineteenth century there was a subordinate population of slaves and pawns whose offspring were shunted with some rapidity between powerful neighboring *bankazi*, whose clan names they and their descendants, alive and dead, now bear: NSAKA of Manteke, MFUTU of Manteke, NTUMBA and MFULAMA NKANGA of Ndemba, NKAZI A KONGO of Ntombo a Nkazi, and NA LUKUTI of Ntombo a Lukuti. Some of this population is now called NTAMBU or NA LOMBO, and much of the relevant material on them has already been quoted. Another lot, said by NTAMBU to be "really NTAMBU," are fairly obviously a single descent group, genealogically speaking, which has been shared by MFUTU, NKAZI A KONGO, and NA LUKUTI. Part of the evidence for this conclusion is the story of the origins of YANGA DYA TONA and NZIMBU A TONA, given earlier in this chapter. Other lineages with similarly obscure pedigrees are found in most houses.

The dissensions in the NANGA clan section are notorious. Mabwaka, the prophet at Kemba, attributed them to the exceptional sinfulness of the Manteke population. We have reviewed the affairs of NSAKA and MFUTU, with some reference to DISA and NKUTI; all these houses consider that they ought to own the chiefship.

Since NZUZI, the remaining house of NANGA, cannot aspire to chief-ship, it is relatively peaceful. It has developed an alternative estate under the patronage of the Protestant mission. NZUZI is divided into three lineages. Representatives of one of them live in Kyanga, and have apparently withdrawn from the affairs of the rest of their house and clan. "We invited them to live here, but for some reason they don't want to." The other two lineages benefited from the circumstance that the mission complex was built in Yongo on NZUZI land, and the mis-sion's protégés, redeemed slaves and servants, were settled in the adja-cent suburb of Kivulusa, meaning "Salvation," where they became, in the context of village politics, clients of NZUZI. Individual NZUZI distin-guished themselves in the mission service and named their children and nephews after Richards and other missionaries. Now the mission has gone, most of the children and nephews are putting their education to work in town, and the population of Kivulusa settled around the moldering NZUZI mansions is thinning out. The *nkazi*, a relatively wealthy ex-sailor and merchant who owns the only functioning auto-mobile for miles around, tends to regard traditional affairs with dis-dain, prompting another elder to remark that those who do not care to contribute at other people's funerals may find the attendance short at their own. Although the two lineages are distinct and apparently free of disputes, their membership is in doubt; until one of the wealth-ier elders dies, no one can say which of the hundreds of NZUZI in town will appear at the funeral to claim a share in the inheritance.

Peace also reigns in MVIKA NTUMBA, about whose lineages nothing much is known except that there are only two, one of them with almost as many members as the whole of MFUTU. So, at least, thinks an in-formed outsider; my own genealogical data, showing descent lines and marriage patterns, indicate more divisions than two but it is possible that they are merely emergent. Because NANGA were the first to get the ear of the colonial government, the whole of NTUMBA was excluded from consideration for the rule of government chief. On account of the chiefship, so people say, the members of NANGA began to accuse one another of slave descent. Yet similar conflicts arise elsewhere, even when no office is in question; internal conditions are probably as im-portant as external ones in originating political struggles. Important variables, external and internal, include personal ambitions and abili-ties and the demographic structure of the groups concerned.

As the stories show, the processes by which persons were transferred from one group to another include slavery and pawnship (discussed in chap. 10). The point to note here is that the descent groups that make up present-day social morphology result from the working out, in relatively recent times, of political conventions; each generation inherits a confusion of debts, assets, scandals, and grievances which it sorts out as best it can according to the resources available to it. Included among the resources is a body of rules, a model — far from consistent, to be sure — of what the social structure should be.

VARIATIONS ON THE DESCENT PRINCIPLE

Descent defines social legitimacy. The difference between a freeman (*mfumu*) and a slave is that the latter cannot, to the satisfaction of the public, trace his pedigree (*lusansu*) in such a way as to locate himself unambiguously in the structure of estates. The disputes reviewed up to this point have been the internal affairs of particular groups. According to theory, questions of pedigree are always the exclusive concern of such groups; if they wish to incorporate slaves, that is their business. On the other hand, the dogma that a slave is always a slave and can never exercise a freeman's rights may lead to the argument that because the present occupants of a given position are illegitimate the rights pertaining to the position should revert to outsiders. Examples of this kind of claim have been discussed in connection with the lineage NDYENGO MYA TONA of MFUTU and the house NSAKA, but all their affairs are internal concerns of the NANGA clan section.

The internal structure of a house may be an issue in a dispute between houses of different clans; such a dispute is likely to be particularly delicate and explosive. In 1965 the most active dispute in Mbanza Manteke concerned, as I have mentioned, the ownership of Mbanza Ntala, an abandoned site in the middle of the Manteke valley. MFUTU of NANGA, led by Hezekaya, claims the site from NGOMA LUBOTA of NTUMBA, a house that has only two adult male members, Joel Albert and Kyanlasu. Joel Albert, an elderly ex-sailor who speaks English, is famous for having once deserted his ship in Europe and lived ashore there for a while before being brought back by the colonial government. Because of infirmities he keeps very much to himself except for occasional forays into the village for a social drink. He cultivates only in the vicinity of his house, which stands at some distance from the other houses. He makes no use of the NGOMA lands, though various relatives cultivate in them. As the head of the senior house he could be the *nkazi* of NTUMBA, but he has no speaking ability and apparently does not care to participate in local affairs. For years, however, he has been engaged in a dispute with NANGA KYA MFUTU over the ownership of Mbanza Ntala and adjacent properties. He is supported by relatives in Manteke and in town, but his principal aide and spokesman is **Kyanlasu.**

Kyanlasu, an aggressive younger man whose usual contribution to any conversation is a violently impassioned speech, lives in the middle of the village in a house left by Johnny Matota, whom he describes as his elder (*n'kuluntu*). He himself was born elsewhere; his pedigree is obscure, and there is no doubt that he speaks in this affair not in his own right but as the voice of Joel Albert. Although the parties have been in court several times, for various reasons the case has not yet been heard in full, and the arguments on each side are not publicly known in detail. The MFUTU argument appears to be that they, as owners of Mbanza Ntala, for which they had no immediate use (having moved to Ntombo), gave it to their Child, NGOMA. As the story goes,

> MFUTU had married an NGOMA girl, from over near the Luima; after she had been brought back to Manteke she gave birth to a child, which died. Her relatives didn't come to the funeral. When a second child died they were sent for, but they said, "It's too far, why don't you just pay us something and keep the girl." [11] So MFUTU accepted their child NGOMA as a permanent resident and gave him land to live on. But now they say that Johnny Matota was the last of these original NGOMA, and that Joel Albert's forebears followed after, and occupied some kind of client status [*bonso mu kimvwa*]. The land was not given to them, nor are they entitled to it.

MFUTU's argument is on two levels. First, there is only one NGOMA estate, conferred by MFUTU on Matota's ancestors; Joel Albert's ancestors lack the pedigree entitling them to inherit the place. Second, Kyanlasu himself (whose background is discussed again in chap. 10) belongs to a third and still less respectable line; this part of the argument is a risky one to pursue in public, because it can be construed as meddling in NGOMA's internal affairs, and for that a penalty can be exacted.

NGOMA's argument is that Joel Albert is the legitimate *nkazi* of the house, and that in any event Mbanza Ntala was originally founded by NGOMA, who settled MFUTU groups on surrounding lands as his clients. Within NGOMA there are two lineages (*mafuta*), one represented by Joel Albert and the other, as far as the outside public is concerned, by Kyanlasu.

If NGOMA should definitively lose the case, they would, in theory, face a choice between moving elsewhere and accepting the patronage of MFUTU, with the prospect of eventual incorporation in the MFUTU

---

[11] Members of the same clan section accept the obligation to bury one another (*baziikana*) (see Van Wing, 1959, p. 89).

house. In disputes referring to the historical priority of different groups (external relations) and to the precedence of siblings within the same group (internal relations), the grammar of the argument in each case turns on the contradictory rules of succession quoted above in connection with the first three lineages of MFUTU: (1) once an original descent group is extinct, its place is taken by the next-senior descent group, but slaves can never inherit; (2) a lineage may assure its perpetuation by incorporating strangers who, as heirs, become freemen.

As we have seen, the field of political action in cases involving this contradiction is not in practice limited to the group whose internal structure is in doubt. The outcome of any dispute depends on the political role of the parties in the community at large. Matrifiliation and patrifiliation are complementary terms in the idiom of political communication, expressing conjunction and disjunction in a field of corporate relations. A group, in the context of its external relations, consists of the descendants of a single ancestress, who are "one place"; internally, the differentiation of elements in terms of authority over the corporate estate is expressed on a scale in which brotherhood (*kimpangi*) signifies equality, seniority (*kikota*) implies relative subordination, and patrifiliation (*kimwana*) implies absolute subordination in some degree of clientage. The scale reappears in the range of meaning attached to such words as *nleeke* ("cadet") and *mwana* ("child, slave").

Although the separation of estates indicated by patrifiliation supposedly makes for a cooperative relationship, the possibility of competition tending to substitute one descent group for another in control of an estate is fully recognized. "Of the chief Na Kwazu it is said that he had many children and grandchildren, but he feared for his life because he had land and they had none." Clients (slaves) are reputed to multiply faster than the real owners of the land because their link with the local *bisimbi* spirits is more recent and therefore more vigorous. The situation is set out in a lament that employs the anthill as symbol of the descent group; anthills also represent the ancestral graves and have phallic associations:

> Mbuta keti nani e? Nani wasaala vana?
> Di menene malundw'e ee, kyadi yay'e![12]
>
> Who is the elder here? Who remains?
> Things are growing on the termite hill, alas!

[12] "Chant judiciaire," in *Ngonge*, 1960, no. 1. In this connection, despondent elders cite Mark, XIII, 12.

The following story, an example of patrifilial conflict, shows the connection between internal and external relations.

In Kyesa Kayenge, Nsyobo's father in his lifetime gave Nsyobo a gun. Kyakumbi, the father's heir, wants the gun back; she says it was never really a gift and that in any event she is entitled to all of her late *nkazi*'s belongings. In the course of the dispute she has insulted Nsyobo, using some very rude language, although she is his Father. Nsyobo took the matter to Kyakumbi's elder [*n'kuluntu*] whose name is Kiyawa. In Kiyawa's presence Kyakumbi said, "It would be good if a dangerous animal killed Nsyobo, so that our clan would be avenged upon his." [This statement is prima facie evidence of witchcraft intent.] When Nsyobo heard it, he thought it best to return the gun.

But Kiyawa, speaking to Kyakumbi and her followers, said, "Brethren, I cannot go into conference [*ku nenga*] with you over this because your lineage [*nzo*] was enslaved; it was Nsyobo's father who paid the money to redeem you, whereby you returned to our clan. Now you are making difficulties for Nsyobo over the gun, but I, Kiyawa, tell you that you have no right to inherit his leavings, but I only, because you are slaves in our clan. You, Kyakumbi, have no right now to eat the heart of Nsyobo's kill, but must bring it to me, *nkazi*, to divide it among the clan." Then Kiyawa gave it back to Kyakumbi and said, "You should bless this gun, so that Nsyobo may kill meat for us."

Presumably there are three lineages, Kiyawa's, Nsyobo's father's, and Kyakumbi's, of which the last has been in slavery elsewhere. Having been redeemed, it remains subordinate to the other lineages, in slavery to its own kin, and is thus excluded, according to Kiyawa's argument, from the exercise of corporate rights, particularly in regard to property inheritance and the *kitaata* link with Nsyobo.

This version of the story comes from Nsyobo's testimony in court, which continued (Mbanza Manteke 97, 1956; cf. Van Wing, 1959, pp. 355–357):

Later I killed an antelope, but one of my Fathers said, "May this antelope be the last you kill." Afterward, when I went hunting and shot many animals, none died. So I went back to Kiyawa and told him I had no luck hunting, because the gun had been cursed. But my Fathers refused to attend a meeting Kiyawa called. On the advice of my family I want to give back the gun, which can no longer be any good to me, but I also want back 1,225 francs' worth of blankets which I gave them to keep, and the contribution I made at the funeral of Kyakumbi's child, namely: 200 francs in cash, 200 for the coffin, 100 in blankets, and 9 for nails. Also the license fee for the gun, 500 francs.

In other words, Nsyobo declares his intent to break off the relationship. Kyakumbi testified that her child had died by a doped glass of beer which Nsyobo had given to Kyakumbi; that is, the child was a victim of witchcraft. The court, which is not competent to pronounce on witchcraft matters except when an accused convicts himself, held that the Fathers had insulted Nsyobo in his own house. Because "it is forbidden to insult a man in his house, or even outside," the court imposed a heavy penalty and damages on the Fathers. Although obviously intending to punish the Fathers for their overall behavior, the court did not sanction the end of the relationship by ordering the return of the funeral gifts as requested by Nsyobo.

HISTORY AND TRADITION

The existence of a range of possibilities, instead of a definite rule of succession, is an essential feature of the present social structure; functionally speaking, it channels the political energies of the public. The BaKongo, however, profess themselves most unhappy with this situation, and say that it is only nowadays, when liars abound in the land, that things have come to this pass.

Tradition describes the constitution of social positions through such events as the birth of daughters to the founding ancestor. It is usually a matter of debate whether the determining events occurred "in Mbanza Kongo" before the migrations began, or in the present *mbanza* of the clan section. The idea that they occurred in the imaginably recent historical past is resisted, although, if the traditions circulating in Manteke have any historical content at all, few of the groups could have originated much before the early part of the nineteenth century. NZUZI showed me the baobab that marks Na Kwedi's grave; when I pointed out that it was quite a young tree, he assured me that the original tree had died and been replaced. On the other hand, testifying on behalf of NZUZI, his Father NKAZI A KONGO said that that clan was still in occupation of Yongo when Richards came to Manteke (Matadi 134, 1958). It is likely that the NZUZI ancestors immigrated after 1886, when an area south of the Lufu River, Mazamba, was abandoned by its inhabitants; NZUZI still claims land there.

Despite the thesis of tradition, the descent groups are clearly revealed as heterogeneous by the traditions themselves, taken as a whole. The themes of seniority by descent (*kikota*), historical priority, and slavery are simply various ways of arguing about assimilation. The migrations that have taken place are those of small groups, even of individuals: refugees, the dissatisfied and the ambitious, and women and children bought, married, pawned, or otherwise redistributed through a network of small local communities. The process continues to the present time in forms not essentially different from those known to Na Mpyoso dya Bazika Nzenza Kavanga Yinkuta and others like him; the war gong (*mondo*) sounds at the government's court of appeal, slavery and witch-hunting are still practiced, though in genteel modern forms, and the dissatisfied still move off to found a new *mbanza* as in days of yore (tradition from Mativa; Mbanza Manteke 88, II, 1964):

> Whereupon the young men were angry. A quarrel broke out, and they dispersed from Mbanza Mbamba. Na Kyangala on the road, Na Futila on the road, Ntukula on the road, and Na Tona. And they sang the song, *Twele kweto ku nsi yikondolo mambu* ["We're off to a land that is at peace"]. They took with them a pig, but when they got to Lwaza the pig went lame. They said, "Let us kill the pig." When they killed it they divided it up, but the entrails remained. Then a quarrel broke out over the entrails of the pig . . .

The difference is that Mfumu Na Mpyoso no longer dances with the sword of his ancestors in the assembly of the clans; instead of chiefship (*kimfumu*) there is only *kinkazi* ("authority").

The stories about the internal problems of MFUTU and NSAKA give some idea as to how the processes of dispersal and reassimilation operated in the past. Apparently such processes continue to operate, as indicated by extracts from a land case in Mbata Kimenga, where a number of DISA and MFUTU offshoots have settled. Mbata Kimenga is a riverine village four hours' walk west of Mbanza Manteke. Communications by truck are poor. Inhabitants of the two villages do not usually attend one another's funerals or other affairs.

In a dispute arising over a mahogany tree, Malemba Nsi of MBENZA tried to show that his opponent Lutete Nkunku of NANGA held land only as a gift, not by right of first occupation. The court transcript shows the importance attached to marriage as an index of accompanying rights in land, and the kind of interrogation to which a litigant should be prepared to respond.

> Now listen. MBENZA NA KONGO left Mbanza Kongo; the woman who came with him was NANGA. We arrived first of all in Songolongo, Kongo dya Lemba, Mbanza Nkazi, Paaza, and then Mbanza Ndingi. The chief who swept up the droppings of the elephant [13] was Na Toma Nsi. After him Na Lalamu, and then Na Tasi, who was Na Ndingi a Lwangu. Na Ndingi brought the woman Zinga Diatona (*luvila* NANGA); the man alive now is Lutete Nkunku.

In Paza, continued the witness, they met NDUMBU, who was already there. Na Toma Nsi stayed in Mbanza Nkazi, Na Lalamu and Na Tasi in Paza. In MBENZA there are four houses (*mafuta maya*): TONA DYA NTANTU, WANGA, NKENGE, and SUBI. On reflection, he thought that

---

[13] *Mfumu yakomba tuvi twa nzau*, "the pioneer who first penetrated the forest."

"SUBI himself is TONA." The point would seem to be important, but he was not sure.

The witness continued:

I, Na Ndingi a Lwanda [*sic*], was the first to leave Paza. [A woman of his lineage married into NANGA, but the witness does not know when.]

COURT: The person you met was NDUMBU, and yet you married into NANGA. Who arrived first, you or NANGA?

WITNESS: NANGA came first, but only from Mbanza Ntala.

COURT: What did you do? After they had married did you give them a place or did the girl go back to Mbanza Ntala?

WITNESS: She went back to Mbanza Ntala.

COURT: So where did Lutete Nkunku come from, Mbanza Ntala or where?

WITNESS: I married the NANGA woman by whom I had these children in Mbanza Kongo.

COURT: What was the woman's name? How many children? Who was given a place to settle [*lufulu*, "house foundation"]?

Because the witness was unable to produce good answers to these questions, the court decided that he was lying and knew no tradition. Lutete Nkunku did know the answers. Comparison of the genealogy he gave and the fragments cited by Malemba Nsi reveals that the latter had confused the original marriage of Na Ndingi a Lwangu with a more recent one. Lutete is content to demonstrate the descent lines resulting from the original marriage, without dwelling on the later one, but independently obtained data from Mbanza Manteke confirm that his parents were born there, and that the Zinga Diatona mentioned by his opponent is Ndona Nzinga of SWETE KYA TONA (see fig. 2).

The court held that if a man wishes to eat off his kinsman's land he must first ask permission, for *kinzingani ye kindelani*, the affinal relationship between MBENZA and NANGA, is not yet dead; it administered heavy fines (Mbanza Manteke 85, III, 1964). If the judgment sticks, it means that the line of Lutete Nkunku has been successfully grafted in the place of Na Ndingi a Lwangu.

It is in the course of particular events, like those described in succeeding chapters, that the structure is defined. At any one time the definition of parts of the structure, of particular relationships and rights, is uncertain; it is only accomplished with the passage of time. Thus structure emerges from process; since it is never other than emergent, there is no real opposition between its statics and its dynamics.

A social structure in three levels is characteristic of the Manteke region and apparently of most of Kongo, but it is hard to be sure. Most investigators have not inquired into social morphology except by taking down the statements of informants describing what ought to be. A partial exception is Doutreloux (1967, chap. 3), whose model of Yombe society is similar to the one given here. An exception among my informants was a relatively well-educated Ntandu schoolteacher, from a region east of the Inkisi. His kinsmen had been involved in a protracted lawsuit in which they had had to challenge the standard or government model prevailing in that area. Accordingly, when he was given Van Wing's monograph to study during a course in African sociology at the normal school, he evaluated it with particular interest. He had also attempted to retrace the migrations of his ancestors and found that they had traversed considerable distances and had made several crossings of the Inkisi. He was able to describe in detail the structure of his clan section, which proved very similar to that of NANGA in Manteke and could be tested by the same diacritical questions referring to rights in women, land, and movable property. Observing a Lemfu land case that continued intermittently for several months, I could not be sure of the detailed structure of the groups involved, but clearly the nature of the arguments and the principles at issue were similar to those encountered in Manteke. Nevertheless, I do not wish to suggest that Kongo social structure is and has been the same everywhere. (The question of variations in social structure and of the conditions of variation is postponed to chapter 10.)

The contrast between the picture of Kongo social history presented here and the one usually obtained from informants requires comment. The evidence is that for at least 250 years, probably far longer, there has been continual grouping and regrouping of small population units among whom priority of occupation in any one area is a relative matter at best. The characteristic organizational framework has not been hierarchical but, rather, a bilateral kinship network within which the descent groups are encapsulated. The folk model, on the other hand, emphasizes a single continuous migration into an empty land and a hierarchical and authoritarian framework dominated by a chief whose title is traced in unbroken hereditary sequence back to Mbanza Kongo.

In detail, the one is an inversion of the other. Tradition records a sequence of events whereby an original clan, starting at a particular point, traveled to its present location, segmenting in the process into its constituent groups. History — or at least the cautious speculation that must here pass for history — says that this purportedly diachronic sequence is a projection of a synchronic model, a normative account of a social structure that was actually built up on the spot by the accretion of small groups who arrived at different times and from different places. The BaKongo, of course, are not unaware of history;

they simply deplore it. Any informant, asked to describe his own origin, quotes tradition; asked to describe the origin of his competitors, he recites history.

My analysis would be no different if it could be shown that some modern lineage was directly descended from the first occupants who had displaced the pygmies and swept up the droppings of the elephant. Biological continuity is irrelevant. The degree of sociological continuity, on the other hand, is often impressive. For example, the likelihood is that NKAZI A KONGO has dominated Mbanza Nkazi continuously for 500 years. The name is a title implying that the owners had the right to provide the king, Ne Kongo, with his official wife at the time of his coronation. This woman was probably his classificatory Father or Grandfather (*nkaaka*), and she would be known as Mpemba Nkazi, which is also the first recorded name of the Manteke region. Probably this is what Father Jérôme de Montesarchio referred to when he gave the title of the chief he met in Mbanza Nkazi in 1650 as "Mother of the King of Kongo." [14] On the other hand, the groups now sharing the estate of NKAZI A KONGO are heterogeneous. There is no reason to suppose that the processes of dispersion and assimilation are new, and it is clear that the structure of social estates in any locality, presented in the idiom of descent, is capable of rapid modification.

[14] For further discussion of coronation and the official wife, see Laman, 1953, pp. 16–22, and Doutreloux, 1967, pp. 143–147, 191–192.

5

KINSHIP AND OTHER NAMES

Tout classement est supérieur au chaos.
— C. LEVI-STRAUSS

Politicians in need of a slogan may describe all the BaKongo as brethren descended from the same father and mother,[1] but this metaphor
is not backed even by the idea that all BaKongo, like all Tiv, all
Gusii, and some other peoples, are genealogically related. Politicians,
again, may advertise themselves as descended from the kings of Kongo,
but no one pretends to trace his pedigree that far.[2] The only relations
of this order which receive a kinship label are those uniting members
of the same clan; thus, the prophet Mabwaka used to refer to President
Kasa-Vubu as his brother in the clan NANGA NE KONGO.

Most village affairs are regulated in kinship categories, since the principal rights and obligations of individuals and groups are attached to
kinship statuses. But it is not possible to deduce the kinship relation of
two individuals by observing their behavior toward each other, even
on formal occasions. There are exceptions to this generalization. Old-
fashioned people are reluctant to mention the names of their *bazitu*
affines, and may observe special courtesies toward them. I met one man
who was reluctant in much the same way to mention the name of
another because it was also his own father's name, although nobody
showed similar reluctance to cite the father himself by name. Such
behavior belongs to a pattern that was formerly more obvious, according to ethnographic records.

An NKongo may trace his relationship to another by any one of

1 They were so described by Governor Moanda at Matadi on 30 June 1965:
"L'Abako, dis-je, n'est pas un parti politique mais une famille où les enfants d'un
même père et d'une même mère se sont retrouvés dans un élan unanime aux objectifs
communs."
2 Edmond Nzeza-Nlandu in *La Fédération Congolaise*, 20 March 1965: "Viti-Nimi
Ne-Mpangu. Descendant des rois du Kongo (Ndofunsu Ne-Mpangu Mvemba-Nzinga)."

several kinship principles, the most important of which are expressed by the terms "individually" (*mu kimuntu*) and "by clan" (*mu dikanda*). Of the several possibilities, he chooses the one most suited to the role he wishes to adopt in a given situation. The system in practice is therefore very flexible; the terms used depend on the context. Usage is not so rigid as the following classification may suggest. The most general term is the most common; descriptive modifiers are added as necessary (one could say "senior female father" but ordinarily would not). The modified terms *ngwankazi*, "mother's brother," and its complement, *mwan'a nkazi*, are used when applicable in preference to the more inclusive terms *ngudi* and *mwana*.

Some referential terms are also the preferred terms of address. They are distinguished by asterisks in the list that follows. If no suitable kinship term is available, teknonymy, titles, and other circumlocutions are used in address in preference to personal names. *Taata* and *maama* may be politely applied to anyone, kin or not, in reference and address; unrelated men may be addressed, still more politely, as *ngwankazi* or *mfumu eto*. All relationships, as distinct from the people in them, may be described by the general term for the category with the prefix *ki-* added; for example, *kingudi* means matrilateral kinship. No term in general use describes all kinfolk collectively. The significance of the terms is as follows:

5. Ego's siblings, and all cousins [3]   *mpangi*
   Male Ego's male *mpangi* older than he   *mbuta*;
     mfumu eto *
       younger than he   *nleeke*
     female *mpangi*   *busi*; pl., *bi-*
   Female Ego's male *mpangi*   *mfumu eto* *
     female *mpangi* older than she   *mbuta*
       younger than she   *nleeke*

2. Ego's father and father's *mpangi* [4]   *se*; pl., *ma-*;
     taata; * pl., *ba-*
   Father's female *mpangi*   *se dya n'kento* *
     ("female father")

3. Ego's mother and mother's *mpangi*   *ngudi*; pl., *zi-*;
     maama *

[3] *Mfumu eto*, which applies to men, and *busi*, applying to women, are perhaps the only terms that cannot be used for persons of either sex. In other regions *busi* is not restricted to females.

[4] In types 2 and 3, seniority relative to Ego's own parent may be indicated by descriptive modifiers, e.g., *maama kota*, "mother's older sister," and *maama nleeke*, "mother's younger sister." *Kota*, from the verb "to enter," applies particularly to the eldest of a sibling group; other siblings "follow" (*landa*). "Seniority" in general is *kikota*. The term *ngudi a nkazi* should not be confused with *nkazi*, which denotes the responsible representative of a group and is not a kinship term.

Mother's male *mpangi* — *ngwankazi;* * *ngudi a nkazi maam'a yakala* * ("male mother")

7. Ego's child or child of Ego's *mpangi* — *mwana;* pl., *baana*
Child of male Ego's female *mpangi* — *mwan'a nkazi*

1. All grandparents and grandparents' *mpangi* — *nkaaka;* *yaya* *[5]

8. All children of a *mwana* — *n'tekolo;* pl., *batekolo*

9. Child of an *n'tekolo* — *mwana wa n'zoole* (lit., "second child")[6]

6. Man's wife — *n'kento* (lit., "woman")
Woman's husband — *yakala* (lit., "man")
Spouse's *mpangi* — *nkwezi;* * pl., *ba-*

4. Parents and children of affines[7] — *n'zitu;* pl., *bazitu*

There are a few more terms, but they are of minor interest and limited currency. As in other aspects of language, usage of these terms varies over quite short distances.

The classical ethnography of Kongo, preoccupied with the phenomenon of matrilineal descent, supposed that a "mother's brother," for example, was necessarily a member of Ego's clan, and failed to note that kinship, as distinct from descent, is bilateral. (The distinction between kinship and descent was not clearly made in anthropological theory until the 1920's.) Kinship reckoning *mu kimuntu,* as in figure 6a, has nothing to do with descent. It emphasizes the distinction of proximate generations and the unity of the sibling group, which includes half-siblings. Within the sibling group Ego's own or real mother, for example, can be distinguished only by circumlocution or by the implications of the context. There is therefore no direct Kongo equivalent for such a term in English as "mother"; the use of English terms in the present text as though they were equivalent sacrifices accuracy to convenience.

The following cases, particularly the third, show how kinship reckoning ignores descent:

1) A certain man married two wives from different clans. His son by the first wife calls his daughter by the second wife *mpangi* or *busi,* and calls the daughter's child *mwan'ame a nkazi,* "my sister's child," although he is of a different clan. This situation is very common.

2) Manzambi and Mabasi in figure 4 are *mpangi* through their common grandmother, as are Mabasi and Maswekwa through their father.

[5] The term *yaya* may be applied to an older sibling, but the usage is considered archaic in Manteke.

[6] Great-grandparents are addressed as "senior mother" and "senior father."

[7] The affinal relationship in general is *kinkwezi,* under which *bazitu* are subsumed.

3) In MFUTU (fig. 3) Vingana calls Hezekaya *ngwankazi*, "mother's brother," because he and Nkebasani are *mpangi ye mpangi* ("brethren"), children of "the same father." She might have called him *ngwankazi* because she is a member of his house and of approximately the next younger generation, but she explicitly rejected this possibility. Her reasoning is not idiosyncratic, and the relationship is not a metaphorical one. There is no distinction, in terms or behavior, between a mother's matrilateral and patrilateral brothers. Vingana's lineage *nkazi* is Mbwaku, whom she calls *mpangi*.

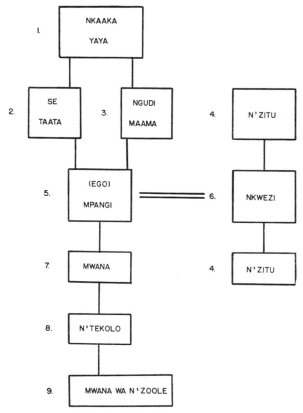

FIG. 6a. Principal kinship terms *mu kimuntu.*

Kinship reckoning of this kind proceeds within a range extending to the limit of Ego's mother's and father's lineages, and possibly the lineages of the grandfathers. A woman, asked to give the proper terms for all adult members of her clan section, NANGA, distinguished generations in her own lineage but lumped everyone else as *mpangi*, except for the men of her house, MFUTU, to whom she referred, regardless of age, as *mfumu eto*, "elder brother."

Exceptions of a different sort occurred in the terms the same woman used for the members of a lineage adjacent to her own in MFUTU. The lineage was NZIMBU A TONA, from which her paternal grandfather came; she said that he was of the same generation as Nkebasani Ndendani (see fig. 3), with whom he was therefore to be identified. (I did not obtain a precise genealogical link, there being some dispute involved.) Applying the principle of the merging of alternate generations, which is explicit in Kongo usage, the informant said that Nkebasani's daughter Vingana was either "child" or "mother"; "child" would be more appropriate, in view of their respective ages. Vingana herself usually addresses the informant as "mother," but other women of NZIMBU have recently stopped reckoning this relationship individually in favor of the less intimate reckoning by clans, according to which the informant is merely their *mpangi*.

In reckoning kinship *mu dikanda*, "by clans," the terms of *kimpangi* (type 5) apply to all members of Ego's clan, who may also be described collectively as *zingudi*. All members of the father's clan are "fathers"; all members of the father's father's and the mother's father's clans are grandparents (type 1). All parallel cousins are *mpangi*, but patrilateral cross-cousins are "fathers" and matrilateral cross-cousins are "children" in this reckoning, whereby the unity of the descent group overrides the distinction between generations (fig. 6*b*).

The choice of which form of reckoning to use depends on whether

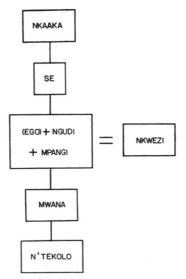

FIG. 6*b*. Principal kinship terms *mu dikanda*.

the relationship between two individuals is regarded as a personal one. This decision in turn depends partly on individual sentiments and partly on structural factors. Within a single lineage personal (genealogical) reckoning applies except when lineage solidarity is being stressed. Within the house and the clan section descent reckoning (*mu dikanda*), according to which all members are *mpangi*, usually applies, but it is readily replaced by personal reckoning if there is a close patrilateral link or if the individuals concerned choose to introduce distinctions of generation. The latter is more likely to occur, as a matter of courtesy, in address rather than in reference.

The difference between the two modes of reckoning is not a matter of group relations versus dyadic, genealogical ones. Interpersonal relationships are frequently traced by dyadic steps until the parties reach, in the second or third ascendant generation, a common *kanda* ("clan section") within which no further genealogical progress can be made. Thus the sequence is completed. For example:

1) Manzambi and Maswekwa (fig. 4) are *mpangi ye mpangi* because each had a grandfather belonging to NKAZI A KONGO; it suffices that each can call himself *n'tekolo a* NKAZI A KONGO without any specific link being traceable.

2) Paul calls Samuel *ngwankazi* because Paul's mother's father and Samuel's father were both members of MPANZU, though their fathers' relationship is unknown; Samuel is a much younger man, and no signs of deference accompany the use of the term.

These usages are not merely matters of courtesy, nor are they obligatory; they simply describe what the relationship is. Merely courteous usages, and those that are "in a manner of speaking," trace relations as far as a common category, a clan (*mvila*). The distinction is illustrated by two examples:

1) Nkomo of NANGA, whose father was a child of NTUMBA, calls his wife *taata* because she also is a child of that clan section and therefore *mpangi* to his father. She is MFULAMA NKANGA.

2) Mabundamene, who is a child of MFULAMA NKANGA, could call his wife *taata* because she is NANGA, the same *mvila* but a different *kanda*; but that, he says, would be only "in a manner of speaking."

The suggestion of these examples, that "real kinship" as distinct from "courteous extensions" is limited by the clan section, is generally but not invariably valid. As already noted, the distinction between *mvila* and *kanda* is less real in practical situations than its analytical importance suggests, and it is not unusual to hear a man refer emphatically to "my very own nephew" (*mwan'ame a nkazi kibeeni*) in a context implying the existence of specific obligations, when in fact the two belong to different sections and have no particular relationship.

Kinship, once established, does not necessarily carry with it any standard pattern of behavior other than general friendliness.[8] That is its importance. Nonkin have no relationship at all, and their meeting can only be awkward until one is formulated. The kinship idiom can provide rationalizations for any degree of cooperation to which the parties may be inclined.

The use by the people of two or more names for modes of kinship reckoning, and by the anthropologist of two or more diagrams (like those used in figs. 6a and 6b), suggests two different sets of kinship principles, two alternative kinship "grammars." In the first six months of my fieldwork I took it that this duality did exist, and as a consequence found life very confusing. In fact, there is only one kinship grammar, and its logic deserves to be spelled out in some detail.

Kinship reckoned *mu kimuntu* ("individually") and *mu dikanda* ("by clans") produces cousin terminologies of the Hawaiian and Crow patterns, respectively. The coexistence of these types is not unprecedented, having been reported, for example, from Truk in Micronesia by Goodenough (1951); in Truk there is also a patrifilial hierarchy of matrilineal descent groups and a corresponding deployment of the two terminologies.

These patterns are distinguished by the labels applied to Ego's cousins when the terminology is projected onto a genealogical diagram (Murdock, 1949, pp. 223–224). The diagrams used in figures 6a and 6b are kin-type diagrams. One of the earliest and simplest statements of the difference between kin-type diagrams and genealogical diagrams is by Hocart (1952; originally published in 1937). I use the former here because they better represent Kongo kinship reckoning which, as shown in this and the preceding chapter, is not genealogical in the usual European sense. Nor is there any terminological recognition, as among the Gusii (I. Mayer, 1965), of a relatively restricted range of kinship that is real in the sense of being genealogical. The nearest equivalent to the Gusii usage is the idea, inconsistently followed in practice, that kinship beyond the boundaries of the clan section is a matter of courteous extension. Within these boundaries, which are those of the most inclusive corporate group, kinship is traced by dyadic steps, to be sure, but not necessarily from individual to individual.

8 Specific patterns are effective within the range of immediate kin, for whom, as already noted, there are no exclusive terms.

A kin-type diagram shows what the relationship between kin types is; for example, it shows that the child of everyone whom Ego calls *mwana* is his *n'tekolo*. This relationship is not directly evident from a genealogical diagram, but the latter shows, as a kin-type diagram does not, the referential content of each term, though only to the extent that kinship is in fact genealogically reckoned, whether historically or fictitiously (see fig. 6*c*).

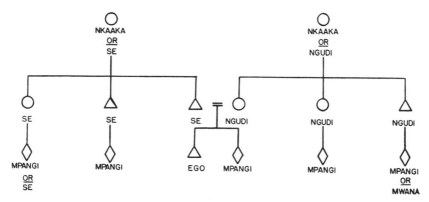

FIG. 6*c.* Cousin terminology.

Kinship takes on role content in a limited number of institutional situations, of which the most important are set out below in chapters 6 through 9. Analysis of these situations reveals four role-types: individual/individual, group/group, individual/group, and the type in which an individual is related to another on the basis of a common relationship to a group. These types are prefigured in the ways in which kinship is established, as in the examples given above.

Kinship terms refer to these roles, which are attributed to persons, not to people as such. Each role is a term of a dyadic relationship. Each person, whether an individual or a collectivity, numbers many other roles as the components of his status. In Kongo, individuals whose role is the same with regard to a particular person are *mpangi ye mpangi* ("brethren"). As such, their interests are similar and their relationship is friendly. On occasions when the role that unites them is to be publicly played, the most senior of the *zimpangi* (or some chosen substitute) speaks for them as their senior (*n'kuluntu*), elder (*mbuta*), chief (*mfumu*), or leader (*nkazi*). Behind the scenes (*ku nenga*) all the *zimpangi* contribute their advice, their cash, and other forms of support to the position taken by their spokesman.[9]

9 *Mpangi* is similar to the Trukese term *pwi* (see Swartz, 1960).

Kimpangi ("brotherhood") may be established because the individuals in question belong to the same descent group; that is, they are *fulu kimosi* ("one place"). Alternatively, *kimpangi* may refer to a common relationship to some other person, collective or individual; for example, the sons of two men who belong to the same descent group, even though the link may be little more than nominal, are brethren and are equally entitled to play a recognized part in the collective affairs of that descent group, to which they are Children (*baana*). A similar relationship, not mentioned so far, unites those who are married into "the same place," whether two men whose wives belong to the same descent group or two women married to the same man or to two "brothers"; this relationship is *kimbanda*, and those who share it may on occasion, like brethren, speak for one another. Like *kinkwezi*, it is permanent and not disrupted by death or divorce.

Such relationships, which are established jurally, depend on public recognition of filiation between a child and its parents and of the allocation of the parents to particular descent groups which "own" them, that is, hold *kinkazi* over them. Usually, jural and biological relationships coincide, but the latter are not critical. Jural relationships can be changed rapidly, and a man may find himself on Monday with grandparents he did not have on Saturday.

A distinction is being made here between people and persons. The two can exist independently. NDYENGO is a corporation that exists in its own right, although to be "perfect" or complete it needs people to exercise the roles attributed to it; at the moment, several groups of people are competing for this right. Conversely, people who are unable to establish claims to any corporate estate are slaves, or kinless people. Strictly speaking, the only completely kinless individual would be some wandering refugee. This status occurs in legend if not often, nowadays, in fact; it is called *kinsoona*. The idea of complete kinlessness, or social death, is vividly present in Kongo thinking. The slave is the man without clan (*wakondwa mvila*), wandering in trackless limbo. The possibility, however remote, of such a fate adds to the intensity of one's pride in his name and tradition.

The distinction between people and persons, an anthropological commonplace, may seem purely analytical and unreal, but I find it necessary in order to explain Kongo usage, which seems to refer more or less consciously to social status, jurally defined. It would, after all, be naïvely ethnocentric to suppose that social structure can be discovered only by a trained observer. As identifications of social roles, kinship terms reveal only one kind of reckoning or "grammar." As a matter of links between persons, kinship expresses relations between

individuals and collectivities according to the four role types mentioned above; on this basis it is possible to contrast reckoning *mu
dikanda* (Crow), *mu kimuntu* (Hawaiian), and others, but the contrast
is superficial. Although superficial, it is real and not simply an unin-
tended product of anthropological analysis; it leads to jural ambiguities
(discussed in chapter 9 and elsewhere).

Situations examined in subsequent chapters show how kinship works
in practice. If Ego's father is SUBI, then all members of that house, as
such, are his "fathers." If Ego's father belongs to a clan such as MBENZA,
then any member of MBENZA is his "father." MBENZA is not a group but
a corporate category lacking internal structure. Further, Ego calls
"father" all whom his father would call *mpangi*; they come from any
number of different clans and form a unity only in that they all share
some role, not always the same one, with Ego's father. The group is
constituted only in relation to the roles of an individual, and there is
nothing corporate about it. On the other hand, the ultimate reference
of a role is always to a permanent, named status, a *fulu*; one is either
a member of a descent group occupying a particular place, or Child,
Grandchild, or affine (*nkwezi*) to such a group.

Fraternity (*kimpangi*) of this kind, as when two individuals are
united by their common status as Grandchildren of a clan (*mvila*),
seems insubstantial, but is patently instrumental in organizing the primary processes of social life in which participation means playing a
role and in which all roles are defined in kinship terms. A Child, for
example, has a right to use his Father's land; at a funeral, a particular
gift is the appropriate one for an affine. Whether a particular Child
or affine chooses to play this role depends on his inclinations and the
total configuration of his social relations. When playing a particular
role in public, as at a funeral, he specifies which it is and draws attention to the appropriateness of his behavior. Those who are entitled to
play the same role are *mpangi ye mpangi* and thus can speak for one
another. This relationship includes the kinds of specific transfer which
anthropologists usually label "succession," but it also includes the
reciprocal responsibility expressed by the verb *vwa*, "to own."

The BaKongo use what we conventionally call "kinship terms" to
discuss statuses and roles. The actor's model for social relationships at
all levels, as Fortes says (1967, p. 10), is the familial situation, particularly "the complementarity of the sexes and the polarity of successive
generations" which are "the basis of a person's conception of his social
identity." This does not necessarily mean, however, that kinship is
"about" familial or genealogical relations. Much anthropological thinking in this area has not progressed beyond that of L. H. Morgan; it is

taken for granted that "primitive peoples" are familistic and that their political, economic, and existential concerns are barely divorced from this context. It could be argued, with some justice but small profit, that the BaKongo have no kinship system in the sense of one specific to familial relations; this argument was in fact standard among those who believed that Africans had not yet reached a degree of individualism sufficient to free the family from its subordination to the clan. Kinship systems are organizational devices whose referents must be determined by inspection. In particular instances, kinship may be about land, property, political office, family, or some combination of these and other concerns.

The distinction between two modes of reckoning kinship, *mu kimuntu* and *mu dikanda*, should not therefore be understood to imply contrasted kinds of behavior. Roles coincide empirically in the individual: the behavior of a member of NTUMBA (*mwisi ki*NTUMBA) who is a Child of NANGA, for example, may be modified by the view shared by all members of NTUMBA that they stand collectively as Fathers to NANGA.

The two modes of reckoning are only the most important, not the only ones. The BaKongo are quite clear on this point; they say that "it depends which route you are following." The route followed, and the relationship chosen, depend on what is convenient. Here is a set of possibilities:

1) Baku of NTUMBA and Ngila of NSUNDI are both children of DISA fathers; therefore, *mu kimwana*, "considering whose children they are," they are *mpangi*, "brothers."

2) Since Ngila's father (DISA) was a child of an NTUMBA father, Baku is Ngila's "classificatory" grandfather, *mu kitekolo*, "on grandchild reckoning."

3) Baku's own father's father was NTUMBA; therefore he is himself both *mwisi ki*NTUMBA and *n'tekolo a* NTUMBA, a member and a grandson of that clan. Since both he and Ngila are grandsons of NTUMBA they could on that account also call themselves brothers (*mpangi*).

The possibilities are multiplied by the operation of two more, related principles: a form of positional succession and the perpetuation of names. Neither of these is followed with the rigor characteristic of Teke society, or with that of some other peoples of the matrilineal belt (Vansina, 1964; Gray, 1953). Positional succession enables Joshua Kingalu to say "I, Na Makokila, welcomed the Protestants" when speaking to Protestant missionaries, and "I, Nsakala Nangudi, welcomed the Catholics" when that statement seems more appropriate, the explicit assumption being that his social identification with these persons, now deceased, entitles him to continuing credit for their endeavors. He is *fulu kimosi* with Na Makokila in the lineage LEMBE KYA TONA, and with Nsakala Nangudi on the ground that LEMBE has inherited the place of NDYENGO MYA TONA (see table 1) or on the ground that these lineages both belong to NANGA, of which he is *nkazi*.

Here are more of his relations:

1) Kingalu's wife calls him *yaya,* "grandfather," suggesting one of those quasi-incestuous arrangements that have caused so much concern to certain ethnographers. She is merely a grandchild of his house, MFUTU. Kingalu addresses his wife (who is not much younger than he and is a great-grandmother herself), as *yaya,* too, because he is a grandchild of her house, MVIKA NTUMBA (see fig. 7).

2) A young girl of NTUMBA, whom Kingalu might also address as *yaya* (though the great difference in their ages makes the term inappropriate), he actually calls *n'zitu,* here meaning mother-in-law, because she is Luzebete Mana; that is, she perpetuates among her names that of Kingalu's wife's mother.

3) Kingalu also refers to another elderly woman, this time of NA LOMBO, as his grandchild; his face shows all the affection expected of grandfathers and the phrase he uses emphasizes the closeness of the relationship: *n'tekolo ame kibeeni,* "my very own grandchild." [10] This woman, whose grand-

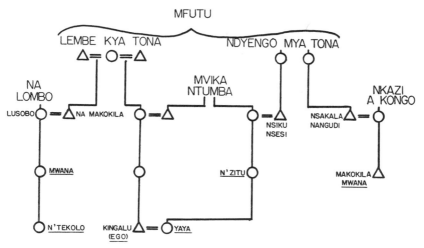

FIG. 7. Selected kin of Kingalu.

[10] Expressions of this kind, and the absence of exclusive terms for close kin, make certain kinds of inquiry — e.g., into the range of marriage prohibitions — extremely difficult. It is necessary to tie the inquiry to specific instances where genealogical positions are known.

mother Lusobo married Na Makokila, is Kingalu's MoMoMoSo (by another husband) DaDa; he arrives at the term "grandchild" not by performing a componential analysis of this series but by noting that he is Na Makokila (LEMBE KYA TONA).

Such calculations make it possible for a man to be simultaneously another's grandfather, father, brother-in-law, son, and grandson. Usually the most direct route is chosen, or the one that has the most appropriately polite connotations. Kingalu himself is very good at this aspect of etiquette, on occasion saluting as *yaya* an elder who represents the father of a classificatory mother of Kingalu's, both parties long since deceased; the same man could have been addressed, but rather less honorably, as *mwana*, since he is a Child of NANGA.

A child need not be given a name until some months after birth (Van Wing, 1959, pp. 220–224). Then he is given a name that probably suggests some family circumstance at the time of birth, such as the sufferings of his parents, the jealousy of the neighbors, the threat of witchcraft. The name is the beginning of a phrase that will not necessarily be known to the world at large (*ibid.*, pp. 257–263; Bittremieux, 1934, *passim*). "Wungyena Vovo" is short for " 'When I'm there' you speak well of me, but when my back is turned you say offensive things." Upon baptism the child gets another name, which is usually French in origin; formerly, in Manteke, it was often English and biblical. At some point the name of a parent, an ancestor, a friend or benefactor of the family, or of some great man may be conferred upon the child. There is a tendency to choose the names of grandparents; a child may perpetuate a man's or a woman's name regardless of sex. When he becomes adult he may choose a name of his own. The result is that he has several names, more or less publicly known, each with a different meaning regarding his past and present statuses. There is nothing obligatory or systematic about such series of names. Some biographical examples follow.

1) **Nsiku Damison** was christened Howard by a missionary. When he grew up he went to work for the transport agency OTRACO, saving his money every month until he had accumulated 1,800 francs and felt like a millionaire. So at Christmas he bought a large pig for 150 francs, a demijohn of Portuguese wine, and all kinds of other food and drink and threw a tremendous party at his house in Thysville. He still had 450 francs in his pocket, and he thought to himself, "All these people came to my house on my account; I am become a person of wealth and importance, just like a white man." So he took the name Nkanda Kacenjwa (English: "change"), meaning "His Skin Was Changed." The next day he called his houseboy and had his meals served in European style. Then he bought an expensive European blanket and two sheets; when he had had the bed made, he got into it, drew the bedclothes over his head, and slept

like a king. For a long time he was Nkanda Kacenjwa, and still responds
to the name, but then he took on the role and name of his *n'kuluntu*
Nsiku Makuta, lately deceased, and moved into the house Nsiku left.
Afterward he happened to get into a fight in Kinshasa, where he did so
well that one of his friends said he was "Samson." In time this name
was corrupted to Damison.

2) An NTAMBU man perpetuates the name of Nkunkuta Mbende of NZUZI
who was shot in 1903 in an affair over a woman. Although Nkunkuta
Mbende is his official name, everybody calls him Dubu. He also has a
magical name known to relatively few and used, as he says, *mu kivanité*,
"as a praise name": Makwende Mawula Nkodya, referring to the charm
n'kisi Makwende.

3) An Angolan who had long lived in Vunda called himself Kifwidimbwa,
"A Dog's Death," because he said that as a stranger without brethren he
could not expect a proper funeral. (When he died, all kinds of people
rallied round to bury him in a style that, though admittedly not elaborate, undoubtedly amounted to a proper funeral).

On the other hand, a name is not a trivial matter.

4) Timothy and his wife, probably in response to a dream, called their
child "Joseph Kasa-Vubu" after the Abako leader who became president
of the republic. In 1964 the parents had an argument while they were
working in their fields, and Timothy went off in a huff, taking the house
keys with him and leaving his wife to sleep in the kitchen with His
Excellency the Chief of State Kasa-Vubu Joseph; whereupon His Excellency, not being used to sleeping in the kitchen, caught a cold. His
mother complained to a councillor, who took Timothy to court. The
court, whose record refers to the child throughout as "the Chief of State,"
awarded him an extremely expensive goat as damages to be paid him by
his father (Mbanza Manteke 70, III, 1964). In 1965, perhaps as a consequence of the cold, the child died, whereupon the commune sent out
formal announcements of "la mort de Monsieur le Chef de l'Etat." The
mayor, wearing his sash of office, attended the funeral.

To be named after someone is *lukwa*, and the bearer of such a name
is *ndusi* (from the same root). *S'andi kalukwa*, "He was named after his
father." The *ndusi* is not to be confused with *ndoyi*, "namesake," one
who merely happens to have the same name. Homonymy may provide
a means of relating two persons, but in this instance the relationship
is explicitly fictive. A Manteke woman calls me *nkwezi* because she has
the same name as my wife's sister.

An individual is not necessarily known by the same name to everybody. When he takes a new name and a new role he does not thereby
drop other names and roles. The device permits him to do things he

might not otherwise be able to do and provides for the fulfillment of roles that might otherwise remain vacant. The active assumption of such a role may cause the individual's relatives to play associated roles.

1) Lukoki's father Lunama was one of a group of ex-slaves, clients of the mission. Because the group has died out there is no one to sit as Lukoki's Father when necessary. However, Lukoki's son Matondo is also Lunama. As a mere youth he could not play a responsible role, but his *nkazi* could, if he wanted to, and his entire clan could be "father's clan" to Lukoki.

2) Ngila Samuel is the youngest of a group of NSUNDI brothers who say that they may sometime return to their own village of Kyesa Kifwa. He would remain in Manteke, however, because his late father, also called Ngila Samuel, committed the care of his grave to him. When a sister was about to be married and a paternal curse or injunction that would have impaired her fertility had to be removed, a meeting of the appropriate relatives straightened out the matter and then called upon Ngila to represent his father in conferring a counteractive blessing.

3) Zansola, according to her own testimony (Mbanza Manteke 2, 1941), brought a child called Thomas to Manteke when she married an MFUTU man. Thomas married Nswele. "Because I had had a hard time bringing up Thomas, I said to him and Nswele, 'Now that you are married . . . , if you have a daughter call her Zansola, because I have had a hard time on account of you.' Later, Nswele gave birth to a girl, whom they called Zansola, and to whom I gave clothes on account of the name. And I began to call Nswele 'mother.' Then one day I asked her to prepare food for us, but she didn't want to. We quarreled over this, and she changed the child's name. I said, 'Very well, but give me back the clothes'; I took them and cut them up."

In this instance the respect due between *bazitu* was overcome by the adoption of an alternative role (cf. Laman, 1957, p. 54; De Sousberghe, 1966, p. 397).

Women sometimes take a new name after bearing children, and other important events may be similarly marked. A healer may give a new name to his patient and the patient's immediate relatives as part of the cure. A religious conversion may merit a new name: a Kimbanguist has the name Kamalandwangakokwanzambi, "The Lord does not hold [your sins] against you." At the time of national independence a correspondent of the newspaper *Kimbanguisme* signed himself "The-things-that-have-been-revealed-shall-not-now-again-be concealed Faustin." Many names have no active role implications at all, and their meanings are forgotten. Most of the names in Manteke refer to roles in the Nkimba association, but hardly anyone is aware of the connection, or knows what the roles were. Other names are those of forgotten charms (*min'kisi*, usually translated "fetishes").

Kinship may also be traced through slaves who are assimilated to the role of Child (*mwana*) with respect to their owner. If necessary, a distinction can be made by some euphemistic periphrasis, such as "child of the top of the head" (*mwan'a mbat'a n'tu*), meaning one not begotten in the ordinary way; but the jural consequences of the slave's position are the same for his offspring as for those of any other *mwana*, and not much different for himself. The difference lies in that his patron is not only his father but his *nkazi*, and it is not possible for him to play off the one against the other as freemen do. Otherwise, his position may even have certain advantages; the slave, as Child, may marry into the patron's clan section and, in favorable circumstances, may be accorded the privileges and responsibilities of its other Children; but he is also, in effect, *mwan'a nkazi*, or classificatory nephew, and a member of the clan section as far as all outsiders are concerned. If he ranks behind all free members of the descent group he is merely on the lowest rung of the ladder, and the person on the next-higher rung is not much better off. The difference will be still less for descendants of a female slave, who will gradually be excluded from marrying into the owning house and tend to acquire external, patrilateral links. This process, quite independently of any formal integrative ceremony, tends to incorporate slave lineages into the exogamous clan section; gradually, they and their owners come to be *fulu kimosi*, "one place."

Kinship links other than those of filiation are equally traceable through slaves. Nkomo refers to Henry Richards as *nkwezi* because "Richards," meaning another missionary who stood "behind him" (*ku nim'andi*), bought the father of Nkomo's first wife; the slave was Nkomo's *n'zitu*, and his "father" was therefore *nkwezi*. Usages of this sort are not "as if," and it makes no difference that Richards was a European, except that, in practice, some other role pattern would have taken precedence.

Bankwezi are, in general, the members of any clan with which one's own clan marries and cooperates; the term connotes a relaxed and friendly relationship: "Since long ago, we have lived together and looked after one another" (*tuuka ntama, twazingana, twalelana*). Consequently, any two people of approximately the same generation can be *nkwezi*, since, if necessary, a past or present affinal link could probably be discovered. Young men commonly address one another using the French "beau-frère," or "bo'" for short; when a passenger-carrying truck pulls into a village on a Saturday, the air is thick with dust and cries of "Beau-frère! Beau-frère!"

The proverb frequently quoted to describe the affinal relationship is *longo lufwanga kansi kinkwezi ka kifwanga ko,* which means that even if the marriage breaks up the affinal relationship created by it is not destroyed. A large number of links are traceable between any two clans in persistent contact. A marriage contracted outside the normal range of *kinkwezi* approximates slavery. The "neighborhood" of any clan section (*kanda*) is thus statistically endogamous, although, of course, all such neighborhoods overlap and no endogamous group exists.

Part II
PROCESSES

6

ETIQUETTE AND EXCHANGE

They are accustomed to hold frequent assemblies
for the public consideration of
every question which in any manner
affects the general interests.
—HENRY RICHARDS

When I was newly in Congo I was told, "There are two things you should know about the BaKongo. The first is that we all came from Mbanza Kongo. The second is the importance of good manners. When someone calls your name, you don't answer 'Huh?' like an animal in the bush, you say 'Kongo!' Like this, 'Kongo!' "

The rules and procedures of polite behavior mark the existence of civilization, of an ordered community. These criteria of conduct let people within that community know where they stand, with important psychological and sociological consequences. When no polite relationship can be established, a man is frightened; he may either withdraw altogether or forget his manners, even to the point of offering some kind of violence. Insistence on extreme formality helps to reduce tension.

Sociologically, etiquette consists of the rules of social communication. The basic communicatory device is the *mbungu*, which means literally a cup of palm wine. There are *mbungu* of many kinds and quantities, but without an *mbungu* nothing can happen in a formal, public sense. The *mbungu*'s nearest European equivalent is, or was, the visiting card, but it is also the refreshment offered to a visitor and the present he brings with him as a token of goodwill.

Not long after I settled in Manteke I visited Kinkanza, in many ways the most interesting village in the region. It has the largest population, but although a large number of residents implies plentiful production resources and hence some prosperity, hardly anybody in

Kinkanza besides a few ex-sailors has built a house of durable materials. The jealousy of neighbors is probably an inhibiting factor. Kinkanza is notorious for witchcraft, and court records of resultant quarrels substantiate the reputation. Manteke people say that until recently they would not willingly visit the village; very charming people, your Kinkanza hosts, but you never know when one will slip something into your drink. The Kimbanguists and other prophetic churches have had a beneficial influence in recent years, but even in this respect Kinkanza shows its individuality: it has a church all its own, founded in 1959 by a native son, Kinene Jean.

Kinkanza is dominated by NLAZA, and not the least of the village's remarkable features is the head of that clan, a tall, thin old man in a decrepit pith helmet bestowed upon his predecessor, he says, by the Congo Free State. He may be the only *nkazi* in the region who still lives in an old-style *luumbu*, a chief's enclosure of tall African poplar trees. He is one of the few local men old enough to remember the early days of the Free State, and one of three surviving initiates of the Nkimba cult. On my visit I was accompanied by a man who came from nearby and who had a sociology degree from an American University — well qualified on both counts, it seemed, to introduce me. Chairs were placed outside the chief's smoky little house, and we explained what we had come for. In the middle of the explanation NLAZA exclaimed, "Look here, Kingani, you're a local boy, you know better than this; I can't hear what you're saying!" We had offered no *mbungu*. We sent a boy to buy beer; while he was gone we placed a leaf on the ground to represent the gift we were making, and repaired our breach of etiquette by making a formal speech explaining the significance of this particular *mbungu*: that is, the purpose of our visit.[1]

The next step was for the chief, having "heard" what we proposed, to retire (to go *ku nenga*) to decide whether he would accept the *mbungu*. This procedure is always followed, even if acceptance is a foregone conclusion. *Ku nenga* ("off the record," "out of earshot of the other side") is the necessary complement to *mbungu*. Here the discussion is conducted informally; rules of precedence are dropped so that anyone who can make himself heard, even a woman, may add his views. When the group returns to the circle, the spokesman expresses the consensus by returning another *mbungu* with his formal reply.

This simple exchange of tokens is the basic procedure for all traditional social transactions, including marriages, funerals, and adjudications. If, in connection with a given affair, a man has received no

[1] A common formula for the opening of such speeches is *Kiizidi mpamba ko*, "I have not come idly or empty-handed."

token, "he doesn't know, he hasn't heard." Conversely, if he has received one, he recognizes the ensuing obligations. On one occasion when I had arrived late at a meeting, the participants were reluctant to tell me what it was about; but when it came to the final distribution of *mbungu* to all those present, binding them (in theory) as witnesses to the transaction, I refused mine, saying that I did not know its significance. They found this argument convincing, so I got what I wanted. Manteke people love to play games with their own procedures. One day I found Paul outside his house sharing a bottle of beer with another elder. "My brother here," he explained to me with a straight face, "has brought me this *mbungu* to tell me that tomorrow is Christmas Day; otherwise I should have no means of knowing."

The more important the affair, the more complex the exchanges and the higher the value of the *mbungu*. For more important communications a series of conventional units complements the *mbungu* proper. For each commodity there is a cash equivalent that approximately matches its market price (in francs), as shown in the following list of the principal tokens:

mbungu	cup of palm wine	1–25
sangala	demijohn	120
nsusu	chicken	250
vunga[2]	blanket	500
nkombo	goat	2,000
ngulu	pig	4,000

In 1951 the equivalent of a goat was 200 francs; of a pig, 400. Ten years earlier, according to Manteke court records, the equivalents had been 25 and 75 francs, respectively.

The smallest coin, 1 franc, is the minimum *mbungu*; 2 francs is considered more polite. If the matter communicated is of some importance, and if no more substantial token accompanies the *mbungu*, 5 or 10 francs is commonly offered. Such a cash token is called *mbungu ya yuma*, "a dry cup." Four thousand francs is a "dry pig"; if a real pig is specified it is *ngulu ya miika*, "a pig with the hair on."[3] (I once heard a man pursuing this logic to its humorous conclusion refer to a real or wet glass of palm wine as *mbungu ya miika*.)

Valuable flexibility is introduced by the principle of cash equivalence. Although 4,000 francs is currently the equivalent of a pig, a

---

[2] This term is used almost exclusively at funerals.

[3] V. Mertens (1948, p. 1104) records that a dry bar of soap, actually 100 francs, was used to "wash off" an obligation; in Palabala at the turn of the century "a gun" meant about 4 shillings in cloth or trade goods. Cf. the "slave with hair" of the Nkundo-Mongo (Hulstaert, 1938, p. 158).

pig with the hair on may well cost more, or at least be more difficult to obtain. On the other hand, by agreement between the parties, a much smaller sum, such as 2,000 francs, may be substituted without losing the name or the significance of *ngulu*. Such an arrangement is likely between parties who are on very friendly terms. In court cases and other adjudications the principle allows the punishment to fit the crime: a woman who insults her husband may be fined a goat, which is the appropriate penalty, but how expensive the goat is depends on the judge's view of the provocation she suffered.

The return *mbungu* is or may be referred to as the original donor's *n'subu*. (Most of these usages are not so precise in practice as in theory.) The *n'subu* is the sample glass of palm wine or the like which the vendor or donor drinks to show that the jug is not poisoned.[4] The ordinary *n'subu* for a demijohn is 20 francs, but the idea of a return gift is more important than its value. I once dropped into the Polokele bar in Manteke where I found Jessy, to whom I felt I owed a debt of hospitality. By way of contributing to the occasion and recognizing my debt I presented him with a bottle of beer, explaining that since we lived at opposite ends of the village we had not been seeing much of each other lately; this *mbungu* indicated my regret. He replied with a grave little speech (no more serious in fact than mine) and an exactly similar bottle which he said was my *n'subu*. For the larger denominations the return gift is usually valued at about one fifth, and in such instances it is called *matondo*, "thanks." (Examples of such exchanges are given in chapter 7.)

These gifts, in various denominations, are more than just tokens, though that is their primary function. Those that are liquid, in particular, are intended to be consumed on the spot,[5] and commensality is an essential part of the idea of a properly concluded agreement. All those who partake of the feast are witnesses to the content of the agreement. The parties immediately concerned are those who eat the lion's share, but there is at least an *mbungu* for all those present. *Dya*, "to eat," is in fact the proper verb to describe acceptance of marriage payments, for example. Accordingly, the gift transferred must be large enough to be divided among all the members of the receiving group. The more important the affair, the larger the group. Size of group depends basically on the level of segmentation involved, although too

4 This antique custom turns up in the story of the Nsimbila War.
5 At a well-organized event there are soft drinks for teetotalers, who may also choose to take their *mbungu* dry. There may be quite a few people who abstain, though drinking habits vary noticeably from village to village.

much should not be made of this principle because the segmentary structure is not so precise as the principle suggests.

The most important affairs have to do with the primary social status of an individual or group; that is, they concern lineage affiliation. Concretely, they are landownership and slavery, for which a pig must be transferred, giving significance to the story often repeated in the missionary literature that at the end of the nineteenth century the cost of redeeming a slave was a pig. Brought into such an affair on each side are at least the elders of one house, plus representatives from other houses of the clan, plus various categories of patrilateral relatives. Nowadays it is rarely a question of redeeming a slave, but rather of clarifying someone's pedigree, usually in connection with a land quarrel, which may well be brought to a head by one of the parties formally presenting a "pig" to the other before an assembly of elders as a challenge.

If you wish to know someone's tradition on a certain point (which really means, if you want his cooperation in a quarrel with someone else), you take palm wine with you and make known your needs. But if the reply is *Kanga ngulu*, "Get ready a pig," you have been rejected. It amounts to something like this: "We consider you a person of no account; bring your pig, and we will hold a gathering of all concerned, at which your pedigree will be expounded and the worthlessness of your claims revealed." The phrase can therefore be intended as a deliberate insult. Names are closely associated with status; parents, after having given their child a certain person's name, must pay that person a pig if they subsequently wish to remove the name (Mbanza Manteke 53, 1946). Attempted suicide merits the fine of a pig.

Lesser affairs, such as marital disputes, can be settled more quietly, and for some that involve only a few people a chicken will do. If a woman has no children and her father's ill will is believed to be responsible, her husband may go with her to see the father, taking along a chicken or two as an offering (*kimenga*) "to ask him what are his intentions." The query concerning intentions is a stock phrase. One of my neighbors, with whom I had attended a funeral, came to my house that evening, borrowed a small coin from my wife, and gave it back to her[6] as an *mbungu* to ask "what I had in mind" because I had not walked home with him. But he was simply indulging in playful sparring.

Since the money is divided up among the members of the receiving group according to their roles in the affair, as a rule not even the most

[6] Etiquette forbade him, of course, to present the coin directly to me.

important of them gets very much. Nevertheless, the token's economic value is by no means ignored. Consequently it may constitute, or be closely equivalent to, a price paid or compensation given in exchange for a service. At the very least, a generously reckoned *mbungu* has a better chance of bending the chief's ear or loosening his tongue. This consideration is more important when its purpose is not simply to negotiate a routine transaction between friends and equals, but to persuade the opposite party to confer a favor. Moreover, the gift, though still the same "goat" or "chicken," may become a true prestation, a recognition of a difference in rank. In modern Manteke it never is, but who is to define the jural significance of some exchange recorded in the traditions of the clans? Here in the heart of the language and of the process of social communication is embedded a fundamental ambiguity, permitting the same institutions to result in quite different structures, hierarchical or egalitarian,[7] or at least permitting one structure to exist concretely in conjunction with the illusion of the other.

The *mbungu* also has a religious significance, although it is now so weak as to be scarcely perceptible. Palm wine (*malavu ma nsamba*) is, with kola nut, the essential ingredient in all that is customary (*fu kya nsi*), all that most profoundly stirs the NKongo's heart to feel that he is at home. The wine is poured as libations to the ancestors; in Mbanza Manteke this practice hardly survives, although occasionally someone pours the first few drops from his glass as *n'subu* to those who are underground or, more often, having accidentally spilled some, he draws attention to the custom. But there are many who feel that a wedding cannot be performed without palm wine; not even beer or *lungwila* will do, and certainly not cash. Of importance also in ritual observances is the pig, particularly the domesticated pig (*ngulu ya vata*), whose ritual equivalence to man may be deduced from witchcraft beliefs and magical practices.

A whole system of *mbungu* is used at, or once was used at, formal gatherings. So at least one hears from the elders, although even a week-long land affair I attended, a gathering of the clans from many villages at which the *mbungu* passed constantly from side to side, was not marked by such formality. According to the theory of etiquette, when

___

[7] Because of this ambiguity I prefer "token" to "prestation" as a translation of *mbungu*, despite Radcliffe-Brown's usage (1950, p. 47) in reference to the corresponding Mongo practice. The definition he quotes from the *Oxford English Dictionary*, the "action of paying, in money or service, what is due by law or custom," is misleading; the complete definition makes it clear that "prestation" implies a difference in rank. It seems useful to preserve this sense. (In French, on the other hand, *prestation* means simply gift.)

Na Kingani has something to discuss with Na Ntutu a Vidalu, he first sends a message announcing his coming, accompanied by an *mbungu* of 1 or 2 francs, called *leeki*, to show that he means it. The advance notice gives Na Ntutu a chance to prepare food and, still more important, to warn his kinsmen and supporters. Failure to give proper notice can still be a serious offense. When MFUTU called on NGOMA LUBOTA without warning (*kondwa mbungu*) to discuss a matter connected with their perennial feud over Mbanza Ntala, a row broke out and he was subsequently fined by the Manteke court (Mbanza Manteke 154, 1962).

When Na Kingani arrives at Na Ntutu's and enters the house prepared for him, where he is first of all to eat, he presents another *mbungu* called *n'kotu a luumbu*, "the entry into the compound," which signifies that the two clans have always got on well together (*nzingani ye ndelani*).[8] This *mbungu* may also be called *mbungu a fula dya vata ye kakatula meeso nsoni*, "the *mbungu* of the entrance to the village and removing shame from the eyes," or "the icebreaker." As such it draws attention to one of the most important functions of *mbungu*, as of etiquette in any country: to provide a standard behavior pattern that overcomes embarrassing pauses and gets things moving. The BaKongo, a nation of politicians and orators, are intensely sensitive to the mood of a gathering and correspondingly nervous when it is not quite clear how they stand, or what is to be done next.

Having eaten, Na Kingani, as he explains the purpose of his visit, may offer *na tambi maatu*, "lend me your ears." If the matter is of some importance it may be put off until the following morning, when the host, if the entertainment of the evening before has "dried up," offers another jug to "wash his guest's eyes" (*sukula meeso*); this action complies with the law of hospitality, that the guest should go away contented, saying, *Ndiidi, ndwini*, "I ate and drank and was well received." The discussion may go on for some days, but always it is axiomatic that "tomorrow is another day" (*mbaatu i n'syuka*), that no important decision should be announced until the parties have slept on it. The custom allows time for mature reflection; formerly, it allowed time for the ancestors to communicate with the chief during his sleep.

The book of Kongo etiquette has not yet been written. Ideas vary widely as to what the proper procedure is in practice. Na Kingani gives Na Ntutu a Vidalu something to express and secure goodwill; especially if he is a little bit old-fashioned, he applies a suitable name

---

[8] *Zingana*, "to embrace" (recip.); *lelana*, "to look after" (recip.). The phrase is a standard description of the relationship of intermarrying clans.

to the offering, calling it *mbungu a fula dya vata ye kakatula meeso nsoni*, whereupon the recipient's eyes light with pleasure as he recognizes *fu kya nsi*, the custom of the country. It is the wrapping on the gift.

The importance of the spokesman, *mpovi*, corresponds to that of the gift. His role is related to those of *nzonzi* and *nkazi*. *Nzonzi*, a term now usually reserved for the judges of the communal court, means judge or advocate and refers to the litigious role of an *mpovi* or *nkazi*.[9] *Nkazi*, the leader and representative of a descent group, need not be a competent speaker but should be. It is to him that gifts are addressed, although he may choose an *mpovi* to speak for him, usually but not necessarily a junior member of his group. The *nkazi*, however, is responsible; the *mpovi* is only a delegate. This distinction introduces a valuable ambiguity, allowing different interests to put different interpretations upon the same actions. Thus all of NANGA, except DISA, regards Kingalu as the *nkazi* of NANGA, as does everyone else; for DISA, however, the *nkazi* can only be the head of the senior house (DISA), and Kingalu is his spokesman.

One man "knows how to speak"; another does not, *kazeyi vova ko*. The nonspeaker may speak most effectively in private, where substance counts for more than style, but lack the imagination to execute the contrived figures of the successful public speaker; or he may be too blunt and impatient. A speaker's repertoire includes stock phrases and images, well-tried sentiments, proverbs and anecdotes, biblical analogies, and images often so subtly and deeply rooted in traditional culture that only the experts in the audience can comprehend them.

One Kasangulu *nzonzi* prides himself on being able to weave into his discourse songs ridiculing the competence of the court of appeal, without its highly experienced judges being able to understand what is going on. He means that his grasp of custom is more profound than theirs, but such an identification of true custom with the debris of archaic custom, though often made, is eventually self-defeating.

A common opening is the phrase, *Tu mfumu ye mfumu, nganga ye nganga*, exactly equivalent to "Ladies and gentlemen . . ." It indicates that no aspersions are being cast on anyone's pedigree; all those present are either chiefs (*mfumu*) or at least ritual experts, not slaves. Some speakers contrive a prologue to which this phrase forms a neat and ingenious climax. A common concluding phrase is *Inokene, ikyele*, "It

---

[9] *Zonza*, "to argue." In other Kongo dialects the word means simply "to speak," and *nzonzi* is equivalent to *mpovi* (from *vova*, "to say"). For an excellent account of the *nzonzi*'s traditional functions see J. Mertens, 1944-1952.

has rained, it has cleared," indicating that everyone may now go about his business. The speech itself proceeds with heavy reliance on the technique of the elicited response,[10] in which audience participation is so active that the expert speaker resembles the conductor of an oratorio. A really fine speech has themes and subthemes, counterstatements, inversions, and recapitulations; songs and proverbs are interspersed, all pointed to the argument, and the proper courtesies are observed toward persons mentioned by name. Such a performance is admired and enjoyed by everyone.

Speaking styles differ markedly: Kingalu's gently elegiac recollections of half-forgotten kinship; Damison's rabble-rousing; the prolixity of a grand old man who has been head of his clan for thirty-five years; the baroque ingenuities of Matuta; the rude, barking style of the man for whom it has earned the nickname of Palaka-Palaka. The best style of all belongs to Makola of Mbanza Nkazi, who in the fifth hour of the fourth day of a noisy and seemingly interminable debate spoke for sixty minutes, scarcely raising his voice, and was heard out in complete silence. The disputants were so impressed by his subtle and complex demonstration of the art that they almost composed their differences on the spot. An attentive audience must be earned; irreverent heckling may greet a poor performance: "We're all in church; Damison's preaching." Younger men practice on unimportant occasions within the family, under the eye of an expert. Any small gathering attended by a first-class *mpovi* turns into a miniature public meeting, a rehearsal for soloist and chorus.[11]

Some speakers use a staff or the fly whisk *nsyensye* (not to be confused with a broom). Neither is much more now than a device to occupy the speaker's hands, but both once had a significance related to the Kongo view that public gatherings are religious occasions, or more exactly that the spirit (*mpeve*) may be revealed [12] in the midst of the

10 The impossible task of recording elicited responses in writing has been valiantly attempted by Laman, 1957, pp. 124–126. The technique is called *kumbisa bantu*, "to cause the people to shout."

11 "Il semble superflu de faire remarquer la beauté de la prose des chefs Bakongo. Si les discours sont un peu longs, les auditeurs, hommes ou esprits, ne s'en plaindront pas. Ils savourent avec délices cette langue sonore et cadencée, syllabes musicales et sans heurt, où les pensées coulent limpides en un parallélisme sans recherche. Les formules, héritage ancestral, sont stéréotypées, mais leur agencement est l'œuvre de chaucun, docile au souffle de l'inspiration. Ce souci esthétique du beau langage crée des artistes du verbe, là où la légende a inventé des sauvages ou des dégénérés" (Van Wing, 1959, p. 343).

12 *Telama*, "to come forth," "to stand up." It would be unwise to attempt to specify which spirit. Cf. Durkheim on "the particular attitude of a man speaking to a crowd, at least if he has succeeded in entering into communion with it. His lan-

circle. The power of the spirit is manifest in the ability of *mpovi* to stir passions, in the power of the decision maker (*n'zengi*) to make decisions that stick; its voice is heard in the sound of the *ngoma*, *mondo*, *ngongi*, *sangwa*, and all kinds of music.

The staff *kolokolo* [13] was a sign of office, but also a means of communicating with otherworldly powers. A chief placed it at the head of his bed while negotiations were in progress so that his ancestors might reveal to him the true tradition and teach him in his dreams what to say on the morrow. The fly whisk looks very ordinary, but I was told that only one old man is left who knows how to make them. He is one of the three surviving Nkimba graduates, and the whisk is evidently of the same type as the one with which Nkimba novices were once flogged (Bittremieux, 1936, p. 44). At one long-standing land dispute one of the parties began by using the whisk provided by their hosts, but on the second day they brought their own, explaining semiseriously to me that there might be something about the other one which would lose them the case. The one they brought was thirty-odd years old, almost as old as the quarrel it was to regulate.

It is probable that the word "Kongo" itself implies a public gathering and that it is based on the root *konga*, "to gather" (trans.). The usual interpretations, admittedly unsatisfactory (Laman, 1953, p. 10), make the mistake of being too concrete; for example, they may claim that "Kongo" comes from *n'kongo* ("hunter"), hunting having been a characteristic activity. On the other hand, Mbanza Kongo is the mythical scene of the original gathering, and Ntotila, one of the titles of Ne Kongo, comes from *toota*, "to gather" (trans.). Related words are *n'kongudidi*, "judge"; *lukongolo*, "circle," "horizon," "rainbow"; *dikonga*, "species," "group"; *n'kongo*, "navel," "descent group," "origin." In the Kimpasi, Nkimba, and other rites the sacred enclosure is called "Kongo." A KiKongo treatise on social organization begins with a chapter on the art of the public meeting (Kamuna, 1966).

---

guage has a grandiloquence that would be ridiculous in ordinary circumstances; his gestures show a certain domination; his very thought is impatient of all rules, and easily falls into all sorts of excesses. It is because he feels within him an abnormal oversupply of force which overflows and tries to burst out from him; sometimes he even has the feeling that he is dominated by a moral force which is greater than he and of which he is only the interpreter" (1961, p. 241). This force is called, in Kongo, *mpeve*. The air stirred up by the whisk is also *mpeve*.

13 The usual Kongo word is *mvwala*, which means not only the staff but the man who carries it and who thereby indicates that he is the agent of a higher power; in Manteke, however, *mvwala* is usually associated with the prophetic sects. Nowadays it is only among the prophets that the religious aspects of gatherings are explicitly symbolized; if they have to be looked for elsewhere, they are nevertheless very much present.

Sociology of Information

Communication of information, like Mauss's "gift," is a total social phenomenon having political, religious, economic, and aesthetic dimensions. Information cannot be separated from the circumstances of its transmission unless analysis of it is to be largely phenomenological or literary. The information received by anthropologists in the field is no exception, as all modern fieldworkers know. I emphasize the point because of the assumption commonly made by the BaKongo and their ethnographers that behind the contradictory and incomplete communications received every day there lies an original and perfect truth toward which the investigator must strive, discarding false testimony and preferring authoritative to less authoritative sources. In most situations my method in this study is quite different. Every communication, like a gift, helps to define the relationship of the participants and their status in the community at large; all information, from this point of view, is sociologically true, though it may not be historically true.

One is told that the way to obtain information is to visit, with proper ceremony, the elder who owns it, presenting him with palm wine at least, and maybe a pig. In practice, since the request is a request for recognition of an alliance, the suppliant must also belong to the community, must already be related as "child," affine, or "brother," for example, to the elder he addresses. He must have a "need to know." The information is then constructed to meet his need, in terms of the relationship between the parties. Apart from such relationships the information exists only as a lumber pile of genealogical fragments, legendary incidents, scandalous rumors, and potent but obscure symbols. It takes shape in the telling; often the teller, besides being a politician and advocate, is a poet and philosopher, an artist in words, and the shape he imposes on his material is of the kind that also characterizes wood carvings and rituals. Gossip, a "broadcasting of judgment" (Paine, 1967), turns out to be much the same thing as formal communications. When there is no crisis, no question of debt, prestige, or land to be settled, gossip is stilled and tradition disintegrates. MVIKA NTUMBA attempted to collect and write down the traditions of his group but, finding only contradictory fragments, had to give up, saying that he was an honest man and would not record lies; in this conclusion he was unfair to his relatives. NLAZA in Kinkanza, confronted by a strange European demanding traditions, was at a loss to know what to say; eventually he settled on the story of his forebears' dealings with the Free State.

One is also told, by everybody, to listen only to qualified elders and shun the company of slaves and upstarts, but good ethnographic method requires that all communications be received impartially. The observer must also through constant participation in community affairs, seek information not initially directed to himself. Only by this means can he obtain a corpus of communications sufficiently large and various that he can begin to abstract common denominators and evaluate the sociological significance of single communications, including those specially constructed for his European ear. Manteke includes a number of men, particularly among those regarded by Europeans as chiefs and those regarded by their fellow villagers as slaves, who have specialized over the years in traditions for such inquiring foreigners as missionaries and administrators. By themselves, these communications are misleading, more or less deliberately so, but as part of a larger corpus that can be related analytically to the structure of the community they are as significant and as valuable as any others; the biases in them are primary data, rather than sources of error.

I was able to approach the optimum level of control over data in only four villages: Mbanza Manteke, Vunda, Ndemba, and Tendele. In other Manteke villages, and on my visits to other areas, inquiry related to structure (as in the incident at Kyesa Kifwa recounted at the end of chapter 2) proved much less profitable than questions about processes and ideal systems. In collecting information I used no assistants. A local man who gave and received data corresponding to his social status could be informant but not assistant. An outsider would have been as handicapped as I, and perhaps more so if he were a Congolese. Several times informants remarked that there had been a change in this regard since 1960; with the increasing politization of indigenous society after independence people became more reluctant to share "secrets" with their fellows and correspondingly less afraid to talk to Europeans, whose political role had diminished.

Field inquiry is a process of communication shaped by the roles of the participants, that is, by their perceptions, not necessarily consistent and reciprocal, of the relationship in which they stand. There is no such thing as a neutral observer; even a machine — and, in some situations, especially a machine — modifies the information transmitted. The observer himself, no matter how well he has gained the confidence of his informants, is always an outsider; in Africa, with few exceptions, the anthropologist has always been a European, and the primary dimension of his research has been the relationship of Europeans and Africans. With the decline of empire that relationship has changed. It does not follow that recent fieldwork is better, but it is different. The fieldworker is still a European, but he is no longer allied with the government; some kinds of information are now more difficult to obtain, some easier, and the shape of all communications has changed slightly.

Formal interviews I found to be marked by awkwardness on both sides, and it soon became apparent that the information to be gained was "cold." The most fruitful questions were posed in the context of the affairs to which they referred, others in casual conversations. A rewarding procedure was to accompany a man to his clearing in the forest, where he could be expected to talk freely during long hours of work in conditions of privacy. My desire to hear all points of view was matched by each villager's care not to be seen too much in my company; young men spoke of "what the elders would say" and elders of "what other people would say." These fears, though characteristic enough of Manteke life, were probably exaggerated; it was clear, however, that association with me would be regarded as an attempt to establish a competitive advantage, and that "other people," feeling threatened, would gossip to redress the balance.

A number of informants thought at first that I would pay them for traditions. By an instinct I subsequently discovered to be appropriate, I declined to do so. "Tradition is not bought," and informants themselves recognized that payment, as distinct from an exchange of tokens (*mbungu*), would introduce distortion. Nor was it possible to facilitate interviewing by compensating people for the time spent. Although cash has been in general use in Manteke since about 1897, its circulation is still largely a function of social relations. Cash purchases are effected only in the markets, which traditionally were placed outside the village, or in a limited number of market-type transactions in the village, as when a housewife offers a spare squash or two on a ledge outside her house for sale to any passerby. Wages are paid only to Angolans and received only from Europeans or in the context of European institutions, such as government employ. Purchase, designated as such, defines the participants as strangers; therefore, as I have pointed out, the parallel communication of normal social information becomes almost impossible.

Hortense Powdermaker (1967) speaks of the anthropologist as "stepping into" and "stepping out of" a foreign milieu. One cannot live in two houses at once. The boundary is not, of course, spatial; it is defined by behavior and expectations. Two schoolboys banged on my door one evening and demanded smoked fish; both the demand and the extraordinary rudeness that went with it were explained by their assumption that I must be a trader. On occasion I would be in conversation with a stranger to Mbanza Manteke who, on finding me there, assumed that I was on the other side of the boundary, and spoke to me as one speaks to Europeans; noticing his way of speaking, a neighbor would correct him, whereupon his attitude, his facial expression, even his grammar, would instantly change. According to Manteke people, what marked my "membership" in their community was my participation in their affairs and particularly my economic policy; "He contributes at our funerals, and when offered a gift he neither refuses it nor tries to pay for it." Toward the end of my visit I came to know how money could be put into circulation unobtrusively. Once, when I was clumsy about an exchange, the conversation went like this: "You're not paying for it, are you?" "Oh no, I'm giving you a present." "Ah, that's alright then; thank you very much." In relation to gift exchanges, the verb to express thanks is *fyauka*, which implies an intention to continue the relationship, rather than the usual *tonda*, which implies a termination.

These chapters contain many examples in which the fact of communication is at least as important as the information content. They suggest a modification of Meillassoux's model for societies of this kind, in which a primary source of the elders' control over their cadets is a monopoly of social information, such as customs, genealogies, history, and marriage rules (1960, p. 48). Manteke people say the same thing, but in fact the dogma of secrecy serves primarily to authenticate information in terms of its source rather than in terms of its content; the elders monopolize the administration of public affairs by refusing to accept communications from unauthorized persons. Any statement with political and structural significance can be rejected, if necessary, by pointing out that the social position of the informant is such that his information cannot be correct. "Don't believe anything he says, his mother came from elsewhere, his father was a slave, he's too young . . ." All these disabilities are summed up in the word *nleeke*, "cadet," the antithesis of *mbuta*, "elder."

The wide availability of supposedly secret information is a public norm as well as an observable fact. Fathers and Sons, who are necessarily members of other clans, are approved guardians of tradition, honored as aides and instructors of the chief or the *nkazi*; in the frequent disputes between members of the same descent group the word of the Oldest Child (*mwana wa mbuta*) is often decisive. Anthropologists are familiar with the corresponding inconsistency, superficially puzzling, in the situation reported by Malinowski (1935, I, 349) from the Trobriand Islands, where a lineage headman may give to his own son magic designated as the exclusive birthright of members of the matrilineage. In Kongo the dogma of secrecy serves to discredit all statements except those made at the right time and in the right place by the recognized authority, who by this act confirms his position. The dogma also permits the authority to vary his statements and traditions as policy indicates. It is essential that the investigator not allow himself to be bound by this dogma.

Social secrets thus parallel the marriage goods of Meillassoux's model, which may be circulated only by elders although any cadet may produce them (1960, p. 52). Limitations are imposed on the elder's control by two factors, one structural and one political. The social information that defines status in customary society refers to a limited range of transactions, mainly transfers of rights over land and over persons, which form the heart of custom *(fu kya nsi)*. In noncustomary affairs, such as relations with the provincial government and other European institutions, the elders are often powerless. The second factor is that cadets who become dissatisfied may attempt to reject existing authority as a whole, attaching themselves to new leaders and honoring new traditions *(kinkulu)* and new sources of legitimacy. These two factors, analytically distinguishable, are spectacularly combined in such major upheavals as the messianic movements of 1921 and other years, and the events leading to national independence in 1960; in day-to-day politics they provide recurrent themes at the village level and in provincial affairs.

7

MARRIAGES

The judge is the most married man in Mbanza Manteke, and acknowledges more children by more different women than anyone else. He is also the best speaker by virtue of an enormous crowd-quelling voice, a demagogic style, and a personality as robust and weighty as his body. As a shrewd elder and *nkazi* of NSUNDI, he is an experienced and respected Manteke figure. His oratorical talent helped qualify him for the post of judge, which he has held for twenty-five years; half of the court's time is spent on marital disputes, he says. Here is his account of how to get married.

First the young man (*toko*) asks the girl for her consent. She gives it: "*Inga*," simpered the judge, glancing coyly out from under his eyelashes and a moment later shaking with laughter at his own performance. Then the young man goes to buy seven things: (1) a head scarf; (2) "smelly soap," as the judge chooses to designate perfumed soap; (3) earrings; (4) thread for tying the hair; (5) laundry soap; (6) a bottle of eau de cologne; and (7) a box of talcum powder. He has a friend[1] give these offerings to the girl, who takes them to her father, her mother's brother, and her two grandfathers in turn to tell them that the young man wants to marry her.

It is no longer necessary to ask the question through an intermediary. Marriages are not arranged by the older generation, although one youth who had just joined the army wrote to his mother to find him a wife as soon as possible because, he said, the food in the mess was terrible. The list of presents is not so standardized as the judge seemed to think, and may include food as well as toiletries. In any event, the girl (*ndumba*) must notify her relatives if she receives any gifts. One evening loud voices came from a reed shanty in which a group of men were scolding their sister; she had been given sardines by a stranger, a government clerk, but had failed to mention the fact. Any presents a

---

[1] The word for "friend" is *matwadi*; *kintwadi*, "cooperation." The *ma*-prefix, or the singular form *di-*, is used to designate roles, especially offices.

girl receives as engagement tokens are returnable if the *bankazi* do not approve of the match.

If the girl reports to her suitor that her relatives agree, he buys and sends to her *nkazi* a demijohn of palm wine which is *leeki*, notification that he will arrive with his relatives on a certain day to ask for the list of gifts demanded by her relatives. Her *nkazi* then collects the three other chiefs (*mfumu*) on her side, and on the appointed day they present the young man's *nkazi* with the list of demands. A typical list (with values given in francs) follows.

1) *Nkazi a ndumba* (the girl's *nkazi*)		1,000–1,500
2) *Se dya mwana* (her father)		2,000–4,000
3) *Mfumu a n'teekudi ku nim'a se* (her paternal grandfather)		300–600
4) *Mfumu a n'teekudi ku nim'a ngudi*		
	(her maternal grandfather)	300–600

Each payment, when handed over, is called *kuta dya longo* (*kuta*, "a packet").

There are also certain presents to be made to the girl's parents, some specifically requested, some required by custom. The most important in the latter category are a suit length and a blanket for her father and a dress length and a head scarf for her mother, "to cleanse the dirt" (*mu sukula mvindu*). The explanation given for the phrase is that these presents compensate the parents for the trouble they had in bringing up the child, in the course of which their clothes were soiled. Its use in other contexts signifies recognition of obligation, especially on the part of a clan toward the father of one of its members.

The suitor's *nkazi* returns home and reckons up the cash available. Then he, not the youth himself, goes to inform the youth's father (*se dya toko*) of his son's intentions. He also informs the two grandfathers (*mfumu za n'teekudi*), taking with him an *mbungu* each time. Each decides what he can afford to contribute. When a young man of NZUZI wanted to get married, his *nkazi* called a meeting of these relatives "to ask for their help." Representatives of the Children of NZUZI were also present. Although NZUZI will on balance benefit from this appeal, its real purpose, as NZUZI said, is to announce the forthcoming marriage; "It isn't right to do things secretly."

Weddings occur on Saturday afternoons or Sundays. They are held in public under a convenient mango tree or other shade, and anyone can attend. People with nothing better to do drop in, or stroll over to a neighboring village if there is no wedding in their own. On a particular Saturday, when an NTUMBA man is to marry an NSUNDI girl, chairs and benches are arranged in a circle outside Makima's house.

At one side Makima is presiding, although he is MVIKA NTUMBA and the youth is NGOMA LUBOTA. Makima is acting as *nkazi* in the place of Joel Albert of NGOMA who is ill. The four chiefs (*mfumu ziya*) on the girl's side sit around the circle in no particular order. Behind them, on mats on the ground, sit groups of women, some doing each other's hair for the weekend. Food is being prepared in several houses in the village. The ceremony consists of the exchange of gifts between the young man's *nkazi* and the four chiefs, who are the owners of the bride.

THE OWNERS OF THE BRIDE

The roles of owners of the bride are prescribed. They are the representatives (i.e., the *bankazi*) of her mother's, father's, mother's father's, and father's father's descent groups. Designation of the actual individual who plays such a role depends on the internal structure of the group in question. We shall consider the NSUNDI, NA TUMA, and NTUMBA weddings illustrated in figure 8, and a fourth in MFUTU of NANGA.

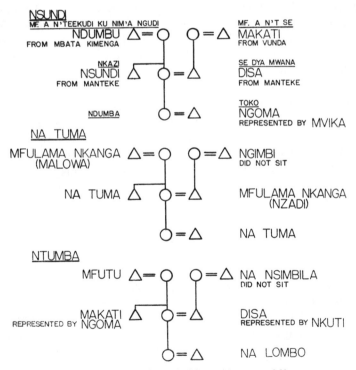

FIG. 8.   Owners of the bride at three weddings.

NKAZI

At the NSUNDI wedding Damison of NSUNDI is the girl's *nkazi*; he is of the same house as the bride in their clan section, but belongs to a different lineage. Damison is her *nkazi* because in her lineage there is no suitably mature man. He also regards himself as head of their house, but on this point he is challenged by the *nkazi* of the third lineage, Tusikila, who says his lineage is senior. Since both are living in Mbanza Manteke, they compromise by sharing the role of *nkazi*; on this occasion as on others, sometimes one speaks and sometimes the other. Together they represent not the house but the clan section, the exogamous unit, NSUNDI, which happens to lack an accepted *nkazi*; that is, the three houses are unable to agree on one. In Manteke village, however, the house KYANGALA NA NSUNDI acts independently in most affairs, and public controversy over the *kinkazi* is avoided. Neither Damison nor Tusikila has any traceable genealogical relationship to the bride.

On another occasion an MFUTU girl was married. Her mother's brother was a young man who asked that a shirt for himself be included in the marriage list but did not otherwise figure in the proceedings. Her MoMoBr, Nkomo, was primarily responsible for all the arrangements, including the preparation of the list and the provision of food and entertainment. Nevertheless, many comments regarding the allocation of funds and resources were made, not by him, but by the other senior member of his lineage, Hezekaya.[2] At the wedding itself Nkomo did nothing and said nothing. The *nkazi* to whom all speeches were addressed was the *nkazi* of NANGA, Kingalu, who presides at most NANGA marriages and funerals. The clan section is the unit of exogamy, although the popular conception of the rule betrays an uncertainty that corresponds to the tendency to identify *mvila* and *kanda*. One afternoon in Vunda the circle for a wedding was just forming when I happened to pass by. When I asked who the young man was, he was pointed out to me, but when I asked the name of his clan the reply was, "We don't know. We haven't heard." The presentations had not begun. Both bride and groom, it turned out, were NA TUMA, but the bride was local, the groom from Matadi. They were thus of the same *mvila* ("clan") but from different *makanda* ("sections"). There was some discussion whether a pig should be killed "to cut the kinship," but nothing was done because (1) the parties were not both local and (2) "that is an old custom which there is no point in observing nowadays."

A similar situation occurred in Manteke when an NTUMBA man se-

2 This lineage is SWETE KYA TONA (see table 1 and fig. 2).

duced an NLAZA girl. Her father wanted them to marry, but some outsiders commented, "How can they? It's all in the family [*bau ye bau*]." That is, they belonged to the same *mvila*. The burden of discussion, however, was the matter of seduction, not incest; when marriage was ruled out, it was for other reasons. One NANGA man is actually married to a NANGA girl from one of the riverine villages, from a section said by Kingalu to be of Manteke origin, but the two groups no longer maintain any relationship. On the other hand, when a youth of MVIKA NTUMBA wrote to his *nkazi* that he was wild about a girl of MAKATI MA NTUMBA he had met in Matadi, and would willingly pay for the necessary pig, he was rebuffed.

At the NA TUMA wedding, because two of the four chiefs on the girl's side came from different houses of the same clan section, the *nkazi* of each house was present. One of them said, *Yeto kweto twawuta, yeto kweto twatekula,*[3] "We ourselves are both Father and Grandfather." This situation arose because the girl's mother was the father's "child" (*mwana*), that is, a Child of his clan section.

At the NTUMBA wedding the parties to the affair had little prestige, few of the important village elders came, and the payments were unusually low. For the bride's house, MAKATI, Joel Albert of NGOMA, who had nothing else to do on a warm afternoon, sat as *nkazi*, though he said nothing. All the arrangements were handled by MBENZA, who has married into this lineage which has no elder of its own. DISA as Father of the Child was represented by NKUTI. As "maternal grandfather" Kingalu of MFUTU, the only recognized orator present, made most of the ceremonial speeches for the bride's family. As the *nkazi* of the entire NANGA clan section, he could properly speak for DISA as well as for MFUTU.

The *nkazi*, therefore, is in principle the representative of the clan section (*kanda*), and the other three chiefs represent homologous units. Principle may be modified, however, when two houses of the same clan section have roles to play. The individual who actually sits as *nkazi* of the clan section is not always the same at different affairs; selection depends upon political accommodations at the level of the house and of the lineage. In any event, primary managerial responsibility behind the scenes belongs to the *nkazi* of the lineage, the primary money-sharing group. Here again the individual acting as *nkazi* may not be a member of that lineage or even of the same clan.

3 *Wuta,* "to engender." Regrettably there is no English equivalent for *tekula,* a word describing the action of a grandfather in producing a grandchild. According to Laman, 1936, *tekula* means "to ramify."

SE DYA MWANA

The Father of the Child (*se dya mwana*) is the bride's father's *nkazi*, whoever that may be for the occasion. The father may be present but the *nkazi* plays the role. Ultimately the marriage payments are received and distributed by the father's lineage. The *mvindu* ("compensation") goes to the bride's parents only; her father gets the suit length, for example. If he is dead, though, the gift goes to his immediate successor. The money (*kuta*), on the other hand, is divided among the members of the lineage, the father getting the most substantial allocation.

At the NSUNDI wedding the girl's late father, of the DISA house of NANGA, was represented by a DISA man of different lineage who lives in Manteke because, like Tusikila, he has a government job there. The *nkazi* of DISA is an old man who lives in Ndemba and comes to Manteke only for more important affairs, such as funerals. The substitute on this occasion is not genealogically related to the girl.

In this instance the girl's mother and father had been married and had brought up the child. Sometimes, however, there may be a question as to whether the marriage payments due *se dya mwana* go to *m'buti*, her genitor, or to *se dya n'sansi*, the man who had the trouble of bringing her up (*sansa*, "to bring up"); divorce is frequent, and the roles are often shared. The money payment, and the kind of wedding at which it is transferred, are recent developments attributable largely to mission and government influence (see below). Since the money itself is a new element, there is no traditional prescription for the division of the spoils. The question is settled, in each instance, by argument leading to compromise.

The judge cites the case of a certain man who married a girl whom he later discovered to have been pregnant by someone else. He wanted to return the wife, but her *nkazi* recommended that he treat the child as his and gave him a goat to ask his forbearance. When the child, a girl, grew up and was to marry, both Genitor and Upbringer put in demands, for 2,800 francs and 3,500 francs, respectively. The girl's *nkazi*, who was compiling the list, saw that the total would be too high. In the course of the tremendous row that ensued the Upbringer was about to renounce his participation in the affair when a compromise was reached, 2,500 francs for the Genitor, 2,800 for the Upbringer. In other cases, says the judge, the *nkazi* might privately allot part of his own share to the Upbringer as compensation for his trouble, but the suit and the blanket, constituting the *mvindu*, can go only to the Genitor. If they did not go to him the girl would fall ill and be barren.

This special ritual relationship to the child is not shared by the Upbringer.

Other elders are divided in their opinions, even when discussing the principle in the abstract. One says the Upbringer gets all the money; another, that the Genitor gets it, even though he may not have done a thing for the child: "Europeans know that the upbringing is what's difficult; *kansi yeto mu kindombe*, we Africans, ppht!" Others say the paternal share of the list should be divided; there are further possibilities for argument if the child was brought up in more than one household. Under no circumstances is there a role for a man whose only link with the child is that at some time he was married to her mother. The partition view was upheld by the court in the case of a woman who had been in concubinage to two men, one of whom had been declared by court decision to be the father of her daughter. When the daughter grew up the other man married her off, pocketing 2,000 francs *kuta dya longo*. The court required him to pay half to the Genitor, citing the proverb usually applied to the rights of partners in an enterprise: *Nwatamba n'tambu n'zoole, nukokula wo n'zoole*, "You set a trap together, inspect it together."

If the Genitor is unknown, or completely inaccessible, the girl's *nkazi* takes over his role. A certain woman had been the concubine of two men in succession. When her daughter grew up and was about to be married, one of the men accused the other of stealing "his" child and of planning to pocket the marriage money. The girl's *nkazi* said that as far as he was concerned both men were thieves, since he knew nothing about either of them marrying his *busi* ("sister"). Since there was no evidence to indicate the paternity one way or the other, the court decided that neither would-be father had any right to the child (Mbanza Manteke 467, 1951). The judges capped their decision with a proverb, *Twala kuulu yabindikila nzo ame, kizolele nzonza ko*, translated in the record as "Donnez moi votre pied pour pouvoir fermer la porte de ma maison car je ne voudrais pas avoir des querelles." The proverb shows explicitly that the decision was a makeshift one. In such situations the child's status approaches that of a slave; he has only two chiefs, his *nkazi* and his maternal grandfather.

MFUMU A N'TEEKUDI

At one time it was general Kongo custom to accord a ceremonial role at weddings to the Grandfathers, but only in some areas is the custom still maintained (see below). The role of Father of the Child is in any event much more important than that of Grandfather, in Manteke as elsewhere. The representative of the Grandfather's group is called *mfumu a n'teekudi* (from *tekula*, "to ramify"); this term, like *nkazi*, designates a responsible role in relation to the Child, but it is not a kinship term. These two chiefs (the Grandfathers) are distinguished by the additional phrases "behind the father" and "behind the mother" (*ku nim'a se, ku nim'a ngudi*).

At the NA TUMA wedding the paternal Grandfather could not or would not come; all *mbungu* were therefore addressed only to the other three chiefs. An anterior dispute probably kept the paternal Grandfather away, but there is a slight tendency for his role to be dropped anyway. The two Grandfathers are often spoken of as one when the roles played at such an occasion are discussed. Similarly, although the paternal Grandfather did not put in an appearance at the NTUMBA wedding, his share of the marriage money was forwarded to him, or so I was told. The original grandfather, however, was a man whose origins are controversial, so perhaps the vacant seat was simply the easiest solution.

MARRIAGE MONEY

When the *bankazi* have assembled the marriage moneys (*mbongo za nkwedolo*) are distributed among them. At the NSUNDI wedding Makima had with him, as provided by the young man and his *nkazi*, enough money to pay the *kuta ma longo*, certain associated gifts and *mbungu*, and five demijohns of palm wine. He also had a reserve fund of contributions by the youth's Father (550 francs), Grandfather (320 francs), and other relatives. Some of these contributions, usually from 5 to 50 francs, were made by individuals out of their own pockets; others represented collections made from members of a lineage.

Makima says that if the youth had been a member of his own house he would have had to make the speeches himself. As it is, he does not care for public speaking, especially at weddings because in his view they occasion, in the name of custom, a deplorable squandering of money. So Kyanlasu of NGOMA does the talking. At Makima's direction he distributes two demijohns (*sangala byole*) to each of the four chiefs of the bride's party. One "demijohn" in each pair is paid in cash "for those who don't drink." An *mbungu* of 2 francs goes with each pair. Each chief also gets an envelope containing his *kuta dya longo*. Several small tokens of from 5 to 20 francs are handed around, but most of the remaining payments go to the Father of the Child, including those that are gifts to the girl's mother. The list of marriage moneys paid in the NSUNDI wedding (see table 2), based on Makima's

TABLE 2
MARRIAGE MONEY, NSUNDI WEDDING, IN FRANCS

1. Nkazi Damison Nsiku			NSUNDI
Thermos mosi	500		The girl's MoBr, her *nkazi*, who compiled this list, had asked for a thermos for himself. He died the week before the wedding.
Costume kaki	830		Cloth
Malanda mamosi	200		Machete
Mbele yimosi	100		Knife. These things requested by the bride's brothers.
Kuta dya longo	1,500		
	3,130		Paid in cash
2. Mfumu a n'teekudi			NDUMBU
Kuta dya longo	600		
3. M'buti a mwana			DISA
Kuta dya longo	3,000		
Kotika	100		Knife requested by member of the lineage
4. Mfumu a n'teekudi	600		MAKATI
	4,300	7,430	List total, paid in cash
5. Mvindu			
M'vwatu wa se	1,500		Father's suit
Kitambala kya ngudi	250		Mother's kerchief
M'fisu myole	100		Two reels of sewing thread
		1,850	
6. Mbungu			
Mbungu	10		Accompanying the demijohns
Funda dya nyanzi	20		Food given to the bride by the groom for her to prepare
Vayikisa ndumba	10		Paid to *se* to "bring out the girl"
Baka mabiika	20		5 francs to each of the four to request their farewell advice to the girl
Nanguna se	140		Representing one demijohn for the Father "so that he may be in a good mood"
Sangala kya nwa di kanda se	140		A similar demijohn to entertain the father's clan
		340	Paid in cash
Total		9,620	

accounts, does not accurately reveal the payments actually made; although the total is the same, the breakdown was slightly different. In addition to the amounts on the list, the youth's *nkazi* handed over the "wine" already mentioned, half of it in cash, and a blanket and a woman's dress length.

While these amounts are being handed around with explanatory speeches by Kyanlasu, arguments break out continually. People sitting around the circle interrupt to tell Kyanlasu that he has omitted an *mbungu*, or given it to the wrong party, or put down 1 franc when it should have been 2 francs. This wrangling is usual. The procedure is never the same twice, although the principal payments to the four chiefs — the "list," the palm wine, and the *mvindu* — are required. The various courtesy payments (listed as *mbungu*) represent a modern summary of the payments formerly made on a series of occasions (Laman, 1957, chap. 2). Customs vary from one region to another, but the principal occasions, in Manteke terms, are (1) *leta kya ndumba*, the initial agreement between the parties, after which the couple are *makangu*, "engaged"; [4] (2) *nkwedolo a longo*, the wedding proper; and (3) *kotisa ndumba*, when the girl is taken to her husband's house.[5] The process of condensation has left many *mbungu* with no other function than to contribute to the etiquette of the occasion, which is the more gratifying and honorable the more elaborate it is.

Table 3 shows the payments made at the NA TUMA wedding as reported by the groom, who was given this responsibility because he had nothing else to do during most of the proceedings. Here the number of courtesy payments, left over from more expansive times, is larger than in the NSUNDI wedding. The "bill" or "list" is *leta kya ndumba*, which had in fact been obtained without ceremony some time before; accordingly, the amount was reduced from the normal 3×120 francs. Item 3 represents a gift of food, but my informants were unable to explain the name (*funda*, "a packet"; *nyanzi*, "a fly"). The *vinu* of item 7 is a bottle of Portuguese wine requested on the list; 400 francs more "wine" was added because "one bottle is easily forgotten." Items 9 and 10 amount to two demijohns for each of the chiefs present, one of which is labeled "liver of the pig"; in nearby villages this label

[4] *Leta* = "letter" = the list, which is requested at the time of engagement.

[5] Nowadays the girl goes to her husband's house anytime after the wedding, without special ceremony. In most of the weddings I witnessed the couples were to be domiciled in town. In one instance the girl came to join her husband two or three weeks after the ceremony, which had been held in her village; she was accompanied by a small group of kinswomen who brought food they helped her prepare for an informal meal eaten by the husband and some friends of his. It is unthinkable that the newlyweds should begin living together until public attention has withdrawn from them.

TABLE 3
MARRIAGE MONEY, NA TUMA WEDDING, IN FRANCS

1. Ndombolo a facture	3 × 40 =	120	Asking for the "bill"
2. Ngyuvudusu nkumbu a ndumba		10	Paid to the Father "to ask the girl's name"
3. Funda dya nyanzi		50	
4. Nsokolo dya mpidi a ndumba	3 × 40 =	120	"Stuffing the girl's basket." To pay for food given to the girl by her family.
5. Nkazi NA TUMA			NA TUMA
Kuta dya longo		1,500	
6. Se			MFULAMA NKANGA
Mfisu		50	Sewing thread
Kuta dya longo		5,000	Marriage payment
7. Mfumu a n'teekudi			MFULAMA NKANGA
(Kuta dya longo)		600	
Vinu		400	
8. Mfisu kwa ngudi		50	Sewing thread for the mother
9. Langa dya ngulu	3 × 120 =	360	Literally, liver of the pig; three demijohns
10. Malavu longo	3 × 120 =	360	Marriage palm wine
11. Mokesa ndumba	3 × 1 =	3	To inform the family that the young man is "talking to the girl"
12. Yuma bya leka kyandi yamuna	3 × 40 =	120	Palm wine "to warm up the dryness of sleeping"
13. Ngi lubundidi yalu	3 × 1 =	3	Request for the concerted decision of the chiefs
14. Nlombu a biika	3 × 5 =	15	Request for farewell speeches
15. Lavu dya nsi	3 × 3 =	9	Libation to the ancestors
16. Nsengo a duuki		20	Notification to the village headman that the girl is leaving
17. Témoin NTUMBA		130	Paid to the local house that represented the groom's house
Total		10,760	

applies only to gifts due the grandfathers. Item 12 is otherwise "washing the eyes," which would once have been presented on the following day.

When the groom's party has placed each sum of money separately at the feet of the proper recipient, a spokesman explaining the significance of each, the girl's *nkazi* replies, reiterating the account. The money is counted, and the bride's party retires to discuss its reply. The participants include all those present to whom custom allots a role in the affairs of the bride's clan section, or, rather, all those present who enjoy participating, do not belong to the groom's immediate lineage, and can if necessary claim for themselves an appropriate kinship status. At the MFUTU wedding the loudest voices raised were those of other members of NANGA, such as Mbelani of NSAKA; of children of NANGA, such as Yoka of NA LOMBO; and of grandchildren of NANGA, such as Damison of NSUNDI. When they had argued it out, they told *nkazi* Kingalu what to say.

There are usually two things to argue about: whether the payments are commensurate with their significance, and how much return to make. At the NSUNDI wedding Damison replied to Makima that 1,500 francs for the father's suit and 250 francs for the mother's kerchief were not enough, considering the market price of such items. At the MFUTU wedding, where the Father had specified he wanted a white suit instead of the usual, cheaper khaki, it was discovered that the length of cloth offered was not long enough. Completion of the negotiations depended on the youth's *nkazi* making up the deficiency. It is only in this marginal sense that any haggling is resorted to; the entire exchange takes place within conventional limits. The same thing is true even of the list itself; people say that "a good man" will ask a little less, but the eventual sum varies more in accordance with prestige than with goodwill. A much more important aspect of the proceedings is the dominant role accorded to the wife-givers; they are cast as the ones whose demands have to be met.

The return gift made by the girl's *nkazi* is approximately a fifth or a sixth the value of the original gift. The Grandfathers almost invariably receive 600 francs and give back 100. At the NSUNDI wedding Damison returned *matondo*, "thanks," so that Makima's actual *kuta* expenses (in francs) were as follows:

nkazi	3,130 — 500 =	2,630
se	3,100 — 500 =	2,600
mfumu a n'teekudi	600 — 100 =	500
mfumu a n'teekudi	600 — 100 =	500
		6,230

In addition, the return may include the alcoholic part of the gift, *n'subu*. In Vunda each chief was given four bottles of beer, of which he returned one. In this instance the arithmetic of thanks was (again in francs):

$$
\begin{array}{rrrr}
nkazi & 1{,}500 - & 500 = & 1{,}000 \\
se & 5{,}000 - & 1{,}000 = & 4{,}000 \\
mfumu\ a\ n'teekudi & 600 - & 100 = & \underline{500} \\
& & & 5{,}500
\end{array}
$$

The Father also asked that 1,000 francs be transferred to the price of his suit, so that the final figure in the Vunda wedding was 4,500 francs. It is this figure (6,230 francs in the NSUNDI wedding) which is returnable in the event of divorce, and which the government records as the marriage payment if the marriage should be registered. Most of it goes to the Father, but it is the *nkazi* of the girl's lineage who is responsible for the repayment; he sometimes has difficulty getting the others to contribute. None of the 5,000-odd francs handed over by the young man's *nkazi* in the NSUNDI wedding under various rubrics as "food and drink" is returnable, as Makima gloomily noted.

When the gifts have been exchanged, the girl is summoned to sit in the middle of the circle. Asked if she accepts the agreement, she indicates her acceptance by clapping her hands. She is then led off to a robing room where the good clothes she is already wearing are replaced by a spectacularly rich outfit. At the circle armchairs covered with embroidered cloths are arranged for the final stage, not without loud and confused argument as to how it should be done. The groom, hitherto inconspicuous among the young men present, takes his place as a procession of singing girls and youths brings the bride from the robing house. Bride and groom sit side by side with their arms around each other's necks; the gesture is an imitation of European behavior which always raises a laugh and increases the evident embarrassment felt by the couple. The groom maintains a stoic face; the girl sulks. She is on his left; at his side is a female *mpangi*, kinswoman of his clan, at hers a kinsman of her clan. The details vary widely and fashions change, but it is common for the groom to wear the bride's kerchief and she his hat; their companions similarly wear headgear of the opposite sex "to show that that which was separate is now joined together."

There follow the *mabiika*, farewell instructions from the *bankazi* and other members of the two families. The young man is instructed to look after the girl, particularly so at the NA TUMA wedding because they were of the same clan — if he wanted to divorce her where could he

send her? The bride is advised to be diligent in household duties —
wash the dishes, sweep the house, do the laundry, raise the children —
and to speak the truth and keep off alcohol. The list of obligations
is always longer for the bride than for the groom. Some speakers lead
songs, some make ribald remarks, each according to his style. Makima,
as Grandfather at the MFUTU wedding, said only, "There is just one
thing that matters: mutual respect."

By this time quantities of food prepared by the bride's relatives have
been brought to the groom's kin, usually by a group of girls singing
indelicate songs. After the *mabiika* the couple usually rejoin their
friends, each his own, and the final event is a wedding feast eaten by
men and women separately, the men being served first. Most of this
food, lamented Nkomo the day after the MFUTU wedding, was paid for
by the girl's lineage, which was also supposed to send the groom back
to his village with further provisions so that his family could not spread
the word that they had been to Manteke and had come away starving.

Men of the bride's lineage meet, usually the next day, to dispose of
the marriage money received. Some of it goes to expenses such as the
bride's identification card which she will need in town where she is
going to live, train fares for certain relatives who came to the wedding,
and the like. Those who played a special role may be allotted a token
reward; Kingalu gets from 10 to 25 francs each time he is *nkazi* at a
NANGA affair. The *nkazi* of the lineage may be given 200 francs, as
Nkomo was after the MFUTU wedding, on the ground that he had borne
the larger part of the expenses. This sum, together with the case of
beer he had put on the list because he and his wife like nothing better
than to share a bottle together at home in the evenings, amounted to
only a part of his actual expenses; the real gainer, he moaned, was the
Father of the Child, whose receipts were large and whose contribution
was little or none. The rest of the money may be divided among the
members of the lineage, men as well as women, most of them getting
only a few francs each. Small amounts may be sent as *mbungu* to relatives resident elsewhere to notify them that the event has taken place.
The *nkazi* may keep a part of the receipts in the lineage's common
fund.

These arrangements are made in private and are very difficult to
observe. It is clear, however, that the allocation of marriage money is
a function of the unstructured internal political situation of the lineage and the house to which it belongs. A strong *nkazi* will make the
decisions himself, and in a well-organized lineage such as Makima's in
MVIKA the common treasury controlled by him is drawn upon for contributions to family affairs of various kinds. In theory, the accounting

is strict; in practice, in most lineages, little bits of paper lie about unreckoned. Kingalu, describing the procedure, emphasized the communicative value of the distribution; after an MFUTU wedding, he said, an *mbungu* might or might not be sent to DISA or NZUZI "to tell them that we have married off our child."

In the Kasangulu area the procedure is considerably different, as are the prices. The dignified preliminary salutations, so characteristic of Manteke, are reduced to a minimum. The speakers, who are not the *bankazi*, sit facing each other on a mat in the middle of the circle. The bride's party's spokesman warms up the meeting with a speech, at the end of which he produces from his pocket a slip of paper with "50,000 francs" written on it. The other speaker receives the paper with expressions of surprise and indignation: "What! Is this a marriage or a market?" Waving the slip of paper, he addresses himself to the gathering: "All you young men, take heed! Before you get keen on some girl, just think — 50,000 francs!" Then he reaches into his own pocket and produces another slip on which is written "5,000 francs." This offer is suitably ridiculed by the recipient, and so it goes. Eventually the youth's party agrees to pay 40,000 francs, of which the other side returns 10,000, leaving a balance of 30,000, the going figure for such a marriage in the area. The difference between these and Manteke rates is a function of proximity to Kinshasa; the entire affair is much more extravagant, with the groom hiring trucks, for example, to bring his friends from town.

In this area the accounting also is done differently. In the event of divorce the bride's *nkazi* will deduct from the 30,000 francs transferred to him in Kasangulu the amount of his expenses for the feast. "If he is a good man he will say, 'I have made several children with this woman, and in my old age they will remember me and give me a shirt now and again; so I will renounce the marriage payment.' But others will claim everything, from the pig they provided for the feast right down to the last bottle of lemonade." Persistent efforts to limit the sum of payments by limiting the amount the courts will return in case of divorce (10,000 francs in Kasangulu in 1966) have been unsuccessful.

FORMS OF MARRIAGE

It is also possible, observes the judge, to marry by *sangata*. "*Sangata* is like this: if I find a knife in the street and make off with it without saying anything, that would be theft. But if I hold it up and say, 'If nobody wants this, I'm taking it,' then the owner has the chance to say, 'Yes, that's mine, but you may have it.'" In this form of marriage the girl's *nkazi* is notified by the offer of an *mbungu*; as the judge's explanation suggests, the offer fulfils the necessary condition for any social transaction — that it be communicated in proper form. The *nkazi* later communicates the arrangement privately to the Father of the Child.

More conjugal unions among Manteke residents are based on *sangata* agreements than on weddings. Most of the village weddings marry off men and women who already live in town, or men who come back to the village to marry at less cost than in town. An accurate estimate for the Manteke population is rendered difficult by the delicacy of the question and impossible by the discord that usually surrounds any status definition: one party says the wedding occurred, the other says it did not, and a full-scale judicial hearing would be necessary to find out. Usually, however, the obvious question is whether even the *sangata* has been observed. A few of the most respected and longest-established households are unquestionably based upon a wedding; perhaps half of the remainder originated in no ceremony at all.

The question is complicated by the terms in use. *Sangata* was mentioned specifically only in response to my inquiries. The ordinary term is *kimakangu* (*kanga*, "to tie"), which formerly referred to the engagement period between the first and second ceremonies, as noted above. It is now translated into French, by the people, as "concubinage," and refers to two states: (1) *sangata* and (2) cohabitation without ceremony. The confusion is due in no small measure to colonial policy. Before the 1920's, when there was no marriage money, a would-be bridegroom took a packet containing sugarcane and plantains to each of the four owners of the bride. This gift, together with palm wine, was divided among and consumed by members of the receiving group. Other foodstuffs were exchanged, but the ceremonially required items were sugarcane and plantains. Makima, who exemplifies the Protestant ethic and keeps meticulous records of everything, has evidence that this custom was still observed as late as 1928. At a later stage in the arrangements, according to the judge, two chickens were necessary. On the Bangu and elsewhere, chickens and palm wine alone were required. It was generally the rule that the girl's *nkazi* sent a pig with her to her husband's house.

Since the civilizing mission of the colonial regime called for strengthening the family as the basic social unit, the government was prepared to recognize and sanction unions that corresponded approximately to the European idea of a family. Discussions of the application of this policy (e.g., in the review *Congo* in the early 1920's) centered on an institution called Bantu marriage in which, in accordance with contemporary theory, it was held that the transfer of bride-price stabilized the union, compensated the bride's clan for the loss of her services, and performed other useful functions.[6] The content of the discussions and the use of the word *lobola* indicate that East African custom provided the model for Bantu marriage.

As in all discussions of the impact of colonial policy on customary society, it is important to note that individual officials differed considerably in their interpretation of the law and of custom and in the models they attempted to impose in their areas of responsibility. Ordinance 21/164 of 16 May 1949, which governs registration, does not mention bride-price, but registration forms in use in the Matadi district do. Despite the wording of the ordinance, which calls only for the testimony of the proper parties as designated by custom, the Kasangulu appeal court held in a particular case that there had been no customary marriage because no money had been transferred (Pool 79, 1958). Wily litigants were able to escape their customary obligations by arguing that since no money, but only gifts and palm wine, had been handed over, no contract had been made (Matadi 865, 1951).

In practice, therefore, the government recognized two categories: (1) customary marriage, identified by the occurrence of a wedding *(nkwe-dolo)* with marriage payments; and (2) concubinage, which included simple fornication, lacked jural content, and was simply immoral. Customary marriage could and should be registered with the government and would be sanctioned by the courts. Most Manteke people believe, erroneously, that a marriage cannot be registered until a sufficiently high price has been paid, and it is clear that customary marriage in the form of bride-price marriage has evolved under government encouragement. The elders speak of this institution as resulting from the policies of named officials operating during the 1930's from headquarters in Matadi. Such court records as exist from that period tend to confirm this view; they show, in part at least, the emergence of *la dot*, under judicial questioning, from the long and varied lists of gifts that were transferred in the 1920's, mostly to the bride herself (Matadi 40, 1935; 77, 1936).

From the popular point of view, in Manteke at least, the situation was more complicated. A series of marriage types now exists, differentiated according to the persons who have been made party to the contract. The simplest type is traditional: before the 1920's, "if you didn't want to get married, you could build a little round house of a kind you don't see nowadays; you and the girl could move in, but her *nkazi*

---

[6] Later on, persistent advocacy by A. Sohier earned wide acceptance for the view that marriage payments are instruments of proof and publicity (1954, Titre III and p. 165; 1943, pp. 115 ff.).

would not know about it." This type still exists and is called *kimakangu* (*kanga*, "to tie"; *makangu*, "a concubine"). Its jural existence depends on a gift to the girl, usually of cloth and store-bought food representing the husband's domestic obligations. If the couple later fall out and come to court, the judges ask (of a particular transfer), "Was that piece of cloth intended to pay her or to clothe her?" (Manteke 83, 1957). The agreed significance of the transfer, making it a gift rather than a payment, is critical. Neither the court nor anybody else, however, is under any obligation to hear the dispute, since no one besides the man and the woman concerned "knows" about the contract.

When I was conducting a census of Mbanza Manteke Kinkela listed his daughter as a member of his household. I subsequently found out that she was living with an NSUNDI man at the other end of the village. The judge's comment on Kinkela's action was, "Well, he couldn't very well say she was living with a man, could he, since he knows nothing about it?" "Couldn't he sue the man for seduction?" "Yes, he could, but first he would have to go to his daughter's *nkazi* with an *mbungu* and say, 'Am I the father of this girl or not? Where's the 5,000 francs I'm supposed to eat?' Whereupon the *nkazi* would come to me and say, 'I hear your *nleeke* has Kinkela's daughter in his house without permission; now Kinkela wants his money.' I would have to call a meeting of NSUNDI and other relatives to help my *nleeke* to raise the money. But in this case," continued the judge, "Kinkela hasn't done anything because his daughter has had several affairs, and he knows he couldn't ask for much. Besides, he's probably glad to see her settled down."

If the *nkazi* or *se* is to "know" about the union, the information must be conveyed by means of an *mbungu*, meaning at least a demijohn of palm wine or the equivalent. The wine is distributed among the members of the girl's lineage so that they all share the information and the responsibility. This union is *sangata*, more usually called *kimakangu*. In practice it is not clearly distinguished from a more elaborate transaction, "to marry by palm wine" (*kwela mu malavu*), in which palm wine is conveyed to all four owners of the bride; they accept the obligation to help settle eventual disputes in the new household, to apply pressure to the wife if necessary, and to pay penalties she may incur by misbehavior. In the event of divorce, all that they received is normally returnable; representative lists include the usual presents for the girl and eight jugs of palm wine: four to the Father, two to the *nkazi*, and one each to the *mfumu za n'teekudi*.

A complete formal wedding "with money" (*mu mbongo*) creates no new customary obligations but is the only type of union the government registers. Registration means, to the people, that the government "knows about" the union. To those who live in the village, the government's knowledge of a marriage means that the courts must constrain an errant partner. It is important for those who live in town, where identity papers are necessary, to have dependents entered in the papers.

In practice, all sorts of uncertain and sometimes strange compromises are worked out. Whether the *bankazi* will intervene depends partly on the prevailing goodwill. A woman whose *nkazi* "knows nothing" may still go to him and her husband's *nkazi* with a complaint, and, even though they are not obliged to, they may well entertain the complaint informally. Sometimes the parties agree that a number of gifts over a long period suffice to convert concubinage into marriage (Manteke 52, 1947), and the husbands in most *sangata* unions express the intention to pay someday. Empirically, there is a continuum on which any union can be precisely situated, if necessary, by formal inquiry, though there may well never be any such inquiry. The judges of the government courts are commonly prepared to intervene in any dispute brought to them, although during the colonial period their judgments relating to unregisterable marriages were upset by reviewing officers and appeal courts on the ground that to enforce obligations upon partners in concubinage was to condone immorality. In 1950, after the government imposed a tax on plural wives, a number of Manteke men divorced themselves, in the eyes of the government, from women with whom they were still living fifteen years later.

This review of marriage procedures suggests that the wedding is primarily a particular exercise in the standard techniques of social communication. The payments ensure the legality and publicity of the act, as a result of which certain rights are transferred. The procedures may also bear an economic as well as a social interpretation, the two being by no means exclusive, but there is no indication that any party except the Father is financially benefited; and the Father's gain is apparently a new element, resulting from European influence and the introduction of cash. The same conclusion can be reached on the ground of the theory of exchange. Most African peoples have a special category of prestige goods for transactions carrying major status implications, such as membership in title associations. In relation to marriage, such goods circulate in exchange for rights *in genetricem*, that is, rights to recruit the woman's offspring and thus enlarge the prospective membership of the receiving group. East African *lobola* is a transfer of this type which may be regarded as a conversion (P. Bohannan, 1955). Precolonial Kongo also had a category of prestige goods, including camwood and gunpowder, with which rights *in genetricem* could be obtained through the institution of slavery. Since marriage transferred only rights *in uxorem*, it had relatively little importance for the maintenance or enlargement of the matrilineal descent group. Under such conditions transfers are reciprocal and communicatory and do not include conversion or require prestige goods; divorce also is relatively easy and frequent (cf. L. Bohannan, 1949).

In principle, no *nkazi* would agree to less than a full wedding for an unmarried girl of his lineage. Anything less is considered proper only for a woman who has been married before and has borne a child. The respectable ideal is not always realized, however. Younger men say that the cheap way to get a wife is to seduce a girl. Sexual relations in themselves are of no great moment. If the girl becomes pregnant the consequences depend on the pressure her family is able and willing to bring to bear on the man. The party principally offended is her father, who will demand 5,000 francs on the ground that when it comes time for her marriage the payment he can expect as his compensation (*mvindu*) will have been reduced. In this instance the offender might as well marry the girl. One Manteke man is notorious for having several daughters each of whom has been seduced several times, greatly to the father's profit. In the ordinary way, a man might expect to satisfy the family with an *mbungu* and the promise to pay later. Why then does any young man go to the expense and trouble of a wedding? He does so because it is the respectable thing to do, because it honors (*zitisa*) the girl and the resulting household (*nzo*). It also guarantees that the fullest range of sanctions will be available to regulate any subsequent dispute. If the girl already has children to be supported, a man may be reluctant to marry her, and particularly reluctant to raise the large sums needed for a full wedding. Consequently, the likelihood is that such a girl can expect only a *sangata* marriage, unless the new husband is unusually affluent.

The minimal condition of marriage in customary law is domesticity, which creates an exclusive bond as far as the woman is concerned. She may not lightly cook food for, or sleep with, any man not her husband. It is an affirmation of the marriage bond that the partners call each other *n'kento ame*, "my wife," and *yakala dyame*, "my husband" (*n'kento*, "woman"; *yakala*, "man"). A man must provide his *n'kento* with a house and she must sleep in it. The removal of her kitchen equipment from his house by either party is tantamount to an announcement that the agreement is ended. The man may choose to set up house in his wife's village (possibly as a client of her father or *nkazi*), in his own village, in his father's village, or in town.

A widow often continues to live in her husband's village. Leviratic marriage is unknown in Kongo, but widow inheritance is practiced by the BaLemfu and others. In Manteke I was told that if God has cut off the marriage that is all there is to it. The marriage money is not returnable. In former times, however, the widow's clan might go to the husband's clan and say: "Who is to look after these children that your brother left, and provide them with meat?" Another eastern custom, sororate, may have existed, according to the oldest man in Manteke, in connection with exchange marriage. When two clans exchanged women, a replacement would have to be found for one who died. Sororal polygyny is emphatically forbidden.

It has often been written that because of *le matriarcat* a Kongo husband has no rights over his wife and children and that the family, being swallowed up in the clan, has no jural existence. This view overlooks the fact that one of the functions of marriage is to transfer part of the responsibility for a woman from her own clan to her husband's, although the woman remains a member of her clan and continues to refer to the same individual as her *nkazi*. Three examples will illustrate the question of rights:

1) Manase of NSUNDI died after a long illness during which she suffered considerable neglect. Her sisters of her own lineage lived at a distance and failed to help her as they should have done. At the funeral the *nkazi* of NSUNDI formally accused them of neglecting their sister. He addressed himself not to them but to their husbands, *bankwezi* of NSUNDI, represented by the husband of the eldest sister.

2) An MVIKA girl who had married an MBENZA man subsequently committed adultery. MBENZA requested a meeting with her relatives (i.e., *nkazi, se, mfumu za n'teekudi*), together with certain Children and Grandchildren who were sufficiently interested to attend, in order to demand redress. When the meeting convened under Makima's mango tree it was found that the girl was absent. MBENZA became indignant, but MVIKA replied that he was himself responsible for the girl: "After all, we gave her to you; how should we know where she is?" The meeting adjourned until MBENZA should produce her.

3) A certain woman was required as a witness in a land case. The summons was not sent to her or even to her husband, but to her husband's brother. "After all, you couldn't expect him to speak for his own wife, could you?"

When a divorce occurs by agreement between the original contracting parties, the responsibility that was transferred to the husband is restored to the girl's own *nkazi*. The affinal relationship established by the marriage remains unbroken. In a sense the affinal relationship may be considered to antedate any particular marriage. The proverb cited in this connection is, "Where the needle goes, the thread follows" (*mwele ntumbu, mwele luwusu*). A particular marriage, however, establishes personal as distinct from group relations of affinity; these personal relations, represented by the use of appropriate terms, survive divorce. The proverb *longo lufwanga kansi kinkwezi ka kifwanga ko,* "the marriage dies but the affinity does not," which describes this situation is frequently cited by ethnographers in a radically different sense, mistranslated to mean that marriage may die but matrilineal kinship will persist, as proof of "une prédominance complète du groupe clanique sur le groupe proprement familial" (De Cleene, 1937a, pp. 3, 8); the ethnographers then draw a horrid picture of the wife's lack of respect in her husband's village, the father's lack of rights over his children, and the clan's right to appropriate a woman's earnings. Van Wing actually quotes a proverb in KiKongo which translates in this sense, but De Sousberghe's recent inquiries in the Kisantu area failed to discover anyone who had ever heard of such a proverb. As De Sousberghe remarks, ethnographers of the Lower Congo have started with the preconceived idea that affinal ties depend on the de facto union of spouses (Van Wing, 1959, p. 155; De Sousberghe, 1966, pp. 378, 387).

THE FOUR CORNERS

When notice has been taken of the importance of the father, it has been attributed to European influence. Nineteenth-century ethnographers, observing that Kongo practice did not correspond to the thoroughgoing matrilineal model required by theory, announced the decline of the clan; during the 1930's there was serious discussion of alternate institutions that might counter the threat of anomie.[7] Obviously, the obituary was premature: "Nous ne pouvons pas nous empêcher de voir que le système familial des BaKongo, le matriarcat, a mis et mis encore beaucoup de lenteur a évoluer" (Decapmaker, 1959, p. 98). On the other hand, the importance not only of the father but of the paternal and maternal grandfathers in Manteke custom can scarcely be due to European influence. Further inquiry shows that Manteke practice is based upon general and fundamental Kongo concepts.[8]

[7] Although the colonial regime sought by legislation and other means to strengthen the paternal role, its influence was not entirely favorable to patriarchy. In Elisabethville, a Congolese writer complained, the government courts endowed maternal uncles, in the name of custom, with rights they never had (Kalenda, 1958).

[8] Most indigenous commentators on custom have accepted the European model of *le matriarcat* and the European evaluation of it as an impediment to progress. (See the many articles on this subject by Daniel Kanza and others in the early 1950's in *La Voix du Congolais*, a journal published in Léopoldville.) An exception is R. Batshikama, who (in *Kongo dia Ngunga*, May 1956, p. 2) cites the proverb, *Tata na moyo ganda Lemba*, "[If your] father is alive, [you can] join the Lemba," as part of an argument to demonstrate the traditional importance of patrifiliation.

The four portions (*bikunku biya*) are paid to the four owners of the bride, who represent the four corners (*bikonko biya*) or four limbs (*bito biya*) of an individual's kinship which define his status and social personality. The idea is universal in Kongo, although it is not always given ritual expression. *Mu sina dya muntu kafiti kala mu ndambu ziya: se, ngudi, ye nkaaka zoole,*[9] "The origin of a person is in four parts: father, mother, and two grandparents." In Manianga a man recites the names of the four clans with which he is affiliated as a protective charm (Laman, 1957, p. 55). In the Ngombe region, on the Bangu, and around Kasangulu the principle is explicitly stated, but in weddings only the Father (*se*) and the Mother (*ngudi*), the latter being the *nkazi*, have roles allotted to them. All the BaMboma follow the *nzila ya kinkaaka*, "the grandparent practice," as do most BaYombe (Doutreloux, 1967, pp. 109–119). At Mpangu weddings in the Kisantu area bride and groom formally locate the four corners on each side in the ceremony of *ta mvila*, "recite the clans" (Van Wing, 1959, p. 168). Farther south, according to J. Mertens (1942, p. 199), the grandfathers get none of the marriage palm wine. This author also mentions 10 francs as the figure for bridewealth in precolonial times, and says that unions can be legitimate and stable without a transfer of money.

V. Mertens' commendably detailed account (1948) of marriage procedures in the same Kisantu area is summarized here. Formerly, exchange marriage at reduced cost was common, but now the parties usually choose for themselves through intermediaries. If the girl is willing to marry, she is given presents to show to her family. The first ceremony, called *kuvika* [*vwika*] *mwana nkento* ("endowing the girl"), takes place in the girl's village after the youth has sent a notification of his coming. He brings a cloth, a kerchief, soap, a comb, a mirror, bracelets, and other small objects (corresponding to *leta kya ndumba* as it existed in Manteke in the 1920's). For the girl's father and mother he brings live chickens and palm wine. The girl's *nkazi* is not present. The parties drink together, and after this ceremony man and woman are to be faithful to each other (cf. *kimakangu*).

The second ceremony, *kuyambila* ("discussion"), also takes place in the bride's parents' village. The young man gives nine jugs of palm

9 My field notes for Kimpese. *Sina*, "origin, root"; synonymous, according to the informant, with *bundu*, "constitution," and *tuuku*, "source." *Sina* is related to *zina*, "name" (see *xina* in Dennett, 1906). Dennett writes (p. 154) that any "person with any pretensions to birth" should have four *bina* — two *xina xixinkaka* (*zina za kinkaaka*), one *xixitata* (father's clan), and one *xixifumba* (mother's clan) — "but it is astonishing how few can trace their pedigree back to their grandfathers." It is apparent that some of Dennett's informants lacked the full complement of corners because of slavery among their ascendants.

wine to her father, who gives two of them to the men of the village, one to the women, and two each to the maternal grandparents (*kinkay ki nkento*) and the paternal grandparents (*kinkay ki yakala*). All three chiefs make return payments. The *nkazi* has no role of importance until the third ceremony, *fulu mambu*, at which the youth's *nkazi* and his Father (i.e., his father's *nkazi*) go to the girl's *nkazi*'s village; curiously enough, they take no palm wine with them. Here the list is agreed upon. A representative list, for a small village in 1945, included (1) 75 francs to the girl's clan, plus 60 francs to her *nkazi*; (2) "a hoe and a cloth" (120 francs) to her mother; (3) other items, such as umbrella, lamp, knife, and so on (75 francs). The young man finds most of this money, and the recipients divide it up among the members of their group. Total expenses may amount to about 2,000 francs, but V. Mertens (1948, p. 1109) states explicitly that the agreement rather than the amount is the essential of the contract. The amount is paid over in the young man's village at the fourth ceremony, *kukaba longo*. The girl is not present; her *nkazi* brings gifts of food and drink. The final event is *kinsi longo*, the wedding feast, which takes place usually in the groom's father's village. Thus, as Mertens concludes, "toutes les cérémonies préparatoires au mariage découlent avec une impeccable logique de l'organisation sociale des BaKongo," involving four persons (*se* and *nkazi* on each side) and the four villages in which they reside. A similar distribution in space and time also characterized Manteke procedures, according to my informants, until they were consolidated in accordance with policy established in Matadi.

It is difficult to be certain of the practice in other areas because informants do not clearly distinguish between the idea of the four corners and a specific ritual embodying it; thus I found that the Ba-Lemfu do not follow grandparent practice, after having been assured that they did. Since the structure of kinship gives alternate generations a relationship analogous to that of affines, the contrast here is not so sharp as it seems at first sight. Lemfu ceremonies allot to *bankwezi* the roles played in Manteke by grandparents and grandchildren. The BaTeke south of Kinshasa, who are not BaKongo, have similar arrangements: marriage money goes to the girl's Father, her clan, and "la famille du grandpère" (Pool 72, 1958). The court's note on this case adds, "Among the BaTeke the first daughter is given in marriage by the father, the second by the maternal uncle, the third by the grandfather. They are the ones responsible for the money handed over" (cf. Vansina, 1964).

The four chiefs regulate all the formal concerns of an individual. They are the ones to whom he turns for all kinds of assistance, and this dependence explains the endogamous tendency of Manteke marriage, the high incidence of marriage into the father's clan, and the preference expressed for marriage into the grandfather's clan. The same people may also confer if the individual falls ill, or if he is involved in litigation. One of the best-known customary obligations of a son in Kongo is to give his father the heart of any animal he kills. The best Manteke hunter, whose father was a slave of MBENZA, hands over the hearts of all large game to the *nkazi* of that clan section. In theory, each of the four chiefs gets a portion, as in the following incident. A man who has quarreled with his wife is awarded by the court damages of "a goat," his wife having unjustifiably removed her hearthstones (*makukwa*) from their house. The goat, worth 2,500 francs (less the court's fee of 750 francs) is divided among the four chiefs (cf. Weeks, 1914, p. 67). The father is informed of what has transpired and is given 200 francs as the "heart" that is his due. The *mfumu za n'teekudi* each get "a kidney and a piece of meat to go with it to make it look better." The wife gets 300 francs or so as *lusadusu* ("help") to assist her in paying the fine. Of the remainder, which goes to the husband's house, the husband gets a substantial portion because he is the one who has suffered, the *nkazi* receives a largish share, and other members are given token amounts. The same partition of the individual himself would take place should his owners decide to "eat" him (i.e., cause his death by witchcraft); at least this suggestion is conveyed by De Sousberghe's analysis of Ndibu proverbs (1967*b*, p. 197). The father's consent is essential before the deed can be done, and the "heart" is his share.

   Another illustration of the same theme also helps to show how the BaKongo conceptualize the elementary structures of their society in simple geometrical forms. On either side of the door of a house in Ndemba are two plaster figures; on the left side, as one faces the door from outside the house, is a serpent, and on the right is a circle divided into quarters colored alternately black and white. This kind of ornamentation is unusual, but these signs appear elsewhere in Ndemba. When I asked what they meant I was told they were merely ornamental, or that if they had had any meaning it had died with the builder of the house. But it was also suggested I address my query to Mfumu Tomi, the Nkimba graduate from Mbanza Nkazi who was visiting Ndemba for a funeral, as I myself was. Tomi, when asked, replied immediately: "The meaning is this. When a candidate for Nkimba initiation presented himself to the expert in charge he would be tested to see if his reflection appeared in a round bowl of water." The test was a fourfold one, each phase associated with one of the four chiefs or owners of the candidate. If the image failed to appear the presence of some kind of animosity (witchcraft) was indicated, and the candidate would be told to come back after he had straightened out the relationship in question. "That, at least," said Tomi, with due ethnographic caution, "was the way we did it around here; in other regions they may have done differently."

Two or three roles are filled by the same representative only when there has been a history of slavery. The relationship of owner to slave is that of Father to Child, kinship terms being used. Therefore, when an *nkazi* marries his slave himself, or gives her to a member of his lineage, he is *nkazi, se,* and *mfumu a n'teekudi* to the resulting offspring; only one of the grandfather roles is left for an outsider, and even that could be assumed by the same *nkazi* if both spouses were his slaves. As already noted, however, unions of this sort are cohabitations but not marriages proper, since no tokens have been transferred; an *nkazi* cannot exchange *mbungu* with himself to let his left hand know what his right hand is doing. Even though the girl is a concubine the parties have reciprocal rights which are sometimes upheld by the modern court; formerly the slave had no recourse.[10]

The four corners establish, mystically and socially, an individual's constitution and existence. They also prescribe the constitution of the committee that meets to regulate affairs of importance in which he is concerned. The committee is identical only for two persons who are full siblings (*ngudi mosi se dimosi*), the archetype of a collectivity occupying the same position (*fulu kimosi*). Other members of the lineage, whose committees are composed according to their parentage, are nevertheless represented by the same *nkazi*, who is related to the other members of the committee by affinity. In the regulation of any particular affair, therefore, the descent principle is excluded except insofar as it serves to range concerned persons "behind" their particular *nkazi* or spokesman (*ku nim'andi*).

On a larger scale than weddings, funerals and land disputes demonstrate the same system of committee government. In more formal anthropological terms such a committee is a set, designated in a network of patrilateral linkages by reference to a particular Ego (A. Mayer, 1965). The intersections of the network are corporate persons (matrilineal descent groups) and the set itself is a quasi group of the type called commissions (Smith, 1966).

10 MFUTU man versus NDAMBA NGOLO woman (Mbanza Manteke 43, 1947; see also 318, 1950; Pool 101, 1957). Peigneux, describing Ngombe practice (1934, p. 116), says that a man may take his slave into his house without formality but may not marry her. The distribution of rights over persons, in relation to marriage and slavery, is further discussed in chapter 10.

Marriage Rules and Social Structure

The following analysis of marriage rules is presented with some diffidence because I did not ask in the field all the questions I now consider relevant. Moreover, I believe it is necessary to allow for a certain looseness of fit, so to speak, between the formal model and actual practice, and it is likely that a comparison of sufficient data from different times and places in Kongo would show some elements of the model to be less stable than others. My interpretation therefore refers primarily to the social structure of Mbanza Manteke.

The rules at issue are: (1) marriage of a man with his granddaughter (*n'tekolo*) is possible, even preferred; (2) patrilateral cross-cousin marriage is preferred on the ground that "where the needle goes, the thread follows" (*mwele ntumbu, mwele luwusu*), or "the honeysuckle twines around the bindweed, and the bindweed twines around the honeysuckle" (*mwenze zingidi lukasa, ye lukasa zingidi mwenze*);[11] (3) patrilateral parallel cousins up to four generations removed from a common male ancestor may not marry; and (4) marriage within the *kanda* is prohibited on the ground that "those of one blood may not marry" (*menga mamosi kamakwelana ko*) (Van Wing, 1959, pp. 154–159).

The first rule exists in Manteke, but none of the hundreds of marriages, past and present, which I noted shows a man married to his own granddaughter; the elders say such a marriage is impossible. On the other hand, marriage between a woman and a man she calls *yaya* ("elder brother," "grandparent") or *toko dyame* ("my young man") is fairly common. The rule seems to be that she may marry into her grandfather's clan section and house, but not into his lineage. My results are not entirely conclusive on this point; the subject is particularly difficult because there is no vocabulary for distinguishing a "real" relative from a "classificatory" one, and because the boundaries and even the existence of lineages are controversial, as previous chapters have shown. What I believe to be the rule is consistent with the patterns of communication in marriage. If it were not so, a Grandfather (*mfumu a n'teekudi*) would be in the position of both donor and recipient of marriage tokens, since the lineage is indivisible and cannot produce more than one *nkazi*. This consideration alone would not, however, prevent concubinage, that is, a private agreement about which no one else "knows"; such a situation would parallel that of the *nkazi* who enters into a domestic arrangement with his own slave.

The standard anthropological term, "patrilateral cross-cousin mar-

11 Translation offered with acknowledgments to Michael Flanders and Donald Swann.

riage," may be misleading in a discussion of the second marriage rule because it injects a criterion of generation not present in the KiKongo phrase, "we marry our fathers" (*tukwelana mase meto*). The phrase means, "we marry into the father's clan section," as indeed many people do; so far as I know, nobody in Manteke has married into the father's lineage. The argument relating to this point is the same as the argument for grandchild marriage, given above.

On the third rule, as stated by Van Wing (1959, p. 156), we have the helpful elaboration of De Sousberghe (1965). Those who are "siblings on the father's side" (*mpangi ye mpangi mu kise*) may not marry if they are descended, up to four generations removed, from one man, or from a group of brothers, who had children by several women from different clans. On the other hand, if there was only one woman, or several women who came from the same lineage, the descendants would be eligible to marry intragenerationally. It is necessary at this point to recall the kinship terminology and the argument offered in chapter 5 concerning kinship and social structure. All those who occupy the same position, including those whose role relative to a particular corporation is the same, are "brethren" (*mpangi*). All cousins are brethren by patrifiliation or matrifiliation (as the Hawaiian terminology expresses it), but cross-cousins can in addition differentiate themselves according to descent-group reckoning (*mu dikanda*). In the Crow terminology they are of different "generations," no longer "one place," and may intermarry; this terminology can therefore be regarded as making available spouses who would otherwise be forbidden. The prohibition thus overcome is acknowledged, ideally, by the sacrifice of a pig or a goat "to kill the shame" or "to end respect for patrifiliation" (*vonda zimi dya kitaata*; cf., in grandfather marriage, Van Wing, 1959, p. 154).

The same sacrifice is called for, as we have seen, in marriage between parties who are united, at least in principle, by *kingudi*, as members of the same clan (rule 4). A number of ethnographers have accepted the explanation that the rule is "no longer" observed because the matrilineal structure is breaking down. This sociological use of the past calls for no further comment; the conceptual relationship between *mvila* and *kanda* has already been discussed at some length. In practice only the *kanda* is exogamous (V. Mertens, 1948, p. 1117). This is consistent with the fact that it is the largest corporate group. Groups represent the intersection of a particular *kitaata* ("patrifiliation") and *kingudi* ("matrifiliation") and their members are brethren "by one mother and one father" (*ngudi mosi, se dimosi*). The blood (*menga*) that unites them, however, is the father's and not the mother's. Informants from different parts of Kongo agree that a child derives its entire bodily substance, as well as its spirit, from the father; the mother is merely the container, a borrowed vessel contributing nourishment. As Laman says (1957, p. 108), the "child stems in its origin entirely from the father, not from the mother. But the kanda-connection is with the mother's kanda, not the father's." And the proverbs agree: "The father gives birth, not the mother. The mother is a bag to keep the child in" (Doutreloux, 1967, p. 106). This physiology provides the rationale approving both grandchild marriage [12] and patrilateral marriage: to return the blood whence it came (*vutula menga*).

I am asserting here, as in chapter 5, that the rules and the reckoning are not fundamentally genealogical, but refer to social status. From this point of view, Van Wing's rule (no. 3) might be rephrased as follows: "All those who are already united by a common role may not marry unless they are also divided by an alternative role." In this form the rule closely resembles the fourth, "those of one blood may not marry." Some senior elders in Manteke hold that the first rule obtained even in an extreme classificatory sense: "If I were a great-grandchild [*ntekudila*, a term not often used] of NTUMBA and so were you, we could not marry." Others hold, however, that if the great-grandfathers were of different houses marriage would be possible. The entire discussion of these remote relationships was artificial; Kingalu smiled, as though I had reminded him of an old song. In practice some closer relationship would be traced, in terms of which marriage would be possible or forbidden.

There is another problem here: Why is the limit four generations? Kingalu said, "Well, it used to be four, but now we don't reckon to more than three." But is it sufficient to conclude that a rule specifying "four" represents simply the average range of genealogical awareness? The roles allotted to Children and Grandchildren in many situations make three-generation reckoning essential; there is no reason to suppose that the four-generation rule was ever standard. On the other hand, it is characteristic of the ideal conceptions of the BaKongo, which they impose on empirically indefinite situations, that four events constitute a complete series; a fifth event simply repeats the first one.

The nature of matrilateral cross-cousin marriage is relatively obscure, some informants affirming and some denying the possibility (De Sousberghe, 1965, p. 420). Patrilateral marriage is, or may be, a form of

12 The correspondence between the roles of *nkaaka* ("grandparent") and *nkwezi* ("affine") has already been noted. In some areas, including Manianga, patrilateral cousins are called *nkaaka*; the merging of generations appears again in the archaic Manteke term *yaya* ("grandparent") applicable to an older sibling. A woman may call her grandfather *toko* ("young man") as well as *nkaaka*, just as a man may call his brother's wife *ndumba* ("girl") as well as *nkwezi*, but these familiar terms are not associated with a possibility of sexual relations (cf. Doutreloux, 1967, pp. 100–106).

hypergamy, and hypogamous matrilateral marriage is not favored. In addition, the kinship designation and role of *mwana* applied to MoBrDa apply also to mother's brother's slave, and marriage with a slave, as distinct from concubinage, is impossible; since slavery is a matter of degree, the situation is inherently ambiguous when considered in the abstract. Ndibu and Manteke informants, using identical phrases, found grounds for recommending matrilateral cross-cousin marriage: by marrying his MoBrDa a man can become his mother's brother's *n'zitu,* a person of respect in his uncle's compound: "lenda mpe kwandi kun'kwela vo n'kento, kadi fwiti kenga luumbu lwa ngwankazi, mu kituka se n'zitu ku luumbu lwa ngudi a nkazi." I do not know how this rule would work out in practice (cf. Van Wing, 1959, p. 158; V. Mertens, 1948, p. 1118).

The ethnographic literature, though often deficient in critical details, indicates that in different times and places the forms of marriage and the privileges of spouses and their relatives have varied. There are suggestions that a role of village wife existed in some areas, and that term marriage was (and perhaps still is) legitimate in some areas. According to Van Wing (1959, p. 156), a man may marry his father's divorced wife, but Manteke people deny the possibility. Undoubtedly the rules regarding cousin marriage are not uniform.[13]

[13] All variations must be evaluated in terms of Kongo marriage as it is, not as it has been imagined to be. A minor idiosyncrasy in the domestic arrangements of the ASolongo has been exaggerated to such a point that some writers believe they have identified an island of patriliny among the otherwise matrilineal BaKongo.

The ASolongo live on either side of the mouth of the Congo River; historically, they are related to the Soyo Province of the former kingdom. The evidence published so far offers no convincing evidence of patriliny. A legend (Marchal, 1947) that supposedly explains the origin of this deviant trait in fact deals only with the patrifilial aspects of chiefship and is in no way exceptional among such traditions. Other evidence relates to kinship, not descent; allocation of children to the father in case of divorce does not of itself create a patrilineal clan (Pauwels, 1965). In any event, the allocation is contingent, in Solongo custom, on the father's renouncing at least part of the marriage money, as elsewhere in Kongo. Milheiros' version of the argument, the strongest, shows that the deviation of Solongo custom is measured from the ideal matriarchy, not from actual matriliny:

"Among the Solongos at the present time patriarchy predominates. Of matriarchy, now almost extinct, a few vestiges remain, as for example in the preference shown toward uterine nephews, the *candas* [*bisi kanda*].

"The present condition of patriarchy is confirmed, moreover, by the superiority of the man, the modification of the rule of succession, the obligation of paternal uncles to look after nephews, the ascendancy of husband over wife, the power of father over daughter . . ." (1954, no. 83–84, p. 19).

"Heredity succession to tribal office passes to (1) the oldest son, (2) the oldest brother, (3) the oldest grandson" (no. 85–86, p. 22).

It is clear that the patrifilial relationship is strong among the ASolongo. One of my informants vigorously upheld the marital privileges allocated to him by custom: "If I buy a bag, everything I put into it is mine, isn't it?" Even he, however, belonged to his mother's descent group, not to his father's.

8

FUNERALS

Circles and right lines limit and
close all bodies, and the
mortal right-lined circle must conclude and
shut up all.
—SIR THOMAS BROWNE

Funerals are the most important events in Manteke; even a land affair is not an event in the same sense, for it usually is only a crisis, more or less deliberately staged, in a continuing dispute. Marriages happen on weekends, in intervals between routine preoccupations, but when a death occurs most of the routine activities are suspended for four or five days. A larger crowd assembles and more money changes hands in more complicated ways than for any other event.

A funeral, unlike a marriage, can scarcely be observed in its entirety; it is too complex, too extensive in time and space. Because the whole village is involved, certain features of its structure are manifested with unusual clarity. Relatives whom nothing else could summon arrive from town and from other villages. At funerals one has some idea of what the real population of Manteke is.[1]

Two funerals, those of Lina Lufumba and Nelly Azeyi, occurred in successive weeks in September 1965; the deceased belonged to the DISA and MFUTU houses, respectively, of NANGA. My discussion of them is supplemented by data drawn from the funerals of Elayi of NSUNDI and others. The organization of a funeral is used as a framework for the introduction of other material relevant to the structural features it reveals.

Relatives are immediately notified when a death occurs. Young men are dispatched on bicycles to other villages and to the railway at Lufu

---

[1] A speaker at a wedding once referred to three feasts: birth, marriage, and death; my inquiries discovered no birth ceremonies at all, except when twins were born.

The funeral of Lina Lufumba: *mayaala*

The funeral of Lina Lufumba: the enclosure

The funeral of Lina Lufumba: building the coffin

Funeral in Ndemba: *mafundu*

The funeral of Lina Lufumba: women cooking for visitors

The funeral of Lina Lufumba: *nganga za nsimba* dancing

The funeral of Lina Lufumba: *koka nlombwa*

Tombs in Bete

to send telegrams to the towns. If the deceased has been seriously ill, the relatives will have been notified of his condition, and a number will already be present in the village. The group of "relatives" includes affines and cognates of the lineage and also, but less imperatively, the cognates and affines of the house and the clan section.

Failure to attend the sickbed of a close relative may in some instances be regarded as an indication of responsibility for the sickness; sickness can be caused by witchcraft, which is an extension of ill will. A child's or a husband's failure to appear may be adduced against him later on, although sanctions do not necessarily follow. Most of the attendants seem motivated by no such specific threat. They want to help and are fascinated by the event of death. Although some of the helpers prepare food or change the bed, most of them simply sit, watching, like so many crows. Anyone whose last agonies are particularly prolonged is believed to be suffering a stringent interrogation, on the border of the beyond, concerning his sinful activities in life. The watchers, all women, sit by the hour on the floor, as many as twenty or thirty crowded into one room of a reed shanty. Men make occasional visits.

The vigil, which continues after death occurs, is punctuated by outbursts of wailing and sobbing as a new arrival prostrates herself at the foot of the bier. If the invalid had been removed to a hospital, the body is usually brought back to the village for the wake and the burial. To remove it to another village for burial would cause serious offense, because it would imply that the relatives with whom the deceased had been living were responsible for his death. The violent manifestations of grief are to some extent put on; women arriving on foot or by truck begin an uncontrollable sobbing and shrieking when they reach the approaches of the village (*mafula ma vata*). A missionary writing from Palabala in 1881 (*The Regions Beyond* [Nov. 1881], p. 318) reported on the demonstration following a death:

> The other day a woman died after some days of illness. The mourning and wailing by numbers of both men and women was excessive. A number of women could hardly be kept from committing suicide, and many others seemed frantic with grief. Women ran here and there sobbing out their usual cry of pain "oh, father! oh, mother!" the men firing off their guns and yelling out the most dirgelike ditties in Fyote, all in the minor key. The next day they wrapped the body in cloth, at the same time sounding their canoe-shaped drums, and chiming some native handbells, making outrageous noises.

The overt behavior also marks profound and entirely unaffected grief; Manteke people are deeply saddened by any death in their neighborhood, not only by that of a relative. "When one man dies, we all die a little bit." The mood is expressed by the funeral laments reproduced and translated by Van Wing (1959, pp. 263–278), although none of the corresponding songs in Manteke has anything like the same beauty or complexity.

The role of the governing committee of kinsmen, many of whom are themselves *bankazi* of descent groups in neighboring villages, is one of the outstanding features of funeral proceedings. Just as the emphasis at a wedding is placed on meeting the demands of the owners of the bride, so at a funeral the emphasis is on the will of the three patrilateral owners of the deceased, especially the Father of the Child. Their permission must be sought by the *nkazi* for each stage of the proceedings.

LUPANGU: THE ENCLOSURE

As soon as possible a rectangular enclosure (*lupangu*) of palm leaves is put up outside the house of the deceased or in some other convenient place. It must be large enough to accommodate all those who attend the overnight wake. In the center is a flat-roofed, unenclosed shelter where the body reposes, usually on the deceased's own bed. It is wrapped in sheets and blankets with the face showing, or just the eyes and the forehead, and is covered with embroidered bedspreads or the like. When Lufumba's body was brought out the women present were actively curious, some of them scrambling for the best places close to the bier. As soon as the body was in place one of the Children led the group in a little ceremony frequently repeated throughout the mortuary rites: everybody, kneeling, raises his forefinger to the sky, then points it downward, then claps his hands; the handclap is repeated, on command, five times, this number being mentioned aloud. Informants were not sure what this ritual meant; one elder supposed it was intended to honor the deceased, "but she's dead, so what good is that?"

In the four sides of the *lupangu* there are, or should be, four doors belonging to *nkazi*, *se*, and the two *mfumu za n'teekudi*, each of whom closes his door when he arrives by hanging up a blanket or bedspread in the opening. After a door has been closed people who wish to go through are supposed to make an obeisance (*sakila*), though few do. An extra entrance provided for informal going in and out does not count as one of the doors. The body in the shelter is respectfully referred to as "Kongo."

These dispositions vary from year to year and from village to village. In Manteke a white flag on a long pole is mounted by each door "to

warn people coming from that direction that there has been a death."
The flags are put in place even when, owing to the configuration of the
village, people could not be expected to approach from all directions.
"The flag is called, in white man's KiKongo, *dalapo* [French: *drapeau*],
or in real KiKongo, *mpeve* ["breeze, spirit"]." In Ndemba only two
flags are hung, subsequently to be carried at the head and foot of the
coffin in the funeral procession. These and other differences occur although the two villages are in frequent contact, particularly in attending each other's funerals.

When I began to ask about the doors in the enclosure — how many
there should be, and why — no consensus emerged from the responses.
Some said there should be only three, the grandfathers sharing one.
The tendency for the paternal Grandfather's role to be dropped has
already been remarked; moreover, people often speak of the Grandfathers in the singular even when there are two present. At a Manteke
funeral there are normally two, and there seemed to be no machinery
for notifying one of them that he need not arrange to close a door.
Others said that the whole business of doors was a recent fad, unknown
in their youth.

Further inquiry revealed that a ritual enclosure always has a specific
number of doors, even though people do not always know why it
should have, and the number itself varies with the type of enclosure
and the region. In Manteke a chief's enclosure, I was told, had two
doors; in Palabala a similar enclosure would have had three, allotted
to the Children and Grandchildren, the wives, and other chiefs, respectively. A ritual enclosure is frequently thought of, in the abstract, as
having four doors, one toward each cardinal point, even though there
are in fact fewer. The doors of a funeral enclosure are simply one of the
manifestations of the idea that a person has "four corners," and the more
general, unconscious idea of a sacred space as bounded and oriented.

Lufumba's enclosure had only three doors because for her only
three chiefs sat: DISA, *ngudi* or *nkazi*; MFULAMA NKANGA, maternal
grandfather (*n'teekudi*); and NSAKA, father and paternal grandfather
(*se ye n'teekudi ku nim'a se*), Lufumba's father having been a slave of
NSAKA. Or had he? At the outset DISA refused to give any *mbungu* to
Mbelani of NSAKA on the ground that Mbelani was a usurper and the
NSAKA inheritance rightfully belonged to himself, DISA. Thereupon
several people objected that a funeral was no time for political squab-
bles; at funerals, amity and cooperation should predominate. This was
on a Saturday. On Monday, when I returned after attending a meeting
elsewhere, I found that tradition had changed over the weekend.
Lufumba's father Nsyama, it was now agreed, had been a slave of

NSAKA, married to three women from DISA, NSAKA, and NTAMBU (which was classed at the time as a branch of NANGA); by all of them he had had children. In gratitude for these services he had been returned to his original clan, NA LUKUTI, whose representative therefore sat as Father of the Child. The ex-slave's real or original Father, NA MAZINGA, sat as paternal Grandfather. Both NSAKA and DISA claimed credit for this solution to the problem. No extra door was built.

The following week, Azeyi died. Her enclosure had only three doors, her father having been bought by NA LUKUTI. By this time, however, I had asked so many questions and had drawn so much attention to the significance of doors that some stigma may have come to be attached to so public an announcement of slave connections; be that as it may, the next day a fourth door was added, seemingly an afterthought. It remained open, however, because there was no chief to close it.

At this funeral a dispute of a different kind arose. Azeyi and her brother Mbwaku had suffered for some years, according to them, from the witchcraft attacks of Maleso, whose position relative to them in NDYENGO MYA TONA is discussed in chapter 4 (see table 1). Azeyi, who lived in town, was Mbwaku's only sister; her children are all male. A certain tension exists between Mbwaku and the children of Nkebasani Ndendani, whose numerous progeny promise indefinite continuity to their line (see fig. 3). Some of them have been associated with Maleso's occult attacks against Azeyi, which were perceived in dreams and by the help of a diviner. At Azeyi's funeral Mbwaku refused to tolerate Maleso's presence. The accusation of witchcraft is part of a quarrel extending over at least fifteen years; it has helped to embitter Maleso and to drive him into partial retirement from village affairs, though it has not prevented other people from consorting with him. Part of his trouble is that although he believes in witchcraft in general, he has no patience with particular accusations, least of all those in which he is the target.

This attitude toward witchcraft is common among the more astute and pragmatic elders; there is perhaps only one man who can be said not to believe in it. Yet there is so much general skepticism that the subject is not much talked about in Manteke. In the inland villages it reaches the public ear more often, but even there the contrast with Kasangulu, for example, is clear. In general, as in the story of Azeyi, a connection exists between witchcraft accusations and political tensions; the elders themselves say that secular quarrels always lie behind them. Yet no specific source of this tension could be discovered in the only other witchcraft episode of any consequence in recent Manteke history, an exchange of charges and vilifications between MBENZA and Mbwaku's lineage of MFUTU.

It is clear that in precolonial times a funeral, particularly of the *nkazi* of an important group, was an occasion for political adjustments. The idiom of these adjustments was witchcraft (*kindoki*). According to the traditional model, witches are antisocial persons, enemies internal and external; the successful *nkazi* keeps them at bay by deploying powers that themselves partake of witchcraft. In secular terms, he keeps the peace and defends the interests of his people by making effective decisions which are in part arbitrary, a function of his personal political ability. One of the procedures used is the identification and trial of witches responsible for death, accomplished by the diviner, the *n'kasa* poison ordeal, and the executioner. Divination and the poison ordeal are political media; execution of the witch, on the orders of the chief, confirms the regime. "When the chief dances [*sanga*] with the sword of power [*mbeele a lulendo*] the Children and Grandchildren rejoice, because there will be feasting and drinking." The sword is thrust into the ground, where its trembling reveals the presence of the spirit (*mpeve*) and proclaims the death sentence. Should tensions remain unresolved, dissident factions sever their kinship and depart to another region (Van Wing, 1959, pp. 252–256, 368–370).

The background to the political process, still according to the traditional model, is the funeral itself, which, when an old chief has died, may last for months or even years. He is not buried until his successor is designated, and meanwhile his body is smoked over a fire tended by his widows. Richards describes what he saw in Manteke in 1881 (Guinness, n.d., p. 412):

About three months ago a small king died, and of course it was supposed that somebody had killed him. . . . They were going to kill a woman and her child, as they were *ndoki*, and had killed the king. . . . The first thing we saw was a hut full of women and children crying in a sort of agony. I went to them and asked where the woman and child were. They only shrieked and rushed out of the hut into the woods crying, "We are under a vow to the inkissi!" We went further on, and everybody declared they knew nothing about the matter, and even before we met them the people would cry out *Kazadiko!* . . . Next day we learned that they had taken the woman and child some miles away, where they first shot her and then cut her throat! The man appointed to do the horrid deed took the child and dashed it to the ground, but a woman present snatched it up and ran away.

. . . The king about whom all the fuss was made is not buried yet, and will not be for some time. The affair keeps the people occupied, firing guns, yelling, drumming, by day and by night, and they say it is "all about the king." They roll mats round the body after it has been smoked, forming a bundle about three feet in diameter, and six feet high. When holding a service in the village on Sunday the odor from the body was unbearable, and we really could not stay.

In modern times deaths in Manteke are not routinely attributed to witchcraft; nor, when they are, is there any effective means of resolving the issue, except in the rare event of a confession by the accused. Execution and the poison ordeal have been forbidden since the European penetration. Funerals are still, however, quite clearly occasions of social reckoning. There is a diffuse sense of crisis; relatives and neighbors feel an obligation to participate, and by so doing to state where they stand. The relatively enormous sums of money expended and circulated, now as in the past, are a crude index to the importance of the occasion.

MAYAALA: THE CHILDREN OF THE CLAN

Construction of the enclosure, as well as all other necessary labors, is the responsibility of the Children and Grandchildren of the clan section who live in the village, plus those who have come from elsewhere for the occasion; they are assisted by any other available workers. Elders are excluded, since no *mbuta* does any work when there is an *nleeke* to do it for him, and since their function lies elsewhere, in the exchange of gifts and *mbungu* and the regulation of the crisis death has occasioned. Junior members of the clan are also excluded, more particularly members of the house of the deceased, who are ritually immobilized at such affairs; they own the event, but executive responsibility is in the hands of the Children and Grandchildren. Such, at least, is the theory. When I found a senior member of MFUTU helping to dig Azeyi's grave he admitted he had no business to be there, but said there were not enough Children.

Each house of a clan section has its *mwana wa mbuta*, "Senior Child" (pl., *baana ba mbuta*). This term means different things in different regions. In the east it refers to a member of a descent group, the first child of a given mother, who would be called *mwana kota* in Manteke (Van Wing, 1959, p. 88). In Manianga it means any child born to a male of the descent group, not necessarily the eldest child. In Manteke the children of each house are ordered by relative age, and the oldest of all is *mwana wa mbuta* to the clan section as a whole. Seniority among Children is explicitly not governed by descent because an important function of the Children is to reconcile their disputing Fathers, among whom one of the likeliest terms of dispute is precisely the order of their seniority by descent, that is, the seniority (*kikota*) of the houses to which they are filiated. Grandchildren are not ordered, and no office represents them in particular.

The *baana ba mbuta* to the houses of NANGA are (1) DISA-NKUTI: Makima of MVIKA; (2) NSAKA: Maswekwa of NTAMBU; (3) MFUTU: Makokila of NKAZI A KONGO; (4) NZUZI: Matuwanga of MPANZU. All are permanent residents of the village; nonresidents and incompetents are disqualified. For important affairs nonresident children visit; if the resident *mwana wa mbutu* should die, another might move in to take his place, but all those on the above list have always lived in Manteke, or at least have regarded it as their home village; in most instances their own clan sections are domiciled there.

Nsiku Damison of NSUNDI, Oldest Child to NGOMA LUBOTA, belongs to a house of NSUNDI which has been represented in Manteke for generations; other members of it live in Kyesa Kifwa, where their tradition domiciles them, but it is possible that Damison's own stated intention to return there and assume his rightful role may be more a psychological prop than a fixed purpose. He says he lives in Manteke because he was born there. If his fathers died out, he might stay on if invited to do so by MVIKA NTUMBA. His actual father, a slave of NGOMA, died long ago; "his fathers," in this context, might refer to the entire house of NGOMA, to a lineage of it, or simply to the group of men of the same lineage and generation as his genitor. In other words, his decision to stay depends on his assessment of his position. An important factor, as already indicated, is his relations with his own clan. He says that his brethren in Kyesa at one point brought an *mbungu* to Joel Albert of NGOMA asking him to release his "son" to live with them and be their spokesman (*mpovi*), but Damison declined because of his dispute with them over the precedence of their houses.[2]

Even as a generalization, the statement that a Kongo boy leaves his mother's home to live with her brother between the ages of eight and fourteen (Van Wing, 1959, p. 229; Richards, 1950, p. 221) misrepresents the situation. The importance in a clan's affairs of resident children has frequently been noted; the discrepancy between this situation and the pure matrilineal model has been attributed to European influence which is supposed to have permitted the reassertion of natural over artificial kinship relations. Alternatively, it has been overcome by merging the Child's role with the slave's; thus De Cleene asserts that

[2] "Dans certains villages . . . l'ancienne coutume subsiste encore, à savoir que l'oncle maternel, moyennant compensation à donner au père de famille, réclame un jeune homme pour qu'il s'installe chez lui et vive sous sa dépendance" (Decapmaker, 1959, p. 98). The same author (1949, p. 97) describes as "la coutume evoluée" that some young men live with the father until his death. See also Weeks, 1914, p. 119.

the *bana ba dikanda*, children of the clan, whose governmental role he notes, are clanless (1937*b*, p. 50; Malengreau, 1939, p. 38). In modern times the residence of children over six, especially boys, is governed chiefly by educational possibilities. Manteke is crowded with children because of the school there, but many other children go to live with relatives in town.

After finishing school most boys spend the best part of their working lives in town. Whether they ever return depends partly on the roles available to them. The modern flight to the cities has something in common with the migrations of individuals and small groups in pre-colonial society; the restless search for greener pastures, characteristic of many matrilineal societies, is frequently remarked among those of Central Africa.

N'SIKI A NGOMA: THE VOICE OF THE DEAD

While the enclosure is being built, other preparations are underway. The family of the deceased must obtain food and drink for the enter-tainment of visitors, buy planks and nails for the coffin, and call in a drummer. A pig is almost a necessity at the funeral of an adult, and a substitute, perhaps fish, must be procured for those who do not eat pork. The price of the pig needed for a funeral is probably reduced somewhat by the vendor; similarly, sticks of plantains are contributed by relatives and reckoned at a reduced value. The foodstuffs are kept in a storehouse guarded by a senior Child (at Lufumba's funeral, by Maswekwa); members of the clan that "owns" the funeral are strictly forbidden to enter. Food is prepared by the women, who congregate for the purpose in a convenient place in the village.

Hand-sawn planks are obtained from someone who happens to have felled a suitable tree, or who makes a business of lumbering. Manteke residents can get planks only at some distance from the village. (The pig may have to come from near the river because Manteke has no pigs.) Coffins are made under the supervision of Mbelani of NSAKA, who re-gards himself as the village's head carpenter; his description of this position suggests the existence of a guild of carpenters, but in reality reveals his own ambition to be chief of as many concerns as possible. When a coffin is being made, all those who fancy their hand at car-pentry join in, whether residents or visitors. The coffin is built with a vaulted lid; the more eminent the deceased, the more baroque the vault. In precolonial times the body was wrapped in cloths, whose ostentatious multiplicity also served to declare the importance of the deceased (Manker, 1932; Fukiau, 1967).

If the family can afford a master drummer,[3] one of the three said to be in the region is brought in; otherwise local talent is used. A master drummer is a musician of a different order from most drummers; he is a knowledgeable master of ceremonies as well as a musician. His arrival is heralded by a gunshot fired at the entrance to the village. At various stages he should be presented with palm wine, both as *mbungu* and as an incentive to play better. He may have other musicians to assist him, principally drummers and players of the double bell, *ngongi*. He alone, however, knows the drum phrases through which the dead speak and which regulate a number of little pagan ceremonies in which the chief participants are women. A composite portrait of a master drummer shows a man of about forty-two, noisy, unruly, assertive, who likes his liquor, enjoys a good time, and inclines to lascivious dancing. More than anyone else at a funeral, he tends to organize people and chivvy them into getting things done.

One of the drummer's first tasks is to lead a group of female Children to clear the grass from the cemetery and from the road leading to it, as required for any ritual in which the cemetery is used. On their return to the village the drummer leads the Children in the forefinger ceremony described above. The cemetery in which most adults are buried in Manteke is a new one, only some ten years old. The burial places that most houses have on their own lands have been abandoned, although none of them is very old. None has the magnificent enclosure of poplar trees, with one entrance, which marks an old site. *Bisi Manteke* are not very particular about their burial places. There is no cult of the ancestral basket, as among the BaMpangu; even in the nineteenth century the chiefs relied more on magical devices than on their ancestors. Although many people are indifferent to the dead and believe that death marks a complete end to existence, few care to spend the night near a cemetery. Quite a number take it as a matter of course that the dead can follow and participate in human affairs, but no particular awe characterizes their attitude.

In Kyanga, and perhaps in other villages, the cemetery is cleared once a year at the end of the dry season when the communal hunts are undertaken. The drummer summons the clans one by one. When the cemetery is cleared, prayers are offered at the grave of the first headman of the village (whose office was instituted by the government). Then two men and two women, described as Children and Grandchildren, sprinkle the place with palm wine to cool it. The year I was

[3] *N'siki a ngoma*, "drummer"; *sika*, "to sound." Manteke drum phrases are not the same as those used in Kasi. See Decapmaker, 1951, for a description of a Kasi funeral similar to one in Manteke.

there it needed "cooling," a fight having broken out in the midst of the proceedings; this was the only physical fight I saw, and not a very violent one at that. Afterward the party who considered himself aggrieved made a speech at the head of each of the graves of his Fathers and Grandfathers in order to draw their attention to his troubles.

In Kyanga it was obvious that half the village did not bother to turn out for the cemetery cleaning. Those who did participate said that if the cemetery was not cleaned the ancestors might be annoyed; as a result, the hunting luck would be no good, and women and crops might not be fruitful. When I asked why nobody cleared the cemetery in Manteke for the hunting I was told, "Well, we used to do it. One year, after it had been cleared, the hunting was tremendous; the next year we did a specially good job on the cemetery and afterward killed practically nothing. So we were fed up and haven't cleared it since."

Laman observes that "the ancestor cult is based upon the power that is ascribed to the father in relation to his children" (1962, p. 44). Other ethnographers seem to have taken it for granted, without inquiring very closely, that the ancestors are matrilineal. In various parts of Kongo, and in several ways, members of the matrilineal descent group are dependent on the ritual services of the Children. Among some BaLemfu, for example, the ritual insignia of the *nkazi* are kept by a chosen Child, the *nkazi* himself being forbidden to touch them except in special occasions (cf. J. Mertens, 1942, pp. 105, 319). In Manteke, where few such insignia remain, a Child or a Father is the approved though not the necessary guardian of the insignia, as also of the traditions; possessions of this kind, both material and immaterial, are helpful in advancing political claims and may themselves be competed for by different branches of the descent group. The most appropriate guardian of secrets, as of graves, is the youngest son, and thus a kind of spiritual ultimogeniture balances the secular rule of primogeniture. This role of the youngest also recalls the role of the Third Child (lineage), who fills the office of guardian of the secrets (*sangila*) and is always described as likely to be of higher intelligence than his politically privileged elders; it recalls also the adage, "The authority [*kimfumu*] of the father is the authority of the son," and the idea that authority or sovereignty is a paternal gift shared among the children.

KOKA NLOMBWA: BURIAL

About 1892, when Henry Richards returned to Manteke from leave in England, he found that in his absence there had been backsliding among his flock. "The principal customs which caused our people to fall," he reported, "were 1) Immoral dances, 2) Palm-wine drinking, 3) Firing of guns about the houses of the dead, 4) Polygamy, 5) Fetishism." The last of these failings has declined somewhat since then, but dancing, the drinking of palm wine, and the firing of guns are essential to a good funeral. For an adult a wake is held every night for three or four nights, while the coffin is being built and the grave dug, and other arrangements are being made. The body cannot be buried until the more important relatives have arrived. During the day nothing much happens in the funeral enclosure, although there are always some women in attendance and occasionally they may sing.

At about eight o'clock at night most of the village women and female visitors gather in the enclosure, bringing their children and their blankets and sleeping mats. Fires are built and coffe is brewed. Guns are fired. Younger men and boys gather in one corner and constitute a choir for the first phase of the wake, which is a short religious service on the Protestant model: hymns, Bible reading, sermon, prayer. If the deceased was a Baptist the service is usually conducted by Kingalu; if a Kimbanguist, by a representative of the Eglise de Jésus Christ sur la Terre par le Prophète Simon Kimbangu. Everybody joins in regardless of church membership; a rousing hymn sing is part of every good funeral. The unofficial anthem of the BaKongo is always sung:

Mpasi zingi vaava nza	Exceeding troubles here on earth,
Mayeela tweti monanga	Troubles we see;
Mansanga meti dadanga	Our tears pour down.
O wiiza, watusadisa.	Come to help us.
O mpeve wiiza, o wiiza,	O Spirit, come,
O wiiza, watusadisa.	Come to help us.

The service over, the customary phase (*mu fu kya nsi*) begins. It is explicitly pagan. During the service the drum must be silent. At Azeyi's funeral her family, dominated by Hezekaya, would not allow drumming afterward either, to the disgust of a number of gay spirits. At Lufumba's funeral, on the other hand, there were no such restrictions. Pressure lamps and small lanterns illuminated the enclosure. Around the coffin sat a row of female Children and Grandchildren, waving little white flags in time with the song; this behavior is called *vuvila mafwa*, "fanning the corpse." At the head sat the *mfumu za n'teekudi*, in this instance the female representatives of the grandparental clans; at the foot of the coffin sat the affines (*bazitu*). Around them danced counter-clockwise a second row of women, many carrying a tin rattle (*sangwa*), the woman's principal musical instrument. The songs and dancing continued most of the night to the sound of the drums, the *ngongi,* and the tin rattles of the women.

It was only on such occasions in Manteke that I saw respectable married women dance; they performed with more grace than most of the teen-agers one sees at the Saturday night hop. The dance around the coffin is not restricted to women, but few men care to join in and it is distinctly the women's affair. This aspect is particularly pronounced when there have been twins in the deceased's descent group — whether in the lineage only, or anywhere in the house, I was unable to determine. In that event, special rituals are conducted by a woman who has herself borne twins (*ngudi a nsimba*) and who is thereby qualified to act as *nganga a nsimba*, the operator of these rituals. The principal *nganga* is assisted by other *ngudi za nsimba* in sprinkling a palm-wine concoction over the coffin and singing "the songs for twins." The content of the ritual, as distinct from the attention paid to twins, varies a good deal. Despite the unmistakable gleam of religious fervor in the eye of Manteke's resident *nganga*, the prevailing mood is that of a party. The purpose of the wake is to keep off the unpleasant spirits that haunt the village at such times, or to cheer up the family, which is essentially the same thing. The elders keep their own wake around their own fire at their usual place of assembly, snoozing, conversing, and passing the palm wine.

The same division of labor is still more evident in the day of the burial. The elders sit in their circle listening to speeches by contributors of funeral gifts; many attend the service when it is held, and then return. The Children and Grandchildren (i.e., the younger men in this category) tear down the enclosure. Before Lufumba's coffin was moved from the bier to the stretcher on which it was to be carried to the cemetery, the mothers of twins danced once more.[4] Instructions for moving the coffin onto a stretcher are given in drum phrases: *Malembe, malembe!* ("Gently!"); *Ntondele* ("Thank you"); *Kangeno* ("Now tie it"). Before the coffin moves off, all those who have any claims against the deceased are asked to state them; on one occasion there was the matter of a chicken jointly owned, whose offspring had not yet been partitioned. The Children and Grandchildren demand a demijohn of wine before they will move off, and may try to exact several more on the way. Shots are fired if the family has enough gunpowder, but there

---

4 There was no dance at this point in the funeral of an Ndemba man whose family had no twins, but there was a separation rite for his widow "at the parting of the ways," which should mean at the edge of the village. In fact, the rite took place at the nearest bifurcation within the village. I have very little information on the role of the surviving spouse in a funeral; none of those who died in Manteke village during my stay left a spouse.

may be an argument about whether to fire two, three, or four shots, and why. Such arguments are typical of Manteke rituals.

Lina Lufumba was danced to her grave by the Children and Grandchildren, singing and swinging her coffin violently to and fro. In front went the drummer and a group of female Children and Grandchildren; at either end of the procession was the *mpeve* on long poles. People took turns at the work of carrying the stretcher, which is called *koka nlombwa* (*koka*, "to drag"; *nlombwa*, "a corpse for burial," from *lomba*, "to become dark"). Azeyi's family would not allow her coffin to be danced in this way, but when the procession reached the cemetery another alternation of Protestant and pagan ritual occurred. Some of Azeyi's MFUTU brethren stood in turn at the head of the open grave and beseeched her, if it was true that she had not died by the will of God, not to visit any displeasure on them. Then the pastor in a last prayer referred to the sins of the deceased, which were reputedly many. After the earth had been filled in the drummer made a final obeisance.

The elderly women most concerned with the pagan rituals were extremely secretive about some of them and still more so about the exchange of small sums of money among themselves after they got back to the village. As the leading women in village affairs, they are pillars of the Baptist church; one of them is the catechist's wife. I did not enjoy their confidence as I did that of the men.

The Manteke funeral provides an excellent example of true syncretism, a juxtaposition of traits of discrete origin manifested as separate phases of the ritual by different groups of people.[5] Although everybody participates in the Protestant phases, the funeral ritual is run by the elders, the senior men, whose primary and exclusive concern is the exchange of gifts. Women and young men also make gifts, but get one of the elders to speak for them. The old women, with the drummer if there is one, are in charge of rituals specifically contrasted with the Protestant or Kimbanguist ones; the elders profess ignorance of the significance of these rituals, and openly despise them as the sort of foolishness enjoyed by women.

The young men and women perform service tasks, but in the *koka nlombwa* and related rituals the young men run the show; the changing fashions that govern these rituals are beyond the control and to some extent beyond the comprehension of the elders, whom the *baleeke* are in a position to defy, to a certain degree. When the young men demanded another demijohn before proceeding on their way to the ceme-

[5] This syncretism is quite different from the fusion of African form and European content, as in Kimbanguism, which is, structurally speaking, interchangeable with Protestantism.

tery with Lufumba's coffin, the Judge had to come out and harangue them in his best crowd-quelling style, speaking as a senior Grandchild but also as an elder of the community.[6]

At a Lemfu funeral the coffin was carried to the grave on the shoulders of a group of men who seemed unable to keep control of it. The deceased insisted on being taken down a side road to visit an old friend — a visit that might have been taken to point to the witch responsible for the death, but, I was assured, the deceased had no such intention — and later, in a particularly skittish mood, she attempted to turn around and go home again. After being sternly lectured by various relatives, the dead woman consented to be transported in peace. The voice of her sister was said by the others to be irritating the body rather than soothing it; when the sister was told to keep quiet, progress became smoother. It was evident to me that some of the bearers were responsible for the performance, but everybody apparently took it quite seriously.

Most villages at one time used wooden hearses with wheels for carrying the coffin to the grave, but they are no longer built or repaired. An elaborate example rotting in a village on the Angolan border, south of Manteke, has two seats on each side for the Children and Grandchildren and a window by each seat permitting the passengers to look into the interior of the vehicle and watch the coffin.

MAFUNDU: THE RECEIPTS

Beginning the morning after a death occurs, the elders sit under a convenient mango tree, listening to the presentation speeches of those who bring *lusadusu* ("help," from *sadisa*) to the clan of the deceased. This procedure is called the *mafundu*. At one time contributions took the form of blankets in which the body was wrapped. Speakers refer more or less elaborately to their gifts in terms of the blankets and other cloths for which money is now substituted. Children and *bankwezi* are expected to contribute "the blankets that go underneath"; the Father offers "blankets to go on top." Various other denominations are possible. In addition to cash gifts, actual blankets, sheets, and bedspreads are given, particularly by closer relatives. Many of these bedclothes are in fact wrapped around the body; others go into storage as part of the funeral fund of the lineage. People who give blankets usually give cash as well.

[6] In relation to a given Ego, it is to be noted, grandparent and grandchild are senior and junior within the same category; a man may therefore describe himself as *nkaka* or *n'tekolo* in a given affair, choosing the term that corresponds to the role allotted by the community to a man of his age.

"Money contributed to funerals is never wasted. When a death occurs in your house, all the other people to whose funerals you have been contributing 20 francs here, 50 francs there, will look in their notebooks and bring a corresponding amount, or probably a little bit more." "Well, that's the idea, but with people with whom you get on well, frequently attending one another's affairs, you don't bother to look in your book, you just take along what seems appropriate, or as much as you can afford." Actual practice falls somewhere between these two opinions. "It all depends," as another man said, "on the closeness of the tie, the degree of goodwill, and the state of the purse." When a childless old woman died in Ntombo a Lukuti, Makima of MVIKA looked in his records and found that on 17 June 1947 the head of NA LUKUTI had brought a blanket to the funeral of an MVIKA woman. He made a point of returning a blanket and recalling the gift received eighteen years before, and considered the obligation honorably redeemed. The parties to this exchange are closely related and on excellent terms.[7]

All gifts are recorded by a competent Child who is chosen by the house to keep the accounts for the affair. He may be courteously addressed as Mayala, "the one in charge" (*yaala*, "to govern"). Although all Children of NANGA participated in the funerals of Lufumba (DISA) and Azeyi (MFUTU), primary responsibilities were borne by a different selection of them in each instance. MFUTU gave the accounts to a NA LOMBO man, a grandchild, and went so far as to import another grandchild from a neighboring village to take charge of the stores and other arrangements. He described himself as both Child and Grandchild because his father was MFULAMA NKANGA and his grandfather NANGA KYA MFUTU (see chap. 3, n. 3).

Gifts are recorded under the name of the donor's clan, not on the basis of his relationship to the affair. Etiquette calls for the *nkazi* of the clan section, or at least of the house, to present the contributions of "those who stand behind him," but nowadays many individuals like to present their own so as to draw more attention to their own names. At Lufumba's funeral some 220 individual contributions were recorded, ranging from 5 to 1,000 francs. The actual number of contributions, many of them from persons related only distantly, nominally, or not at all, was larger than that. The total receipts, at an ordinary funeral, may run to about 18,000 francs; at an important funeral as

[7] Although I refer here to the house, I believe the "debt" is thought of as a matter between two lineages; I cannot be sure, because the exchange is spoken of as being between clans and, as already indicated, the boundaries of the lineages in any one house are difficult for an outsider to determine.

much as 45,000 francs, which in the village economy is a prodigious amount of money, may be contributed. Once, in Ndemba, a mentally deficient youth brought 2 francs as his *lusadusu*. The presiding *nkazi* was inclined to ridicule the offering, but those present admonished him to respect his Father (*zitisa s'aku*) and accept the gift in the proper manner.

The categorization of contributors illuminates the nature and function of the clan (*mvila*). At Lufumba's funeral five groups were classed under NKAZI A KONGO: (1) persons who are *bankwezi* with some personal affinal relationship to DISA; (2) persons belonging to the same clan section (*kanda*), with no particular link, who are *bankwezi mu dikanda*, members of a clan section that habitually intermarries with NANGA; (3) Children and Grandchildren of NANGA; (4) strangers, temporarily resident in the area, who happen to be of the clan (*mvila*) NKAZI A KONGO; and (5) Angolan refugees, clan unspecified, who live in Mbanza Nkazi and are clients of NKAZI A KONGO. Parallel categories included other clans and the following: MANIANGA — six individuals, all born elsewhere; ANGOLA — eight refugees in Manteke; AMERIQUE — Mr. Macgaffei Mundele; BAMONITEUR — Manteke schoolteachers, all strangers; and COMMERCANT — a passing trader.

There is an *mvila* called MANIANGA, but it is not known in Manteke; the label above refers to the Manianga region. When the spokesman for this group made his gift and said his clan was MANIANGA, there was some outcry because there is no such clan and because everyone knew that the speaker was Albert Luwawa, that he has lived in Manteke for thirty years, and that his clan is NLAZA. He explained that he and Tekasala of MPANZU and some others like them felt themselves to be strangers; they did not want to join themselves individually to appropriate local clans, but on the other hand they did not want to be classified with another lot of strangers, the recently arrived Angolan refugees. So they had invented a clan for themselves.

On another occasion, when there was a crowd in the village for a wedding, word arrived that Luwawa's *mpangi* had died in his home region, at a considerable distance. An impromptu *mafundu* was held on the spot. Some of the group of long-resident strangers who are close friends of Luwawa's constituted themselves his clan. First they accepted contributions from all the other clans and then made their own gift. These sums were added up by other Manteke people who took on the role of Children and helped Luwawa make the appropriate returns.

The wife of the nurse in charge of the government dispensary in Manteke once gave birth to a stillborn child. Both he and she were strangers, but because her clan was NANGA NE KONGO the local sections

of that clan acted as her brethren; it was the only time, as someone remarked, that NANGA KYA NA NSAMBA, MFULAMA NKANGA, and NA MVEMBA
had ever acted in concert. People contributed planks and foodstuffs
and labor, just as though they had been close kinsmen. Village women
took over the house and cooked food; at the wake many of them were
in tears, although there was no shrieking and howling. This demonstration of sympathy was remarkable. The nurse, as a stranger, feels
little at home in Manteke. His wife gets land to cultivate, but she
merely tags along behind the village women without being invited to
join them. Like other strangers, such as the teachers, the nurse finds
it hard to have to buy all his food, especially as there may be none for
sale; his nominal kinsmen do not offer to let him participate in the
local distribution system. Although he is extremely circumspect in his
relations with the villagers, a flow of anonymous letters denounces his
supposed sins and failings to his superiors. Yet when his child died,
bisi Manteke lived up to the highest ideals, their own and anyone else's,
exerting themselves especially on his behalf "because he is a stranger,
and because he does so much for us. It is hard for him to be a
stranger, and to lose his own child after delivering so many of ours."
When the contributions were all in, *bisi ki*NANGA went into conference
with their Children and Grandchildren, paid all the expenses, and then
presented the balance to the nurse — not directly to his wife, of course.

These examples demonstrate the role of the clan as primary category
in the organization of Kongo society. They also show that relations
among the clans, with reference to any specific affair, are at once relations of kinship, space (or direction), and function. The model for this
situation, already given in the form of the diagram connected with the
theory of land tenure, is embodied in the structure of the funeral enclosure. The arbitrariness of empirical relations, as compared with the
formal organization of process, is noteworthy: everybody, to play his
role, must belong to a category coordinate with other categories, but it
does not greatly matter how the category is composed. Component functions of the process must be carried out by actors appropriately designated, but there is room for choice in the allocation of roles, provided they are kept distinct.

The people themselves speak initially of their participation in
funerals as community participation and refer to visitors as representatives of other villages. These participating villages form the neighborhood of any particular village such as Manteke; Manteke people recognize a certain gulf between themselves and the inhabitants of, for
example, Mbata Kimenga, Kemba, Kinkanza: "We don't attend one
another's funerals any more." Most marriages link parties within the

same neighborhood. When there has been a marriage beyond the bounds of the neighborhood, participation in funerals is physically more difficult and is likely to be limited to immediate kin.

The participating community includes, in principle, the whole population of the village in which the funeral occurs; failure to participate causes unfavorable remarks. The active population adopts roles appropriate to the primary communal categories: elders (*bambuta*), cadets (*baleeke*), and women. Within these categories more specific roles are adopted according to kinship relations, although these roles are sometimes adduced as a kind of afterthought: of two men helping to dig a grave, one says, when asked, that he is doing it because he is a Grandchild of the owning house; another says that he has no particular kinship tie but is doing it to help out.

All speeches at the *mafundu* are addressed to the *nkazi* of the clan section that owns the affair; speeches for both Lufumba and Azeyi were directed at Kingalu of NANGA. Some clans have no *nkazi* because the constituent houses, though agreeing that the office exists, cannot agree who should fill it. MVIKA NTUMBA and MAKATI MA NTUMBA, both large groups with frequent weddings and funerals, have a solution: when one owns the affair, the other provides the *nkazi*. (It has already been noted that "MAKATI" is a label for a diverse group; some of them prefer to have Joel Albert of NGOMA LUBOTA, a relatively neutral figure, act as their *nkazi*.) Other compromises are possible.

Each speaker, on first addressing the gathering, salutes a representative of his father's clan. The salute is a soft handclap (*nkofi*). The donor, standing, bends his knee; the recipient, responding with a similar handclap, pushes his hat to the back of his head or sometimes takes it off. This routine, called *kundasana*, is the essence of polite behavior according to custom (*fu kya nsi*): *tukundasananga*, "we respect one another." Old friends, however, play all kinds of humorous variations on it. It is particularly honorific to reply to such a salute by initiating another exchange.

The father's nearest representative, structurally speaking, will do as the recipient of the greeting; if there is none of the clan present, the speaker claps toward the horizon. He next salutes his grandfathers — that is, his own grandfathers, not those who may be sitting as *mfumu za n'teekudi* in relation to the affair in process — and continues around the circle exchanging greetings with other persons of importance, using the appropriate kinship term and clan name and perhaps mentioning briefly the particular link upon which he bases the usage. The money he brings is placed on the ground in front of the *nkazi*; if he presents several amounts they are placed and described separately. He announces in whose name he speaks and what is being contributed. He may wrap the whole business up in quite an elaborate speech, detailing perhaps the circumstances in which news of the death arrived in his village, or recounting some anecdote. The *nkazi* may reply himself or have an assistant do so.

These ceremonies continue all day for about four days. If no gifts are coming in, the elders converse, or drift off to eat or to see to other business. A few younger and more efficiency-minded men regard the procedure with some impatience: "We wait here for two days for Na Mpamba to bring his 2 francs; when he comes, he says he is *nkwezi* Na Mpamba, and how sad he is, and here is his 2 francs."

Concurrently the *nkazi* exchanges a series of *mbungu* with the Father of the Child and the Grandfathers, informing them that their child is dead and requesting permission for the body to be placed in the coffin and buried.[8] The other chiefs formally inquire of the deceased's matrilineal kin (*ngudi*) who is to take his place. The more important the deceased and his family, the heavier the contributions and the more elaborate the exchange of *mbungu*. After a last-minute influx of big money from Kinshasa at Lufumba's funeral, the ritual courtesies became more intricate and more expensive, with each speaker embroidering still more elegantly upon the figures introduced by his predecessor.

When the burial is over and the majority of the *lusadusu* has come in, the total is announced and those present are told that the *mafundu* proper, the public phase, has come to an end. A demijohn of palm wine is offered, plus a dry equivalent for those who do not drink, and a small coin (*mbungu a kimbangi*) is given to each of the witnesses.

The next day the clan section with its Children and Grandchildren discusses the disposition of the receipts, including the contribution made by the section itself to the lineage of the deceased. In addition to the contributions listed by clan, at Lufumba's funeral Mayala had noted the following (in francs):

1. Mbuti NA LUKUTI		1,660	Father of the Child
Tuveta tua nlele	4		Four sheets
Tiya tukobe	3		Gunpowder
Mbungu		4	
2. Nsiki a ngoma, mbungu		2	Drummer
3. Nsiki a ngongi, mbungu		20	*Ngongi* player
4. Ntekudi MFULAMA NKANGA		5,760	Grandfather
Nlele	1		Sheet
Mbungu		6	

[8] Cf. the Ndibu proverb, *Mono i nsizi; nkete dia loombwa nsotelelwa dio lwa nkewa*, "Je suis le *nsizi* [sorte d'agouti]; pour que je mange les fruits, il faut que le singe les laisse [fasse] tomber pour moi" (De Sousberghe, 1967*b*, p. 197).

5. Ntekudi NA MAZINGA	251	Grandfather
6. Nkazi NANGA KIANSAMBA	2,452	*Nkazi*
7. Atekolo ye ana	520	Children and Grandchildren

The first item of expenditure is a return gift to the Father, proportional to what he himself contributed and always discussed as a single sum even though it is presented as two: (1) *matondo* (e.g., 100 francs), return gift; (2) *mvindu* (e.g., 150 francs), a recognition of the Father's right to the deceased's personal clothing and some other belongings left in the house. Each of the three chiefs is entitled to (1) 20 francs, representing palm wine; (2) *mbungu* (1 franc), *ikudedele va mbulu* ("I smooth your forehead"), which signifies the end of mourning and entitles the recipient to shave his hair, buy new clothes, and the like (mourning observances are not elaborate in modern Manteke); and (3) *mbungu* (1 franc), *ikusumbudisi mavambu a nzila* ("I cause you to cross over the parting of the ways"), which bids farewell.

Then expenses are met. Food is paid for; if a relative brought a stick of plantains without specifying a price, a reasonable price is decided on. If the drummer played well and did not sleep on the job he gets at least 150 francs. If he is not treated generously he may decline to come next time. Also, the *ngongi* players and the women mourners who rattled *bisangwa* are paid. Planks, nails, gunpowder . . . Here is a partial list of expenditures at Lufumba's funeral (in francs):

Masalampanti, gift to the carpenters who made the coffin	450
Yingongi, ngongi player	40
Ngoma, drummer	400
Tengula mabundu, a demijohn for general consumption	120
Mbuti a muana (the Father of the Child)	
A blanket and	400
Ntekudi NA MAZINGA (Grandfather)	
His blanket and	100
Ana ye atekolo, tonda salu	
Thanks to the Children and Grandchildren for their work	1,040
Bana ba Leopoldville	
Special return gift to Children resident in Kinshasa whose help had been particularly generous	600
Allele mu lumbu	
For the women who had slept in the house of the deceased during the wake	150
Tengula bundu diaka	
Another demijohn, the first having been insufficient for so large a crowd	120

At Elayi's funeral the question of disposing of his house, an admittedly miserable shack, came up. The Children, some of whom were leading local elders, conferred with the *baana ba nkazi* (juniors of the lineage) and decided after much argument that the house should go to Elayi's wife and children. Hezekaya, as Senior Child to NSUNDI, returned to the circle and informed the *bankazi* of this decision.

Settling the accounts is actually a process that goes on for days after a funeral, as late contributions come in and other expenses turn up. After a week or two the members of the lineage, with their *nkazi*, hold their own entirely private meeting at which they may decide to give 1,000 francs, or some other sum, to the widow to help her with the children: so much for a brother whose personal share of the expenses had been high; so much toward another's train ticket. This procedure was followed after Elayi's funeral. In the end each man present, including the anthropologist as honorary *mwisi kiNSUNDI*, got an *mbungu* of 10 francs. Manase's funeral, also in NSUNDI, produced a deficit which the members of her lineage were publicly required to make up; she was an old woman without children to remember her.

N'KALA: THE TOMB

In the east, some nine months or a year after the funeral, the house holds a party called *sukula maza* ("washing in water"), nominally to signify the end of mourning. Contributions from friends and relations are accepted in the usual way. Manteke people disparage this custom as non-Kongo, and say it is just one more modern excuse for extravagance and probably immorality. The custom appears, however, even in Manteke: a man who was unable to be present at the funeral may bring a gift, weeks afterward, and say, "This 50 francs is soap to wash off the mourning dirt [*mu sukula mvindu*]." A young stranger who had lately taken up with an NSUNDI girl in town came to visit his *bankwezi* and used the excuse of Manase's recent funeral to make a gift which he said was the *nkwezi*'s blanket. By such means, relations are cultivated.

Another feast, common to all parts of Kongo, celebrates the construction of a monument. The Children of the deceased must give permission for the monument to be erected, and they alone may remove objects placed on a grave. The money needed may be provided by the Children or by the lineage of the deceased; the latter is in any event ritually immobilized and cannot actively participate in the event. In theory it is disgraceful for a grave to be left unmonumented or unmaintained, but such neglect is usual; it may be many years, even generations, before a memorial is put up, if at all.

Tombs are built in the dry season, when the concrete will not be rained on and palm wine is plentiful. The feast is called *matannga*, a term also used for a party given by a man to celebrate his getting out of jail or, in the old days, surviving a witchcraft ordeal. Besides its manifest function, a *matannga* marked by lavish expenditure may reveal the lineage's social importance. For example, at a village near Kinganga a whole cow and four hogsheads of sugarcane liquor were among the refreshments provided for the hundreds of guests at such an event.

NZUZI in Manteke built tombs for his mother and sister. Although cutting all possible corners and ignoring all the extravagant customs such as drumming, gunshots, and all-night dances, he still spent more than 20,000 francs. He sent *mbungu* to the other houses of his clan and to the Children and Grandchildren, notifying them of the event. Each group held a separate meeting at which individuals made their donations. Then all gathered outside the house of the owner of the affair, Lutete Mbanzu. His brother of the same lineage, who shared the expenses, opened the proceedings by giving 5 francs *mbungu* to Kingalu, *nkazi* of NANGA, to say that the work on the graves had been completed. In thus speaking out he was in error, for the owners of the affair should say nothing. Mbelani of NSAKA, replying on behalf of Kingalu and addressing himself to Manzambi of the second lineage of NZUZI, presented the contribution of the other houses. Then Luwawa, a Child of NANGA, presented 300 francs on behalf of the Children. This sum included the original *mbungu* of 120 francs which he as treasurer for this affair had received but had not yet physically distributed. More substantial help was rendered at the graves by Children who labored on the monument.

The elders of NANGA who were present — Kingalu, Maleso, Hezekaya, Lusala, Kinkela (all MFUTU), Dyasa (NKUTI), Mbelani (NSAKA), and others — decided that 1,500 francs should be returned to the Children. The sum was divided into (1) 1,000 francs, *ngulu*, the pig always required for work on cemeteries; (2) 300 francs, fixings to go with the pig; (3) 200 francs, *malavu*, palm wine. These items are described as *matondo* and as sustenance for those working on the tombs, although in fact their purpose is primarily communication; most of the recipients did not go near the graves. At this time all members of NANGA were excluded from the cemetery; trespassers would be fined. Kinkela said he would feel obliged to pay this customary penalty to avoid bad feeling; Lutete Mbanzu said it was just one more device for extorting money.

The exchange of moneys on this occasion was complicated by the intrusion of a member of NTUMBA who, as a Child of NANGA, had already been informed of the event, but who complained, as the bearer of Lutete Mbanzu's father's name, Lukoki John, that his wife's and daughter's graves were being interfered with without his knowledge. His manner throughout was of one playing the fool. After being heard he was requested to withdraw, but later he was recalled and was given three *mbungu*: 5 francs for *mbiikulu*, "apology"; 5 francs plus 5 francs for information concerning the two graves; and 5 francs for announcing completion of the work. But he decided this payment was not enough: "After all, you gave *sangala* 120 francs to the Children, and another to your brethren, what about me, Father of the Child?" So he returned the *mbungu*, thereby rejecting them. The clan, however, added only another 10 francs, and he, having made his point, contributed *lusadusu* of 150 francs, a relatively substantial amount. Since the original Lukoki had been purchased by the mission, and since in the village context it is NZUZI who speaks for him (because he married an NZUZI woman and because of NZUZI's relationship to the mission), Lukoki's clan is usually given as NANGA, although his home clan NZUNDU is known. His namesake would not have been entitled to another *mbungu* if the two of them had belonged to the same lineage.

The cemetery where his mother and sister are buried was described to me by NZUZI as "the cemetery of the chiefs." Other people deride the expression. All the chiefs from Na Makokila onward are buried there, but it is the mission cemetery located on NZUZI land. It contains the graves of missionaries as well as those of Ne Kwede and members of NZUZI, but most other adults are buried in a communal village cemetery. When Panu of MVIKA NTUMBA died he was taken to Ndembolo, the ancestral burying ground and *mbanza* of his house, but some members of MFUTU saw the burial there as a political gesture, a statement of territorial claims referring to the fight for Mbanza Ntala. Every village has a separate cemetery for children.

Like marriage ceremonies, the feasts connected with death vary regionally. A Manianga writer lists the following: burial, removal of mourning, and building the tomb. *"Matanga"* is the term he uses for a general feast of the dead which is held after a number of deaths in the same group. Removal of mourning centers on the rite of shaving the head, beginning with the ceremonial cutting of a few hairs from the top of the head of the surviving spouse. All these events are marked by *mafundu*, in which different categories of relatives bring gifts and receive food, drink, and other gifts in exchange (Kamuna, 1966). Kamuna insists, however, that gifts of cloth, money, or palm wine on such occasions are not simply presents (*ka n'kailu ko*), but payments of debts (*mfuka kibeni*). Failure to pay is actionable at law.

He distinguishes three kinds of *mafundu*: (1) *fundu dia mbakisa,* or initiating an exchange; (2) *fundu diamvutula,* which returns the gift one has received at an earlier event of one's own; (3) *fundu dia nsoma,* the initiation of a new exchange (*soma,* "to augment"; Laman, 1936).

In the committee form of government as revealed by weddings and funerals procedure is formally regulated, whatever conflicts and structural uncertainties prevail informally (*ku nenga*). The owning matrilineal clan section is functionally distinguished from its patrilateral kinsmen and its affines; its Fathers and Children are represented as the principal repositories of authority, although the owners may well be able, informally, to procure the decisions they want. The sole sense in which the owning *nkazi* may be said to be the "chief" is that the entire committee, in its structure and procedures, focuses on him; he is not, even in name, the primary decision maker. The focus and membership of the committee change according to the location (ownership) of the affair.

Within the clan section a similar displacement operates. The owning house receives the collective contribution of the rest of the clan section (in the event of a funeral). Decisions are once again made by a committee whose responsible member, formally at least, has the smallest say. Moreover, the spokesman of the owning house represents, within that house, a lineage other than the one that is actually promoting and paying for the affair.

The pervasive principle thus revealed is that nobody speaks publicly for himself; his "owner," at the appropriate structural level, speaks for him.[9] This practice recalls the importance of the clan (*mvila*) as category; in a structural sense the individual person does not exist in Kongo society. This fact is an aspect of social organization, however, and not, as Europeans have commonly supposed, a product of a collectivist habit of mind.

[9] Cf. the Ndibu proverb, *Mono vumu yavimbwa, lwenda kwa X,* "Moi, je suis le ventre qui a été gonflé, allez chez X," the speaker designating the proper person to speak for him (De Sousberghe, 1967b, p. 197). The calculus of representation is further illustrated by this incident: Albert of NKAZI A KONGO has a daughter by his NLAZA wife. The daughter has been seduced, but Albert himself does not raise the matter of the compensation due him. Instead his *mbanda,* Joseph of NANGA KYA MFUTU, whose wife is also NLAZA, goes to see NTUMBA on Albert's behalf; NTUMBA acts as "*nkazi* of first instance" for the NLAZA women resident in Manteke. The overture is rejected, however, because MFUTU and NTUMBA are not on good terms. Instead Pierre, who belongs to a different house of NKAZI A KONGO but is recognized in the context of Manteke village affairs as spokesman (*nkazi*) for members of that clan, acts as go-between. NKAZI A KONGO, like NLAZA, is domiciled elsewhere, though some members live in Manteke as Children of NANGA.

9

LAND

Although there is no shortage of land in Kongo, the areas nearest to the villages and most likely to be productive, such as the Manteke valley, are heavily cultivated, especially in contrast with the forests which are plundered rather than cultivated. Proof that much more intensive use is possible is provided by the dry-season gardens of a man who works in Ntombo with rake and watering can, and by the plantation maintained in Kivulusa by another who is lame and is thus forced to make the best use of land close to home. In each instance intensive and rational use of a small area of forest produces a much admired crop. In contrast, most men who want fruits like *nsafu*, plantains, bananas, avocados, and grapefruit collect them when they are ripe from trees planted by themselves or by their forebears, which grow untended among the other vegetation. Even at this level of exploitation, however, large areas of reasonably accessible forest are not used. Convincing evidence of the availability of land is that in 1964 eight households of Angolan refugees were given plots in the Manteke valley and elsewhere; in other villages a much larger number of Angolans have been accommodated (see chap. 1, n. 5). Land use falls into four principal categories: hunting, field cultivation, forest cultivation, and growing of tree crops.[1]

Individuals and small groups hunt all through the year, but the big communal hunts occur at the end of the dry season, beginning in the Lunyonzo valley about 15 August and moving west to reach the Congo River around 15 October. When these hunts were described to me, I expected to see ritual establishment of boundaries in which affines and Children and Grandchildren would play appropriate roles, but nothing of the sort occurred. The owners of a particular

[1] Houses are built in the village on sites acquired according to rules of succession and filiation. The resulting patterns are complex. Rights in a house site resemble those in a cultivated plot.

tract decide when it is to be burned so that hunters may shoot the fleeing game, but the decision is really a communal one, for wherever the fire starts it soon spreads to many different tracts.

Anyone, whether local or not, may join the hunt. At the end of the day the hunters gather with their catch. Portions are allotted to those who set the fire, to the dog handlers, and to the owners, but the procedure is extremely informal. The only disputes that commonly arise relate to young plantations destroyed by the fire, but it is surprising how seldom anything is destroyed; in 1965 no complaints were heard in Manteke.[2] In fact, most of the grassland burned in these hunts is uncultivable.

On the fringes of the riverine forests, where the women's field crops are grown, the soil is more fertile. Plots are rectangular and measure about 30 yards by 35. The agricultural agent in the 1930's recalls that up to that time plots had been much smaller, but the government required that they be enlarged.

On a certain day the owners of the land go to divide up a new tract for cultivation, having informed their friends and relatives; in practice, almost everybody goes along for the division of a large tract. Half a dozen large tracts may be in use at one time, plus many smaller ones opened by perhaps two or three individuals only. A survey of one large tract, owned partly by NSAKA and partly by NZUZI, showed that all the users claimed rights to their plots as landowners, as children or grandchildren of the owner's clan, as wives of NANGA men, or as wives of children or grandchildren of NANGA. On so wide a basis, almost any woman could share in the tract. A few people, all strangers, were specifically clients who had asked for permission to use plots of land. Boundaries are marked by a furrow made with the hoe.

On new plots are planted peanuts, *wandu*-peas, and manioc, which mature in succession. October peanuts are harvested in February; manioc, after about fourteen months. As the ground is cleared after harvesting, subsidiary crops of sugarcane, sweet potatoes, tomatoes, and corn are planted. Before all these are cleared, the plot may have been in use four or five years. Those who have had luck with peanuts may try a second crop; one or two experiment with ideas of crop rotation learned from the mission. The large NANGA tract mentioned above may have been in use, in part at least, for as long as ten years, but it was impossible to obtain believable estimates. *Bisi Manteke*, particularly women, have little notion of calendrical time; I once heard an educated youth trying without much success to explain to a mother what

[2] Communal fishing is organized after the first rains, but large streams are few and in 1965 so little water was running that fishing was a failure.

her son meant when he wrote that he would be home in March. It may be fifteen to twenty-five years before a tract is used again.

On a working day most of the villagers work in one place, a place designated by some informal process. The nurse's wife complained that as a stranger she did not hear when the women would be going to this or that field. One who often goes to the fields by herself is likely to be suspected of theft. Whole households go together; nowadays the men even help with such work as planting peanuts in addition to doing the heavy clearing, a task that is traditionally theirs. The division of labor is not obligatorily specified, and the men have opportunities to be lazy which are denied to the women. The idlers are well known to public opinion.

On the whole, the village works hard, much harder than one would suppose from the pronouncements issued by the government in town, which suggest that the rural economy would be transformed if the peasants would only bestir themselves. The low productivity of the village is attributable rather to the shortage of laborers. In 1965 there were only twenty-three men between the ages of twenty and fifty; of these, four left in the course of the year and one was a dangerous lunatic who had to be tied up most of the time. Quite a few women, usually widowed or divorced, have no man in the house.

The men are chiefly concerned with forest cultivation. At the end of the dry season they cut down tracts of forest which are approximately the same size as the field plots. A week or two later, just before the rains, the cuttings are burned. The principal crop is beans, followed by an optional assortment of corn, sugarcane, tomatoes, pepper, pineapples, and bananas. Each plot is worked by a man individually, with the assistance of his wife at planting and harvest; there is no communal expedition to a designated forest, and each plot is relatively isolated. If the man does not own the land, he asks the owner for permission to work it; often he cultivates the land of his father's clan, which would never normally be refused him, but he may ask a patrilateral *mpangi* or anyone else for permission to cultivate. Such permission, once given, may not be withdrawn, even if relations between the parties deteriorate. In the dry season beans are planted in the valley bottoms, together with tomatoes and vegetables of European origin, such as cabbage and lettuce. Some people also put in, in the drier places, a peanut crop. Forest land is black and wet and full of leaf mold, but crops are damaged by fungi and excessive moisture.

Men also extract from the forest the fruit of planted and unplanted trees. Unplanted trees are those that have reseeded themselves, such as the mangoes growing along the truck routes. All palm trees except those planted near the village by individuals grow naturally and may be exploited by anyone, including casual visitors to the village.[3] There are a few restrictions: (1) no one may take fruit from a tree someone else has reserved by hanging a sign on it; (2) Children and Grandchildren may tap wine from producing trees without asking specific permission because it is theirs automatically, but all others must first ask the owner of the land (*mfumu a n'toto*); and (3) no one should take all the palm nuts from a tract lest the owner, if left with none for himself, become angry.

The exception is made for palm wine because of its commercial value and relative scarcity. Palm oil and palm kernels are salable, but their production requires a great deal of work; the raw material is not scarce. Timber trees, such as mahogany (*n'kamba*) for planks and, near the river, the silk-cotton tree (*m'fuma*) for canoes, are also appropriated by the owner of the land even though they grow naturally. An element in the dispute for Mbanza Ntala is that an MFUTU man has cut down a mahogany tree. In recent years, certain scarce materials used for house building have been appropriated by landowners. In areas where there is a commercial demand for palm nuts, a similar development may have taken place.

Planted trees are usually found on sites formerly cultivated. Citrus trees and *n'safu*[4] are the most popular, but bananas, plantains, and avocados are also widely used. Such plantings are made as investments for the future, in anticipation of the cash to be expected from selling the fruit in town. Rights to trees are clearly distinct from rights to the land on which they grow; the trees are identified individually by the name of the planter, sometimes have names of their own, and are inherited matrilineally; that is, they become the corporate property of the lineage, the inheritance group. Trees are owned by women as well as by men, though it is always the men who do the harvesting. Children and Grandchildren may help themselves to fruit without asking, but the owner of the land may not do so unless he also falls into one of these categories.

No tribute (*vaku*) is payable to the owner of land by a man who cultivates it or plants trees on it, although the villagers say that in the 1920's the government tried to define landholdings and told the owners they ought to demand a prestation in lieu of rent. A view

---

[3] Richards (1950, p. 221), followed by Douglas (1963, p. 33), suggests that the oil palm represents a permanent property basic to the existence of corporate matrilineages in Kongo.

[4] *N'safu* = *Canarium schweinfurthii* or *C. saphu; m'fuma*, the silk-cotton tree = *Ceiba pentandra* or *Eriodendron anfractuosum; n'kamba* (known by different names in other regions) = *Chlorophora excelsa; n'sanda* = *Ficus dusenii*.

commonly held by Europeans was that custom demanded such payments to the hereditary landowner. In fact, payments similar to rent, acknowledging a landlord-tenant relationship, could be made only by a foreigner. Within the community obligatory payments are made between kinsmen on kinship occasions. A stranger long resident in Manteke may, if he so desires, offer fruit from his trees to the owner of the land, but such a gift has no jural significance. On the other hand, modern squabbling over land is partly motivated by the idea, derived from Belgian planning and instruction, that the rural economy will be commercialized in a Utopian future; in that day people expect to collect rents, leasing their lands in perpetuity to some company or other.

The ritual basis of the association between women and grassland, between men and forest, is clear, even though not so well developed, at least in modern times, as it is for example among the BashiLele (Douglas, 1955). The woman's implement is the hoe, associated with peace; the man's is the machete, which, with the sword and the axe, is associated with war and chiefship. Women are supposed not to be able to handle a machete skillfully, though some of them do, and cultivate forest plots if need be. Grassland, secular and cultivated by women, is identified with the treeless and trackless plains crossed by the ancestors on leaving Mbanza Kongo; it is contrasted with the forested hills and valleys where the villages of the living and the dead, sacred and ruled by men, are dominated by the silk-cotton tree and the baobab (*n'kondo*). At the conscious level these distinctions come out most clearly in connection with communal work on the roads, where men clear the forested stretches and women the grass; the distinction is not always botanically clear, and is governed in practice by the principle that men are entitled to work in the shade.

A certain amount of agricultural produce reaches the market through devious commercial channels designed to profit middlemen. Four of the village's younger men are part-time traders who collect sacks of dried manioc, peanuts, or beans — the chief exports — and take them to town; they have no means of knowing what price they will get, and sometimes an expedition results in a loss. An alternative to marketing the produce in town is to sell a sack or two to one of the full-time local traders, or to the trucks that come through from Matadi and elsewhere in search of foodstuffs. The price offered is so low, however, that most people prefer to send their surplus directly to relatives in town, who sell it or eat it.[5] The producer is repaid in gifts of cash

5 Ndongala (1966, p. 31), expressing the conventional wisdom on peasants who lack economic foresight, writes: "Il est difficile d'expliquer, sans une enquête socio-psycho-

or in services of various kinds, the exchange serving to fulfill social obligations and to distribute the equivalent of the middleman's profit between producer and consumer. The relatives in question are children or lineage brethren, or very often an assorted household. Makima of MVIKA, a prodigious worker who hates to be long away from his forest, Nkenge, says that he never sells anything.

Information on the circulation and accumulation of money is harder to come by than information on politics, which is otherwise the most secret topic in village life. The absence of rational calculation, which has been and is still dwelt on at excessive length in the discussion of African and particularly Congolese peasant economies, only partly explains the reticence in financial affairs. It is true that no one keeps accounts, and that few people could; Congolese lack the budgetary habit. On the other hand, every woman knows approximately how many sacks of peanuts she produces in a year and exactly how many she sends to town — but she probably will not tell you.

The circulation of economic as of political information is inhibited by the characteristic obsession with the necessity of defining and preserving rights of all kinds, an obsession that reveals the pervasive insecurity of Kongo society. The insecurity is indicated by the frequent iteration of the tag, *kyame, kyame; kyangani, kyangani,* and its variants, which may be translated, "To each his own." Insecurity is revealed also by the constant fear of theft, which is quite out of proportion to the actual incidence of theft, even of reported theft.

The thieving believed to occur is effected mostly by witchcraft: by such devices as funny-money which flies back to its originator's pocket, taking with it all the cash in the victim's pocket; or by charms that steal peanuts from under the plants and transfer them to a neighboring plot, despite countercharms arranged along the boundary to prevent theft. Hence the dominant idea is: "If Kingani knows I have it, he may contrive to deprive me of it; any more information he gets will assist his purpose." Hence the secrecy over tradition and boundary marks; hence a woman's assertion that she has forgotten her mother's name, although that is one thing a woman never forgets. But political information, if it is to be useful at all, must circulate occasionally, at

logique approfondie, les causes fondamentales de l'absence de calcul économique comptable chez les paysans ba-kongo." The problem is not psychological but social; the economic milieu of the modern Congolese peasant is profoundly irrational. It is a commonplace that rational economic initiatives are repeatedly frustrated by unpredictable political and economic developments originating in town and having to do mainly with such factors as price and transportation. On the lowest level, commercial buyers of palm nuts in Manteke routinely refuse to tell village women the price they are getting per kilo, lest the women seek out better offers.

least; with economic information this need never arises, except in connection with inheritance. Consequently the formulas for the dissemination or dissimulation of such information are deficient, though for political information they are highly developed.

A reasonably industrious woman, it appears, may have from four to six field plots from which she feeds her household. The yearly surplus she sells or distributes may amount to four sacks of manioc and four to six sacks of peanuts. Her husband owns half of what he has helped to produce, but the rule is not fixed; distribution of produce depends on the context of social relations. A good wife, the women say, gives her husband money from her sales, or more likely gives him foodstuffs he can sell himself, whether or not he has helped to produce them. A number of couples in the village, young and old, seem to operate in close partnership. A husband's obligation is to provide meat, store-bought foods such as sugar, and clothes for his wife and children; if he fails to do so, the obligation may be cited against him, but the "good husband" nowadays does much more, whatever may have been the custom in the past.

Both men and women, apart from their consignments to relatives in town, frequently give meals and small amounts of food to kinsmen of all kinds; for this reason commensality is no guide to the definition of the household. Those most frequently found eating together are close kinsmen, those who trace dyadic kinship links. Circulation of small amounts of food is one of the many functions of kinship; anyone who refused to participate would be renouncing his kinsmen and ultimately his own status. Many feel obliged to be more openminded in order to acquire as many friends or clients as possible, to demonstrate goodwill, and to counter jealousy and hostility. Persons with more money or greater prestige are more often called upon for small gifts, meals, and other assistance; how they respond depends on personal temperament, consideration for their own security, and their sense of what is right. These factors vary from one individual to another.

CONFLICTS

In principle, the big communal tracts used for field crops are exempted from conflicts over land rights. Whatever their political disagreements, NTUMBA and NANGA work adjacent plots in harmony; each could justify his use of the land by calling himself either the owner or the Child of the owner. In any event, the crop belongs exclusively to the producers, who are often a NANGA man and NTUMBA wife, or the reverse, but use of the land for a crop cycle of four or five years establishes no permanent right to the land itself.

Retrospectively, land usage may be confounded with landowner-ship, but the ambiguity is useful. MFUTU, NSAKA, and NKUTI say they own the land on which Mbanza Manteke is built, except for Yongo, which belongs to NZUZI and was given to the mission; and they can show the boundaries of their holdings. NZUZI's dogma is that the entire hilltop belongs to him, and that the boundaries remain from the days when the land was used for peanut cultivation. Thus the parties can agree to differ.

In practice, land disputes seem not to arise in connection with the field tracts (*maviye* or *bilanga*); at the present time the focus of con-flict is elsewhere. Disputes frequently arise in connection with the men's forest plots (*masole*), usually on account of fruit trees. A man alleges that another's slash-and-burn activities destroyed his fruit trees in the same or an adjacent plot, or else the possession of fruit trees is linked with possession of the land itself. Fruit trees once planted and matured produce a cash crop with little more labor; they are in-herited, and constitute a permanent asset of the lineage. On the other hand, after twenty years it may be hard to say who originally cleared the land and planted the trees; judgment turns on the testimony of witnesses and neighbors and belongs to the realm of the political, to the context of a lineage's relations within the clan and outside it.

Fruit trees thus form the perfect mediator between the economic and political spheres, the former characterized by communal coopera-tion, the latter by sharp competitive individuation of status. The men penetrate the forest and "found" a settlement, an act that establishes a complex of social relations but involves no productive labor as such and brings no direct economic return; the women plant peanuts in the grassland, an act in which productive effort produces an economic return in a few months, but does not modify the social structure. A conflict over fruit trees has immediate economic relevance, and its political obliqueness often makes it more expedient than an all-out confrontation over ownership of the land.

For what follows, the reader should recall that NANGA is divided into five houses — DISA, NKUTI, NSAKA, MFUTU, and NZUZI — of which MFUTU is divided into the five "TONA" lineages: SWETE, LEMBE, NDYENGO, NZIMBU, and YANGA. NZIMBU and YANGA, with their clients NA LOMBO, are the chief element in an MFUTU faction led by Hezekaya of SWETE which is at odds with almost every other landowner in the village.

The court cases examined here show how a limited dispute mobilizes political allegiances throughout the community.

In 1951 SWETE brought suit against NTAMBU for harvesting *nsafu* from trees on the tract in Ntombo in the Manteke valley; in the preceding generation both groups had planted trees there, but NTAMBU said that MFUTU's had burned. The court held that the land was NTAMBU's, but that his trees were the ones that had been burned (Mbanza Manteke 536, 1951).

This tract is one of several in the same area which were given to NTAMBU as a Child of NANGA. An element in the controversy is the division between NTAMBU and NA LOMBO; the latter, clients of MFUTU, regard themselves as the true NTAMBU and owners of all NTAMBU land rights. In describing the landholdings to me, MFUTU men tended to divide the entire landscape between themselves and NA LOMBO, with a few patches allotted in mere charity to MVIKA NTUMBA.

In 1957, as part of the continuing tension, Luwawa accused NTAMBU of working an MFUTU tract in the same area, damaging in the process some of his *n'safu* trees. Luwawa is a stranger, but spoke for his YANGA wife. According to him, NTAMBU had said, "You think your wife owns this land, but Makokila owns it." Makokila is a Child of NANGA; specifically, he is the son of Nsakala Nangudi of NDYENGO. He is on friendly terms with his "brother" NTAMBU, who is also a Child of NANGA, and the two extend cultivation rights to each other. Moreover, they share the view that the NZIMBU and YANGA lineages of MFUTU are illegitimate and have no land rights at all. NTAMBU's allegation is that his friend Makokila may speak on the use of this land, but that YANGA is not entitled to.

In his testimony NTAMBU said that his forebears had been given the land by NDYENGO and that therefore he was entitled to cultivate it. According to the court's summary, "NTAMBU says this is NANGA land which they gave long ago to their Children NTAMBU; [in reality,] because NTAMBU owns *n'safu* trees there, he thinks the land belongs to his clan," which the court called "NTAMBU or NA LOMBO." In that ambivalence lies the real point of the dispute, which extends far beyond the boundaries of any one plot of land. The court, holding that Luwawa was partly to blame for the damage, divided the expenses between the parties without settling anything (Mbanza Manteke 4, 1957).

MFUTU VERSUS NZUZI

Use of forest tracts for tree planting tends to appropriate lands to particular lineages of the owning house, as in the preceding case, in which NDYENGO is said to have particular rights to a certain tract. In grassland such rights are exerted by women; if the lineage has no women, the rights lapse. NDYENGO had cultivated land in a tract called Makasakasa, but his rights passed to LEMBE on his death. Since LEMBE has no women, the first say in the use of the land passes effectively to SWETE. This lineage also has no women active enough to cultivate, but when Nkomo of SWETE found a group of NZIMBU and YANGA women off "to divide up the land in Makasakasa" without mentioning the matter to his wife, he deemed their behavior part of a tendency toward territorial aggression on the part of those two lineages. As noted earlier, Nkomo is excluded from the faction led by Hezekaya.

In 1956 NZIMBU A TONA, speaking as MFUTU, disputed ownership of the forest of Mayombe with NZUZI. His tradition described Na Myposo as the original founder of Mbanza Ntala, to which Mayombe is an outlier. As neighbor and witness he called MPANZU. Asked how MPANZU came to have land in the valley, he explained that MFUTU had married an NGOMA woman to whom Mbanza Ntala had later been given, and that NGOMA had similarly imported an MPANZU woman who had been given land on the borders of Mayombe. NZUZI, he said, had cultivated in Mayombe as slaves of MPANZU, or something of the sort (the record is obscure).

MPANZU, denying MFUTU's account, claimed that he was the original settler in certain lands and that he also owned half of Mayombe, which had been given to him by his father NZUZI. Certain NZUZI women who were not slaves had come to live in that half because their *nkazi*, Ne Kwede, threatened to kill or enslave them, and they had sought refuge. MPANZU's testimony therefore contradicted MFUTU's.

NGOMA LUBOTA, called to testify, said that he knew nothing about having been married by MFUTU, but that in 1932, when there had been a dispute concerning Nsakala Nangudi, MFUTU and the other houses of NANGA had called their Child, Malanda Mika of NKAZI A KONGO, to show them their boundaries. (Malanda Mika, explained NZUZI to me, was the oldest man for miles around and had with his own eyes seen the land dispositions taken by elders long since gone.) He had told them, said NGOMA, that NZUZI of NANGA owned Mayombe, but that NGOMA was the founder and owner of Mbanza Ntala. Thus NGOMA seized the opportunity to assert that MFUTU really owns no land, in Mayombe or anywhere else.

NZUZI recited his claims to Mayombe (detailed on pp. 43–44) and then explained why Na Vuba of MFUTU had worked in the forest. It was agreed that Na Vuba had done so, and the fact that he had seemed to indicate that he owned the forest. NZUZI said, however, that Na Makokila of the LEMBE lineage of MFUTU, *nkazi* of NANGA, once killed Na Kinwani Kyatana Nzingu of NZUZI; NZUZI's Father NKAZI A KONGO was ready to declare war when Na Makokila agreed to hand over Na Vuba of MFUTU to replace Na Kinwani as the mainstay and *nkazi* of NZUZI. For this reason Na Vuba had cleared land in Mayombe and planted *n'safu* there. (Na Vuba belonged to NZIMBU A TONA; if the reputed origin of this lineage is correct, one of its members would be a likely choice to repay an MFUTU blood debt.)

MFUTU retorted that Na Vuba worked in Mayombe because he owned it, and his sisters' sons after him, but the court decided in favor of NZUZI (Mbanza Manteke 60, 1956), and MFUTU appealed to Matadi. Both sides told me that they had won the appeal; NZUZI even showed me a copy of the judgment to prove it. When it was pointed out to NZUZI that the copy showed the case resulting in a draw (as described below), he explained that the decision formally announced was merely a politic device to prevent hard feelings, and that the Belgian president of the court had privately assured him he was in the right.

This incident is typical of all situations in which Manteke people are required to witness to rights and wrongs. Like other upholders of authoritarian ideologies, they believe that truth is manifest, that to any problem there is only one right answer, and that in any conflict there is always one party at fault and one in the right. As Henry Richards described it, they believe that if a man is not a child of God he must be a child of the Devil, "for they have no concept of a neutral condition." In the words of Thomas Kanza, NKongo from Manianga and experienced politician, "For the Congolese, a discussion can only end with winners and losers, those who are right and those who are wrong" (Kanza, 1968, p. 58). If this black and white pattern is not immediately apparent, that is only because the party at fault is obscuring it to his own advantage; he is guilty, that is, of "politics." The French word *politique* is used almost interchangeably with the KiKongo *kindoki*, "witchcraft." Ordinary men are deceived by the devices of witchcraft which it takes supernatural resources to see through.

The same rigorous denial of the essential grayness of truth leads NZUZI to misrepresent the facts. If he were lying, he would be clever enough not to hand me the paper that disproves his statement. Yet his behavior is typical, and as a result truth is very scarce in Manteke, even among those who patently believe every word of their most preposterous accounts. Everybody forces the facts as he sees them into the pattern he feels they must fit. This is a universal human trait, but what seems to be the special development of the art in Kongo is related, I suggest, to institutional homogeneity combined with extreme politization. If NZUZI were to admit that judicial investigation had not declared MFUTU in the wrong when he cut down trees in Mayombe, he would admit that his entire tradition, which is the charter of his status, was questionable. In institutionally heterogeneous societies a defeat or status modification in one institutional field leaves the individual's status unchanged in other fields, but in homogeneous societies all institutionalized activities take place within the same structure of statuses and relationships. Yet, in Kongo, the structure itself is fundamentally ambiguous with regard, for example, to the rules of succession; experientially nothing is fixed, despite the definite patterns of the ideology. Uncertainty extends into everything; one can never be sure that another has done, or will do, what he says. Few people feel sufficiently secure not to attach more importance to the making and mending of alliances than to anything else.

The record of MFUTU's appeal from the Manteke judgment introduces the topic of the government's view of custom. On this occasion MPANZU testified that Mayombe belonged to MFUTU; his change of mind cost him a goat. NA LOMBO supported MFUTU, saying that she "had always heard" that Mayombe belonged to MFUTU. NTAMBU supported NZUZI, stating that Nsakala Nangudi, in the course of his quarrel with the rest of MFUTU, had publicly declared what all the landholdings were: "From his mouth I learned that Mayombe belonged to NZUZI, but I am not sure that what he said was true." Makokila of NKAZI A KONGO, Child of NANGA, confirmed that his father Nsakala Nangudi had said so.

Maleso of NDYENGO also appeared for NZUZI, as did a younger man of the rival NDYENGO line, who said, "My mother told me I shouldn't collect *nsafu* in Mayombe because NZUZI owned it."

COURT: You know that . . . [MFUTU] is your maternal uncle; why do you want to intervene in this affair?

YOUNG MAN: I testify against him because he said I was a slave, and must buy a pig to become a chief [*mfumu*, i.e., a freeman].

Faced with this contradictory evidence, the court told the parties to patch up their differences and said they could both go on using Mayombe as their ancestors did.

This kind of nonjudgment was frequently given, in like cases of intraclan conflict, by courts over which Europeans presided. Ignorance of the internal structure of what was believed to be a single land-holding collectivity, as revealed by the characteristically irrelevant use of the term "maternal uncle," made *la coutume* an impenetrable thicket and rendered rational decision impossible. On the other hand, in this case the judgment turned out to be politically wise, whether deliberately or not (Matadi 134, 1958); a definitive solution to the problem encompassed by the case is impossible.

DISA VERSUS MFULAMA NKANGA

Severe conflict between two factions, in which the most conspicuous issue is the ownership of a piece of land, erupts in other contexts, resulting in parallel accusations of witchcraft, seduction, insult, and assault. Such a situation prevails in Ndemba between DISA and MFULAMA NKANGA. DISA, whose tradition has been mentioned several times in this study, says that MFULAMA NKANGA fled from the ravages of NA NGOMBE in the Luima valley, arrived in the Manteke area "with his ears cut off," and sought refuge with DISA, who gave him lands. On the other hand, MFULAMA NKANGA, calling himself the original settler, gave a different account of the origins of DISA:

MFULAMA NKANGA married a woman called Tumbuka. The man's name was Nsyama Malombwa of Mbanza Mboma in Manteke. Her *nkazi*'s name was Nsakala Mbadi; his *nkazi*'s name was Na Kukuta. Tumbuka had a daughter called Myezi Bwa who married Masunda Fumbi of MFULAMA NKANGA, and another child, Nsyama Menga; then her husband died and she went back to Mbanza Mboma, but Nsyama Menga stayed in his father's village of Kinsona.

Mbanza Mboma belongs to NSAKA of NANGA, but the testimony does not indicate to which house of NANGA the *nkazi*, Nsakala Mbadi, belonged. Anyway, at the time these events are supposed to have taken place the structure of NANGA may have been considerably different. Nsyama Malombwa was apparently a Child of NANGA, into which he married and to which his children Myezi Bwa and Nsyama Menga belonged.

Myezi Bwa's *nkazi* Nsakala Mbadi borrowed money from his *nkwezi* Na Kukuta of MFULAMA NKANGA, and then again from Masunda Fumbi. Later he said to his *nkwezi* Masunda, "It would be a good thing if you took my *busi* Myezi Bwa as one who belonged to you [i.e., as a slave], since I have no money to repay you." Myezi Bwa was pregnant at the time with Kazayi Hana, conceived out of wedlock; Masunda Fumbi was annoyed and was jealous of the other man, Na Nlongo a Kwela. Later he and Myezi, now become his slave as well as his wife, had a child called Kambwasiku.
Some time afterward Nsyama Menga came to redeem his sister Myezi Bwa,

Kazayi Hana, and Kambwasiku, and paid the pig of rubbing with chalk.[6] Since these people had only their father's land to eat off, they were given these tracts. . . .

Then Kinkela Nzonza of NTUMBA in Ndemba married Madede Nlandu of Mbanza Mboma, but she left him. So he went to her *nkazi* Nsakala Mbadi to ask for his money back. Nsakala Mbadi had to borrow money from our ancestor Na Kasa of MFULAMA NKANGA, to whom he pawned[7] his *busi* Madede Nlandu. By her Na Kasa had a daughter, Manase Kyezi, and another called Nswami. Manase married my *n'kuluntu* Nsyama Ntengo and had several children. . . . They occupy the land given to Nsyama Menga, but to this day they have not redeemed Madede Nlandu. If you think this story isn't true, call DISA and have him show you, if he can, his villages and the old trees left by his ancestors, and their names and tombs. . . .

At present we suffer a good deal on account of these people. They sleep with our women, steal our money, and play the fool with the girls in the grass. They sought the death of their fathers by witchcraft, but the gun did not go off.[8]

This story shows that NANGA of Manteke and MFULAMA NKANGA of Ndemba regularly pawned dependents to each other. The origin of the group that calls itself the DISA house of NANGA is traced back to two different but linked transactions of this kind. The situation is confused by the presence in Ndemba, as clients, of a lineage recognized as slaves of NSAKA. As in other cases, it is extremely difficult to analyze tradition stratigraphically, to find out at what level in a long series of exchanges a particular modern group originated. The confusion resembles the telescoping of generations in a genealogy.

THE LANDOWNER'S SON

During the 1950's an area northwest of Mbanza Nkazi was the scene of a particularly violent and complex struggle which is still going on. The traditions on all sides, giving the usual histories of wars and slavery and offering fascinating glimpses of an antique social order, are too long-winded to be detailed here. A case concerning an unfortunate individual called George, however, reveals an interesting set of political alignments. The groups involved are apparently all landowning houses; one or two may in fact be lineages, but the court

6 *Ngulu ya kuswa luvemba.* Marking with white chalk, ordinarily on the temples, signifies purchase, separation, victory in court, innocence, and going free (Laman, 1936).

7 *Simbisa,* "to cause to hold."

8 Mbanza Manteke 85, 1956. This record is written in KiLeta. The word translated as "witchcraft" is *bunduki,* which means "gun" but has the same root as the KiKongo *kindoki,* "witchcraft." The word in the record translated as "gun" is the ordinary KiKongo word for gun, *n'kele.* The ambivalence between shooting and witchcraft is fundamental to Kongo magic and witchcraft theory. In 1965 the continuing dispute between MFULAMA NKANGA and DISA produced another accusation of shooting, characterized by the same ambivalence.

record does not permit discrimination; anyway, the segmentation of the descent group is not directly relevant. George was claimed as a slave by NANGA II and NTAMBU I (related only nominally to sections of these clans in Mbanza Manteke) who disputed possession of the tract of land he worked.

NTAMBU I said the land was his, not because he first settled it, but because it was given him by his Father NSUNDI I. He also said that the original NTAMBU I, Na Lungu, Child of NSUNDI, married a NANGA woman. She had two children. When one of them died no *nkazi* came to bury him, and none came when she herself died. So the remaining child, founder of NANGA I, became our "slave by default" (*mwan'a fundu*). Later on NTAMBU I moved across the river, giving the land to NANGA I but imposing by oath (*nloko*) the restriction that NANGA I could not dispose of it without first asking permission. The text says he was forbidden to eat it, that is, to exercise the prerogatives of *mfumu a n'toto*. The sequel shows that these prerogatives include the right to receive strangers.

To prove the existence of the restriction, NTAMBU I told how an MBENZA refugee had come to submit himself to NANGA I as his slave, and how NANGA I had first gone across the river to ask NTAMBU I if he could accept the slave.[9] NTAMBU I's complaint to the court was that NANGA II was appropriating the land and breaking the restriction.[10]

NANGA II said that his ancestor had bought the land from NTAMBU for three boxes of gunpowder and a gun, and called NTAMBU II as his witness. There was some question as to whether NANGA I and II were or were not the same group.

Each side called his Grandfather NSUNDI to testify; that is, they called NSUNDI I and NSUNDI II, respectively. The paternal, land-giving relationships may be summarized as follows:

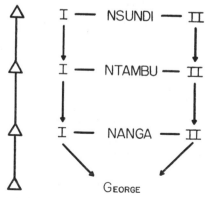

9 The submission procedure also involves *nloko*.
10 *Lembisanga nloko*, "calming the oath."

The court attempted to solve the problem by giving the land to George, but when the case was appealed to Matadi the higher court found the judgment unreasonable. It decided that NANGA II could not have bought the land because NTAMBU had it only as a gift from NSUNDI in the first place and therefore was not himself entitled to sell it (Mbanza Manteke 67, 1965; Matadi 406, 1966).

The NSUNDI groups called as witnesses had a land case of their own pending. The preceding year (1964) NANGA I had engaged in a dispute with NSUNDI II in which they called as witnesses, respectively, NDUMBU I and II, who had been conducting a running battle of their own throughout the 1950's.

In the course of the latter struggle NDUMBU I cut down some trees planted as a house enclosure by NDUMBU II, for which he was punished by the Manteke court. He appealed the verdict, alleging conspiracy and corruption. In his view planting an enclosure was an assertion of ownership of land that according to him was his own, but the appeal court held that trees were one thing, land was another. During the same period the parties and their allies accused each other of plotting rape and of planting charms of various sorts — all imaginable but mostly imaginary crimes, indicating tension. In such situations the court may have difficulty deciding whether to spend time on a half-dozen emotion-laden disputes or to strike at the heart of the matter by dealing with the land aspect.

In their court appearances NDUMBU I and II predictably involved their Children, NLAZA I and II, respectively. We see therefore a circus of landowners continually appearing in court as one another's witnesses. The situation represented above has been somewhat simplified; there are, for example, three houses of NDUMBU, not two, and two more that have died out. Moreover, patrifilial relationships posited between groups are interlaced with affinal and filial relations between individuals belonging to these and other groups. Nor is the content of such relations entirely predictable; in one case Father I invited Son I to move to his village, which he did, only to be kicked out shortly after by Father II, who suspected him of conspiring with Son II, between whom and Father II a land quarrel was in progress.

In situations of this kind the ambiguity of reckoning kinship by clans or individually acquires jural significance. Most of the elders of MVIKA NTUMBA in Manteke are the sons of NANGA men, mostly of the DISA house. MFUTU opponents of MVIKA therefore argue that MVIKA as a whole resides in the village only as Children of NANGA and that their land rights are merely those of clients. MVIKA retorts that collectively they own their land as *fondateurs*, and moreover as Fathers to MFUTU.

Similarly, in a Lemfu case, Philip argued that since Simon was his Child he could not be the owner of the land in dispute between them (Pool 19, 1953).

The first step toward settling a dispute over rights to land is to call a meeting of the elders of the groups concerned and their Children and Grandchildren. In practice, the elders who come are those who live in nearby villages and who are continually involved in the group's affairs. Others who live in town make an effort to be present if they hear a particular relationship to the parties or if they have a generalized interest in regional politics. A meeting called in July 1965 by NKAZI A KONGO of Tendele, a village some 3 miles northwest of Mbanza Manteke, was attended by upward of 150 people. The men sat around a large *n'sanda* tree, the partisans of the two sides selecting more or less opposite sides of the circle. In general, the more senior the elder the better the chair he was invited to sit in, but there were no precise distinctions.[11] Many of those present were youths, Angolan refugees, and other outsiders. Not all those spoke who had a specific relationship such as Child or neighboring landowner, and not all those who spoke had such a relationship. One or two women also had something to say, but "the fly whisk goes the round of the men before it reaches the women;" the women sat to one side on mats.

The dispute reached its crisis in a quarrel between two women who had been cultivating in a nearby valley. Certain young trees had been rooted up, and insults referring to slave status had been exchanged. One of the women opened the proceedings by presenting a small *mbungu* to the *nkazi* of the lineage NSUKA FUNSU, demanding to know her pedigree (*lusansu*) — that is, whether she was a slave or not — the implication being that, if she was not a slave, she was entitled to use the disputed piece of land without asking permission from someone else. NSUKA FUNSU was not her own lineage, however, and the *mbungu* was simply a device for introducing a debate over the relative status in the clan section of this lineage and of another lineage, NSAMBU FUNSU, neither of which had a direct interest in the land. The promoter of the meeting, NSUKA FUNSU, was carrying on a dispute which turned out to be the main dispute in NKAZI A KONGO, extending back at least thirty years and entangling most of its segments. On the second day everybody went down to look at the land in question and the

[11] I was grateful that a particularly comfortable chair, as chairs go, was reserved for me, day after day.

uprooted saplings, but the scope of the debate soon exceeded this narrow framework, which disappeared from sight.

In the first two days of the debate, the question at issue was presented by the owning lineages to the Children and Grandchildren. Each speaker first made a courteous round of the elders present, as at a funeral. In theory, only he who holds the fly whisk speaks; he yields it when necessary to another speaker. In practice, proceedings were not that orderly, and it seemed at times that the loudest voice carried the day. Speeches were interrupted by songs proposed either by one of the speakers or by somebody else who had thought of one he considered appropriate. Some of the songs are in the traditional idiom, brief, allusive, and frequently incomprehensible to all but local people. Since on this occasion it was a question whether the clan section would split up, unable to reconcile its differences, one song was heard several times:

> E, nsangu, nlangu, e zimwangan'e,
> Nsangu, nlangu, e tala! zimwangan'e
> Katutengulanga kanda dyangana ko.

> See, the news has spread like water!
> It's nobody's clan but our own we're breaking up.

Other songs, in European idiom, are derived from the Baptist and prophetic churches. One that has come to be associated with the forensic search for truth, clearing away deceit and confusion, draws a parallel with the role of the prophet:

E zindoki zazonsono, nukubama kweno;	Witches, all get ready;
Mwan'a muntu se ukangala.	The son of man comes forth.
E kwe! E kwe!	E kwe! E kwe!
Kanutiinandi bangukwa ko;	Do not run from the ordeal;
Zulu ye n'toto se biningana	Earth and sky will shake
Mwan'a muntu se ukangala.	As the son of man comes forth.

Kinene Jean, the prophet of Kinkanza, is said to have originated this song:

Mawonso bu maswemingi,	When all things were hidden,
Ngunza wasolele mo.	The prophet disclosed them.
Mu mbandu yayi	In this generation
Maswekama se masoluka	The hidden things shall be revealed,
Makangama se makutuka	The closed shall be opened
Ntangu bu ilungane.	When the time comes.

A symphony of songs, speeches, and choral responses continued for four days, the orators flogging the air with proverbs and fly whisks without apparently making much progress. No deep mysteries of customary law were in fact being argued; the entire meeting was an exercise in pure politics, a sounding-out of the support for various positions, while the hard facts and precise statements that might have made compromise impossible were carefully avoided.

Toward the end of the session one side addressed an *mbungu* to the *nkazi* of NKAZI A KONGO, who had largely kept silent and who was not presiding over the gathering. He got up, made a speech, and then began to dance. In the tremendous excitement that followed, everyone joined in the song and ululating women rushed out with cloths to tie around the *nkazi*'s waist. Others put money in his mouth. The spectacle deliberately invoked the profoundest sentiments of *fu kya nsi* ("traditional custom"), associated with the image of the chief dancing in the midst of the clans with *mbeele a lulendo*, "the sword of power." At the height of the frenzy he would announce his decision (*nzengo*, from *zenga*, "to cut"), one of those terrifying decisions that mark the true chief: to kill, to burn, to expel.

On this occasion in Tendele NKAZI A KONGO carried no sword, only a staff that despite its brass nails was little more symbolic than a walking stick. The entire meeting, though it lacked the traditional trappings, was nevertheless consciously a religious occasion; as Hezekaya, Child of NKAZI A KONGO, pointed out when he called for an opening prayer one day, any decision arrived at would be an act of God, a function of the spirit (*mpeve*). Hymns, biblical analogies, and references to sin and suffering continued the theme.

After finishing his dance and commenting on his role, the *nkazi* announced his decision: the parties should patch up their differences, sign an agreement not to quarrel over the land, and eat a goat together. The decision settled nothing; NSUKA FUNSU, after a private conference, rejected it. They proposed to pay a pig to the Children and Grandchildren to have them clean the cemetery, after which the parties would take an oath at the grave of the first settler on the land in question. The other side, in turn, rejected this proposal, saying that to support their case they needed to call one of their kinsmen from Matadi who commanded relevant traditions. The meeting then adjourned in discord. According to NSUKA FUNSU, the other side was afraid of the proposed ordeal, which would result in the death of one or more members of the party that was in the wrong. There appeared to me, however, to be widespread skepticism regarding the worth of trial by ordeal.

Graced by the presence of the man from Matadi, the meeting resumed in September. He turned out to be, not an authority on tradition, but a man of huge girth, with voice and personality to match, who could obviously be a formidable aid to his side, like an armored car among infantry. But he also turned out to have little taste for the battle, several times throwing his weight on the side of compromise. After further efforts in this direction, thick with subtle allusions to buried metaphors of *fu kya nsi*, the decision was reached to go into the fundamentals at issue: *se tutima*, "let's dig."

Before this decision was reached, the meeting heard the views of neighboring landowners who discoursed inconclusively for some hours. An *mbungu* went back to the *nkazi* of NKAZI A KONGO at one point, but he returned it with the comment that his proffered solution had already been rejected. The tone of the meeting then lost some of the good humor that had marked it, and there was talk of splitting the clan and of the risk that some of the people most immediately involved, particularly the women, might become sick or die as a result of the ill will engendered. *Mbungu* were presented successively to the Children and Grandchildren, the Fathers and Grandfathers (*mataata ye mayaaya*), in the hope of finding an acceptable compromise. These different means (*nzila*) were consciously differentiated; if one failed to work, another was tried. The proceedings were accompanied by songs, proverbs, and allusive oratory conveying very little solid information:

E bataata, nwiz'e
E mpasi tumonanga mu dyambu dya kindoki e.

You fathers come;
We are suffering because of witchcraft.

Dweta, se tudweta.

Let us taste it, consider the matter carefully.

Kuku, e, vila, vila! [12]

A bird sings in the forest; we do not understand what it says
[some deception is involved].

O mpeve wiiza, o wiiza,
O wiiza watusadisa.

O Spirit, come,
Come to help us.

[12] There were apparently no other words to these songs, except that the first song is a common form into which any appropriate words can be put.

After several days of meetings interspersed with singing and oratory, some of the Children asked to hear the relevant traditions. When their request was granted a quite different kind of speech, recounting traditions like those presented at length in earlier chapters, was heard. The components of NKAZI A KONGO were listed during the discussions as lineages (*mafuta*); usually houses would be listed, at least initially, but here the structure of the houses was the primary matter in dispute (see table 4).

TABLE 4

SEGMENTATION OF THE CLAN SECTION NKAZI A KONGO
ACCORDING TO NSAMBA FUNSU

House[1]	Lineage[2]	Representative
NSIMBA [3]		
NZUZI	NSAMBA FUNSU	Maleka
	ZALA DYA FUNSU	Kinkela Mpaka
	WUMBA WA FUNSU	Yobo
NLANDU	NSUKA FUNSU	Kyangana
	NKENGE A MPANZU	Makola
	NKALA MPANZU	Tsaka
	MVEMBA NDULU	Tsaka
	MAZANGI MA NDULU	Isaac
	NSOMPU A NLANDU	Mayuma
	ZINGA DYA NLANDU	Masampu
NKULA [4]		

[1] The names of the houses are the standard series given to twins and children born after them.

[2] The names of the lineages refer to such charms (*min'kisi*) as Funsu, Mpanzu, etc. The last two lineages on the list belong on the other side of Kyesa Kifwa, near the river, and did not enter into the dispute between NSAMBA FUNSU and NSUKA FUNSU.

[3] This house died out fairly recently.

[4] This house died out long ago.

The three-level structure of NKAZI A KONGO is like that of NANGA, which I have presented as though it were universal. So it is, but only as an abstract model which is not necessarily realized in every clan section at any one time. Examples of variations have already been shown among the groups in Manteke village. The variations occur in the course of the expansion, contraction, and reorganization of the groups in a continuous political progress. The division into houses is supposedly related to an initial division of the land at the time of the original foundation, an act of chiefship (*kimfumu*). People sadly remark that land is no longer portioned out, there being no chiefs. Comparative analysis shows, however, that the process of reorganization and reapportionment still continues, although it is not, and probably never was, made up of specific acts. The material offered in evidence at the Tendele meetings gives an idea of how the uncertainty of group relations is related to change.

Two of the lineages listed in table 4, MVEMBA NDULU and NKALA MPANZU, are said to be represented by the same individual, Tsaka, who is headman of the village of Ntombo a Nkazi. In 1961 or so, in the course of a dispute, some of Tsaka's brethren accused him of witchcraft, and he replied with a statement of tradition pointing out "where each one had come from." After that most of the village moved off to a new site, thus completing a classical scenario. For outsiders it is now difficult to say whether the NDULU groups are subdivisions of NKALA MPANZU or not. We may assume it was more tactful for NSAMBA FUNSU to list the lineages in this way.

Tsaka himself, who was not present at Tendele, was later summoned to testify in court. Because his land is farther east, he recognized NSUKA FUNSU as a neighbor but disclaimed knowledge of its relations with NSAMBA FUNSU. Yet he was positive that NKENGE A MPANZU was senior to NKALA MPANZU and its legitimate heir. His testimony suggests that, from his point of view, the houses NSIMBA, NZUZI, and NLANDU do not exist, or do not properly express the grouping of the lineages, which should be considered as organized (following the indications of their names) into the houses FUNSU, MPANZU, and NLANDU. Tsaka's testimony was marginal to the main dispute between NSAMBA FUNSU and NSUKA FUNSU, which centered on land left by the house NSIMBA whose three lineages had all died out. NSAMBA FUNSU said that NSIMBA's heir was NZUZI, and he claimed the land as senior representative of NZUZI on behalf of ZALA DYA FUNSU, whose members were actually using it.

NSUKA FUNSU, which is domiciled in Tendele near the land in question, told the story given below in order to disqualify NSAMBA FUNSU, which is domiciled in Mbanza Nkazi. Both groups accepted the division into houses as listed in table 4, but it was clear that this structure referred only to rights in land in the region adjacent to Tendele, between Mbanza Nkazi and Ntombo a Nkazi. To NKALA MPANZU of Ntombo a Nkazi, as we have seen, the structure was apparently different.[13]

---

[13] When the ownership of the land in question was settled, a number of other questions were patently ignored, principally that of the status of WUMBA WA FUNSU. The Manteke court, in summing up, specifically excluded NSAMBA FUNSU from the Tendele area but left open the matter of its land rights in Mbanza Nkazi.

THE TRADITION OF NKAZI A KONGO
AS PRESENTED BY NSUKA FUNSU

Dramatis Personae

NSIMBA, an original settler (now extinct).

Slave Group I, bought by NSIMBA (now extinct).

Slave Group II, bought by Group I, now occupying the land.

Slave Group III, of obscure origin, also occupying the land, and known as ZALA DYA FUNSU.

NZUZI, a worthy young man, the true heir of NSIMBA.

NLANDU, sibling to NZUZI and NSIMBA and also an original settler; here represented by NSUKA FUNSU, a champion of justice.

NSAMBA FUNSU, an adventurer, masquerading as NZUZI, but in reality neither a sibling to NSIMBA nor an original settler; in league with ZALA DYA FUNSU.

NKULA, defunct sibling to NSIMBA.

In the Luima valley in the east there were four houses of NKAZI A KONGO [see list above] which suffered from the depredations of NA NGOMBE. Their chief therefore sent young men westward, where they met, first, the predecessors of the group NKALA MPANZU, then those of NKENGE A MPANZU, who welcomed them as fellow clansmen. [NSUKA FUNSU's spokesman insisted that he obtained land in Tendele as a first occupant, and that he was not beholden to his neighbors for it; there was evidently something forced about this assertion, and the relationship between NSUKA FUNSU and the other lineages supposedly of the NLANDU house remained obscure.]

Having settled, NSUKA FUNSU summoned his brethren from the east. The house NKULA had already died out. NSIMBA, having arrived in Tendele and seeing his house threatened with a like fate, bought a woman who subsequently had three sons. In the same period a completely different group of NKAZI A KONGO, the predecessors of NSAMBU FUNSU, arrived from elsewhere and were allowed to live with NSIMBA, NZUZI, and NLANDU. In time, Na Bunga, the *nkazi* of the new arrivals, presided at the burials of the slave woman's three sons, the real NSIMBA having died out by this time. On the strength of this story NSAMBA FUNSU asserts that he is the legitimate successor of NSIMBA, and ipso facto that he is of the house of NZUZI.

Not so [says NSUKA FUNSU]: Na Bunga of NSAMBA FUNSU presided at the funerals and was allowed to inherit certain goods, but only as the delegate of the *nkazi* of NKAZI A KONGO, Malanda Mika of NSUKA FUNSU. The real heir to NSIMBA is a second group of slaves bought by the three sons; their representatives cultivate the land now. The other group also cultivating it, ZALA DYA FUNSU, are not NZUZI either; they are a third group of slaves brought in still later. The real NZUZI is a young man not previously mentioned. NSAMBA FUNSU, though admittedly belonging to NKAZI A NONGO, cannot claim a position in any of the three houses related to the land in question.

In reply, NSAMBA FUNSU based his case on the factors already indicated, the tradition handed down by Na Bunga and two court actions in 1937 and 1939 which showed, he said, that the affair had already been decided in his favor.[14] His presentation, like the preceding one, was interrupted by songs felt by others to be appropriate and by intermezzos such as the following: someone raises a question which the speaker appears to reject; a Child gets up and lays down the law that all questions shall be entertained; eight others express concurring opinions, and two more sing songs. After a final flurry of chanted responses, the speaker is able to resume his theme.

Since no clear answer emerged from the recital of tradition, the Children and Grandchildren were offered an *mbungu* of 100 francs and asked for their views. Their spokesman rejected the offering on the ground that a goat at 500 francs would be appropriate to ask for forgiveness for having already turned down the Children's views. When this sum had been put down, the Children went into conference (at one such conference twenty-seven men were present). The personnel on these different committees frequently overlapped; in particular, the *nkazi* of the clan section is himself also a Child and a Grandchild, his father having been a slave of NKAZI A KONGO. In trying to add weight to the authority of his opinions, the *nkazi* stressed that he encompassed in his person the four regulatory roles, the "four corners" of the affair.[15]

While the search for means was still going on, the *nkazi* made a masterly speech in which he proposed that the matter be referred to the *bambuta* (elders), that is, a select group of senior *bankazi* chosen by himself. The speech was so eloquent that his proposal was adopted, and the new committee decided that the land at issue should be divided. The pressure for compromise and for a result that would permit everyone to get back to work compelled acceptance of the decision, although no one felt privately that that was the end of the matter. It is not land per se that the parties to such disputes are after, but the definition of status, of which the allocation of titles to land is a consequence and an expression. As an experienced elder put it, "What they want is *kimfumu* ["authority"]; if the land is theirs, they may not want to use it, but you have to go to them to ask permission before *you* can use it."[16]

The Tendele affair was taken to court in April 1966 by NSAMBA FUNSU. Much the same evidence was heard all over again by five judges,

14 When I pointed out that the records of these cases are in fact consistent with the claims of either side, supporters of NSAMBA FUNSU said, in effect, "Ah! but you have to read between the lines!"

15 He used the words *ngyatekulwa, ngyabutwa, ngyavuwa,* which are passive forms of the verbs "to ramify," "to engender," and "to own."

16 Where the commercial use of land, trees, and minerals has been introduced, the motivation is usually different. Matadi and Kasangulu records are full of cases explicitly related to cash revenues generated by commercial concessions.

some of whom had been present at the customary hearings. Accepting the position of NSUKA FUNSU, they fined NSAMBA FUNSU for attempted territorial aggrandizement. Much weight was given to the testimony of the Senior Child (*mwana wa mbuta*), who said that he had been instructed in the matter by his father Malanda Mika (cf. Ngoma, 1963, p. 35). This testimony supported NSUKA FUNSU in the main, but contradicted it in some respects. The court also paid attention to the testimony of the representative of the second group of slaves, who admitted freely that his *nkaaka* had been bought; but, he said, "a man is bought, but not an *mvila*, and my *mvila* is MBENZA." He had been left on this land by its late owners and had thus become a freeman (*mfumu*) as the owner of land (*mfumu a n'toto*); nor would he consider going back to MBENZA and his place of origin unless someone were to arise again in the place of NSIMBA. According to him, he *is* NSIMBA, and NZUZI (the young man mentioned above) is his heir. The court accepted this position. Both sides also said that that was what they wanted; each went back to its village and held a victory party, and each side informed me that it had won.

As indicated, NKAZI A KONGO is a complex and far-flung group. It seems to have been held together in the preceding generation by Na Bunga and Malanda Mika, who as rivals for the *kinkazi* zealously attended funerals and other functions for miles around and in the process kept the office alive. There are signs of the incomplete merging of traditions; NSUKA FUNSU is evidently a relatively recent arrival in the area and still maintains good contacts in the Luima valley, where it may even be entitled to land. Also, no two versions of the list of lineages and their representatives are exactly alike; a settlement is possible only by careful exclusion of potential disputes not directly relevant to the point at issue.

The status accorded to "the new NSIMBA" draws attention once more to the ambiguity of succession rules. On the one hand, "No slave can own land"; on the other, "No landowner is a slave." In the dispute between NDUMBU I and NDUMBU II, the former took away emblems of chiefship belonging to the latter on the ground that NDUMBU II was a slave. NDUMBU II replied that he had been a slave but had been redeemed; that he owned land and had acquired the appropriate emblems of *kimfumu* ("freedom"). This answer, of course, denied NDUMBU I's claim to a *kimfumu* ("authority") of a somewhat higher order, paramountcy over the group as a whole (Mbanza Manteke 42, 1956).

From the Manteke court a case may be appealed to the territorial court in Songololo, where the procedure is much the same but costs more. The judges, or rather the assessors who advise the presiding official, are drawn from other communes. From the territorial court appeal is possible to the Parquet (i.e., the magistrature applying the written law of the land), but only on the ground that due process has not been observed; the Parquet does not concern itself with the substance of judgments.

On the whole the system for settling land disputes works very well. It is the only system instituted by the colonial regime which operates in the rural areas not only effectively but as it was intended to do. Its chief virtue lies in the fact that it bridges the gap between government and custom, which are otherwise opposed ideologically, institutionally, and politically. Yet to extol the system for its effectiveness is not to say that a large proportion of land disputes have been settled or are likely to be settled in the near future. On the contrary, it is notorious that land cases drag on for generations, and that once "settled" they erupt again in some new guise. Government and people alike deplore the interminable litigation as the result of "politics," which they feel is a social evil. Land disputes carrying status-defining functions are indeed the primary channel of political activity in rural society, which would be radically changed were this channel not available.

RESIDENCE AND RIGHTS

A majority of land cases are decided, not on the merits of the traditions presented by the parties, but on the testimony of witnesses. Witnesses may produce detailed traditions of their own, but often their testimony is no more than "we have always heard that . . ." or "we recognize Na Mpamba as our neighbor." Success therefore depends partly on how much support the litigant can find in his community. When the fight is fierce and the stakes are high, collusions called *fronts communs* develop, particularly in the event of a circus like the one described above.

Supporting testimony is valuable quantitatively and qualitatively. Although the theory of land tenure validates the testimony only of structurally relevant witnesses, at traditional gatherings noise and physical numbers have their effect, and the government courts will hear several witnesses even from the same lineage. In either situation, the elders say it is advantageous to have a crowd at one's back. Besides offering testimony, supporters can give advice and help defray expenses, which even in Manteke may easily run to 30,000 francs.

Supporters are not all members of the house or the clan concerned in the dispute. *Bisi Manteke* living in Kasangulu can arrive at an approximation of the state of politics at home by watching the Children and Grandchildren going down on the train from Kinshasa to Lufu. Nsiku Damison of NSUNDI, Oldest Child to NGOMA LUBOTA, explained that in the event of an encounter in court between NGOMA and MFUTU he as a judge would not be able to advise his Fathers in private conference (*ku nenga*), but that the next senior Child, an NTAMBU man, would come down from Kinshasa to see to it. The existence of these invisible armies makes it difficult to judge the real relative strength of opposed parties, although it is clear, for example, that NGOMA (two adult residents) is not so weak compared with MFUTU (twenty-four) as might appear at first.

Before the village of Mbanza Manteke was constituted, the *nkazi* of each house lived on his land with some of the members of his house and their spouses and a collection of slaves, classificatory children, and other dependents. Pointing out the old dwelling sites in the Manteke valley, an informant said: "There in Ndembolo sat MVIKA NTUMBA with his Children and Grandchildren; in Mbanza Ntala, NGOMA LUBOTA with his . . . ," and so on.

In an affair with another group (as in the Nsimbila War), Children, affines, and others would be summoned from elsewhere, but the main body of supporters was probably in residence; at least they did not have to come from Kinshasa or Matadi. The residential unit or village (*vata*) associated with each house (*vumu*) might be divided into hamlets (*belo*; pl., *bibelo*) associated with component lineages (*mafuta*). With reference to land, lineages are usufructuary groups; they include slaves and inmarrying women, for example, who "eat off" the land but are not among its "owners" (in the sense of the verb *vwa*, "to own"), but depend upon the favor of the owners. The latter are not necessarily all residents, but it is essential to the maintenance of their rights that they participate in the group's affairs by attendance at funerals, land disputes, and the like.

Table 5 shows the pattern of residence in Mbanza Manteke, by descent group and by four categories of residents, in 1965. Adult men are those who are over school age (i.e., those who are more than eighteen years old). The subclass "sons" includes adult men whose fathers belonged to groups domiciled in Manteke village as landowners or clients. Adult women are marriageable women, which means that they are about sixteen or older. The subclass of married women includes those who are living with or have lived with a Manteke man, whether the latter is alive or dead.

Owners in the strict sense are members of the matrilineal house. The patrilateral affiliates of the house, including fathers, have a privileged

TABLE 5
RESIDENCE OF ADULTS IN MBANZA MANTEKE, 1965

Descent group	Adult men	Sons	Adult women	Married women
GROUPS THAT OWN LAND LOCALLY				
NANGA	19	2	22	11
NTUMBA	9	7	14	8
MPANZU	4	4	8	6
NTAMBU	5	3	6	6
MBENZA	3	1	5	4
Total	40	17	55	35

Total men and women: 95
Percentage of adult men in total: 42.1
Percentage of sons among adult men: 42.5
Percentage of married women among adult women: 63.6

	Adult men	Sons	Adult women	Married women
GROUPS THAT DO NOT OWN LAND LOCALLY				
NKAZI A KONGO	3	3	5	3
NSUNDI	10	7	5	4
MFULAMANKANGA	5	3	4	4
MBENZA	1	..	9	6
NANGA	..	..	1	1
NTUMBA	..	..	5	4
NLAZA	1	..	8	5
NSAKU	..	..	2	2
NKUWU	..	..	1	1
NA LUKUTI	..	..	5	4
NA MVEMBA	..	..	2	2
NDAMBA NGOLO	..	..	2	1
Total	20	13	49	37

Total men and women: 69
Percentage of adult men in total: 29.0
Percentage of sons among adult men: 65.0
Percentage of married women among adult women: 75.5

	Adult men	Sons	Adult women	Married women
ALL GROUPS				
Total	60	30	104*	72*

Total men and women: 164
Percentage of adult men in total: 36.6
Percentage of sons among adult men: 50.0
Percentage of married women among adult women: 69.2

*The difference of 32 between the total number of married women and the total number of adult women includes 12 women who lived elsewhere while married and were either widowed or separated from their husbands, and 20 women born in Manteke who presumably were never married.

relationship: their requests for land to use can scarcely be denied, and whether or not they are using the land they should defend the title to it against challenge by other matrilineal houses. Both owners and affiliates are said to have the right (*luve*) to use the land and pronounce upon its disposition. The traditional village organization has been disrupted, but these rights have not been changed.

Although the distinction between residence and participation is important analytically, the confusion of the two produces another of the ambiguities one may describe as operationally necessary. In disparaging an opponent's tradition a villager may say, "He wasn't born here," or "His mother wasn't born here." The double implication is, "He wasn't on the spot to acquire the knowledge he pretends to," and "If he really had right to land here he would have been born here." [17] Similar ambiguity appears in the excuses most frequently given by those who prefer "not to know" the tradition on a particular point: "We weren't born over there," or "We do not share a boundary with them," and the related "I don't know what happened because I was too young in those days." These excuses, though incompatible with the dominant argument that tradition is a birthright, preserved if necessary by direct inspiration, have the advantage of permitting tactical flexibility.

For the establishment and maintenance of rights, then, filiation is primary, participation necessary, and residence advisable.[18] Thus a group of NTAMBU brothers, whose conflicts with NANGA have been described, live on their land in Nsimbila "to keep MFUTU from stealing it," but their *nkazi* lives in Manteke in order to represent them and because he is Oldest Child to NANGA. The *nkazi* of MBENZA lives in Manteke for different reasons. His village, Paza, was destroyed in precolonial times by war, but the land has since been returned to MBENZA. When I asked him why he did not reestablish the village, he said, "If enough of my kinsmen were to ask me, I might; but they would have to accept my authority, so that I could tell Kingani to cultivate here, and you, Kyankaka, cultivate there. . . . Yes, I might." In that day MBENZA would wear his bracelets once again.

THE EVOLUTION OF TRADITION

One evening I asked a group of friends gathered around the palm wine what motivated MFUTU in its efforts to assert ownership of

---

[17] A woman sometimes returns to her mother's home, which is not necessarily in her own or in her mother's native village, to give birth, but usually it is the mother who visits her daughter for this event.

[18] "L'idée d'un lien de propriété purement abstrait est donc mal integrée; c'est par la présence physique que l'on affirme et que l'on maintient ses droits fonciers" (Dufour, 1963, p. 180).

Mbanza Ntala. They roared and slapped their knees and swore that no stranger, least of all a European, could hope to grasp the root of the differences between MFUTU and NGOMA LUBOTA: "Even MFUTU, when he thinks he's got down to the foundation, has only got down as it were to the concrete floor overlying the foundation. If we really dug down to the foundation there'd be hardly anyone who could go on living in Manteke."

The metaphor is a structural one, recalling the connotations of the word *nsi*, which means a region or a country; *kisi nsi* is the culture of a particular region. *Nsi* also means "the underneath"; *ku nsi a nlangu*, "under the water." The expression *ku nsi a n'kulu*, "in the old days," recalls both senses: the country as it was in the days of the ancestors beneath, and the *bakulu*, who are the foundation. A clan, they say, is like a house; the walls must follow the foundations, although in the later stages there may be accretions and modifications obscuring the original outline. The application of this model to land tenure is two-fold: to the map of landholdings, and to the forensic process in which titles to land are attacked and defended.

An inventory of landholdings in Manteke is little more than a cata-logue of disputes, most of which concern title to the land; only a few relate to boundaries, but there is no universal agreement on these either. If all titles to land were definitively established, litigation would scarcely abate, but would turn on boundary marks.[19]

The usual boundaries are the edges of forests; watersheds are im-portant but, in contrast with Ntandu practice, stream beds are rarely used. The forest on both sides of a valley is usually, therefore, a single holding. Such a holding may be divided into upper and lower portions which belong to different parties. The Nkenge valley is one such hold-ing; MVIKA says he gave the lower half to MFUTU, but MFUTU says that he gave the upper half to MVIKA! Around Ntombo in the Manteke val-ley the holdings are small, comprising perhaps only an acre or two, and the boundaries follow straight lines between conspicuous trees.

The land map (see map 3) gives an idea of the distribution of holdings among the groups claiming them: NANGA, consisting of NKUTI,

[19] "Le problème foncier n'est pas une question de bornage. Il est l'expression du conflit interne de ces sociétés segmentaires. Sa source se situe plus profondément encore que dans la crise d'autorité actuelle. Celle-ci l'aggrave seulement." After making this diagnosis, similar to mine in this study, Doutreloux offers a contrasting prescription: "La dégradation des institutions a entraîné celle des traditions orales. Ils disent souvent 'Ces choses sont trop loin.' 'Nous, maintenant, nous ne savons plus . . .' Il faudrait alors rassembler patiemment quantité de généalogies receuillies à des sources diverses et par une comparaison serrée tenter d'en tirer au moins des approximations" (Doutreloux, 1959, pp. 505 ff.).

NSAKA, MFUTU, and NZUZI; NTUMBA, consisting of MVIKA NTUMBA and NGOMA LUBOTA; MPANZU; and NTAMBU, including NA LOMBO. Each group has more lands than are shown on the map and also has considerable acreage beyond the area covered by the map. The MPANZU estate, however, is obviously smaller than the others. NGOMA LUBOTA says he owns Mbanza Ntala, Mbuku, and adjacent areas, as well as certain tracts in the lower Nkenge valley. He says he sold or gave part of Mfula to Nsiku Nsesi of MFUTU-NDYENGO, Kuba to a predecessor of Kingalu's in MFUTU-LEMBE, and one of the Nkenge tracts to Na Bikadyo of MFUTU-SWETE "who was buried on it, which proves she had no land of her own." All three of the "original" MFUTU lineages are thus represented as having been landless clients of NGOMA; the physical distribution of the lands they were given, in relation to Mbanza Ntala, is said to corroborate their landlessness.[20]

The idea, as frequently explained to me with the aid of little drawings in the dust or on the backs of envelopes, is that the land map, properly interpreted, reveals the outlines of the original territory (*nsi*) centered on the founding ancestor's *mbanza*. Originally (*ku nsi a nkulu*), that is, the land map looked like the diagram given on page 31: a rectangle bounded on the north by NKAZI A KONGO, on the west by MBENZA, and on the south and east by whoever are your best friends in those directions (I try not to take sides). Even granting the reasonable claims of this or that party, the map shows nothing of the sort; but one can imagine the universal shout, "Ah! but you've only got down to the floor; what about the real foundations?"

The tendency of BaKongo to organize the visible and historical landscape into simple, bounded, and symmetrical forms has already been noted. The tendency results from the nature of their religious thinking and has little to do with geography and mapping in the European sense (cf. P. Bohannan, 1963). For Manteke village no maps of landholdings exist. Although every elder can give a list of his lands and indicate more or less exactly their boundaries, the assumption that a kind of unwritten map exists is unwarranted. The notion of *nsi*, the large exclusive territory of an original *mbanza*, cannot refer to a deduction from such a protomap; it exists as an ideological function. Alternative possible interpretations of the physical distribution of holdings are as much sociological as geographical in their referents.

The structural aspect of the forensic process is expressed in the application of the principle of the ripeness of time. A considerable degree of indefiniteness in the empirical social structure is not only

---

[20] Kimpumpu, to the south, was the subject of a lawsuit in 1941; MVIKA lost after Malanda Mika testified in favor of MFUTU (Mbanza Manteke 40, 1941).

tolerable but necessary. Every elder considers that his rights are being infringed, but only in some cases is he ready to take action. He accumulates his list of grievances and waits until the time is ripe.

In a dispute taking the form of rival claims to land the present distribution of lands may be taken more or less as it is, with the implication that the testimony of any of the present occupants is admissible. Should the dispute be more far-reaching, the parties seek "to dig deeper," denying validity to the testimony of those whose local antecedents are supposedly more recent. In theory, the segmentary reduction of the land map and of the social structure could be taken simultaneously to the level at which only the direct heir of the original settler remained, confronting four homologous figures across the boundaries of his impressive domain. The possibility, though illusory, guides people as mirages can guide them.

For the ultimate reduction to occur would require a perfect tradition (*kinkulu*). It is unreasonable to suppose that any elder in Kongo is master of the answers to all the questions that might reasonably be asked of him, although people frequently judge actual examples of tradition by this standard. "It won't do to say, 'In Mbanza Nkulu we met Na Nkala Nene,' and leave it at that. You should be able to say how long you remained there, what gifts were exchanged . . ." In practice, the more elaborate *kinkulu* is the more persuasive. It appears, moreover, that *kinkulu* of this sort is a relatively new development, a response to the new rules laid down by the government.

Ku nsi a n'kulu, a meeting such as the one at Tendele would have been attended by the opposing *bankazi*, each backed by his warriors ready to surround him if need be. The evidence of tradition is that negotiation over fine points of title did not last long, and that little wars over minor issues occurred frequently. Warfare was a highly magical business, virtually an ordeal in which the parties, after suitable ritual preparation, submitted their opposing claims to otherworldly powers; the first side to lose a life lost the verdict, and the war was over. Inside corporate groups divination and ordeals of other kinds served a similar purpose. During World War I Henry Richards found it hard to explain to the elders of Mbanza Manteke why Europeans kept on fighting after thousands had been killed; they found this practice "a great wonder, a great revelation, and a great puzzle."

One cannot be sure what kind of tradition was offered to support land titles before the institution of courts; ethnographers have recorded fragments from tradition, but Bittremieux's "Mayombsche Reisboek" (1920) and "De geschiedenis van Kangu" (1924) are among the few extensive reports of relatively primitive tradition.[21] In the stories Bittremieux records, explicitly magical events — the planting of trees, the division of animals, and the fabrication of charms — play a more important role than villages built and alliances contracted.

Court records contain evidence of the evolution of tradition for forensic purposes, away from the magical in the direction of the evidential and refutable. The evidence is not conclusive because in the beginning records were kept in a perfunctory way and only later approached adequacy; whereas one or two pages once sufficed for a court case, the record for the Tendele affair runs to about sixteen pages of single-spaced typescript. Moreover, in the 1940's the forensic art in land cases was by no means as sophisticated as it is now, as shown by hearings at the Matadi court of appeal, where cases were heard by a European judge and recorded under his supervision. As late as 1949 an expanded demand for concessions caught some landowners unprepared.

In a typical case NDUMBU asserted that because VUZI was his son he owned no land, having only the right to occupy certain sites, and that therefore he was not entitled to a share in concession revenues. Tradition offered by the parties and their witnesses was so feeble as to amount to no more than, for example, "I have always heard that Ntoto Wowo belonged to NDUMBU." The indigenous expert appointed to inquire into the boundaries was unable to find any, and a witness declared that the ancestors (*bambuta*) did not concern themselves with precise boundaries. Other witnesses had "never heard" that VUZI was Child to NDUMBU. The court had to base its judgment on the government's political file which identified NDUMBU as the first occupants of the area; but because the two groups had so long cohabited, and because "to establish a limit now would only give rise to quarrels," the two were enjoined to share the land and the profits "as before" (Matadi 645, 1949).

The records indicate that the litigious learned rapidly; those whose traditions lost a case came back a year or two later with better traditions. The successful litigant nowadays is the one who has learned to foresee that if he asserts he was *given* a piece of land he cannot also, within the rules, assert that he gave or sold part of it to someone else. The point may seem obvious, but it has not yet dawned on so shrewd a politician as NZUZI in Manteke, or on most others. The mere organization of tradition for forensic purposes is an art in itself, and it

[21] It is a pity that some of the enthusiasm devoted to collecting folklore had not been diverted a little; the bias against politically significant data is, however, systematic and predictable.

does not come naturally; I have watched a bench of experienced judges trying for forty-five minutes to elicit simple facts of tradition from an honest but bewildered elder.

A litigant in Manteke rarely hires an advocate (*mpovi*); the idea is disapproved, ostensibly because truth should be self-sufficient but more profoundly because the use of an advocate is not considered fair. In Kasangulu, where land is valuable for plantations, chicken farms, and the like which cater to the Kinshasa market, and where village politics is caught up in provincial and national politics, enormous sums can be expended in litigation; semiprofessional advocates began to appear before the courts in the mid-1950's. Tradition is in fact not enough; cases are won by oratorical ability, grasp of the law as a system, and political resources. Conventionally, however, the issue is understood as one of truth and falsehood; the losing party is deemed to have lied, and many a presiding judge prides himself on the severity with which he fines losers to punish them for their "attempt to steal the land" of the winners. In Kasangulu the scale of fines and of court expenses is governed by the urban rather than the rural value of the franc; litigation is financed by the profits of bars and trucking businesses in Kinshasa. To lose a major case appealed to the territorial court is to suffer a crushing economic blow, to which is added the stigma of dishonesty and possibly a jail sentence for false witness.

The announcement of one such judgment brought jubilation to the winners, who brandished the traditional tokens of power, but left the losers visibly numbed; the last scene of the day took place in an ancient Chevrolet chugging back to Kinshasa through the darkness: "What can we do? The judgment was a farce, the court was corrupt. How can we appeal? Do we know anybody in the Parquet? [Turning to the anthropologist] What would *you* do?" The winner in this case, an astonishing showman, knew perfectly well what the other side had in mind. "You know what I would do in his place? I'd accept the judgment; yes, accept it. Then after a while I'd pick a quarrel over a boundary . . ."

In the evolution of tradition the touchstone of merit was very often the presiding judge's concept of customary society, derived ultimately from two sources: the model put forward by indigenous experts, and a lingering European image of the African kingdom of Prester John whom Diogo Cão sought. Two trends are distinguishable, however, in the administrative policy of the Lower Congo: the idealistic and the pragmatic. The former sought to interpret custom as it ought to be, the latter as it evidently and historically was. The point is illustrated by the differing reactions of two officials who presided over Kasangulu courts during the 1950's to a common situation, that of two groups from different clans wrangling over land to which neither clearly had an exclusive claim. One of the officials, discovering that the two groups had long cohabited, had exploited the land in common, and had settled their affairs in concert, considered that they constituted a "federation" and judged that the land belonged jointly to both. The other official, who always came to a different conclusion when faced by this kind of evidence, based his reasoning on the authority of custom (Pool 7, 1950):

The lands of each community represent a collective patrimony left by the ancestors. According to custom, they may not be alienated by the *mfumu kanda*, who is by right of seniority the representative of the ancestors in the eyes of the living. He is also responsible for the management of the common patrimony and may divide it into as many estates as there are clan segments installed in the area of the community. The *mfumu kanda*, who is thus also the *mfumu nsi*, divides the lands among his followers. Since the natives of the community are under his tutelage, they have usufructuary rights in the collective properties. The *mfumu kanda* may levy a tithe on the produce of the earth, even though he rarely exercises this prerogative. Fruit trees and vegetables planted by a native remain his property, but the chief of the clan may demand part of the fruit. The same is true for naturally seeded trees.

The foregoing is an excellent summary of the hierarchical or "royalist" model as it might be gathered from DISA in Manteke or from the work of Van Wing. Its practical application runs into the contradictions analyzed in earlier chapters, but it permits political resolutions not possible under the analytical approach. With the departure of Europeans from the territorial administration after 1960, the preeminence of the royalist model has been firmly established. Taking at face value the authoritarian and historical implications of tradition establishes a procedure through which land tenure may eventually be rationalized; in the process, the domain of custom (*fu kya nsi*) in rural life would be brought under administrative control.

Very slowly, tradition is ceasing to be oral. MBENZA in Manteke now speaks of the transcripts of his successful litigation in much the same tone as he speaks of the grave of Na Nkazi Makonko. He confided the documents to me in great secrecy, although they are a matter of public record; he said they contain all the necessary tradition pertaining to his lands, although in fact the story they record is far from complete and seems open to challenge. The really valuable statement in them is one that unequivocally attributes the land to him; since official policy is not to reopen such cases, his title seems safe with or without tradition.

At the Tendele affair bright young men on both sides busily took notes, over the objections of certain elders. According to theory, tradition does not need to be written down; an *nkazi* who really owns the land has the tradition in him and need consult no book. On the other hand, once his tradition has been written down by others he no longer has absolute control of it, and in a sense it has been stolen from him. Objections in this sense were overruled on the ground that keeping a written record was the modern and European thing to do; "and besides, if the tradition is true why shouldn't it be recorded?"

Rationalization is beginning to affect the role of supporting witnesses as well as the content of their testimony. At the territorial courts of appeal, where a body of archives and a staff equipped to use them are being built up, a litigant may now be asked to explain why he challenges another's ownership of land when a few years before he accepted the other's supporting testimony against a third party. If this process continues, rural society will be stratified into a class of freemen (landowners) and a class of slaves (clients).

Part III
CHIEFSHIP

10

AUTHORITY AND POWER

Evidences of symbolism are occasionally
to be met with.
—HERBERT WARD,
*Ethnographical Notes Relative
to the Congo Tribes*

The materials set forth in chapters 6 through 9 illustrate the degree of uncertainty prevailing in the empirical structure of Mbanza Manteke. Much of the time it is impossible to say definitively who has what rights and obligations in regard to this or that person, group, or landholding. In part, this uncertainty is an aspect of process, which takes time; disputes cannot be settled instantly as they arise. More fundamentally, it reflects a characteristic and pervasive disequilibrium, defined by Radcliffe-Brown (1950, p. 11) as a condition of marked disagreement concerning the rules.

Historically, the empirical structure may be regarded as resulting from the continuous immigration and progressive assimilation of heterogeneous groups, initially constituting descent lines but later integrated in the clan section as lineages. There has also been a continuous process of internal adjustment to accommodate demographic imbalance, personal ambition, and other occasions of political strain.

Currently unresolved organizational problems appear at the level of the clan section, the house, or the lineage. It descent were the only or even the principal structural factor, such problems would seriously interfere with the necessary conduct of affairs. The burden of regulation, however, falls mainly on committees constituted in terms of patrilateral and affinal links in such a way that status ambiguities phrased in terms of descent can be accommodated and the legitimacy of social transactions is assured. In a multitude of informal situations in daily life, having to do with residence, cultivation, and utilitarian activities, cooperation and compromise are stressed. On the other hand, the formalities of a land case constitute a specialized arena in which competitive energies can be exercised. Even here the uncertainties of status definition, forming the subject of argument, contrast with the formal patterns of the procedures by which such argument is publicly conducted.

The structure of rights in land, which differentiate landowning houses from one another, is established, in theory, by an original apportionment. Historically, the present situation results from the infiltration of heterogeneous lineages which came by different routes and at different times. As a practical and political matter, their respective land rights are determined, insofar as they are determined at all, in the course of disputes over particular tracts. Such disputes occur between neighbors, and between such neighboring lineages emerge conventions of inclusion and exclusion which differentiate the houses, as far as those neighbors are concerned. Other lineages, whose land is at some distance, are involved in these particular disputes only indirectly, although all groups maintain the ideology of a common estate of the clan section. What identifies the clan section as a unit, however, is the rule of exogamy. Different groups of lineages, each with its own set of boundary relationships relating to land in its neighborhood, may entertain conflicting conventions regarding the ways in which all the lineages of the clan section are organized into landowning houses. If this condition persists, fission of the clan section becomes likely.[1]

As noted earlier, the status of a house and a clan section, but not of a lineage, is defined by the intersection of a particular *kitaata* and *kingudi*. The same is evidently true of the status of an individual. The lineage, which is not internally segmented, is the only unit that settles its affairs privately; consequently, lineage affairs are difficult to observe. The affairs of all other units — apparently including the chiefship as it formerly existed — require the cooperation of persons designated as Child, Grandchild, Father, Grandfather, and affine. Each status has its role in relation to the "owner" of the affair, and the role is filled by an individual drawn from the appropriate category. On a particular occasion the man who actually "sits," who visibly fills the role, is the *nkazi* of the group or category. At the risk of banality, it must be emphasized that the role attaches to the status and not to the individual, who may fill several roles in the space of half an hour at the

---

[1] In the case of NKAZI A KONGO the ground is already prepared. For some elders NKAZI A KONGO is the name of a clan, with three sections represented in Mbanza Nkazi: NKALA NLANDU, MBENZA, and NKUTI A NIMA. For others, Nkala Nlandu is merely the name of the charm owned by the section whose proper name is NKAZI A KONGO. When the division occurs, one of the new sections will call itself NKAZI A KONGO, the other NKALA NLANDU, and each will conserve traditions showing it to have been there from the beginning.

same affair. He can move from one to the other by invoking patrifiliation; on the basis of descent he can occupy only one. The function of descent, from this point of view, is to articulate the different organizational levels (Smith, 1956, pp. 65–66).

KINKAZI

In Manteke the only customary office at present is that of *nkazi*, whether of the clan section (*nkazi a kanda*) or of a smaller unit. Externally, the *nkazi*'s function is to represent his group; within the group he is only one among several elders, by whom he is selected for the position. If he represents the senior descent line, the prestige thereby accruing to him may influence the selection, but other factors, both personal and political, are likely to carry more weight. Representation is pervasively necessary: nobody (except a stranger, someone who lacks an *mvila*, i.e., a nonperson) ever speaks for himself. Men speak for women, seniors for juniors, the father for the child; in some circumstances, junior speaks for senior, child for father. These pairs recur as the irreducible units of social relations.

An *nkazi* represents his group in the affairs that concern it, but he derives no authority from the definition of his role to make decisions on his own. Decisions relating to the affairs of the group he represents are made by a committee composed of representatives of related groups and categories: Father, Grandfathers, Children, Grandchildren, collateral groups, affines. Although the structure of such a committee is approximately the same in all instances, the membership varies according to the group owning the affair and the kind of affair in question; the committee is not the same for a DISA and an MFUTU funeral, although the *nkazi* of NANGA presides at both.

Within the group he represents the *nkazi* does not play an authoritarian role. It is said that "one man cannot kill a marriage"; nor can he, on his own, make any similar decisions. He consults the other elders of his group, principally the men but also the women. Explaining the system, an *nkazi* said: "If an affair is brought to me, I would have to ask my younger brother about it. He is, strictly speaking, my *nleeke*, but he is a person of some importance just the same. I would also have to ask my sister[2] Topsy, although she is a woman, because she is very elderly and cannot be ignored." An *nleeke* of the lineage or a *mwana* (Child), or anyone else who wanted action taken in affairs concerning the lineage, might approach the elder or the younger

[2] "Classificatory sister," *busi* or *mpangi*; here "member of the same lineage" is meant.

brother or Topsy, or another of the elders of the lineage, and the elders would jointly decide what to do.

If the elders are unable to agree or if the *baleeke* fail to consult them or to accept their decisions, the group disintegrates. For example, NTAMBU and NA LOMBO should be two lineages of the only house of a clan section; now, because they refuse to arrange their land affairs jointly, there are two houses of one lineage each. Whether there are also two clan sections or only one is still uncertain. The two groups refused to cooperate in such matters as contributing to funerals, but the definitive incident, having to do with the characteristic corporate affairs of a clan section, will probably be a marriage between members of the two groups, or a refusal of the elders to allow such a marriage.

On the other hand, as shown in earlier chapters, the *kinkazi* exists as long as the group continues to regulate its common affairs, even though there is no single *nkazi* identifiable. NTUMBA, for instance, has a *nkazi* for each house but none for the clan section; the *bankazi* of the houses share the position of *nkazi a kanda* according to rules that they have developed.

Thus there is no chief in Manteke. The landscape is organized not into a checkerboard of sovereign territories (to revert to the image used in chapter 2) but into a network of cognatic and affinal ties. The representative roles are occupied by *bambuta*, "elders." Over a period of time the same faces appear and reappear in neighboring villages. NA LUKUTI, for example, is seen in Mbanza Manteke as *se dya mwana*; the following week, as *nkwezi* in Ndemba; then as *mfumu a n'teekudi*, also in Ndemba; as *nkazi* in Ntombo a Lukuti; as *mwana . . .* , and so on. Collectively, therefore, the elders run the affairs of the community, but there is no council of elders for any and all affairs. There is not even the specific rank of elder; other cadets from time to time occupy the chair of authority (*kiti kya kinkazi*) and eventually become *bambuta*.[3]

The most important elders at the village level are those whose houses own land locally or whose talents have earned them a strong voice in local affairs; Nsiku Damison of NSUNDI is an example in the latter category. Elders who are clients of other elders are in effect cadets (*baleeke*), regardless of age and of the fact that they may be heads of lineages. The distinction between elder and cadet is not rigid; it is

[3] The "council of elders" nevertheless exists in the ethnography. It seems to be difficult for Europeans to imagine a form of government that lacks a chief or at least a college to embody it; a situation with "no one to give orders" is regarded as "anarchy." Of Manteke, the government report of 1931 said: "Power is exercised by the agency of a council of notables called Nenga." In such reports the answers fill in details of the scheme that dictated the questions.

merely a tendency revealed, for example, when people run over the names of those whom they would expect to consult on a matter of general interest.

An *nkazi* represents his group in relations with other groups and protects the interests of his dependents. He performs the following specific functions: (1) marrying off his dependents; (2) burying his deceased dependents; (3) sponsoring dependents and clients, which means speaking for them in general and finding land for them to culti-vate; and (4) exercising authority over slaves, especially in questions of sale or redemption. These four functions have a jural value; they tend to define the *kinkazi* upon which the corporate character of the group depends. The key questions for the definition of corporate rela-tions, internal and external rights, as asked in court, are: (1) Who was the *nkazi* who married off this girl or this youth (referring to some history of the group's affairs)? (2) Who was *nkazi* at the funeral? (3) Who received this stranger when he arrived? (4) Who bought and who sold the slave? Good traditions provide satisfactory answers to such questions; examples are given in earlier chapters.

TRANSFER OF PERSONS

Authority over persons may be transferred and shared in various ways, although at present there is little agreement in Manteke as to the names or the nature of the various institutional forms of marriage and slavery in which the principles of transfer, as applied to persons, were formerly embodied. The vagueness results partly from the trans-formation of the political system which occurred when warfare and slave trading were abolished and new sources of power were intro-duced, and partly from the political importance of distinguishing between freemen and all others (i.e., slaves). The statements of in-formants, the records of tradition, and a survey of the ethnography suggest that the varieties of slavery and marriage are merely permuta-tions of a simple set of variables, although particular institutions, that is, standardized arrangements for the transfer of rights, vary from re-gion to region and over time as well.

Ideally, rights over persons and land may be transferred by loan, pawn, gift, or sale, or by default. An individual can be pawned, sold, or redeemed only by his *nkazi*, normally the representative of his matrilineal descent group. If he is bought or redeemed by a person other than his original *nkazi*, that person becomes his *nkazi* by virtue of the transaction; it is possible for an individual to be "free," in the sense of having no *nkazi,* only by being the founder, like Ntinu Wene, of a new, entirely autonomous domain.

The right of an *nkazi* to dispose of his dependents applies equally to slaves and freemen. In the past, however, slaves were sold or pawned more readily than freemen because they possessed relatively little influence within the group to which they belonged and had no kin in other groups to speak for them. A father was, and is, expected to protect his child against unreasonable competition within the child's descent group, but could use only political means to this end. If a *nkazi* decided to sell a dependent he did not have to consult the individual's father first. The father might himself buy the child in order to defend him from the witchcraft of his matrikinsmen, who would be relatively powerless after the transfer.[4] The father might also acquire his children as pawns (Claridge, 1922, p. 157). Pawns enjoyed a relatively privileged position in that they could not be sold so long as their redemption remained a possibility, that is, so long as their original *nkazi* retained a claim to them.

Pawnship (*kinsimbi; simba,* "to hold") is related to partnership (*kimbundi; bundana,* "to join together") in that the *kinkazi* is shared. If two groups jointly bought a female slave, her offspring were divided between them; the same is done nowadays with pigs and chickens and with productive machines, such as manioc grinders, whose output can be divided. It was possible to combine these institutions — for example, by buying a slave and pawning a share — and evidently similar combinations occurred in certain forms of marriage. Pawns were transferred as surety for debts, their own or their *nkazi's.* A pawn might become a slave, but the initial transaction was not intended to be permanent. As long as the impermanence was recognized, a pawn could not be sold. A similar privilege was accorded to those who voluntarily enslaved themselves under the procedure known in Manteke as *koma nloko.* The phrase, which may be translated "nail an oath," recalls a class of charms consisting of a figure covered with nails. A man dissatisfied with his *nkazi's* treatment of him approached the head of another group, upon whose forehead he wiped his foot (*dyata va mbulu*). In other areas he sat on the chief's bed or committed some other ritual sin amounting to an insult so gross that he was immediately enslaved. Bittremieux's version of the chief's response to the pollution of his forehead, the site of his soul (*lunzi*), is "A! zal ik mij zoo laten vertreden door een voet die drek vertreedt?" (1922–1927: *s.v.* "dibanda"). The candidate was supposed to bring a white chicken

4 Laman, 1957, pp. 59, 106. This custom may still be resorted to at the present time (J. M. Janzen, pers. comm.).

with him, and the chief announced acceptance of his allegiance by firing shots. Apparently whole groups of people might swear allegiance to a powerful chief by this means. (Others are reported as subordinating themselves to someone with no mention of *koma nloko*; the type situation shows a woman with dependents but no adult to speak for her.)

Another aspect of the institution of pawnship is revealed by a story about Na Sangala of NSAKA:

His juniors [*baleeke*], it is said, accused him of witchcraft, whereupon he renounced NSAKA and submitted himself [*komene nloko*] to Na Makukisa of NSUNDI in Matenta. [It is likely that Na Sangala and Na Makukisa were sons of the same father, Na Kwindi of NGOMA LUBOTA.] His action caused a great scandal. Na Makukisa demanded the payment of a man and a woman to be his slaves before he would return Na Sangala to NSAKA. The *baleeke* said this was too much, and offered instead a man and a slice of the forest Kinsala; but Na Makukisa wanted money, not land, so they pawned the forest to NKAZI A KONGO and paid over the money and a man called Na Lumingu, who was redeemed only after the Word of God came to Manteke.[5]

The last pawns in Manteke village were redeemed in 1964. They are the group NDAMBA NGOLO, a number of whose women continue to live there. The men live in Matadi. (A similar group of NTUMBA women were formerly pawns of NTAMBU). After redemption a man, in particular, may want to move to town, because even though he is now free he has no land and hence no local standing; if he were to return to his original place he could scarcely expect his new found brethren to move over to make room for him. The problem for women, who usually are not directly involved in politics, is less serious; they live where they or their daughters have married. When necessary, Kingalu of MFUTU acts locally as *nkazi* to his erstwhile pawns, NDAMBA NGOLO.

Gift, like pawnship, is a limited transfer. Marriage is structurally similar to gift, particularly to gifts of land. In both the recipient has the use of the object transferred, but ultimate ownership, expressed as control of the *lusansu* or *kinkulu* ("tradition") relating to it, is retained by the giver. Marriage may be described by the verb *vewa*, "to be given," although the usual word is *sompa*, "to borrow"; both terms are explicitly contrasted with *sumba*, "to buy," and *kanga*, "to capture." Institutional forms of marriage undoubtedly varied from place to place, with resulting differences in, for example, the types of contract possible and the related rights of the father over his children

---

[5] This version of the story was given to me by the present NSAKA himself, but it lends support to the opinion of NKUTI that Na Sangala was the last of the "real" NSAKA (see fig. 5).

(Laman, 1957, p. 106). Manteke people now disagree on the question of what contractual form corresponded to the designation *longo lwa nkita*, which occurs in traditions, and variously explain it as sale of the woman (*kita*, "to trade"), pawning, sharing, and the equivalent of *longo lwa fundu* (see below). The oldest man in the village, "the man who shook hands with Stanley," suggested in some of his faint recollections of nineteenth-century institutions that *longo lwa nkita* might have been the term for exchange marriage (cf. Bittremieux, 1922–1927: *s.v.* "kita").

The *nkazi* who "eats" the marriage payments for a girl "owns" her offspring. Similarly, a lineage falls under the authority of the *nkazi* who has repeatedly officiated at its funerals; it is axiomatic that members of a group recognizing a common *kinkazi* bury one another (*baziikasananga*). Thus a marriage may become *longo lwa fundu*, as in the story of the origins of NGOMA LUBOTA: a girl marries in, in the usual way, but the marriage is converted into the equivalent of a purchase and her descendants become slaves (*baana ba fundu*) when her *nkazi* fails to come to funerals (*mafundu*). The Ntandu proverb that describes this transfer is *Kisambu kibweke mu simu nzadi, kansi kulendi kio zenga ko*, "The palm-nut cluster ripened on the other shore, but you may not cut it" (Van Wing, 1959, pp. 183–184). At other times conversion is accomplished by an additional payment, the girl's *nkazi* having discovered that he "needed money."

The lending of land is better documented than the lending of women because it involved long-term relations between groups. Some information about the lending of women is available, however. The girl Dwingi appears to have been lent to Nsakala Joseph by NTAMBU, and other instances that occurred near the turn of the century are mentioned by missionaries and travelers. In such transfers, if the man was a stranger, the girl's *nkazi* retained control of any children born to her, filling the role of *nkazi* and Father (*se*) toward them. The same thing happens nowadays if a girl, during a visit to town, has an affair with a stranger. Her children, though not slaves, lack the full complement of kin.

Although *bisi Manteke* now refer to all persons who were the objects of *longo lwa nkita*, all pawns, and the descendants of both as "slaves" (*bakimvwa, bansumbidi-nsumbidi*, etc.), we may distinguish by this term those who were transferred in a transaction intended to be permanent. Three types of transaction existed: gift, purchase, and indemnity. (1) Kingalu Musesa is said to have given a slave to his father Na Makokila, but it is unlikely that this kind of gift was made very often. Slaves were also transferred as title fees (Doutreloux, 1967, pp. 169–

170). (2) Slaves could be bought locally at markets; if so, they came originally from the periphery of the purchaser's political neighborhood, or still farther away. (Boys who broke the rules of the Nkimba cult and people who persistently annoyed the elders or chased other men's wives might be spirited away at night to the north, across the river, or to Angola or Palabala). (3) Slaves could also be acquired as indemnity or blood compensation. The owner's title to the slave depended on his ability to recite the story of the circumstances in which the slave was acquired. A slave captured in war or stolen could run away if he got the chance because no transaction was involved (cf. J. Mertens, 1942, pp. 116, 119), whereas in legitimate slavery the transaction, not the slave's location, was decisive.

Slaves belonged to the man who acquired them, if he did so in his own name; otherwise they belonged to his lineage, which would in any event inherit them at his death. As the descendants of a slave began to acquire property and social responsibilities they became a separate lineage within the house of their owners. If, because the owners died out, or by political success, the slave group acquired land in its own name (i.e., as a foundation and not as a gift from its Fathers), it ceased to occupy slave status. (This development sequence is not recognized ideologically, of course, but occurs in history.) Slaves, like other Children, were entitled to help themselves to the fruit of the Father's trees and to use his land; conversely, Fathers could take fruit from the trees of any of their Children. The degree of autonomy of slaves, in deploying their labor and in owning personal property, evidently varied a great deal.

There are still some slaves in Manteke village; that is, they admit that their *nkaaka* was bought. The "abolition of slavery" meant that all those who wanted to redeem themselves could not be prevented from doing so. Should the remaining slaves choose to buy out at this late date, they would have nowhere to go. On the other hand, though they may suffer an occasional insult, they cannot be referred to publicly as slaves because they "stand behind" their owners, in this instance MPANZU.[6] Only inside the MPANZU group can they be discriminated against, but if there are no intragroup conflicts they have all the privileges of freemen (*mfumu za kanda*). The ambiguity that may arise is seen in the story of Kyanlasu, the belligerent spokesman of NGOMA LUBOTA.

[6] The polite introductory phrase, *Tu mfumu ye mfumu, nganga ye nganga*, signifies "We are all gentlemen, there are no slaves present." When a distinguished visitor arrives in a village all members of his party are given chairs, even those whose lowly status is so well known that ordinarily they would be ignored; discriminating among the visitors would be most impolite.

The fragmentary evidence from court records suggests that Kyanlasu's mother was of NA MAZINGA in Kibunzi, across the Congo River
to the north, and that she was sold or otherwise transferred to NA
MAZINGA in Kinsala, near the Luima River. The history is a tangled
one. When her daughter's child was to be married, Johnny Matota of
NGOMA LUBOTA in Manteke presented himself as her *nkazi*. Upon being
rebuffed he took the matter to court, saying that his predecessor Na
Mabonga of NGOMA had arranged to buy back Kyanlasu's mother but
that the owner had refused his offer of one pig, a piece of cloth, and
another slave. The case was heard in 1936, when the dispute was at
least twenty-two years old.

The Manteke court held that the slave's owner, NA MAZINGA of Kinsala, was not entitled to refuse to sell her back and that she was to be
free, "freedom" here presumably meaning transfer to NGOMA LUBOTA.
It was far from clear, however, what interest NGOMA had in the matter.
When the case was appealed to Matadi, Matota explained that "le
clan Mazinga avait pris sous sa protection le clan Ntumba [NGOMA]
de Kibunzi et qu'ils se considèrent comme étant les parents de Mazinga." This statement evidently has some bearing on the origins of the
Manteke NGOMA LUBOTA and on what MFUTU regards as NGOMA's dubi-
ous pedigree, but a good deal remains unexplained.

The appeal court in Matadi held that the Manteke decision was
wrong, and that no change should be made in the situation because
the slave and the owner belonged to "the same clan." This judgment
ignores the crucial distinction between the unorganized *mvila* and the
corporate *kanda* and leaves the status of the slave or ex-slave obscure.
At about this time Kyanlasu moved to Mbanza Manteke, where eventually he occupied the house left by Johnny Matota, whom he describes
as his *n'kuluntu*, and became the principal spokesman for NGOMA
LUBOTA. (It seems likely that Matota's motive was to recruit new dependents, since his lineage was faced with extinction.) It is particularly
galling for MFUTU to have to confront him instead of his less aggressive
nkazi, but any public suggestion that Kyanlasu is "illegitimate" merits
the fine of a pig.

The question of Kyanlasu's status was raised again in court in 1963,
in what connection it is not clear, but the case was suspended by the
government on procedural grounds (Matadi 248, 1936; Mbanza Manteke 266, 1963). It seems that as long as NGOMA regards Kyanlasu as
belonging to him, and no new judgment is handed down, Kyanlasu's
position will remain as obscure as it now is. MFUTU's hopes in the
matter caused him to delay repeatedly appearing in court to confront
NGOMA in the affair over Mbanza Ntala. When at last MFUTU did pre-

sent himself, the bench of judges aroused his indignation by bursting into the chorus of the old Baptist hymn,

> Wiza ku nzo ame, yiyazibudi;
> Ntama ngyakutombele, u mwan'ame.

> Come to my house, which I have opened for thee;
> Long have I sought thee, my son.

Various procedures, ranging from capture to voluntary subordination, admit individuals to the status of client; in that status they are dependent on the sponsorship of another group from which they are excluded by the principle of descent. In practice, the extension of *kinkazi* tends to assimilate clients to the owning descent group; conversely, junior descent lines tend to be excluded from the exercise of authority and to approach the status of client. The distinction between chief and slave, absolute in theory but empirically a matter of degree, is subject to adjustment over time.

The most clearly subordinating procedures for entry into clientship — enslavement by capture, purchase, and pawn — have been abolished, but the extension of *kinkazi* to aliens continues. Several examples from current Manteke affairs illustrate the practice.

A small group of women in Mbanza Manteke belong to NLAZA in Kinkanza. Since it is a long way to Manteke, their *nkazi* has delegated routine supervision of their affairs to NTUMBA–NGOMA LUBOTA, NLAZA and NTUMBA being the same *mvila*. Accordingly, Joel Albert sits as *nkazi* at their weddings and appears in court for their divorces. In serious matters, as when one of the girls was seduced by an NTUMBA man, the real *nkazi* comes to Manteke. Should he fail to do so, his dependents would be effectively transferred to NGOMA.

Complete strangers who have chosen to settle in Manteke may or may not become incorporated in local houses in their lifetime, but they will be incorporated posthumously if they have descendants. The principle is that patronage is converted into common descent. For example, the patron of the slaves redeemed by the missionaries was NZUZI, who spoke for them in village affairs; their clan is given now as NANGA, although further inquiry reveals their original clans. The slaves whom these ex-slaves themselves acquired, and their descendants, are claimed as Children by NZUZI. In another example, a man who, while living in town, married a woman from elsewhere, has a son who belongs, of course, to a foreign clan but for whom he speaks in Manteke; this son is said, on first inquiry, to belong to his father's clan.

Angolan refugees seeking a place to live need a sponsor. It is noticeable that sponsors tend to be those who feel they need support in their struggles with other *bankazi*. There are nine refugee households in Manteke. One is dependent on NTAMBU; the other eight are dependent on NZIMBU of MFUTU, who acts as their *nkazi* in affairs that relate them to the village, such as a funeral. The refugees do not work for NZIMBU, and they are only beginning to participate in village affairs by contributing at funerals. Most of them brought spouses with them, but in time there will be intermarriage. Their mere presence enlarges the *kinkazi* of NZIMBU. Such a development may be resented by others, as when DISA imported Angolans into Ndemba; MFULAMA NKANGA said that his consent should have been asked — Who did DISA think he was, anyway? Some villages have refused to admit any refugees.

A number of men have acquired wives in the course of military service in the Upper Congo. Such women are not described as slaves, but admittedly their status is similar to that of slaves, especially after the husband's death, and may be held against them in quarrels ("naked savage, landless witch"; Mbanza Manteke 459, 1951). The husband's *nkazi* is not only *se dya mwana* to the offspring of these women, but also *nkazi* and *mfumu a n'teekudi*; it is the concentration of these roles in one position which jurally distinguishes slaves from freemen.

SOCIAL CONTROL

A man remains a cadet (*nleeke*) until he is about forty, perhaps longer. As a cadet he is likely to be assigned to service tasks at funerals; only occasionally is he invited to practice being an elder by being given secondary speaking roles at weddings and the like. His advancement depends on his personal character, his ability, and the number of his older relatives. As they become infirm he will have increasing opportunities to serve as *nkazi* at some of the less important events. Otherwise he is at the beck and call of his elders, whose tone toward him is often peremptory. Young men speak of the elders as jealous and faultfinding.

The status of "young man" is that of client; all young men are clients, but not all clients are young men. Slaves are permanent clients (*baleeke*).

The control exercised over their dependents by the elders is a function of their managerial monopoly in routine public affairs. This monopoly is precarious. In precolonial times the ambitious but underprivileged could depart for greener pastures, perhaps founding a new *mbanza* "free of disputes" (*yikondolo mambu*), where their version of their pedigree and social worth stood a better chance of acceptance. This process continues to the present. Many of NTAMBU and their adherents, though still officially resident in Manteke, have moved to Nsimbila where their cultivations are. (Because their residences at Nsimbila officially are simply field huts convenient for overnight stay, they need not comply with public ordinances relating to hygiene, for example; as one of them says, "I'm the mayor here." As some of them also have houses in the village, population totals must be qualified in various ways.)

In modern times the principal way for young men in search of independence to escape is to go to town. One can see at a major funeral what the impact on the political system would be if even a quarter of the absent population were to return to the village to live; the physical presence at such an event of so many powerful, intelligent, opinionated people — housewives, stationmasters, truck drivers, janitors, directors of companies, traders — temporarily transforms the village.[7]

The *baleeke* who remain in the village chafe under the restraints put upon them. For those who are young in years a degree of compensation is provided by the Dikembe, a social club catering to the unmarried men, the most junior of *baleeke*. Dikembe culture, an interesting caricature of the serious magico-religious beliefs and practices of the older generation which it defies, contains the seeds of an antisociety. The membership includes unmarried girls; the club's principal functions are to circulate the latest songs, to organize dances, and to facilitate premarital sex. The doors of bachelor huts bear such inscriptions as "Palais d'Amour" in Gothic lettering, and the theme is continued in nicknames and personal praise names adopted by the young men. An example is the nickname Kiwaya from the English "wire" (i.e., wire netting) for one who "entraps girls." A slogan on a door is "Ennemi de la liberté" (of girls, of course). The praise names, recited *mu kivanité*, like those of the clans, vaunt the personality of the owner; one of my friends called himself "Zorro le Fantôme Noir, Genti Cawboy, Amateur de Djazz." The last phrase means "jazzy lover," not "lover of jazz."

Each village chapter of the Dikembe has officers who are elected annually; they are president, vice-president (female), *docteur* and secretary. The secretary had inscribed on the door of his hut in Manteke the word "Secret" exemplifying the KiKongo pun to perfection: "secretary" and "secret" (sexual adventures). A *docteur*, in general, is one who knows ways of attracting women; the function of the officer who bears this title is to "read the Bible," that is, play the drum at dances.

The culture of the Dikembe is that of *billisme*, most highly developed in town where it occasions much editorial hair-tearing and scandalized comment in the Kinshasa press. Billism, whose heroes are the

---

[7] Although the various censuses conducted in Manteke have been based on different criteria, the adult population since 1912 has apparently remained close to 160, despite the tendency to migrate to the cities.

stars of romantic French and American movies, takes its name from Buffalo Bill, "sheriff du quartier Santa Fé de Paris, métro d'amour." The Bills are the principal fetishists of the age, circulating recipes for love charms among themselves. One who was so careless as to drop such a recipe on the path was taken to court by the elders of Vunda in righteous indignation. The recipe, for a potion to be slipped into the loved one's coffee, was composed according to authentic magical rules: (1) three palm nuts; (2) fingernails and toenails; (3) skin from the soles of the feet; (4) root of *fwititi*, a tree that is the image of man; (5) hair from the forehead; (6) pubic hair; (7) axillary hair. The potion is irresistible, but the defendant said he had not used it.

A favorite charm, or rather class of charms, is Mpungu, which was formerly made up in the snail shell *kodya* but is now usually put in perfume bottles (Raymaekers, 1960). The ingredients for charms are sold at the cosmetic counter in the market, the purpose of both kinds of commodity being the same — to entrap people. The owner of Mpungu, according to Claridge, "is commonly a rogue of the worst dye" (1922, p. 123). The Dikembe of one Manteke village found itself in court facing the collective wrath of the elders after the parents of one girl had refused to allow her to join the club and the girl herself had refused the advances of members. In retaliation the Dikembe had sung songs likening her face to that of Prime Minister Lumumba and her father's chronic cough to a phonograph record. The most serious charge, however, was that the Dikembe's vice-president had shut the girl up in Mpungu to keep her from conceiving (Mbanza Manteke 8, 1964). In 1965 the Manteke village chapter folded up for lack of members.

Another outlet for self-expression is provided by the Kimbanguist church, although the Baptist church lays claim to the upper echelons of village society. The elders are nearly all closely associated with the mission: Kingalu, *nkazi* of NANGA, is catechist of the Baptist congregation, and the committee that nominally supervises congregational affairs is made up of NANGA and NTUMBA men, supported by a parallel committee of their NTUMBA and NANGA wives. In contrast, all those who now belong to the Kimbanguist church, and apparently all those who did belong even during the enthusiastic period of national independence, are, for various reasons marginal to the village establishment. Each of the original prophets who sprang up in the region during the period of messianic fervor in 1921 belonged to a client lineage (see below). Moreover, they were all young men, just reaching the age at which they would begin to feel the effects of discrimination. The few who returned from exile in 1959 included Elayi of NSUNDI, who was invited by the *nkazi* of NSUNDI in Manteke to build a church there. Such sponsorship is just as necessary for the church as it is for refugees; in villages where the Baptist establishment is strong Kimbanguism can get no foothold. In Manteke, despite his invitation to Elayi, NSUNDI has never belonged to the Kimbanguist church. He represents the majority, the Christmas Christians who appear in church once a year; as he put it, "I believe that God is in heaven, but I'm down here, and I like my glass of beer" (Baptists in good standing are supposed to be abstainers). After Elayi died in 1965, NSUNDI, strongly supported by the village elders, led the movement to throw out the Kimbanguists, who were forced to rebuild their church outside the village on land controlled by the headman.[8] Kimbanguist sermons throughout the year sounded the note of embittered righteousness, on such texts as "He that is not with me is against me" and "How is the faithful city [*mbanza*] become an harlot!"

The dichotomy between those who matter and the rest, and the latent discontent of the latter, were apparent during the great Manteke witch-hunt, a disorder that lasted for twenty-four hours in June 1966. As noted earlier, the village is not so devoted to witchcraft as is Kasangulu, for example. Nevertheless, there had been some accusations and arguments. One of these affairs had to do with a girl of sixteen, married for two years but not yet pregnant. Her husband, who slept away from home a good deal, had syphilis. Her resentment at her barren condition (*sita*) had led to a number of domestic explosions, and it came as no surprise to me when she suffered an attack of violent pains diagnosed at the hospital in Nsona Mpangu as hysteria. She herself blamed the pains on the witchcraft of a neighbor. This accusation was dealt with in the ordinary way, by a meeting of the owners of the parties called by her father. Nothing was achieved, however, because the traditional magical means were unavailable and because in the circumstances it was impossible to obtain either a confession by the accused or convincing evidence of expressions of ill will on her part.

This proceeding was managed by the elders. The tensions it aroused, and other discontents, coalesced some months later when one of the village girls, unmarried although beautiful and at least seventeen, drew her father's attention to a diviner practising in Lufu. Since she and her father alike were convinced that her continued celibacy must

---

[8] The headman is an apparent exception to the generalization that the congregation is recruited from nonentities; but he is overshadowed in his own lineage by his brother, and in this village his job has never been highly regarded. His reason for joining the Kimbanguists, a common one, seems to have been that the Baptist church, before independence, expelled him for some marital offense.

be attributable to someone's ill will, they decided to call in the diviner, who was variously described as a magician (*nganga*) and a prophet (*ngunza*). A dozen or more other people in the village, likewise convinced that something was eating them and that they could stand it no longer, signed a written invitation promising to pay the diviner's "expenses" if he would come and clean up the village once and for all. When he appeared it soon became obvious that he was a charlatan rather than a serious practitioner of any of the established techniques. He wore a white suit, a sharp hat, and a sharp moustache, while his assistants wore charade costumes including a turban and a long red shirt. The diviner's behavior was so lacking in the dignity, courtesy, and discretion that are ordinarily necessary in village affairs that it was astonishing he should be countenanced at all by a people who habitually regard even the best intentions with uncharitable suspicion.

The séance began in the evening before a large crowd composed mainly of women and (among the men) marginal people. In attendance were some (but not all) Kimbanguists, who are forbidden by their church to have anything to do with witchcraft or magic. The expert and his assistants trembled (*zakama*) spectacularly, danced artistically through the fire, identified most of those present as potential witches, and "discovered" villainous-looking charms buried on four roads leading into the village. He brought the charms back to a parody of an altar he had set up and, handling them very gingerly as though they were as noxious as they looked, dunked them in the chalice to neutralize them. While the more skeptical village youths were gleefully showing one another just how the "discoveries" were made, connoisseurs of the magical arts noted that the four roads were not the ritually correct ones (*mafula ma vata*), which any true possessor of second sight would have had no trouble identifying. Anyway, because they were buried on the wrong roads, the charms could not have had the malign effect the diviner attributed to them.

The séance continued the next day at the cemetery. The expert hinted that all the illnesses of local residents were caused by a pot containing nine *kodya* shells maliciously placed in the village water supply; he would remove the pot if a sufficiently large fee was raised. By this time, however, most of those who had promised to share the costs had become sufficiently disillusioned to renege, and the beautiful girl's unfortunate father was left with most of the bill. By the next day hardly anyone had a good word to say for the witchhunt; an attitude of noncommittal disinterest was popular.

Obviously the charlatan should have been run out of town, and he could have been had enough elders made up their minds to get

rid of him. But all the elders except one found urgent business in distant forests, and that one stayed at home only because he did not want
to be suspected of running away. "Let anyone come in here saying
I'm a witch, and I'll give him a piece of my mind." Of course, no one
did. Meanwhile, with the elders away, the "prophet" took advantage
of the opportunity to harass defenseless women and extort money from
the foolish. The communal government did nothing to stop him. "Until someone brings me a complaint, I am helpless," said the mayor.
Commenting on this dictum, an elder correctly noted that the government never hesitated to take action when it felt like it, with or without
a mandate.

The temporary paralysis of the elders and the government should
be compared with the administrator Saintraint's description of conditions in Madimba Territory just before independence in 1960 (CRISP,
1961, I, 143–144):

> Partout en plus on parle de rejeter les anciennes contraintes, soit coutu-
> mières, soit religieuses, qui avaient maintenu si longtemps et si bien la dignité
> du mariage chez les Bakongo. C'est publiquement qu'on parle de fêter l'in-
> dépendance en prenant une seconde femme, c'est au vu de tous que le con-
> cubinage et le mariage à l'essai sont prônés et pratiqués, c'est partout que
> s'installe une licence à laquelle aucun frein ne s'oppose plus.
> Les anciens — et même pas les anciens, les hommes formés — sont unanimes à
> dire qu'on ne les respecte plus, qu'ils n'ont plus rien à dire aux jeunes gens;
> ceux-ci, dans la meilleure hypothèse, passent leurs journées dans l'oisiveté,
> courent les marchés, vivent d'expédients divers aux crochets des villageois
> actifs.
> Tout le monde sait que le fétichisme revit dans tous les villages; les rites
> du ‹Vwela› du ‹Ngimbi› se déroulent au grand jour; devins et dieudonnés
> circulent sans cesse en consultation. Et réapparaît le triste cortège des accusa-
> tions de sorcellerie, des haines familiales et des soupçons longtemps remâchés,
> de l'exploitation de la crédulité publique, des escroqueries, tout ce qu'on
> résume en peu de mots: un dramatique retour en arrière.

The modern flight to the towns, unlike the earlier migrations of
rural groups, constitutes a permanent escape from the control of the
elders. Unlike rural migrants, town dwellers do not reproduce in their
new locations the social structure of the villages they come from. In
rural society the elders exercise authority in all institutional situations;
in town, the structure is institutionally differentiated. A man depends
for economic resources on his employers; in public affairs, on the government bureaucracy; for ritual services, on one of a number of local
congregations. He rents his house, and his wife borrows sugar from
neighbors who are not relatives. He keeps up his ties with his kinfolk
and his village largely in order to preserve rights that he may someday

want to exercise, perhaps when he retires. In town his elders are of
no particular use to him; their functions are distributed among many
different organizations. Consequently, when elders do visit from the
country, they come as a man's kinsmen and not as elders of his present
community. Not uncommonly, the groom at a wedding is accompanied by a truckload of friends, one of whom is his spokesman in the
negotiations, instead of by relatives.

Funerals and weddings reveal the resulting lack of discipline, extensively deplored in colonial literature and attributed to the declining
influence of tradition on the mentality of the natives. Should these
same individuals return to the village, however, they would have no
choice but to organize their lives in terms of rural society. The village
elders have themselves worked in town for twenty, thirty, or forty
years; as early as 1912, Henry Richards reported that many of the
people were telephone men, engine drivers, firemen, carpenters, nav-
vies, and the like. In a different social structure the dependence of individuals on others to speak for them takes a different form; this fact,
apparent in the realities of daily life, can be studied without recourse
to pseudopsychological quantities.

In town, the organizations through which individuals protect their
interests include religious congregations, labor unions, and political
and cultural associations of various kinds. These organizations function within the concepts and symbols of a political culture common
to rural and urban areas alike (Janzen, 1967). Congregations and
other associations seek to constitute complete societies, establishing
schools, dispensaries, and economic cooperatives for their members,
but they succeed in aggregating members only in numbers corresponding to the pattern and type of authority instituted in them. Those with
the weakest and least differentiated authority structure split most
readily, amid the usual charges of witchcraft and arguments over tradition. To the despair of Marxist intellectuals in Kinshasa, the labor
unions notoriously fail to display the solidarity that consciousness of
their economic role should stimulate: "It often happens that when you
think you are addressing a group you find yourself confronted only by
individuals." [9] Like the churches and the innumerable *unions de res-
sortissants*, the labor unions continually place notices in the newspapers
indicating that the leadership has been repudiated or reconstituted,
displaying the shifting allegiances of associations whose prime function is to channel patronage in an unstable society. Political parties
are similarly ephemeral, activated principally for the sake of election

[9] *Le Progrès* (Kinshasa), 19 April 1966.

campaigns in which those who seek access to the privileges of government describe themselves as *les jeunes*, in opposition to the group in power, *les vieux*.

The *nkazi* exists everywhere in Kongo; his role is essential to the ordinary processes of government. Sometimes he is referred to as a chief (*mfumu a kanda*), but it is agreed that an *nkazi* as such is not a real chief. One may address the head of a clan section in Manteke as "chief," but to refer to him as such invites derision. To find out what a real chief is, we must know more about the contexts in which the expression occurs.

There is no word in KiKongo which can be unambiguously translated as "chief." The usual word, *mfumu*, means many other things as well. It means owner and responsible person, as distinct from slave, and in this sense is used with the verb *vwa*, "to own," which as we have seen applies to the relationship among members of a descent group: *Mono mvwidi baleeke bame*, "I own my dependents": *Mono mvwidi mambu*, "It's my affair"; *Mono mvwidi n'toto*, "I own the land." These expressions suggest exclusive rights; "It's mine and no one else's." All suggest aspects of *kimfumu*, "chiefship": *mfumu a n'toto*, "owner of the land." No slave can own land, no slave can be *mfumu*. Hence, *mfumu* (*mfumu a kanda*) means "freeman," even "ordinary citizen." *N'tinu*, usually translated "king," is similar to *mfumu* and interchangeable with it in ordinary phrases such as *n'tinu a n'toto*, "landowner."

Manteke informants to whom it is suggested that so-and-so is a chief are likely to snort, "Who invested him?" (*Nani wan'yaadisa?*) or alternatively, "Whom did he invest?" Investiture confers symbols of power (*bidimbu*) such as the sword (*mbeele a lulendo*), the staff (*mvwala*), the bonnet (*mpu*), the bracelets (*minlunga*), the leopard skin (*n'kand'a ngo*), the buffalo-hair whisk (*m'funka*), and others. These symbols identify chiefship as a sacred function; moreover, chiefs are credited with supernatural powers, including influence over fertility and prosperity and the power of second sight. A comparison of Kongo rituals and ritual figures indicates, however, that none of these features is peculiar to chiefship. The chief, the diviner, the prophet, the magician, the healer, in all their varieties, share a common lexicon of insignia and a common repertoire of special abilities associated with them.

The common feature of all these ritual functions is that the functionary has power that he has obtained from the otherworld and uses in this world. The power may be good or bad, but it is something the natural man has not got. It is apparent in the ability to stir up assemblies, to heal, to kill, to see clearly "the things that are and the things that are to come," to promote good (such as health, happiness, and hunting luck) or evil (illness, quarreling, food shortage). It may be equated with *mpeve*, "the spirit," with light (*kia*), intelligence (*ndwenga*), and knowledge of all kinds, including tradition. The power is sometimes recognized by the signs of possession (*zakama*) but above all by the ability to get things done. The various ritual functionaries represent standardized configurations of powers, procedures, and insignia, varying fashionably in time and space.

According to the Kongo conception, a chief was chosen by a committee of his relatives from among the elders of his descent group. Thereafter he submitted to a rite of passage which included seclusion in a temporary camp or enclosure and some sort of ordeal which indicated that supernatural forces approved of his candidacy. These forces are represented in various ways: as ancestors or as spirits of various kinds, including local spirits (sing., *n'kisi nsi*) and those embodied in powerful charms (*min'kisi*). In practice it is extremely difficult to tell these forces apart, since definitions vary from one informant to another; nor, since they all serve the same function, is it necessary to do so in the present context. Some candidates were required to spend the night in cemeteries, in caves, or near certain large rocks associated with the otherworld; one who died, or disappeared mysteriously, was considered to have been found unacceptable and was replaced by another candidate. Some depended on a successful hunting or fishing expedition. Those who obtained a sign of approval were invested with the insignia of office, through which the same supernatural forces conferred upon the holder the characteristic powers of the chief, their delegate. The characteristic sign of this delegation was the staff (*mvwala*) which the chief could in turn entrust to his own representatives. His standing as a chief was confirmed when he himself invested others with special powers, thus removing himself definitively from the status of cadet (*nleeke*).

In the imagination of modern BaKongo, what clearly distinguished the old chiefs as a category was the power to alter both the personal status of others and the boundaries of groups. They killed and burned and enslaved; they decided unequivocally who was free and who was not; they put down evil, maintained order, and assigned land to their dependents. The idea of such power horrifies and fascinates the people of today. A modern text for use in schools sums up chiefly power in these words (Tshinkela, 1965, p. 32):

L'autorité des chefs actuels n'a pas la même étendue que celle des «Bamfumu» de jadis. Le Mfumu orgueilleux et cruel avait tous les pouvoirs et ses décisions étaient irrévocables. Ordonnait-il la mort de quelqu'un? On exécutait la sentence le même jour. C'est dire combien l'autorité inspirait la peur. Ainsi pour impressionner le peuple, dans certaines régions, en présence des notables, le nouveau chef tuait son neveu ou sa nièce et la tête de la victime était exposée à la vue de tout le monde. Cela voulait dire, si le chef n'a pas pitié des siens, à quoi les autres ne doivent-ils pas s'attendre?

Zenga, "to decide," also means to kill by decapitation. The power of death, which is diacritical for chiefship (*kimfumu*), is a power of darkness not available to uninitiated people. The above quotation refers to an element in the initiation ritual which is also a proverb — "The king in Kongo buried his kinsman alive and upheld his opponent" [10] — which is usually interpreted to mean that a chief must judge impartially among his dependents and clients; it also expresses the political truth that one gets to be chief at the expense of lineage rivals by establishing himself as a patron of strangers (including slaves) and extralineal kin. In Manteke tradition, candidates for chiefship who failed to execute a number of dependents, that is, who wielded insufficient power to obtain the consent of the community, were replaced. Commonly the execution took the form of burying slaves alive with the body of the previous chief, thus accomplishing a double rite of passage for the old and the new. Na Sangala lacked power precisely because he failed to sacrifice slaves.

The chief also wields the power of enslavement, partly as a function of his position in his own group and partly as a function of wealth enabling him to purchase strangers. This power is a power of daylight, available secularly to anyone in some degree. Both the power of death and the power of enslavement must be demonstrated at the inauguration of a Yombe chief, as described by Doutreloux (1967, pp. 169–170): the candidate hands over to the neighboring chiefs who come to inspect his spirit (*mpeve*) and, if they find it adequate, to invest him, a number of girls as slaves; they are called "daylight people" (*bantu ba mwini*). At the same time a corresponding number of souls, the "night people" (*ba fuku*), are handed over to the same chiefs; the owners of the souls die shortly afterward. The invested chief wears bracelets on his arms

[10] *Ntotila Ndo Funsu Na Mvemba Nzinga waziika ngw'andi kimoyo ye lungisa ntantu.* The usual translations give "his mother" for *ngw'andi*, but there is no direct Kongo equivalent for "mother" (cf. Ngoma, 1963, p. 26; Cuvelier, 1946, pp. 288–289).

corresponding to the price of his dignity, night people on the left, day-light people on the right.

The chief also has the ability to divide his dependents into groups and allocate land to them; his *kimfumu* is expressed in the related ability to receive strangers as clients to whom he gives land and insignia. The patronal relationship is expressed in kinship terms as patrifiliation (*se/mwana*). The legend of Ntinu Wene, reported by Cuvelier (1946, pp. 11–14), summarizes this aspect of *kimfumu*. At a feast the king held on the "Hill of Partition" (*mongo wa kaila*) his children danced before him and each received his distinctive lands and insignia (cf. Troesch, 1953). An aspect of the same power to allocate, and thereby to establish order, is seen in legends that describe the chief as dividing his followers into descent groups in order that they might intermarry. Intermarriage is one of the meanings of the chiefly title Na Tona: "Na Tona looked upon [*watona*, "looked at," "had sexual relations with"] his sister."

An essential part of the inauguration of a new chief was the promulgation of his own prohibitions (*min'siku*), with penalties attached. The prohibitions were much alike in all instances: usually no thieving, no quarreling, no adultery. Conceptually, however, each list was peculiar to and characteristic of the *luyaalu* of the chief who announced them. *Luyaalu* (from *yaala*, "to spread out") refers to the inauguration ceremony and the mat or the leopard skin on which the chief was enthroned; in ordinary modern use it means "government." The particularistic conception of *luyaalu* was reflected in the ideal uniqueness of the candidate's success in the ordeal, his insignia, and his prohibitions. We have already encountered this conception in the praise names of the clans: the special virtues of a particular, appropriated praise name incorporating a unique title. To some extent a particular *luyaalu* is part of the heritage of a descent group; it is conferred by the spirits or ancestors associated exclusively with that group. It was also peculiar, however, to the chief himself; he personally had to be accepted by the supernatural powers and, according to the usual ideal, had to move his village to a new site. That is, he founded the *mbanza* all over again. Some of his insignia, moreover, like those of modern prophets, might be chosen by himself in response to a vision.

The prohibitions of the reign, once announced, were vigorously enforced. This part of the ideal is the source for nostalgic statements to the effect that "in the old days adulterers were buried alive." Lack of or uncertainty in the evidence never impeded judgment, because the spirits sustaining the chief indicated the truth to him in dreams or in the way his sword trembled when thrust into the ground.

The idea of chiefship summarized in the preceding paragraphs may be called *kimfumu*. It is clearly different from *kinkazi*, the role of the modern *nkazi*. The contrast opposes not only the two figures of *mfumu* and *nkazi* but the social orders they represent. Under *kimfumu* government was regulated by a benevolent despot, not by a committee. The chief was the focus of a redistributive economy. Lands were exploited by favor of the chief rather than by right. As Manteke people recall it, in the old days nobody was concerned with land boundaries; crops produced were brought as prestations to the chief to give to his people. The men of the village all ate together in their meeting place (*mbongi*), to which their wives sent food. If economic boundaries were vague, social boundaries were precise. Slaves were clearly recognized as such, and among freemen the rule of seniority clearly ranked individuals and groups. Succession to the chiefship was a prerogative of the senior house whose members, particularly the chief himself, monopolized tradition and other secrets. The structure of the clan, therefore, conformed clearly to the ramage or hierarchical type. The aristocracy, comprising the senior components of neighboring descent groups, confirmed its position by obligatory patrilateral cross-cousin marriages in the form of exchanges between equals or hypergamy between ranked groups.

To what social and historical realities does this image correspond? The folk answer is that *kimfumu* is a historical, real system which disappeared because the procedures by which power was obtained and exercised were forbidden by the Europeans. The European answer, in general, is that the colonial regime destroyed the chiefs by failing to recognize them and by substituting upstarts who did not command the respect of the people. Either way, the idea of *kimfumu* is deemed to be a recollection of a real past. This answer is too simple.

In the first place, evidence does not sustain the assumption, advanced principally by De Cleene, that *kinkazi* and *kimfumu* are different kinds of institutions, the first "social," concerned with family affairs and kinship relations, the second "political," concerned with the affairs of a sovereign territory (*nsi*) to which individuals are affiliated by the rule of residence. De Cleene's thesis (1937*b*), developed primarily with reference to Mayombe but elaborated to include all BaKongo and eventually the indigenous population of the Congo as a whole (1946), was that above the *bankazi* there was placed a chief (*mfumu a nsi*) who governed by the aid of an earth spirit (*n'kisi nsi*). The antecedents of this thesis, prevalent in the ethnography of the early twentieth century, are that in the course of social evolution territorial units replace the more primitive kinship units, and that agricultural peoples exhibit fertility rites, earth cults, and matriarchy.

Accordingly, the word *nsi* has been translated "earth" or "territory," whereas in fact it means "region," "locality," or "domain." *Mfumu a nsi* means "local chief," no more and no less, but the assumption that it meant territorial sovereign was built into the European view of traditional African society. Colonial agents were required, during the pursuit of custom consecrated by Colonial Minister Louis Franck in the 1920's, to try to identify the *mfumu a nsi*. A number of them, at least, reported that there was none. For Mbanza Manteke, the responsible official wrote: "Chefs de terre: inexistant. De petits chefs de terre ont existé mais il n'étaient pas puissants et ne réalisaient pas l'idée que nous devons faire d'un 'Fumu na Nsi.' " The district commissioner who forwarded the report concluded that the investigator had misinterpreted the evidence; [11] according to theory there had to be, somewhere, "native chiefs."

An administrator in Mayombe specifically challenged De Cleene's view: "Il est inexact, à mon avis, de prétendre que le 'ntinu-tsi' exerçait une suzeraineté sur une région determinée et qu'il y était reconnu maître absolu" (Nauvelaert, 1938, p. 408). In his view the title was honorific; the holder might be sought out as an arbiter, but no more. In an appended reply De Cleene reiterated his conviction, maintaining that if the available evidence did not support his view it was precisely because the colonial regime had destroyed the chiefs by investing the wrong people with regulatory powers.

What is important here is not one author's mistaken interpretation, but the extraordinary currency of the error, unsustained and even opposed by the ethnographic facts. De Cleene's principal sources fail to justify the construction put upon them.[12] His work has ethnographic relevance only in a nominal or fictitious sense; it imposes on the Kongo landscape an idea of African society classically stated in 1919 by G. Van der Kerken in his influential *Les Sociétés bantoues du Congo belge et les problèmes de la politique indigène*.[13] Here again a model of feudal, hierarchical society ("les grands chefs et les grands feudataires") is defended against the evidence (e.g., reports by travelers on the insignificance of chiefs) by the contention that European policy has destroyed the chiefs by failing to recognize them.

In brief, the basilotropy that governs this kind of ethnography is a function of the policy of indirect rule, which required the existence

11 Rapport d'enquête, n.d., and letter, 17 July 1934, in file on Mbanza Manteke, archives of the Cataracts District.
12 Bittremieux, 1922–1927: *s.v.* "ntinu," "p'aku." Van Reeth (1935) describes a social structure evidently much like that of Mbanza Manteke.
13 Bk. IV, chap. 3, esp. pp. 235 ff., 250.

of chiefs. In some parts of the Congo there undoubtedly were chiefs in the sense of hereditary rulers who dominated a stable administrative hierarchy. Among the BaKongo, however, chiefship was characteristically not an office but a commission, a role open in certain circumstances to a suitably charismatic figure. Commissions may be regarded as a stage in a process of differentiation wherein extremely diffuse political systems gradually establish specialized organs; the institutionalization of office in a political system, that is, may result from the routinization of charismatic roles (Smith, 1956, 1966).

The character of chiefship as a supplementary rather than a basic feature of Kongo government is seen in one type of chief, the *mfumu a mpu*, which has been adopted by ethnographers as the epitome of traditional government.[14] The chiefs known by the raffia bonnet (*mpu*) they wore are described idealistically by Van Wing (1959). J. Mertens used the role as a point of departure for a far-reaching analysis of Kongo culture (1942). He shows clearly that the system of government among the BaNtandu is like that of Manteke, involving an *nkazi* (called *mbuta kanda*) and committees of Children, Grandchildren, Fathers, and Grandfathers. He also shows that the role of *mfumu a mpu* is distinct from that of *nkazi*, although the two are often filled by the same individual. The *nkazi* has a right to the *mpu* if he wants it, but not all groups have one, and not all *bankazi* want the position; some give it to a young child, some allow others to compete for it who are not necessarily members of the group. A line of thirty-two chiefs of Mpangu, all but one of them buried in the chiefs' cemetery (*biulu*), shows six who did not wear the *mpu* (J. Mertens, 1942, pp. 140–141). Competitors had to obtain the support of clansmen and appropriate patrilateral kin and also had to spend more money than most people could command (*ibid.*, pp. 41 ff.).

The *mfumu a mpu* is the priest of the cult of the ancestors of the group. By interceding with them he secures hunting luck, health, and other desirables. The position may remain vacant for some years, until a diviner indicates that the lack of an incumbent is the reason for current misfortunes (*ibid.*, p. 48). In this respect, therefore, the inauguration of an *mfumu a mpu* is one of a series of rituals which might be used "to clean up the country" (*sukula nsi*, see below), and it is still so

---

[14] The ethnographic model is concisely presented by Soret (1959), in whose work the influence of De Cleene is manifest: "En un mot, au point de vue social, la *kanda* 'se présente comme une entité dans laquelle l'individu pratiquement s'efface devant la collectivité' [ref. De Cleene 1946], et sur cette collectivité, l'autorité du *mpfumu mpu* était incontestée" (p. 74). Then Soret supplies reasons why the observable facts do not correspond to his model.

used in Kasangulu Territory.[15] The *mfumu a mpu* conducts rituals connected with a basket (*lukobi lu bakulu*) containing the relics of his
predecessors. These baskets are associated with traditions like those of
the clans in Manteke and are indeed a material equivalent of such
traditions. "Il va sans dire," says Mertens, "que tous les chefs couronnés
prétendent avoir une corbeille qui leur vient en ligne direct du royaume
Kongo" (*ibid.*, p. 40). Every chief also knows that other people's baskets
have been stolen, fabricated, dug up in the forest, combined from
several different descent groups, and the like.

When, as is usual, the *mfumu a mpu* and the *nkazi* are the same person, the combination of ritual powers and secular authority creates a
new role. All the governmental functions proper to a chief are also
carried out by any *nkazi* (e.g., purchase and redemption of slaves, de-
fense and allocation of land, regulation of marriage), but the *nkazi* as
chief is supported by supernatural sanctions of his *mpu*. In carrying
out his role the chief depends on a committee of relatives, although, as
Mertens remarks, "Bon nombre d'ethnologues s'obstinent à attribuer
au chef, partout et toujours, la garde de l'ordre du clan et le contrôle de
la tranquillité publique" (1944–1952, X–XI, 188–189).

In this example, therefore, *kimfumu* and *kinkazi* are complementary
elements of the social structure. Ideal accounts of inauguration rituals
also show the interdependence of the two principles. In the most elaborate account available, the story of Na Menta, the "last" Ma Nsundi or
king of the BaSundi, the chief symbolizes rather than wields the power
of a regime in which the executive element is composed of the *bamayaala*, that is, his Children and Grandchildren. Na Menta, taken prisoner
when he was very young, was badly treated and constantly watched
until he reached marriageable age, when he was castrated. At the time
chosen for his coronation he was required to wage war against his
enemies and capture the *mbanza*. If he lost, he died, but if he won he
had proved his right to be crowned. Coronation was performed by
MPANZU, who received valuable property as his fee; MPANZU also provided the king's wife. After being marked with chalk Na Menta was set
on a leopard skin, with the *bamayaala* at the head and the "enemies" at
the foot.[16] "They then placed a rod over Na Menta's shoulders, set a

15 On one occasion the inhabitants of a village argued whether the *mpu* and the
ancestral basket (*kimpi*) should be reactivated or whether Dieudonné, a modern
antiwitchcraft procedure, should be used instead (Pool 28, 1963).

16 The "enemies" must be the affines, who sit at the foot of the coffin at a funeral.
A similar story is found in the traditions of NSAKA in Manteke, where the last chief
is said to have been castrated because one of his predecessors abused both his office
and the wives of his kinsmen. Required sexual impotence of a chief is a widespread
trait in the western Congo which has been little studied (De Sousberghe, 1963, Pt. 2).

leopard-skin diadem on his brow, a necklace of leopard's teeth round his neck, a plaited cap (*mpu*) on his head and a loin-cloth about his loins" (Laman, 1957, pp. 140–142).

The picture drawn is, in essence, that of the institution of an *n'kisi* ("magical statue," "charm"), which is the chief himself. Other examples from tradition show the same interdependence of the chief and a committee. A Manteke informant, repeating material he probably learned elsewhere, describes the ideal Mbanza Kongo in terms of the king's enclosure and the human body:

> In the enclosure of the king, there where he put his head was a house of his people, NSUNDI; there where he put his feet was another house of his people, NA TUMA. Then, at the door, was another house, NKOTE; also NKUTIKI, that is, LUKUTI. Whenever the king had business to decide he would have with him NSUNDI [*sunda*, "to surmount"], NA TUMA [*tuma*, "to announce"], NKUTIKI [*kuta*, "to gather"], and NKOTE [the doorkeeper; *kota*, "to enter"]. When they had come to a decision, NA TUMA would have NKUTIKI sound the drum [*n'kwiti*] to call the people, and NA TUMA would make the announcement.

> Since the coming of the Europeans government or chiefship has been a matter of fines only, without any real decisions [*kondwa kwa zenga mambu mu kedika*]. In the old days it was our custom that those who did wrong should be killed or sold or jailed.

What is missing, in modern times, is the power to make decisions that stick. When this power existed, it operated through institutions organized in the same way as modern institutions, though with very different effect. As Doutreloux says (1967, p. 191), whatever the extent of a chief's powers, chiefship is inevitably associated with a collection of people who surround the chief at least as much to control him as to assist him. Doutreloux's description of these assistants provides the best insight into the kinship aspects of a governing committee. The principal roles fall into four different groups:

In the Kongo examples it may be no more than a myth expressing the idea that *kimfumu* should be exercised on the part of the group and not at its expense. Some other stories of the last chief are clearly of this order, at least in part. For example, MFUTU tradition speaks of Na Mpyoso, who became chief when his "sister" Na Bikadyo was disqualified. Disqualification of a female candidate by menstruation appears in NANGA traditions from elsewhere, however (Laman, 1957, p. 156); it probably belongs to the class of stories, also widespread in the western Congo, which explain why women do not normally govern.

a) Children, Grandchildren, and cadets.
b) The chief's wives:
  1. Nkama Lemba, who may be a slave.
  2. Tata Nketo, his "female father."
  3. Na Nkazi Vandi Beni, another representative of the Fathers.
  4. Matsabi, a slave, who keeps the keys (*nsabi*).
c) The chief's kinsmen:
  1. Matsafi, the heir.
  2. Mantandu, another cadet, the "chief of police."
  3. Na Mfuka, the chief's eldest son, the judge.
  4. Matsona, a ritual officer (*nganga*), guardian of the insignia.
d) The chief's deputies: Kapita, Na Tsuka, and Zutu, who "go about together." Zutu is in charge of fiscal matters.[17]

POLITICAL RESOURCES: ECONOMIC

Anthropology increasingly recognizes the diversity and flexibility of African political systems. Since much of the study of those systems is conducted in terms of formal classifications, cultural comparisons and historical reconstructions frequently turn on the presence or absence of governments of a certain type. From this point of view modern Kongo society, with its diffuse network structure, belongs to a different type from the old kingdom of Kongo, which was so clearly centralized and hierarchical that it is commonly described as a despotism.

The major changes in Kongo social structure since the fifteenth century are best regarded as quantitative phenomena (cf. Fortes, 1949). The political culture, embracing the basic political concepts, has remained the same, while the exigencies and opportunities of the milieu have changed. The formal structures of government are administrative frameworks; only with the addition of historical and processual data can we see how power is distributed in them. When concentrations of power occurred, the social structure became hierarchical and approached the extreme royalist model of *kimfumu*; when power was relatively diffuse, the more egalitarian, network-type structure associated with the idea of *kinkazi* predominated. Nevertheless, *kinkazi* and *kimfumu* are elements of a single cultural complex. Their opposition is seen whenever a conflict arises over succession, either of individuals to office or of descent groups to a vacant estate. Their complementarity is revealed whenever the political structures of different times and places are examined in sufficient detail.[18] Since the principal

17 From Doutreloux, 1967, pp. 191–195. The material is evidently a synthesis of the statements of several informants. The arrangement given here, based on indications in the original text, is mine.
18 The abundant historical material is only now beginning to be published; see the bibliography in Vansina, 1966.

changes took place, roughly, in 1700 and 1885, the precolonial period may be divided into two phases. The most important factor in each was the pattern of trade (Vansina, 1966).

Mbanza Kongo (later San Salvador), the capital of the Kongo kingdom, corresponds at first sight to the utopian Mbanza Kongo of tradition, and the reign of Affonso I, Nzinga Mvemba, realizes most of the ideal of *kimfumu*. But Affonso is clearly a special case (Cuvelier, 1946; Vansina, 1966). From the Kongo point of view he did not simply succeed, after a struggle, to the throne established by Ntinu Wene. Affonso achieved a new *luyaalu*, a regime peculiar to himself, with a new tradition (*kinkulu*) of its own, Christianity, and a new *mpeve*, the Holy Spirit. Validating his candidacy, he overcame his opponents in battle by the aid of supernatural forces marshaled under a white cross by St. James the Apostle.

Consistent with the rule that Children inherit whatever estate the Father has created by his own efforts,[19] all the descendants of Affonso became eligible to be king. Except when an ambitious charismatic figure preempted it, the throne was given to a successor chosen by a council of nine or twelve nobles. For the seventeenth, eighteenth, and nineteenth centuries there are various descriptions of the San Salvador government and lists — not at all consistent — of court officials. Some of the accounts represent the ideal models of informants; to what extent these models corresponded to actual institutions is a problem for historians. What is noteworthy is the repeated appearance of regulatory committees consisting of sets of four and a triad made up of principal, a second, and a contrasted figure. The last may be a woman but is more often a ritual expert (*nganga*), one such being usually identifiable also in each set of four officers. For example, a mid-seventeenth-century account of San Salvador says the royal council was composed of four principal officials, four lesser officials, and four women; that is, there were four sets, each consisting of a chief and two subordinates, one male and one female.

Kinship roles are not usually identifiable in these committees, but it is known that two of the original four provinces of the kingdom, Mbata and Mbamba, are associated with the role *nkaaka* ("grandparent"). One of these was the fief of Nsaku, who is sometimes said to be more powerful than the king. His responsibilities included the ritual investiture of

[19] The old commentators are not reliable in kinship matters, but the usual interpretation of what they say is clearly forced: "Etant donné le système matriarcal, les candidats à l'autorité suprême ne pouvaient être pris que dans la parenté utérine ou germaine du défunt, donc frères ou neveux. Quand les documents mentionnent les fils, il s'agit ou bien de fils au sens large, membres du clan royal, ou bien d'un cas exceptionnel et abusif" (Van Wing, 1959, p. 42).

the king, who was required to marry one of Nsaku's female dependents. According to Claridge (1922, p. 197), no king in the late nineteenth century could rule without Nsaku the "prime minister," Sengele the "chief justice" (executioner), and Mfutila the "chancellor of the exchequer." These three officials constituted the "three hearthstones" (*makukwa matatu*) of the government.

Some of the functions of government were allocated to committees consisting of the king, at least nominally, a major official, and two assistants. The members of the finance committee were Mfutila the tax collector, Mani Mpanzu, and Mani Samba; the title of the last of these indicates that he regulated movement on the roads. The king's court of justice included (1) the king; (2) Ne Moanda Kongo, principal councillor, and Ne Myala, his assistant; (3) Ntinu a Mbanzi [Mbazi], principal councillor "of the outside"; Mpangu a Kongo, intelligence officer; and Nsaku a Lau, recorder; and (4) Ngudi [Nkuti?] a Ntotila, convener.

In Loango, in Dennett's time, administrative functions were allocated to six committees corresponding to the six ideal divisions of the realm (north, south, east, west, above, and below); each committee was composed of the king, two assessors, and a ritual expert (*nganga*) (Dennett, 1906, p. 24). The titles of most of these officials are recognizable as modern clan names.[20] Dennett's informants described the San Salvador kingdom as composed of Fumu Kongo (Father), Ma Kongo of the province KaKongo (Son), Ma Loango of Loango (Grandson), and Ma Ngoyo, magician (Dennett, 1898, pp. xxxi–xxxii). These relationships were represented in a totemic order: Kongo, the leopard; KaKongo, the eel; Loango, the buffalo.[21] They were reinforced by the required patrilateral marriage of each ruler (Bentley, 1900, I, 22).

The later coastal kingdoms, such as KaKongo (De Rouvre, 1880) and Loango, seem characteristically to have had four provinces each. In Loango the rule of succession provided that the governors of the provinces succeed one another in rotation, the occupant of the highest-ranked province being designated heir to the throne. In Affonso's time it was assumed that the governor of Nsundi Province was heir presumptive, indicating partial survival of the rotation pattern. Initially the Kongo kingdom was composed of four provinces, later increased to six.

In theory, the king could appoint and revoke all his officials, in-

20 An alternative word for *mvila* ("clan") is *ngenda* ("title"), as in *Ngend'aku nani?* ("What is your clan?"). Interestingly, Ngoma says (1963, p. 22) that the twelve clans of Kongo can perhaps be reduced to an original four, but he does not explain further.

21 Dennett, 1905, pp. 390 ff.; 1887, p. 73. "Totem" is *xina* (see Chap. 7, n. 9); Dennett's KiKongo is regrettably erratic. On totemism see also Bentley, 1900, I, 263.

cluding the governors of provinces. We are not told the kinship idiom
for this role, but it was probably patrifiliation; that is, the king appointed his Children to territorial offices. Affonso, for example, was the
king's son and governor of Nsundi before he himself obtained the
throne.

Whatever the details of the structure of the kingdom — and a great
deal is obscure — the power of Mbanza Kongo was real, based as it was
on a monopoly in the supply of *nzimbu* shells used for currency. Apparently the economic function of the kingdom, like that of the kingdoms
of the northern savanna in West Africa, was to facilitate exchange of
products between ecological zones. Administration of trade created a
political estate as well as a source of wealth.

For a time the king was also able to control and benefit from exchange with the Portuguese, including trade in slaves, but after a
series of invasions and rebellions and the appearance on the coast
of the Dutch as rivals to the Portuguese the pattern of trade was transformed. About 1700 the pattern that prevailed until the late nineteenth
century was established. Europeans provided both the media of exchange and the principal demand, which was met by slaves and ivory,
among other products, exported through factories located at a number
of points on the coast. A central administrative monopoly was impossible in an age of autonomous chiefdoms, the most powerful of them
located near the coast. One of the most important inland chiefdoms
seems to have been based on the markets of Manianga; to some extent
it inherited the domain of Nsundi Province of the former kingdom.

In this period chiefship was a formal means of registering success in
public competition. Power could be increased by the accumulation of
dependents in various categories, by ability in argument and war, and
by the acquisition of ritual means of impressing others. Money could
supply any deficiencies of birthright, and groups that controlled markets, caravan routes, and river crossings could combine the wealth
amassed through trade and taxation with the power inherent in commercial administration. By such means greater chiefs emerged and
obtained paramountcy over lesser chiefs, but there was little stability in
hierarchies thus established. In Mayombe the highest title (*bwene,
wene*) was Mbenza, followed by Divungu, Kayi kwa Vungu, and others
(Doutreloux, 1967, p. 181; cf. Laman, 1957, p. 151). Although in theory
the hierarchy of titles formed the framework of the structure of kingdoms, continual competition changed the composition of groups within
the structure.

Most descriptions of San Salvador emphasize the powerlessness of the king.[22] Throughout the nineteenth century, however, concentration of power, where it existed, was clearly associated with pervasive hierarchization of society. Three classes were the rule: a small number of freemen or chiefs (*mfumu*); the "bourgeoisie," free descendants of slaves; and the slaves (Brásio, 1961, p. 137). Differences in dress made the ranking obvious, and marriage patterns confirmed it (D'Hanis, 1890, pp. 146–147). On the other hand, Phillips, describing coastal kingdoms in the 1880's, noticed that many slaves freed themselves and advanced their status by successful trading. The error of his conclusions was pointed out to him (1888, p. 230): "A keen lawyer of the place explained to me: "You see the pattern on this plate, you cannot alter it, the white is made white and the black is made black, and no one can change it. So it is with slaves, they are born so, and the free people are born free, and no man can make it not so."

Even in the nineteenth century the ideal was inevitably at odds with the facts, for the Kongo ideal makes no provision for deviants, the ambitious, and the dissatisfied; since the *mbanza* cannot accommodate them they must depart from it, voluntarily or involuntarily. A missionary in the 1880's remarked that the violence of the chiefs, symbolized by the heads impaled around their enclosures, contrasted sharply with the pacific character of the population at large; homicides and assaults were rare; accusations of witchcraft were frequent. Although the people had a horror of bloodshed, they attended public executions as entertainments (Brásio, 1961, pp. 68–69, 131). The importance of the patron to political processes in the same period is shown in the following comments (Phillips, 1888, pp. 218, 228, 226):

Reliance on the capable man is a very prominent trait in their character. . . . a master of slaves, or the father of a family, may be very exacting towards his dependents, yet they will support him devotedly if only he can protect them from outside annoyance.

Unpopularity of a chief may cause a tribe to desert him, they congregating around a mission station, but this cannot be expected to last: some necessary regulation of the missionary's may cause the dispersion of the new converts.

With the cessation of the slave trade, the chiefs became poorer, and the whole of the working population was turned to produce and sell to the whites.

The structures of government in inland kingdoms were less elaborate and still less stable than those in coastal kingdoms. The principal con-

22 E.g., Jadin, 1957, pp. 327–328. The missionary António Barroso (Brásio, 1961, p. 131), describes an incident in which the king, having wounded his own slave, was judged by a council which fined him; the councillors themselves, but not the slave, shared the fine.

cern of the chiefs, when Europeans began to penetrate the interior, was that their trade monopolies would be destroyed, as indeed they soon were. The slave trade enabled chiefs to dispose of deviants, acquire dependents, and reward their followers with the proceeds of levies on caravans to and from the coast. Later on, when peanuts and ivory were the principal exports (Sir Harry Johnston said most of the "olive" oil sold in Europe was made from peanuts), gunpowder, gin, and rum were the leading imports. Stanley describes a chief who, backed by his young men, sat down in the path in front of Stanley's party and demanded rum; Stanley, never one to observe local conventions, discomfited the chief by refusing to pay. He thought the chief was a scoundrelly boozer, although in fact imported and redistributed alcohol was the mainstay of the political system, ensuring the loyalty of clients.[23]

Traditions refer to the markets of this era as the creations of individual chiefs. Sometimes they were, but usually a market, or a series of markets, was regulated by a group of three or four chiefs. On his first journey through the continent, Stanley encountered several of these market groups (1879, II, 404, 452). At Palabala, an important trade route junction, four local chiefs took turns presiding over local government, each collecting taxes and giving judgment on the day of his own market; the four market days made up the Kongo week. The markets, placed outside villages, were government centers monopolizing the highest authority, specifically the right to execute criminals. Thus difficult political problems were removed from the village proper, and neighboring chiefs reinforced one another's control over dependents.[24]

A Kasangulu informant described the structure of a market governing committee as follows:

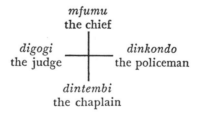

The dialect is KiLemfu. The translations of the terms (into French), and the relative positions of the officials, are the informant's own. The parallels between this committee and other committees described above are evident.

[23] Weeks (1908, p. 427) briefly describes a redistributive economy of the period.

[24] Jacob Munzele (1966) has written the best account of market government, but it has not been translated. See also Weeks, 1914, chap. 19.

When a chief became powerful, in association or in competition with other chiefs in the vicinity, he attracted dependents who were attached to his own group by the use of the *mvila* ("clan") as an organizing device. Each *kanda* ("exogamous local descent group") received from its patron rights to land and insignia from which it took its name, adding the name of the patronal group. For example, MPANZU A NANGA refers to the *n'kisi* Mpanzu conferred by NANGA. In this way a whole principality could be organized in kinship terms. In the mid-nineteenth century the dominant group on the Ngombe plateau was NGOMBE; when the regime collapsed, probably because of declining trade, some of its clients, such as NANGA KYA NA NGOMBE, fled westward into Mbanza Manteke. Other groups displaced in the process were MFULAMA NKANGA and elements of NKAZI A KONGO.

The same system unified the provinces of the old kingdom; the dependents of Ma Nsundi, for example, all assumed the NSUNDI name (Laman, 1953, chap. 3). The various groups of NSUNDI in the Manteke area remain from that era; I have evidence of the assimilation of NSUNDI ancestors into the genealogies of relatively recently arrived NTUMBA houses.

Regimes of the least importance are represented by NANGA in Manteke, whose heterogeneous structure has been discussed above at some length. The best ground for accepting MFUTU's allegation that MVIKA NTUMBA are recent arrivals in the area is the extraordinary homogeneity of the latter, which indicates that they were not in a position to acquire slaves when that was the normal mode of political competition.

POLITICAL RESOURCES: SPIRITUAL

Although the pattern of trade is the most important variable in the precolonial history of Kongo, all social processes cannot be reduced to economics. In the main, areas in closest contact with long-distance trade had the most powerful, most centralized, and most stable regimes, in which concentrations of power were marked by the rituals and insignia of chiefship. Power derived ultimately from commercial relations was confirmed and strengthened by ritual; from the popular point of view, rituals were instrumental in the acquisition and deployment of power, which was, and is, conceived of as a supernatural resource. The ritual system possessed a dynamic of its own; such factors as personal ability, demographic pressures, and soil fertility may have been relevant to the rise and fall of particular individuals and regimes.

The legend of Na Bikadyo expresses the partial autonomy of the ritual factor. After Henry Richards had lived for some time in Mbanza

Manteke, he discovered that large towns a few miles away boasted orderly streets and an air of prosperity, quite unlike Na Makokila's three little "towns." One of these large settlements was Mbanza Nkazi, which, insofar as the region was united under a single regime, was evidently its capital. Mbanza Nkazi was dominated by NKAZI A KONGO, to whom Na Bikadyo of NANGA (MFUTU) turned when she had accumulated enough wealth to make a bid for investiture. When the augury was unfavorable, she ceded her place to Na Mpyoso.

Na Mpyoso apparently wore an *mpu*, although it was not an element of particular importance among his insignia. A modern elder, asked about *mpu* and the chiefs of bygone days, said, "Oh yes, they had little bonnets and bracelets and bells that made a noise when they walked, and all kinds of things." The insignia of NANGA, as listed by the government in 1922, included a long stick with gilt nails, a large saber, a raffia bonnet, a collar with leopard's teeth and claws, and a leopard skin "completely worn out." By 1931 all except the saber, which NSAKA keeps in his house, had been disposed of, reportedly on the advice of the mission. In other villages such objects give rise to lawsuits, invariably in connection with disputes over landownership but essentially struggles for relative autonomy (*kimfumu*). The chronicle of the objects themselves — who made them, inherited them, borrowed them, remade them, and so on — constitutes a political history of the neighborhood.

In 1956 two houses of NDUMBU engaged in a dispute over possession of "government objects" (*biima bya luyaalu*). The first house (represented by Na Nkutu) claimed a monopoly of all insignia, but the third house (represented by Nlalu), composed of ex-slaves, had celebrated their redemption by ordering new insignia. The order of the houses is, of course, itself controversial. The following testimony was given by the representatives of the two houses (Mbanza Manteke 42, 1956):

NKUTU: My forebears Na Kimbuta and Na Lonzi in our clan NDUMBU took buffalo [*mpakasa*] hair and put it in a handle in order to discuss affairs in the midst of the people, and this we call *mfunka* ["fly whisk"]. Also they had a saber or great sword [*mbele yanene*]. Lalu has unjustly retained these things.

When Na Kimbuta died he left the things to his sister's son, Na Lonzi, who gave the *mfunka* to his Father Mavambu Ntwanga of NLAZA to keep, but when Na Lonzi died his Father did not return it. When we looked for the things Na Lonzi had left we found only the great sword. . . . When James Masefi and Nsiku Malanda of NDUMBU went to ask for the *mfunka* they were given only the handle, which lacked the buffalo hair. So they accused Na Nlele [NLAZA] before the chief Makubika, who required him to pay a pig.

Masefi made another *mfunka* which he gave to his senior [*n'kuluntu*], Nsiku Malanda; but in our clan, NDUMBU, Nsiku was only a slave. After his death his heir, Nlalu, refused to hand over the things to us, the true owners.

NLALU: It was my ancestor Na Nsibwavita, otherwise Na Nkosi a Yongo, who made this *mfunka*. Na Lonzi merely borrowed it, later handing it for safekeeping to Nsakala Mwaka of NLAZA in Kibete. When Nsakala died, Na Nlele succeeded him.

Later, Na Nlele and Nsiku Malanda quarreled when a child died in NDUMBU, and Wazayakana and Na Nlele cut boards [for the coffin], but Na Nlele would not give any; so Nsiku Malanda was angry and accused him before the chief Makubika, saying that Na Nlele [NLAZA] had insulted his Father [NDUMBU]. Then Nsiku Malanda asked for the *mfunka* that Nsakala Mwaka had kept, but when Na Nlele handed it over it was only an empty handle with no hair in it, because Nsakala Mwaka at one time went mad and pulled all the hair out. Nsiku Malanda made no complaint but had Mosasi Dikumwa remake the *mfunka*. Because it was remade, it belongs to me and not to Na Nkutu. When the *mfunka* came . . . Nsiku Malanda paid a blanket, and to this transaction his son Nsakala Mosasi can testify. And this is no light matter, for it has to do with our land in Kulu.

Na Nkutu said Nsiku Malanda was bought and therefore could not hold insignia of authority. Nsiku Malanda said he made the insignia himself, but Na Nkutu took them by force and carried them to his house.

When Nsiku Malanda redeemed himself from slavery in the house of KONZO [the second house] he became a freeman [*kwiza mfumu*] in the house [*fulu*] of NGOMBO. Hence he took his *mfunka* because he had ordered it made. The handle that belonged to Na Lonzi is still in my possession.

In present-day Manteke the *mpu* has special significance only for DISA, who wears one. It had its own *n'kisi* ("charm") consisting of a bundle containing red ocher; chalk; red stones; red dye; the skin of a a squirrel; part of a leopard skin; human fingernails; *nsalafu*, red ants that sting; *nkanka*, another kind of squirrel; the head of *tunsi*, a red bird; the head of *sempe*, another red bird; and claws of the fox, the *nzobo* (a feline that eats chickens), and the leopard. This bundle, says DISA, was so potent that "if you put your two fingers inside and then put the powder to your nose and breathed you would be healed in a hurry." [25] Other people regard DISA's *mpu* as primarily a propaganda device whereby he seeks to advance his claims to land against those of MFULAMA NKANGA.

In Ntombo a Lukuti, in days gone by, Na Mbwende a Mona ruled by the *n'kisi* Lukuti, from which his clan section takes its name. NKAZI A KONGO had the *n'kisi* Nkala Nlandu. NSAKA, speaking to a missionary, emphasized that the authority (*kimfumu*) by which his forebears ruled was not the authority of *min'kisi* ("charms, fetishes") or that of military force, but the authority of "white magic."

The diversity of ritual apparatus in the Manteke region is related to the heterogeneity of the population. Immigrants brought with them

25 I am indebted to Mrs. Ruth Engwall for this information. Note the connection between chiefship and healing.

the objects in vogue in the places whence they came. In the east and south, as we have seen, *mpu* predominated, but was associated with other insignia (J. Mertens, 1942). For the north and west, Laman's books on *The Kongo* describe the rich variety of insignia and the way that fashions in them changed. Devices whose ineffectiveness was revealed by prevalent social disorder, especially sickness, lost ground to others.

In Mayombe the characteristic chiefship object was the *n'kisi nsi*, which Bittremieux regards as an earth spirit, or a fetish related to the fertility of the soil. Laman prefers to speak of "government *n'kisi*," and the focus of the rituals connected with this class of objects (usually a sacred stone) is evidently not the soil as such but the domain (*nsi*) (Dennett, 1906; Doutreloux, 1967; Bittremieux, 1936; Laman, 1957). A new political unit, asserting its autonomy by putting forward its own chief, sought out its own *n'kisi nsi* (Nauvelaert, 1938).

Besides the charms and insignia that expressed the local social structure, ambitious and wealthy people went elsewhere to buy charms and titles. Some men in the Manteke region bought stone figures (*n'tadi, n'kisi*) from the coast; nowadays, people favor magic purchased in the east (*ku ntandu*) or brought from Europe if they can afford the price and have the necessary contacts. The king in San Salvador conferred titles that carried particular powers on anyone who was able to pay the fee demanded (Jadin, 1957, p. 328). Such titles were not part of the structure of government in San Salvador. One of them, the title Nkanga Mpaka, was held by the leading chief at Palabala, described by a missionary as "a most superstitious old man. I am told he has killed more than 80 persons since he began to reign, for witchcraft alone." The fact that Nkanga Mpaka regularly sent prestations to San Salvador to confirm his title has been interpreted to mean that he was paying tribute, as a remnant of the political and fiscal system of the old kingdom (Weeks, 1914, p. 47).

Whatever the source of his powers, the chief exerted them on two levels, "by day" and "by night." In order to be able to identify and condemn witches by day he had to be something of a witch himself by night, and as such he would cause the death of a certain number of his dependents in order to satisfy the demands of his nocturnal colleagues. The killing was acceptable as long as the public interest was served in the long run.[26]

Although ideally the chief (*mfumu*) and the magician (*nganga*) were distinct (Van Wing, 1959, p. 152), in practice the distinction between

---

[26] Van Reeth, 1935; Bittremieux, 1922–1927: *s.v.* "kiungu," which means "the dark art of getting rich."

government *n'kisi* and other kinds of charms was slight, and many a chief was a qualified *nganga* (Bittremieux, 1923). The insignia of the magician included the staff (*mvwala*), bells, a bag (*n'kutu*), whisks, and other objects that he shared with the chief. Ordinary charms had the same quality of particularity with regard to their origins and capabilities, and the powers of the magician overlapped those of the chief; he also could "see" the truth, detect witches, heal sickness, and even cause death, indirectly. When the chief was particularly weak, the magical arts provided an auxiliary government for the community.

KINKIMBA

In the nineteenth century, as chiefship weakened with the decline of trade, communal cults became increasingly prevalent: Ndembo in the south (Bentley, 1887, p. 506), KiMpasi in the east (Van Wing, 1959, chap. 6), KiNkimba in Mayombe and Manteke (Bittremieux, 1936). All these cults were periodic rites of passage for the young, but this function alone does not explain their presence.

BaKongo express their sense of anomy in the conviction that sickness is rife, the birthrate declining, and the death rate alarmingly high. These misfortunes are caused, in popular belief, by witchcraft, which is the product of envy and social disorder. Even now, when the population is rapidly increasing, people of all ages shake their heads gloomily and say there is so much witchcraft about that the BaKongo face extinction. Usually the Europeans are blamed for this state of affairs, partly because they themselves, in the popular view, were witches whose hospitals and churches were elaborate devices for stealing the souls of black people, but more especially because the Europeans outlawed the processes of identification and punishment — divination, ordeal, and execution — in which the natives had formerly found protection against witchcraft. Witches are envious, self-seeking people who steal, commit adultery, spread malicious rumors, and use harmful devices against their neighbors. The essence of witchcraft is concealed ill will, whether or not it is actively implemented, and whether or not the means employed are of the kind Europeans would class as supernatural or magical; it is un-Kongo or antisocial behavior. A young man asked me if there is witchcraft in America, and when I answered in the negative, he said: "Don't you have people who steal, chase other people's women, and start quarrels in the village?" My affirmative reply brought this comment: "Well, then, you have witchcraft."

This catalogue of ill-doing by witches is the same as the one against which the chief's inaugural prohibitions (*min'siku*) are directed. When central authority is weak, antiwitchcraft procedures provide a diffuse method of achieving decisions (*nzengo*), eliminating deviants, and resolving conflicts. The very diffuseness of these procedures, and the difficulty of obtaining and enforcing clear-cut decisions through them, led to a constant demand for new devices that would maintain social order. Laman's work on the people north of the Congo River shows that different kinds of charms and symbols of power became fashionable from time to time but eventually declined. In my view, KiNkimba is best regarded as a temporary and contingent device expected to bring society into conformity with the ideal model.

Social disorder, resulting from lack of *nzengo*, is experienced, or at least described, as a condition in which witches multiply and the unrighteous prosper, in which rights are infringed and slaves pass themselves off as freemen. The slave and the witch are closely associated, the one lacking a clan and the other having betrayed his clan out of cupidity. The true chief is one who knows the traditions that segregate slaves and freemen; he can see who is a witch at heart and can restore order by frustrating deceit. KiNkimba served the same functions. It was convened by the chief (*nkazi*) whenever the country was deemed to be in a disorderly condition, that is, when witchcraft was said to be rampant (Bittremieux, 1936, pp. 30–32). A magician with the title Baku was called in to conduct it. The advantages of the cult accrued to the entire community, because prosperity and good health were assured; the chief could even get new houses built by the initiands. Manteke people and other BaKongo recall the KiNkimba as a school for adolescent boys which made good citizens of them and taught them certain skills, including climbing palm trees to tap palm wine (a dangerous occupation), military tactics, dances, the use of medicines and charms, and the KiNkimba language. The initiation lasted for up to three years, during which time the boys appeared in public only on certain occasions, dressed in raffia skirts and covered with white clay, and otherwise spent their time at a secluded site in the forest.

During their training the BaNkimba were taught verses that spoke of killing noninitiates, who were described as kinless persons (i.e., slaves) lacking relatives to protect them (Bittremieux, 1936, p. 78). They were to be killed by the ceremonial sword of the cult (*mbeele a lulendo*) which is also the sword of chiefship. After their graduation the Ba-Nkimba were entitled to insult the uninitiated as "those who lack a clan" and also lack the ability to understand the KiNkimba language (more accurately, the KiNkimba vocabulary), which was the language of "chiefs" (*mfumu*, i.e., "freeman") (Van de Velde, 1886, p. 373). The admission procedure for Nkimba candidates apparently served to exclude slaves, who would be unable to pass the test because they lacked kin in all four corners.[27]

The BaNkimba also destroyed witches. The rite was a continuous battle against witches in general, attracted to the Nkimba camp in the form of mosquitoes, but there were also witch-hunts directed against particular witches in the village or among the initiands. Witches, once caught, could be put to the poison ordeal; the bodies of those who succumbed were hung from a tree. In Manteke the tree stood on the hill Kiyengalele, overlooking the Nkimba site.

KiNkimba was not a necessary transition ritual for entering adulthood. Initiates, like others, were entitled to marry and to undertake other adult responsibilities. The skills taught in the school, insofar as they included productive techniques, were not restricted to initiates; nor did initiates subsequently exercise, individually or collectively, any ritual function derived from their initiation. It may be taken for granted that the periodic performance of so elaborate a rite consolidated the community and provided psychological reinforcements, but it seems that the principal specific function of the Nkimba was to make clear, from time to time, who was and who was not a slave, particularly with respect to young men entering into political life. "The people," noted Henry Richards, "have a horror of slavery."

MESSIANISM

Whereas KiNkimba was under the control of the elders and reinforced their authority, from time to time the BaKongo have resorted to messianism, a different kind of religious movement which has revolutionary potential. Messianic movements in the Lower Congo are mass versions of the chronic tendency of cadets (*baleeke*) to secede and found a new regime of their own. The initiators of such movements are young men, women, and marginal people; they are followed by the bulk of the population when the lack of leadership and therefore of the decision-making power has created intolerable anomy. The last to join are the elders forming the establishment; they have little or nothing to gain by participation in such a movement.

The best-known messianic movement is the one started by Simon Kimbangu in 1921 (Andersson, 1958). Kimbanguism is usually interpreted as a reaction against colonial oppression, although no particular reasons have been advanced to show why it occurred at a time when the colonial regime had been showing steady amelioration for some years.

[27] Compare the idea that a candidate for chiefly initiation must have a complete, i.e., circular, soul (*nsala*) (Laman, 1957, p. 143).

Explanations must also take into account another messianic movement of thirty-five years earlier, known as the Pentecost of the Congo, which began in Mbanza Manteke.

When Henry Richards first arrived, in 1879, he was welcomed by Na Makokila of MFUTU, who probably saw an advantage for himself in associating with this white man. Makokila, "king" of a particularly grubby and insignificant little hamlet, had nothing to lose. His over-lord, Lutete Mbonzo of Mbanza Nkazi, viewing the development as a challenge to himself, brought a war party down to Manteke. He was discomfited by Richards, who, without knowing it, played the tradi-tional role of a magically protected peacemaker and stood between the opposing lines. In due course Makokila reaped his reward in the esteem in which he was held by missionaries:

My husband and I were sitting in our own room this morning, when the door opened, and a black hand, not overly clean, appeared on the inside. Its owner followed immediately, an old man with gray woolly hair and beard, and a rather pleasing expression of countenance. His attire consisted of an old flannel shirt, and a cotton cloth around his loins, both somewhat dirty. And who was our strange visitor, do you suppose? No less a personage than the old King Makokila, of whom we have so often heard from returned mis-sionaries, especially of his kindness in giving Mr. Richards ground to build upon, and fighting in his defence at the beginning. He is chief of a large district, and much held in honor by all his dependents.[28]

For seven years Richards preached the gospel without success, but in 1886 "the bones that had been shaking for some time past began to stand up, and show very evident signs of life. Truly the Pentecostal power came as I have never seen it before; for the people began to bring out their idols for us to burn, and to cry, 'What must we do to be saved?' " Similar movements occurred simultaneously at other mission stations along the river. The background to these developments was the final collapse of the power of the chiefs, who lost control of trade en-tirely and were reduced to the role of labor recruiters for the Euro-peans. The south-bank route to Stanley Pool was opened in 1883, and in 1885 the dominion of the Free State was proclaimed. (The region of San Salvador in Angola, where Portuguese and missionary penetration was effective several years earlier, was swept in the 1870's by the charm-burning movement KiYoka.)

Richards' first convert was Lutete, a magician who had been accused of witchcraft in Ndemba and took refuge with the missionary, accom-panied by his wife. Like all the first converts the couple moved to the

28 *Baptist Missionary Magazine* (Boston) (Jan. 1890), p. 15.

mission compound, called Kivulusa ("Salvation"), where they built a
house. "Now that the people no longer trust in their charms and gods
of their own making for healing of the body I have to be doctor as
well as bishop, evangelist, judge, etc.," Richards wrote. "The converts
look to me for guidance in all matters." The demand of the women for
European dresses he took to be a sign of grace resulting from conversion, but it was, rather, a desire to wear the uniform of the new society.
Women far outnumbered men among the converts, but by 1887 even
Lutete Mbonzo, "that turbulent chief," was asking for baptism.

To use a term that became popular in this sense only in 1921, Richards was *ngunza*, "a prophet," and he is so regarded by Manteke people.[29] The prophet heralds a new regime, with its particular spiritual
identity, tradition, sources and insignia of power, administrative center, and rules. The regime offers a new deal to its clients, abolishes the
old criteria of status differentiation, and requires that the old competitive devices (magic, charms) be abandoned. It expels witchcraft and
guarantees salvation — health, security, and prosperity — to those who
keep the rules.

The Pentecost of the Congo, like other movements associated with
the establishment of effective missionary and colonial control in the
Lower Congo, was a messianic capitulation to a new regime that promised order. Unlike the movement of 1921, this messianism did not
sweep the entire area all at once because a sense of common identity
was lacking; rather, each region and village capitulated separately. Under the new regime, it was anticipated, slavery and land boundaries
would be abolished; there would be a new apportionment of land
by the new chief, who would make all necessary decisions in the light of
the new revelation of truth. Richards himself recognized "the danger of
mass movements. . . . The people think that if *one* is converted *all*
must be." He tried to overcome this attitude by interrogating candidates for baptism individually and by stressing the idea of personal salvation, but he noted also that the first Christian proselytizer usually
became the leader in a village that converted. One of his most successful workers was Thomas of MFUTU, who became government chief in
the *chefferie* of Manteke. As I have already noted, in most villages in
the region the Baptist congregation is the establishment at prayer.

On the other hand, the BaKongo are prepared to be disappointed;
power is ambiguous, and the white man's power, like that of others,
required commerce with darkness. It was believed that Henry Richards
stored the souls of the deceased in his attic before exporting them to

29 The theology of the prophetic role and the ways in which Richards fulfilled
it are too complex to be included here.

the otherworld; when the people were shown that the space was empty they said, "In daytime, yes; but *at night* — ah!" It was expected that anyone who learned the new magic would have to pay a relative as the price (Mabie, 1952, p. 68).

The worst period of colonial oppression, beginning in 1887, was associated with epidemics of sleeping sickness so severe that in 1890 Richards wrote: "I candidly believe that . . . [the population] is dying out." This experience "sorely tried the faithful" but did not reverse the process of conversion to Christianity. Forced recruitment of porters, laborers, and soldiers by the Free State in the 1890's caused many villagers to seek refuge in the forests. "The policy of the State is anything but wise. If their *capitas* or carriers fail to fulfil an agreement according to the State mind they send vagabond soldiers in the villages to take away women belonging to any one as prisoners." These conditions favored rather than hindered the missionary, to whom many people came for protection.

Responding to an international outcry, the Free State mended its ways. After the reforms of 1906 and the creation of the Belgian Congo in 1908, conditions improved. Sleeping sickness was brought under control, and forced labor, now exacted in the name of education, was limited. "Now there is more peace," wrote Richards; "the people are coming together and building larger and better villages on good sites and, as usual, give them other names, and the old names are sometimes forgotten. . . . The people live in better houses, . . . eat more wholesome food, use soap on their bodies, make clothes to wear . . ." What then can have stimulated the messianic upheaval of 1921, a mass reaction against both the state and the missions? If the developments of the preceding twenty years are examined from the standpoint of the villagers, two related factors stand out: the policy of indirect rule and the Protestant missionary policy of congregational self-support.

The policy of indirect rule took shape in 1910 in the form of a decree requiring that all natives be assigned to chiefdoms (*chefferies*), whose boundaries were deemed to be determined by tradition. Before that (in 1891 and 1906), the law allowed for the recognition of local dignitaries by the state, but did not organize the population as a whole. Government agents, particularly in the Lower Congo, were expected to inquire into the social structure of indigenous communities and award the medal of chiefship only to people whom custom had already designated as chiefs. This policy was confirmed and extended by Louis Franck, who became minister of the colonies in 1919 and with whose name the policy as applied to the entire colony is usually associated (Franck, 1921). Where chiefship was particularly weak, Franck provided for the creation of sectors and encouraged the fostering of individuals as artificial chiefs.

The BaKongo were therefore thrown back on their own resources. Whereas they had heretofore looked to Europeans — administrators, traders, missionaries — to make decisions for them in every field, they were now told to turn to their traditional chiefs. But in this part of Congo there never had been chiefs in the sense understood by the Europeans, and the same Europeans had gutted the political system that in times gone by had permitted the rise of those more or less charismatic figures whom the Europeans took to be chiefs; no longer could local bosses tax trade, execute witches, and acquire slaves. The only political resource available was the patronage of the European, whether administrator or missionary. Moreover, native society as a whole was assumed to be apolitical, and an elaborate ideology was invoked to explain how it worked in the absence of politics. This ideological construction, called *la coutume*, is further discussed in chapter 11.

At the same time Protestant missionaries, anxious to see the fruit of grace revealed in communities of prosperous farmers and artisans corresponding to the ideal peasants of European social reformers, and further prodded by the treasurers of their organizations who lacked funds to support growing congregations in the mission field, increasingly stressed the goal of congregational self-support. Christians were expected to support their own catechists and teachers and pay for their own buildings and equipment by tithing. They were also expected to help pay for the cost of medical treatment; this policy was instituted at the hospital in Mbanza Manteke shortly after 1900.

The new policy and the reasons for it ran completely contrary to the principles of the indigenous economy and are still not understood by the village people at large. In the indigenous economy goods are transferred in gift or exchange: the former creates a social bond and is not calculated; the latter is a commercial transaction, for profit, which is possible only in the absence of a bond (see chap. 6, above). In Manteke even a nominal charge for medication is taken as a sign that the physician is making a profit at the patient's expense. The missionary ideal of the Christian — individually saved, economically self-sufficient, and socially autonomous — is the Kongo ideal of complete anarchy.

Richards' annual reports show how much opposition the self-support policy aroused: "Many are saying, 'You are only after our money.'" During the same period the people were learning that the European regime was divided and that it was possible to play Protestants, Catholics, and government against one another. "As the Jesuits are very active out here," wrote Richards, "we Christians must all pull together." After 1910 the newly instituted government chiefs were often the focal points of missionary competition.

In sum, during the second decade of the twentieth century the promise of utopia was replaced by a political order of rival patrons competing for clients. Litigation over land and slavery occupied the government's new chiefs and the territorial agents. In 1913 Richards noted sadly that polygamy, which had been dying out, was on the increase, and that "even our Christian chief, one of our earliest converts," had succumbed to temptation. In 1917 he reported that a new difficulty, the question of the relations between state and Church, had arisen. In one village "about one half maintained that when a Medal chief decided a matter brought against a church member the church must accept the decision and refrain from further discipline"; Richards rejected this point of view, and quoted Scripture to uphold a policy of double jeopardy. At this time the missionaries were less and less in direct contact with the people, who dealt instead with Congolese catechists, pastors, primary school teachers, and medical assistants.

The resources to which indigenous society was forced to return, by government and missionary alike, had been severely curtailed. Congolese were invited to be laborers and assistants, but not managers. The new chiefs were not allowed to make the kind of decision that was regarded locally as definitive, and many of their decisions could in any event be appealed. Such authority as they had was founded upon a European concept of tradition which in native eyes was entirely arbitrary. One could say, erring only by exaggeration, that it has never occurred to most of the people that what the government refers to as "custom" is meant to embody the traditions of their ancestors, *fu kya nsi*.

In a situation so profoundly anomic it is not surprising that a mass movement in search of yet another new regime should begin in a stronghold of the Baptist Missionary Society. The prophet Kimbangu himself, according to some reports, had been disappointed in his desire to become a catechist. In a few days the movement spread throughout the province, affecting Catholic and Protestant regions alike. Everywhere the established elders were the least affected by it. The big mission hospital in Mbanza Manteke was deserted, the sick having betaken themselves to Kimbangu, who charged no money; the local prophet was a young man who had recently been expelled from the church for taking a second wife. Kimbanguism was not, however, a reversion to paganism; as the people saw it, it was a return to the true promise of Christianity, the utopia that the missionaries had preached but then subverted (MacGaffey, 1969).

The Kimbanguist movement was suppressed by the colonial government, but new outbreaks of it and of other movements like it continually recurred (Doutreloux, 1965). The suppression marks the beginning of the modern phase of rural Kongo society, characterized by the petty tyranny of more or less irresponsible government chiefs, increasing litigation over land, unresolved accusations of witchcraft, and flight to the cities. Somewhat later, the modern institution of "customary" marriage was established.

As we have seen, political power in modern Kongo society is diffused throughout a network of affinally linked matrilineal groups, the latter representing the outcome of political processes rather than the starting points. Politics is superficially secular, and ritualized concentrations of power are missing. The same ritual equipment still exists, however, as an expression of an institutional system and a related ideology which have shown remarkable powers of persistence. Many of the ritual behaviors of Mbanza Kongo can be observed today even in secular and colorless Mbanza Manteke. Wherever power is demonstrated or asserted, even in small degree, magical attributions flow toward it. The successful party at a land case brandishes *mvwala, m'funka, mpu, n'kand'a ngo*; an *nkazi* dances, and women rush up to tie cloths around him, transforming him temporarily into *mfumu*.

The most impressive demonstration of this capacity for magical expression occurred before independence. Perusal of the nationalist KiKongo press reveals that the elite were concerned at first to improve themselves by adapting to the European institutional system. Contributors approved of the *carte de mérite civique* and deplored matriliny. Only after the possibility of political opposition had been demonstrated, in 1956, did custom (*fu kya nsi*) and the ancestors merit fervent eulogies. Joseph Kasa-Vubu, leader of the Kongo political movement, was often referred to as "le roi." The ritualistic manifestations hailing the approach of "Kasa's kingdom" included a resurgence of messianic fervor; this, it was felt, was the new regime that Kimbangu had announced. During preindependence agitation, the leaders of Abako maintained good relations with resurgent Kimbanguism in its various forms, but it was only the Kimbanguists who thought of their movement as a national church, as they still do. The politicians, who had developed their power as members of the urban elite and organized it within the European institutional system, were not, in general, Kimbanguists, with two notable exceptions. In Mbanza Manteke, in 1959 as in 1921, the prophets and their followers were marginal people, of doubtful pedigree, in poor standing with the mission, remote from privilege. Messianism thus remained no more than an appeal to alternative power.

After the consolidation of power in the hands of the present privileged class within an institutional structure inherited from the colonial regime, the traditionalistic symbol of Abako, the sword of power (*mbeele a lulendo*) upright in the snail shell (*kodya*) (see fig. 9), ceased to be relevant to the government's real role, as the people saw it.[30] Its irrelevance was explained to me at length on several occasions by authorities on magical matters, and the issues of *Kongo dia Wene*, a newspaper published in 1961, commented bitterly on the distance between the ideal and the real: "Is our bondage ended?" The ideal had been stated in 1959 (*Kongo Dieto*, first issue, n.d. [1959], p. 5):

Kodya represents the tradition, power, wisdom, foresight, and intelligence of our forefathers. *Kodya* rejoices the heart, because it is the source whence came this country, the Kongo of King Ne Kongo.

Independence makes you tremble in your bones, because it returns tradition to our country, Kongo. Tradition means this: first, it will repopulate the country as it used to be, reducing sickness and death. . . . Independence

Fig. 9. The sword in the shell, a symbol of customary government adopted by the Abako party.

[30] Abako withered away after it had achieved the aims of the elite. Now it is no more than the election campaign apparatus of the group that controls the provincial government (see Monnier, 1965). Between 1957 and 1961 Kimbanguism, specifically the Eglise de Jésus Christ sur la Terre par le Prophète Simon Kimbangu, manifested the same crescendo and decrescendo of ritualism as Abako. Kimbanguists are aware of this phenomenon and have explanations for it.

will remove us from the realm of Mfutila, the tax collector, and enter us in the following of Nsaku Ne Vunda. . . . All our people will be blessed with intelligence, foresight, and wisdom, and we shall imitate the times of our forefathers.

The white man brought disease, theft, and divisiveness [*Kongo Dieto*, 13 Dec. 1959, p. 4].

In my dream I saw the King of Kongo at the moment of his coronation; in front stood Simon Kimbangu, behind him the King of Kongo, and behind him also the King of the Americans [see MacGaffey, 1968] and the White King. All of Kongo knelt down and saluted them [*Kongo Dieto*, 21 Feb. 1960, p. 3].

The sword in the shell stands for all that the children of Ne Kongo feel most strongly has been taken away from them.

11

GOVERNMENT AND CUSTOM

Reprenons la question de l'homme.
—FANON

The anthropologist working today in Congo, and probably in most of Africa, is likely to meet the ghosts of his forerunners. It is not simply that he must study the work of his predecessors in order to give depth to his own findings, but that the conclusions of previous generations of anthropologists have become part of the situation he seeks to understand. The earlier phases of the tradition within which he himself works are preserved in the policies of governments and the consciousness of peoples. There are times when it is almost his own image that the anthropologist confronts as in a mirror: in 1966 the leader of a small messianic community which had constructed a large concrete monument to be the scene of the next Bethlehem quoted Cuvelier on the historical origin of the BaKongo as part of his explanation for the design of the structure. Anthropology invented *le matriarcat*, and colonial policy was directed toward this ideal construct rather than toward contemporary historical reality. I have noted from time to time that a more realistic policy appears in a persistent minor tradition, but there is no doubt which point of view was the more influential. *Le matriarcat*, as embodied in legislation and in education ("African sociology"), has become an essential part of modern Kongo culture; it is an explanatory model that tends to orient the thought and action of Congolese as well as of Europeans. This replicated interaction brings new dimensions of uncertainty and requires a heightened self-consciousness on the part of the fieldworker.

Although no professional anthropologist worked in Kongo until just before national independence, there is an extensive body of literature on customary society. It falls into two groups. First, the missionary ethnographers, principally Van Wing, Bittremieux, J. Mertens, La-

man, and Andersson, among whom the influence of the culture-historical school of anthropology is more or less marked, are concerned with
culture; they describe traits that are analyzed and grouped according
to intrinsic affinities, historical sequences, and evidence of diffusion.
From this point of view matriliny is one trait among others; social
structure per se is not studied, even in such a work as J. Mertens' *Les
Chefs couronnés* (1942). A partial exception is Van Reeth's *De Rol van
den Moederlijken Oom* (1935). The resulting gap in the literature on
the BaKongo prompted me to select that group for my own fieldwork.

Second, the writers concerned with *la politique indigène* rely for
their ethnographic data on the work of the first group, in spite of the
fact that for them social structure has a particular significance. Social
structure, especially social morphology (i.e., the structure of groups), is
regarded from this point of view as the primary framework of society
and culture, upon which everything else is dependent. Writers in the
second group discuss customary law: the allocation and maintenance
of rights within the structure of groups, especially in regard to
marriage, the filiation of children, transmission of property, land
tenure, and chiefship. Matriliny, or that more comprehensive model
known as *le matriarcat*, becomes the dominant characteristic of Kongo
life. The leading members of this group are De Cleene, Gelders, and
Malengreau, all of whom have defended the policy of indirect rule and
have used data referring to the BaKongo for generalizations applicable
to the Belgian Congo as a whole.

The context of concern is the colonial situation, and the pervasive
theme is social constraint: the constraints imposed on the individual
by society, and those imposed by the colonial regime on indigenous
society through the courts, the chiefs, and the economy.[1] The basic
assumption is authoritarian: individuals must be constrained by specific institutions, if anarchy is not to result. The clan, it is agreed, is an
anachronism rapidly disappearing in the face of modern conditions and
aspirations; the question is, What shall take its place? Gelders advocates a reformed and modernized clan; De Cleene calls for a bilateral
family of European inspiration. Order in indigenous society and the
persistence of the colonial regime are implicitly allied; to be avoided
are unbridled individualism, communism, xenophobia, delinquency,
immorality, and insubordination.

Ethnographic data in these texts consist of little besides the stock
quotations from Van Wing. Imagination is thus free to construct a

1 "L'étude du clan dans ses rapports organiques avec la société indigène s'impose à
quiconque veut observer le phénomène de la compénétration des civilisations au
Congo. Elle intéresse donc en tout premier lieu l'administrateur coloniale" (De Cleene,
in Gelders, 1943, p. 65).

clan indigène corresponding to no African reality and to put forward such inventions as De Cleene's *mfumu a nsi* ("territorial sovereign"). Examination shows that the problems with which these authors earnestly wrestle are not empirical problems at all but products of European social theory.

There is no point in tracing here the origin of each of the sociological and philosophical ideas for which Gelders' *Le Clan*, for example, is a veritable attic; suffice it to say that the dominant theoretical influence is that of Durkheim, particularly of his *The Division of Labor in Society*. All discussions of *la politique indigène* in the period in question, approximately 1920–1950, are haunted by the same dark shadows that troubled Durkheim: the mob, revolution, anarchy. The hope explicitly held is that in Congo, firmly controlled by enlightened scientists, the errors and evils of Europe can be avoided. Society cannot be left to itself; the result is usually lamentable. Nor, by the same token, can individuals be left alone: "la personalité libérée de ses contraintes détruit l'ordre; il lui faut une tutelle" (Gelders, 1943, p. 6).

This essentially authoritarian tradition in social science poses a problem of concern to Europeans as to all peoples. The problem is the nature of civilization, and proposed analyses and remedies are based on the idea of social structure as the primary force constraining the individual in the interests of order. In the heyday of imperialism the empirical opposition that best represented the polarity between civilization and noncivilization was the relation between European and African. The physical contrast between white and black was used to define by contraposition the nature of civilization (MacGaffey, 1966c); the cultural and psychological attributes of the black race were constructed as negative versions of the qualities deemed characteristic of the white race.

In colonial Congo the negative characteristics of the black race were summarized in the form known as "the Bantu mentality." The absolute difference between the Bantu and the European mentality was a fundamental postulate of the policy of indirect rule, as Monsignor de Hemptinne's critique (1928) pointed out, and the institution of this policy coincided with a turn toward despotism in colonial policy as a whole (J. Sohier, 1966).

A comprehensive catalogue of the deficiencies of the black race is given by Gelders (1943), but its contents are already familiar to students of *la science coloniale* as written in English, French, or Dutch: the black man is sentimental rather than rational; spendthrift, not prudent; passive, incapable of initiative; and so on. His positive aspirations, insofar as he has any, are "cultural and spiritual"

(Gelders, p. 63). Above all, he is neither economic man nor political man, and in black society the individual is not yet differentiated from the collectivity, which is the clan: "Le sens politique, dont les noirs ont toujours manqué" (*ibid.*, p. 13); "Le clan n'est pas favorable au développement de la personnalité humaine" (De Cleene, in *ibid.*, p. 67).

The assumption that individualism (*conscience de l'individu*, etc.) is absent is purely dogmatic. The history of economic development in Belgium, the United States, and other Western countries is a history of the development of corporations and corporation law. This fact does not keep Belgians and Americans from celebrating the achievements of economic individualism and the Protestant ethic. In Congo, where corporate structures have entirely different functional characteristics, the most superficial observation reveals that Congolese, and BaKongo in particular, do not behave as dogma demands; on the contrary, in pursuit of individual advantage, economic and political, they are ingenious, aggressive, conniving, and indefatigable. The discrepancy between theory and fact has been treated by scholars as an empirical paradox: "Les sociétés africaines, bien que nettement communautaires, sont pourtant à la fois fortement individualistes" (Gelders, 1943, p. 9). The scholarly solution was to distinguish between true individualism (commendable) and egocentrism (deplorable). Similarly, civilized collectivism (progressive) was distinguished from its primitive forms (stagnating). Malengreau, explaining that corporations in African society are not really corporate, asserts (1947, pp. 58–63) that although a sense of generality was present the spirit of solidarity was lacking; the natives had "l'esprit sociétaire," but not yet, in his view, "l'esprit communautaire."

The entire theory of the clan as the matrix of native society depends on the assumed characteristics of the Bantu mentality. The apolitical African instinctively reveres tradition and unthinkingly imitates the habits of his ancestors (De Cleene, in Gelders, 1943, p. 66):

Le chef de clan, étant celui qui dans la conception indigène se trouve le plus rapproché des ancêtres, a de ce fait une autorité quasi religieuse sur tous les membres du clan. Personne ne fera opposition à sa volonté, parce que tous sont persuadés qu'il parle et agit au nom des ancêtres. Obéissance et loyauté à son égard sont pour eux des sentiments tout naturels.

The Kongo authoritarian ideal, which I have called *kimfumu*, corresponds very closely to that of colonial science. In both, politics is a threat to order in society. Politics is self-seeking individualism which obscures the truth and prevents rational decision making conducive to the greatest good of the community. Order results from obedience to the chief, not from argument.

In fact, the precolonial Kongo chief was much like the "Big Man" of Melanesia, another figure whom the ethnography of the period frequently endowed with more authority than he possessed. He was a successful competitior in an unstable political system, although the normative principles of Kongo political structure, like those of Melanesia, are also, under certain conditions, capable of expression in centralized, hierarchical, and relatively stable regimes (Powell, 1960; Sahlins, 1963). In colonial times chiefs disappeared not because the colonial regime awarded medals to the wrong people but because it sought to monopolize power of every kind, political, economic, and religious. The rituals of power could not be attached to the regime itself as long as it was based upon an alien (i.e., European) institutional system and as long as its relations with native society were based upon the mistaken idea of custom incorporated in the policy of indirect rule. These conditions both persist today, although Belgian personnel in the government have been replaced by Congolese.

GOVERNMENT CHIEFS

To this day few Congolese comprehend the idea of a state or other political unit based primarily on territoriality rather than on descent. For Kongo villagers in particular, government is not something established to govern a limited territory; a government is the representative of a particular power, for whose operation and influence a center is much more important than a periphery. To *bisi Manteke,* "the commune of the BaMboma" means a group of officials occupying certain buildings in Manteke village. The government (*luyaalu*) has its sphere and the people have theirs; the latter is called *fu kya nsi* ("local custom"), an expression that implies the popular (in both senses of the word) rather than the traditional.

This particularistic concept of government is related to the original meaning of *luyaalu,* which refers to the investiture ceremony of a chief. Investiture entitles the chief to the use of insignia that represent the particular power and authority conferred upon him according to the particular source whence they come, perhaps the ancestors of his group or such and such an *n'kisi.* Eligibility for *luyaalu* is a status from which no man willingly admits his exclusion. Each of seven different elders confided to me that he alone was the true hereditary chief of Manteke. As we have seen, the illusion of solitary grandeur is built into tradition; if the opportunity arises, any clan can visualize its founding ancestor arriving over the horizon from Mbanza Kongo, accompanied by his niece and followed at a respectful distance by his son, to whom the girl is later given in marriage, there being no other inhabitants in the land.

When a chief established himself, representing a clear concentration of power, the entire structure of the group with which he was associated tended to assume a hierarchical form, within which the clan sections and the houses and lineages of each clan section were ranked. Marriage patterns, and the preferred institutional forms of marriage, would tend to conform to the hierarchy. Increasing hierarchization, however, tended toward its own destruction, as junior descent lines and younger sons were increasingly excluded from privileged roles. Hence the instability of any particular structure and the incessant flux of migration.

The new *luyaalu* of the Europeans was not thought of as a fundamentally different kind of institution. It was an expression and a source of power, with its own modalities, which could benefit its clients. The dominant elements in the indigenous communities regarded it as a threat; the less satisfied often expected it to benefit them. New possibilities had been introduced, but the game was the same. Even to speak of "the European regime" is to distort the popular conception, which distinguishes the *luyaalu* of the Free State from that of the Belgian Congo. In 1960, after independence, a number of landowners attempted to take back tracts given to the Belgian Congo (or at least to renegotiate the agreement in the expectation of profit) on the ground that the Republic was a new *luyaalu*.

When the south-bank route was opened in 1883 the Free State sought out chiefs through whom to communicate with the populace. NLAZA of Kinkanza, who was a small boy at the time, gave the following account, on 15 July 1965, of how the chiefs got their medals.

Stanley appeared in this country with his *kalaka* ["clerk"], George, and fifty soldiers and his donkey-drawn machines for transport. He slept, and in the morning he called for the chiefs. Nsakala Mbenza of NLAZA and Nsyama Nzyenda were of one house, and Stanley asked them, "In your descent group [*mu wungudi weno*] who is senior?" They said, "Mwene Nsamu a Yela came first, but he has run away to the forest." Then Stanley went to see the falls in the Congo River, came back, and passed on to Mbanza Manteke. Very early in the morning he departed for Matadi by way of Kongo dya Lemba to have a look at the country, which he saw was good. A European called Lembama whom he sent to look for porters (and there was another one called Mabasi) came to bestow the chiefship. Then Nsakala Mbenza and Nsyama Nsyenda began to urge each other, the one saying, "You wear it," and the other, "No, you." When Mabasi saw what was happening he left two staffs of office, but that ended his responsibility. Then the other European asked for porters; he was given two, and he went back to Tendele and Mbanza Manteke by the road through Nzanza Ntala.

When Mfumu Mbonzo of Mbanza Nkazi heard the story of how Nsakala Mbenza and Nsyama Nzyenda were afraid of the chiefship, he went to Mbanza Manteke where he found the European called Mabasi. He sought out his clerk, George, and said, "Listen, those people to whom you gave the chiefship in Kinkanza have run away, but I would like to have it." George said, "What's it worth to you?" and Mbonzo replied, "A pig and a goat." So he was invested with the medal. When he had got it he went to Mfumu Matombokele in Ngombe and said, "If you want to be chief too, pay me so much and I'll speak to the European about it." So they went to Kongo dya Lemba, where they got the medal, and returned to Ngombe. In the morning Mfumu Lutete Mbonzo collected his payment from Mfumu Matombokele. So Nsakala Mbenza and Nsyama Nzyenda lost the chiefship and had only two sticks to show for it.

As for the chiefship of Mfumu Mboko in Mbanza Manteke, he was the one who received the Protestant missionary, so the missionaries told the government he should be chief. That's how Mboko a Nkosi got his medal.

This story was told us by David Kimbungu in Mbanza Kinkanza. He had with him Makembo Mbengi and Jessy Ndyeki, and there was with us a white man called MacGaffey, and myself, Makima Lutete Samuel. Behind them also there was Isaac Menga, but he drank *malavu* and gradually fell fast asleep, so it was hard to get the story straight. They gave us a stick of bananas, and the white man bought three bottles of beer to give them for their story, according to custom.

"Stanley" means the Free State, though Stanley himself was not in the area until later. The two KiKongo names for the Europeans in this story mean literally "one who is calm" and "one who is bald." One of them probably refers to an Englishman, Major Vetch, who was Stanley's agent in the area for a time. Overall responsibility belonged to Lieutenant Valcke, known as Ntu a Nguvu ("Hippopotamus Head"). NLAZA's story, as usual, expresses a political claim, that although the medal went to Mbanza Nkazi, it should have gone to NLAZA in Kinkanza. Nsamu a Yela may have been prevented by some kind of ritual taboo from meeting Europeans, but my informant could not confirm that he was. A more obvious explanation is that he was frightened; to this day, the first reaction of much of the population of the interior villages, on hearing of a European's approach, is to disappear into the forest. The cadets, as usual, were more ready to confront an opportunity. Lutete Mbonzo of Mbanza Nkazi belonged to NKUTI A NIMA which, whatever his own position at the time, has always been subordinate to NKAZI A KONGO.

As a result of the arrangements made by Stanley's first representatives, what is now the Manteke commune was divided into two chiefdoms (Mbanza Nkazi, Mbanza Manteke) and a subchiefdom (Ngombe)

which eventually came to be treated as a chiefdom equivalent to the
others. The new *luyaalu* ("government") or *kimfumu* ("chiefship"),
represented by the medal of office, immediately became an estate in its
own right for which elders and their adherents competed; it was not
traditional, but it was certainly not something that interested only
slaves and upstarts. The readiness with which medal holders are denounced by others as slaves and upstarts is a measure of envy.

A major difference between the new chiefship and others was the
rule of succession established by the Europeans: the deceased chief's
younger brother or sister's son was the proper heir. This rule was based
on a misunderstanding of KiKongo, in which the rule of matrilineal succession refers to a man's *mwan'a nkazi* ("sister's son") as his heir;
mwan'a nkazi, however, refers to any man who stands in this relationship and would be applied regularly and exclusively to the real sister's
son only where hierarchical stratification had developed to an exceptional degree, if at all. Similarly, *n'leeke* means any cadet, not just the
real younger brother in the European sense. An *nkazi* is selected from
the senior members of the entire group he is to head, not from the
senior lineage only. If the succession is disputed, it is regulated by the
Children and Grandchildren of the group.

NSAKALA NANGUDI AND THE CATHOLICS

When Mboko a Nkosi of NSAKA died in 1905, he was succeeded as
government chief in Mbanza Manteke by Thomas of MFUTU. The
change to another house of NANGA was probably made simply because
Thomas, a literate man who was a protégé of the mission, was regarded
as best qualified for the chiefship; his selection gave rise to much
argument later on. After the reorganization effected by the decree of
2 May 1910, which established the modern institution of *chef coutumier*, Thomas was reinvested according to the specifications of the new
law. A decision made by the district commissioner for the Lower
Congo, dated from Boma, 15 October 1912, and referring to a report
of inquiry of which no record remains in the Manteke political file,
constituted the chiefdom of Mbanza Manteke, "suivant la coutume
indigène," as including Mbanza Manteke, Vunda, Ndemba, Kyanga,
and thirteen other villages. A related certificate of investiture, using
a standard wording, confirmed Thomas as chief of these villages "dans
l'autorité qui lui est attribuée par la coutume, pourvu qu'elle ne soit
pas contraire aux règles de l'ordre public universel, ni aux lois de la
Colonie." The chief bound himself to abide by all the provisions of
the decree of 2 May 1910.

According to the next document in the file, an undated and un-signed manuscript report probably written in February 1917, the chiefdom of Mbanza Manteke had been headed by the same family since the penetration of European civilization. Because the late Chief Thomas' successor, Hezekaya, was very young, Nsakala Nangudi of MFUTU, after a preliminary inquiry made by the territorial agent, was named to succeed Thomas. The agent recommended that his investi-ture be hastened in view of an "intrigue" to nominate Ndombele, "soutenu par la Mission et très aimé de la population, mais étant nulle-ment de parenté avec la famille regnante."

At this point the policy of indirect rule lost all hope of success in Manteke. The villagers, with their acute sense of the link between so-cial status and responsibility for specific affairs, could have accepted without difficulty a new chiefly office with elective succession, but the government had already decided that the African mentality demanded a hereditary chief with responsibility for all affairs in a given area. André Ndombele, a slave of the branch of MBENZA who were clients to MFUTU, did not fit the European notion of an African chief. The gov-ernment reports of this period all take it for granted that NANGA NE KONGO was the first occupant of all the land from the Lufu River to Mbanza Nkazi; that, within NANGA, NA NSAMBA was the original sec-tion; and that the house of NSAKA owned the chiefship, both DISA and NKUTI having died out.

The 1917 report, which envisages Hezekaya as the only alternative, continues by saying that Nsakala Nangudi was recognized as chief in February 1916 and provisionally given the medal in order to cut short argument among the natives. (He had been acting as chief since December 1914.) This provisional appointment, though forgotten in Manteke, had important consequences.[2]

In 1917 Nsakala Nangudi was replaced by Kingalu, then about twenty-seven years old. The record is deficient on the point, but Kin-galu was literate and Nangudi was almost certainly not; the govern-ment probably needed a literate chief. Kingalu wore the medal until 1921, when he was held responsible by the people for the death of a local man who had been arrested for associating with the Kimbanguist prophets. The government reacted to the messianic movement of that year by arresting its leaders in all the villages; the brutality of the

---

[2] All these documents come from the file in district headquarters in Thysville. Some of them are no more than manuscript notes. The contents of the corresponding file in Manteke are known to the elders and constitute their principal source of information for the events of this period. The elders know nothing of the temporary appointment of Nsakala Nangudi because the local file has no copy of the relevant documents.

soldiery at the time is widely remembered. After these events, Kingalu ran away to Angola saying that the people would no longer obey him. "I understand," wrote the territorial administrator, "that when he was invested only three notables voted for him."

The elders then presented Na Lumingu of NSAKA as candidate for the chiefship, but the officials, describing him as an old man of small authority, chose instead his sister's son Samuel Manyonza. For some reason Manyonza's investiture was also provisional; before it was made final in 1932, new complications arose. By 1928 Nsakala Nangudi had become a convert to Catholicism and had interested Father Jodogne of Kasi in the Manteke area, and a catechist was sent in from elsewhere. It was reported to the district commissioner in Boma that the Protestants resented this intrusion. The catechist needed an official residence permit, and it was obvious that he and his small group of converts could scarcely survive the opposition of the government chief, Manyonza, especially since the latter had the full support of the Protestant mission.

Nangudi's action in responding to political frustration by changing his religious affiliation can be matched by instances from elsewhere. A striking example occurred in Palabala in the 1930's. The representatives of VUZI DYA NKUWU, then officially regarded as second in precedence among the four principal local clans, took the occasion of the consecration of two local chiefs, attended by the district commissioner, to sound the war gong, playing such phrases as "I came first, I am the senior." For this "insult" they were taken to court by NSAKU A NE VUNDA, to whom the phrases were addressed. NSAKU, having replaced the San Salvador title owned by their late chief Nkanga Mpaka with a more important one, replied to the insults by saying simply, "Nous sommes des chefs, des médaillés, reconnus par le gouvernement" (Matadi 71, 1935). Shortly afterward the entire body of VUZI adopted Islam, a religion that, unlike Kimbanguism, was then acceptable to the government. They built a mosque and took on the dress and occupation of itinerant Hausa traders, known locally as "Senegalese." They have followed this way of life ever since.

In terms of Kongo philosophy there was more to Nangudi's conversion than pique and political strategy; the purpose of adhering to a specific ritual is to obtain satisfactory results. On this occasion, however, the move was fatal to his cause, for the intrusion of the Catholics threatened not simply the Protestant monopoly but the entire structure of the community.

At that time the village of Mbanza Manteke, built around the school and hospital on the top of Yongo, was a typical missionary community of a kind that no longer exists, at least not in Kongo Central. "However much he might wish to avoid it, the missionary was often given the position of a chief" (Slade, 1962, p. 150). The missionaries themselves probably had no idea how central the mission was to the social structure of the village. If they did inquire into the social structure, they did so in terms of the royalist model and the traditions of the DISA, NSAKA, and MFUTU houses of NANGA. The mission's primary concern was to oppose Catholicism, commonly referred to by Protestant missionaries of the day as "the greater darkness." The village elders, on the other hand, were anxious to safeguard an arrangement that made NANGA, as primary client of the mission, patron to the rest of the village and secured to them individually a satisfactory portion of prestige, influence, and financial security. Consequently Nsakala Nangudi was as strongly opposed by his brethren of other lineages of MFUTU as by NSAKA, the rivalry between those houses being a secondary matter. At some point in the resulting bitterness Nangudi stood up and spelled out the traditions of NANGA, especially of MFUTU, telling who came from where and who was entitled to what.

The provocation for his action was the need of the Catholic catechist for land on which to build a house and a church. Nangudi was prepared to give him some property in the part of the village where the commune now is, but the rest of NANGA declared that Nangudi was a slave and owned no land, a charge now admitted by everyone to have been a fabrication. Commenting on the charge in 1929, the territorial agent wrote:

Il va sans dire qu'à la génèse de ce différend ne sont pas étrangères d'autres querelles telles la jalousie entre membres de diverses branches de la famille-chef, de vieilles disputes relatives à des mariages, des déceptions resultant de fonctions briguées mais non conférées ainsi que des rancunes inassouvies provenant de décisions prises par les chefs médaillés successifs.[3]

Disregarding an administrative injunction, the Catholics went ahead and put up a building, but Chief Manyonza tore it down. He wrote to the government complaining that the catechist taught people to disregard the chief's authority. Father Jodogne argued that the chief's actions threatened freedom of religion; Monsignor Cuvelier added that the chief had threatened the "disappearance" of any converts.

---

[3] According to my analysis of clan structure, ownership of land, evident in the right to dispose of it, is a prerogative of the house and not of the lineage. Although two of my informants, Mbelani of NSAKA and Kingalu of MFUTU (each of whom occupies an isolated and precarious position), asserted that a lineage has this prerogative, all other sources, direct and indirect, contradict their view. The attempt of Nangudi, as NDYENGO, to "sell his land to the Catholics" did not succeed.

Describing these events, one of my informants said: "The *père* came here and wanted to build a church, but Mbanza Manteke had always been Protestant country, so the people prayed to the ancestors to keep out the Catholics; besides, Mfumu Manyonza took the *père* by the beard and threw him to the ground." The *père* in question was Father Decapmaker, whose report to the government (dated 12 December 1929) makes it clear that although he suffered indignities the one who was really knocked down was "le pauvre Sakala."

In 1930 the government decided not to allow the catechist a residence permit, but the fight continued.[4] Catholics pressed charges against Manyonza for abuse of his authority, some of them justified; on one count he spent a period in jail. Protestants accused one of the Catholics of being a hemp smoker.[5] Tactics on both sides verged on the unscrupulous. The Catholics proposed in 1932 to start a regional school in Manteke, even though the pupils as well as the teacher would have to be brought in from the outside.

The government's inquiry into the proposal revealed that only three adult Catholics resided in the village, Nsakala Nangudi and two others. One I can identify as a member of NTAMBU, a marginal group, but even after talking with him I am not sure what his purposes were. The other was Mampuya, the remaining male member, with Nsakala Nangudi, of NDYENGO MYA TONA. Nangudi's son, living at Kasi, was also identified as a Catholic, as were some of the children of the son's wife, by himself and by another father. (This woman belonged to the client house of MFULAMA NKANGA; her children included leading local Kimbanguists of 1921. They remained Catholics until 1959, when one or two of them reverted to Kimbanguism.)

In pursuit of the policy of indirect rule, instructions issued from Boma governing the recognition and investiture of *chefs médaillés* included a form or checklist to be followed by territorial agents in their inquiries into customary government. The model "report of enquiry" refers to such topics as chiefdom, customary insignia of chiefs, rights of a chief over his subjects, mode of a chief's succession, and rights of subchiefs. Occasionally the official literature admits the possibility of units consisting simply of a few natives obeying the authority of the eldest, as of the head of a family. Even in such in-

[4] At this time, while NSAKA was offering its tradition to the government as that of "the chiefdom," partisans of Nsakala Nangudi were providing Monsignor Cuvelier with the tradition of MFUTU, similarly designated as that of the chiefdom. Na Mpyoso, it says, ruled over an area including Kongo dya Lemba, Mbanza Nkazi, and Kinkanza (Cuvelier, 1934: *s.v.* "Nanga").

[5] The Catholic so accused still smokes hemp, and in fact grows it for sale. His principal customers are the students at the Catholic college in Konzo.

stances political links, however tenuous, were to be looked for and fostered. No nonhierarchical system was envisaged, and the emphasis lay on identifying the true chief so as not to upset the local hierarchy:

> Le droit du chef coutumier a ses racines dans le passé; il ne vient à l'esprit d'aucun indigène de le discuter. C'est, des lors, sans heurt et sans difficultés que le chef traditionnel, agissant dans les limites de la coutume, obtient l'obéissance de ses sujets et le respect de ses decisions. . . . Plus donc l'administration se préoccupera de conserver les vrais chefs, mieux elle sera en mesure d'exercer sur les communautés une action efficace et aisée.[6]

Without questioning the assumption that the *groupement* was a traditional unit, the investigator on the spot pursued the question of which house of NANGA, NSAKA or MFUTU, was traditionally entitled to rule over Mbanza Manteke. His dependence on a small circle of informants is revealed by his report that DISA and NKUTI, the senior houses of NANGA, were extinct. A special report dated 17 January 1932 was devoted to the pros and cons of NSAKA versus MFUTU. By this time Nsakala Nangudi was out of the running,[7] and his place as candidate had been taken by Mampuya, another pro-Catholic (and member of NDYENGO). MFUTU-NDYENGO claimed "the chiefship" on the ground that Na Makokila was chief when the Europeans arrived. NSAKA claimed it because Mboko had been the first chief invested by the government (see table 6). Taking all the rules of the royalist model seriously, the investigator was inclined to favor MFUTU, but thought that Manyonza of NSAKA would be the most practicable choice.

After his own tour of inspection in Songololo Territory in March 1932, Assistant District Commissioner L. Hofkens wrote a report based on entirely different assumptions. He said the remarks under the headings "History" and "Genealogy of the Chiefs" in the territorial report of 1931 suggested that the peoples living in the territory had their own political organization which had been consecrated by European authority. Hofkens disagreed; these *groupements*, he claimed, were conventional and corresponded to nothing that had previously existed. Immigration had not been a process of conquest, but one of slow infiltration by small groups following different routes. The modern villages represented recent and poorly integrated concentrations.

[6] *Receuil à l'usage des fonctionnaires et des agents du service territorial au Congo belge*, Royaume de Belgique, Ministère des Colonies (1930 ed.), p. 255.

[7] At an advanced age, Nangudi died about 1933 of sleeping sickness, but rumor still says he was poisoned by his brethren. The argument over his death was so bitter that his son Makokila, who belongs to the house and lineage of Nangudi's own father in NKAZI A KONGO, took the body to Tendele to be buried, denying the *nkazi* (MFUTU) his normal responsibilities. Mampuya of NDYENGO also died shortly afterward.

La chefferie étant de création purement européenne, il est aisé de comprendre qu'il n'y a pas un seul individu qui puisse appuyer ses prétentions à l'investiture sur des droits coutumières. En pratique, et toujours pour la région qui nous occupe, l'interprétation la plus généralement admise est la suivante: l'investiture octroyée par les Europeens crée un titre qui n'est pas seulement conféré à celui qui devient chef, mais aussi à sa famille.

TABLE 6

OFFICEHOLDERS IN MBANZA MANTEKE

Individual	House	Term of service
GOVERNMENT CHIEF		
Mboko a Nkosi	NSAKA	1891–1905
Thomas	MFUTU-SWETE	1905–1914
Nsakala Nangudi	MFUTU-NDYENGO	1914–1917
Kingalu	MFUTU-LEMBE	1917–1921
Manyonza	NSAKA	1922–1944
NKAZI OF NANGA		
Na Makokila	MFUTU-LEMBE	? –1890
Mboko a Nkosi	NSAKA	1891–1905
Thomas	MFUTU-SWETE	1905–1914
Na Mbele	MFUTU-SWETE	1914– ?
Mampuya	MFUTU-NDYENGO	?
Kingalu	MFUTU-LEMBE	1935–present
VILLAGE HEADMAN		
Ndombele	MBENZA	ca. 1914
Mampuya[1]	NZUZI	?
Tukota	MFUTU-SWETE	1940's
Baku	MVIKA NTUMBA	1955–present

[1] This Mampuya is reckoned as a member of NZUZI because he was a slave of Lukoki John, who was incorporated in the NZUZI house of NANGA.

In Mbanza Manteke, Hofkens observed, the so-called history referred only to the Manteke branch of NANGA. The Vunda branch, MFULAMA NKANGA, was somewhat more important. Although NANGA NE KONGO in its several branches was numerically preponderant, it did not enjoy any precedence over other local clans. It was incorrect to say that the DISA house of NANGA was extinct. The earlier investigator, because of his erroneous idea that the senior branch of NANGA exercised authority over the group, had been at pains to decide whether NSAKA or MFUTU was the senior house. This question, however, was of little importance; it was certain that the houses were of equal rank, and that the patriarch was the oldest member of the senior generation, regardless of house. Under the circumstances, Hofkens continued, since the aged Na Lumingu was patriarch it would be appropriate to invest his sister's son Manyonza as chief, the latter being also the choice of the elders.[8]

This more pragmatic view of custom apparently represents the policy that prevailed in the Cataracts District (corresponding to the eastern half of Kongo Central) in subsequent years. The supposed hierarchical character of indigenous government received much less attention after implementation of the reforms of 1933, which provided for the reorganization of chiefdoms to facilitate a program of rural development. Each chiefdom was endowed with a communal treasury, a dispensary, and an agricultural program, all nominally under the control of the chief, representing the community. In fact, however, the innovations enabled the European administration to improve its own control over local resources, particularly labor.

In July 1932 Manyonza was "confirmed in the authority attributed to him by custom." Later, when it was proposed to unite the three chiefdoms into a single unit, all three *médaillés* competed for the headship. Manyonza's strategy was to emphasize traditional autocratic chiefship; he required that he be carried in a litter wherever he went. But he was a very heavy man, and the burden was too much for the young men, who left the village in large numbers in the early forties. They blamed their departure on the chief's weight, but it was also attributable in part to political disturbances in NANGA. In 1944 the chiefdoms were replaced by a single sector with a new *chef de secteur* nominated, after the views of the community had been solicited, to occupy an explicitly noncustomary post. It is not clear what role the heads of the erstwhile chiefdoms, now *groupements*, played in the sector, except that they were among the judges of the customary court. The *chef de secteur* presided over the local court, just as the *chef coutumier* had done under the *chefferie* organization.

THE VILLAGE HEADMAN

The other customary office invented by the colonial government, besides that of government chief, was the position of village headman; the innovation may be considered a success, since the office is now integrated with the domain of the customary (*fu kya nsi*). The head-

[8] It is not clear from the record how popular Manyonza was. In trying to obtain the nomination he mobilized a group described as "the elders," who went to Songololo and signed a petition in his favor. All who can now be identified were clients of the mission or of the NSAKA house. The absence of NTUMBA signatories is conspicuous.

man's responsibilities are to pass on government instructions and other announcements to the people, to supervise required communal upkeep of local paths, and to help keep the peace. In many villages the position is held by a person of importance, who may also be the Baptist catechist and the *nkazi* of a clan section or house. In Kyanga the headship alternates between the two dominant clans, and the first occupant's grave is the scene of prayers for village prosperity, whereas in Mbanza Manteke the occupant has never been a structurally important elder. The difference between the two places may be attributed to the simultaneous presence of the government chiefship in Manteke, on which most of the attention is centered.

The headman's peace-keeping functions take a variety of forms. When some Manteke villagers failed to turn up for communal labor, the headman presented the problem to a village meeting, suggesting that he report defaulters to the commune. "Oh no, let's keep it within *fu kya nsi*; those people impose such unreasonable fines." If, however, the headman had imposed reasonable fines of his own they would probably not have been paid. On another occasion, a villager complained that his latrine had been misused by someone else. The headman held an informal meeting of the parties and some of their relatives, but the culprit himself declined to attend. Fortunately, the headman happened to owe him some money, from which he subtracted the compensation that the meeting decided was due. Otherwise payment could not have been enforced.

Disputes of this kind, falling in the realm of public order rather than of kinship or corporate relations, may be taken to the headman in the first instance. If a case goes to court, the court will receive it only if it has first been presented to the headman. If a matter of some importance, such as theft, is taken to the headman he calls a village meeting, which is the nearest thing to the legendary council of the elders. At such a meeting anyone may speak if he can make himself heard, whether he is an elder or not, and the procedure is not organized in terms of kinship roles.

The typical procedures of a headman's meeting were shown by a case in which a woman was accused by an unrelated neighbor of stealing chickens.[9] Her *nkazi* came from Vunda for the occasion. At the village meeting the headman made the opening speech but did not speak again. The parties and their witnesses were heard, with such elders as NSUNDI playing a prominent part. It turned out that the

9 The word "unrelated" here means that the neighbor bore no important relationship to the woman, though some sort of link can always be discovered. An offense committed by a very close relative is not subject to public arbitration, unless the dispute is so profound as to threaten the relationship itself.

accused had taken the chickens by mistake and that she had admitted her fault to the Kimbanguist congregation, to which she belonged. It also appeared that her husband had threatened the other party with a machete, or had implied such a threat. (Everybody has machetes and knives, but this was the only reference I heard to their possible use as weapons.)

When this information had been elicited the headman selected a group of a dozen men, of whom I was one, from the forty-five present and retired to one side (*ku nenga*). These men, none of whom was very closely related to either of the parties to the dispute, were to decide the case. As the woman's guilt was not in doubt, the discussion turned upon the fine. It was suggested that 250 francs (approximately the market price) be paid for each chicken, but the amount was doubled as a warning against theft. The total for three chickens thus was 1,500 francs, but that sum was reduced to 1,250 francs because large fines characterize the government's judgments, not those of customary gatherings. The threat of using a machete did not actually become a case of assault, which would have had to go to the government, but to remind the husband of the obligations of good-neighborliness it was decided to fine him 500 francs. After further discussion the fine was awarded as personal compensation to the plaintiff. Furthermore, the sum of 100 francs was demanded, in the headman's name, as adjudication fee from each of the original parties and, to associate him officially in the judgment, from the husband as well. The decision was announced to the meeting in the headman's name by Kingalu, the most dignified and most nearly neutral of the speakers present. The others in the selected group had instructed him in what he was to say. The woman, summoned to sit in the midst of the circle, burst into tears at the reproof administered and was told to control herself.

When the fines and fees had been announced, totaling 1,950 francs for the husband and wife and 100 francs for the plaintiff, the husband assumed responsibility for his wife's fine. His action was regarded as normal; it was not suggested that her *nkazi* was responsible for her fine. In informal session (*ku nenga*) the villagers contributed small amounts to help make up the fine: 5, 10, or 20 francs each, with no distinction as to kinship or clan. The usual busy young men who take on such jobs at funerals recorded and counted the contributions, which came to 1,217 francs. The amount due the plaintiff was formally presented by the woman's *nkazi*, with an *mbungu* of 5 francs. A spokesman for the plaintiff (not his *nkazi*, just a friend) announced that he presented 250 francs to the gathering as thanks, including 200 francs as *matondo* ("thanks") and 50 francs as *mbungu a kimbangi* ("tokens to witnesses"). Half of the 250 francs was given to the men, half to the more numerous women present. The headman's fee was divided among those who had made the decision *ku nenga*; they received about 15 francs apiece, with a little more for the headman and Kingalu.

In another case of theft, in which the parties belonged to MFUTU and NSAKA, respectively, the injured one, instead of taking the matter to the headman, issued invitations to selected elders. When the meeting took place, I was told, much the same people would be present as at the headman's meeting, but only those invited would be entitled to speak. If the dispute was not resolved by this means, it would have to go to the headman before being taken to court.

The headmanship is integrated with the customary domain because, in conformity with the principles of customary government, it constitutes a point of reference for summoning a committee to consider certain village affairs. The committee follows the procedures of other customary committees. The headman is also a point of articulation between the administration and the customary domain. The people regard the headmanship as a customary office because it is filled by popular choice and because the headman's decisions, as in the case cited above, are those of the community, even though the people are well aware that the headmanship is a European innovation and not a traditional office.

The idea that the headman is the customary chief of a customary unit, the apex of a minor hierarchy, persisted during the colonial period and still persists today. It persists because it is congenial to an authoritarian policy. Its application is illustrated by the following incident. In 1944, when Tukota was headman, he brought suit against twenty-four women who had fled to the fields to avoid having to fetch wood and water for a visiting official and his soldiers. The record of the case (Mbanza Manteke 9, 1944) clearly states the women's motives. Later, a reviewing authority red-penciled the statements in the record, insisting in a note that the offense was an infringement of customary law, the defendants having left the village without the permission of "l'autorité indigène." "Il ne faut pas citer le nom du Commandant. Le capita [headman] porte plainte parce que ces indigènes ont quitté le village contre son gré pour aller s'installer ailleurs en dehors du village (kifu ya nsi)." Thus is custom prostituted.

THE COMMUNE

The rural commune of the BaMboma occupies approximately the same territory as the sector that preceded it. The basic law establishing the constitution of communes is the colonial decree of 10 May 1957, on native areas, but a study of the laws, difficult and confusing in itself, tells little about the actual processes of communal government.

In the political ferment of the mid-1950's, the 1957 decree was announced as a liberalizing progressive measure. For the first time representative councils were to play a part in rural government. The sector system, established by law in 1933 and instituted in Mbanza Manteke in 1944, seemed to be relatively authoritarian in that the sector chief was appointed; in the late 1950's nearly all BaKongo were governed under this system. In practice, the application of the 1933 law had been liberal; the sector chief in Manteke had, in effect, been chosen by popular vote. The new law of 1957 therefore introduced nothing that was in fact more democratic than before; on the other hand, it actually entrenched the powers of customary chiefs who were ex officio members of the council and who also had the important role of nominating other council members and the members of the executive college. In the Lower Congo, therefore, the new law was regarded as a backward step. The justification for its provisions was that the leaders and authentic spokesmen of the rural population were the customary chiefs; in fact, as we have seen, these chiefs were creations of the colonial regime and were irrelevant to the actual political processes of rural society. As government appointees, they could be counted on to support the interests of the administration.

The provisions of the 1957 decree, insofar as they prescribed the selection of communal government personnel, were rapidly superseded by new policies and by the march of events (see CRISP, 1960, 1962). On the eve of independence the leaders of the Mbanza Manteke section of the political movement Abako became, by popular choice, the executive council of the commune. This development repeated the insurrectionary pattern with which we have become familiar: the leaders of Abako were ambitious, capable younger men, not the elders of the community. The chief of sector was excluded from consideration for the post of mayor of the commune because his office associated him automatically with the colonial regime. He eventually became spokesman for the resentment of the elders, and of the community at large, against the new regime.

The period 1960–1962 is remembered as the time when there was no government. In Manteke the most serious consequence of the deficiency was the collapse of the courts as an agency in the settlement of land disputes. Landholdings in some villages were protected by armed patrols, and there was much talk of impending violence, although none occurred. Under the colony, as we have seen, the government preempted the use of organized violence and instituted the courts as the people's alternative resource.

In 1962 the province of Kongo Central was established. The provincial constitution declares that the capital shall be called Mbanza Kongo, but its location was never decided. Songololo, a politically neutral site near San Salvador, the old Mbanza Kongo, was proposed, but in practice the seat of government was always on the outskirts of Kinshasa. In 1966 it was moved, on orders from the central government, to Matadi.

The preamble to the province's Edict 27/63 of 6 November 1963, on the administration of the province, speaks of the need to effect a dynamic democratization by reforming colonial structures to meet current conditions. Edict 42/63, relating to the communes, enunciates the necessity for radical changes. The decree of 1957 was officially denounced as paternalistic (Monnier, 1964, p. 239). In essence, however, the new legislation recapitulated the main features of the old. An innovation was the provision for the election of a communal council by the adult constituency of a rural commune, but this change was more apparent than real, since popular election had been accepted practice for some time. The new law (Edict 42/63), like the 1957 decree, makes the customary chiefs members ex officio of the communal council. For a commune such as Manteke (BaMboma), with a population of 10,000 to 15,000, the law provides for thirteen councillors, each elected for a three-year term. The executive college (*collège échevinal*), consisting of the mayor and two secretaries, is to be chosen by the councillors from among their own number. In practice, the thirteen seats in Manteke are shared by the three *groupements* (Mbanza Manteke, Mbanza Nkazi, Ngombe) in proportion to their population, and each *groupement* also has one representative on the executive college. This distribution is not prescribed by law, but it is almost necessary when the people have only a segmentary sense of their identity as a commune; that is, they think of themselves as "we" only in opposition to other communes or larger units. Article 16 of Edict 42/63 says that the council, the legislative body (*organe de décision*), is to meet at least once a month. According to Article 18, the sessions are to be public. The mayor and his assistants (i.e., the college) jointly carry out the decisions of the council.

So much for the law. In practice, since only a few typewritten copies of Edict 42/63 exist, the only document the mayor has to guide him is the decree of 1957. Although the provisions of the edict are generally known, actual practice inverts the structure they prescribe.

The executive college spends its time trying to keep afloat in a sea of paper work. In the colonial period the amount of *paperasserie* required of local administrators was notoriously burdensome; since independence it has greatly increased. All official correspondence is written in the pompous style of thirty years ago, and higher headquarters demand increasing numbers of copies of each document. The provincial government has added to the registrations and reports required by the central government; for example, it issues, as a revenue-raising device, its own identity cards. The machinery for handling all this paper — typewriters, filing cabinets, calculators, even carbon paper and official forms — is almost nonexistent. Moreover, the members of the executive college are completely untrained in this kind of work and have difficulty expressing themselves in French, the official language. They devote their energies exclusively to filing reports and trying to make budgetary ends meet.

The commune's assigned responsibilities include housekeeping arrangements for dispensaries, schools, the court, and the agricultural agency, using operating funds obtained from a higher authority. In fact, the commune does virtually nothing in this field; the buildings for these institutions were constructed before 1960, and nothing is done to maintain them. Much the same is true of the commune's responsibility for the roads; a dwindling number of road menders, irregularly paid, make minimal repairs in some areas. The government's efforts to encourage commerce and the use of markets amount only to a spasmodic and ill-sustained intensification of controls. Theoretically the government maintains order, but daily problems are in fact left to the villagers and serious ones to the gendarmerie. It sees to public health by inspecting latrines once a year and requiring that grass in the villages be kept cut. The communal government is effective only in repressive or nonproductive functions. The population is counted, numbered, and taxed; the commune issues marriage certificates and travel permits, sells the provincial identity cards, and sets up roadblocks where such documents can be inspected.

In this situation, administration per se is the principal form of political activity. Governmental decisions have to do with the timing, amount, and direction of levies and controls, which are regarded as the exclusive concern of the executive college. The council proper met only twice in 1965, and its only activity was an attempt to demonstrate fraud and mismanagement of communal funds; the councillors, pencil in hand, spent hours checking the college's arithmetic. All other governmental activities, some of which might in the long run increase revenues, are said to be out of the question because there is no money.

Consequently the people participate in government only at election time; even then, they could not effect any change by choosing new councillors and a new mayor. A profound dichotomy exists between "the commune" (i.e., the executive college and its affairs) and all that interests the villagers. This opposition produces secondary reactions. Feeling threatened, the college and its servants (clerks and communal police) barricade themselves behind the institutional forms and processes that distinguish their roles. Mainly of European origin, these forms and processes become ritual devices emphasizing the autonomy of the government vis-à-vis the rest of the population:

1) Public notices, for example, are put out in French. A clerk addressing a fellow villager who is an offender against public regulations speaks French, of which he has an imperfect knowledge and the offender none at all (sometimes the army language, LiNgala, is used in the same way). This barricading is not deliberate; after I remarked on it, the commune began to put out its notices in KiKongo.

2) Another clerk, in sending out a routine notice, finds that his supply of the appropriate form letter has run out; he takes his typewriter and reproduces the entire form, including all alternative phrases and other items irrelevant to his present purpose. Thus a laborsaving device becomes a labor-increasing device. The clerk's justification is that he must use the appropriate form for this act of government.

3) The communal police set out to arrest a thief who has been seen passing through the village. One of them runs back to fetch a bugle on which he sounds the alarm; since all the policemen, and most of the village, are already present and the thief has already been apprehended, the alarm serves no purpose. He sounds it because that is what policemen do when acting as policemen.[10]

Incidents of this kind, though extremely trivial, are characteristic of the operations not only of the communal government but of the provincial government as well in its routine contacts with the population; dozens of similar examples could be cited. Such behavior is deemed inefficient by Europeans and others, who regard the government officials either as incompetent, that is, incapable of understanding the means and ends of what they are doing, or as alienated, that is, forced to operate in terms of cultural and institutional forms that are alien to them and therefore impose a psychological burden. Al-

10 On this occasion the thief was not only apprehended but was beaten and kicked by six policemen at once; their behavior strongly suggested that as individuals they felt threatened by this offender against the law. When I remarked to the mayor that the offender had merely been accused of theft, he justified the conduct of the police on the ground that he, as mayor, knew that the man was guilty because he could "see" into people's hearts. The mayor was attributing to himself one of the essential powers of the ideal chief (*mfumu*).

though such comments have some validity, they disregard the primary sociological fact of modern Kongo, which is the dominant but precarious position of the governing elite. Government is not simply one role and one means of livelihood among many; it is the one important source of privileges of all kinds. Consequently the primary focus of political activity is the boundary between those who are in government and the rest of the people. Deep concern for the style and circumstantial details of governmental roles — personal titles, elaborate circumlocutions in correspondence, complicated filing systems — corresponds to the anxiety of those in government to preserve the boundary. The same style is eagerly adopted by private organizations whose function is to mediate between the government and its clients: trade unions, indigenous churches, and newspapers, for example. Here government is an end in itself, and the behavior of the governors is efficient in terms of that end.

Privileges begin with income. If the government regularly paid his full salary, the mayor would almost certainly be the wealthiest resident of the commune; the police force is one of the few local sources of steady employment. Privileges also include the prestige and satisfactions of office and relative freedom from all the petty restrictions and harassments the official world imposes on everyone else.

To support the structure of privilege, the government collects taxes. In rural areas the traders, who obtain high prices in town for rural products and charge town prices for the goods they sell in village shops, are almost the only people with money. Trade is carried on at high risk in extremely uncertain conditions, but successful traders profit enormously. The balance sheet for a village store run by a cooperative showed a net profit of 25 percent in eighteen months, a period in which goods of all kinds, even beer, had been in increasingly short supply and in which the store's losses from inventory amounted to more than 7 percent of turnover. The large-scale productive enterprises that exist in some rural communes pay taxes to a higher authority; a percentage of the revenue collected is supposed to be returned to the commune, but in practice it takes political pressure to get the money. For revenue above and beyond the taxes levied on the citizenry at large, the traders are the commune's main hope. Any new enterprise is hungrily regarded. Since accounting methods are unreliable, small-scale enterprises are taxed at an arbitrary flat rate, whether they are making a profit or not. As a result, in 1965 several enterprises that might have benefited the Manteke community were suppressed almost as soon as they had begun. The commercial community is also the chief client of the government, on which it depends for maintenance and administration of roads and markets and, at the higher levels, for the allocation of commercial licenses and quotas.

Because of their economic interests, the traders tend to lead popular opposition to government in such areas as the inadequacy of government services (in connection with roads, bridges, and agricultural extension work) and the repressive effects of taxation and police harassment. When the Manteke communal council, at one of its rare meetings, mounts such an attack, the executive college replies that it has no money. The fiscal facts are, apparently, that good administration alone would enable the commune to overcome its chronic deficit; the college is honest but unskilled. Even good administration would not produce money for the additional services the commune ought to be providing, and it has to contend, moreover, with a general economic decline and the failure of higher authority to release moneys to which the commune is entitled.

Deprived of its managerial function, the council suspects fraud and corruption, but none of its assiduous arithmetic ever touches the basic problem of efficiency. No one points out, for example, that the cost of administering the market taxes — taxes that are particularly resented — is much higher than the revenue realized. The government is not obliged by law to tax markets, but the councillors would not propose that it refrain from doing so. Everybody, in government and out, assumes that it is the government's business to regulate everything; what has not been explicitly permitted is forbidden. The idea that an individual can decide, of his own free will, to do something new without obtaining permission suggests anarchy.[11] If conditions are to be improved, the government must order it; for example, if the economy is to revive, the government must compel people to bring more food to the markets, whether they can anticipate profit from their labors or not. As citizens, of course, the people appreciate government when it benefits them and controls their adversaries, but they resent restrictions imposed on themselves.[12] As citizens, councillors accuse the government (the executive college) of concealing its activities from the legitimate scrutiny of the public; as councillors, that is, as members of the government, they insist that their meetings be closed, in violation of the law on this point.

11 I never could explain that it was my own idea to come to Congo; everybody assumed that I was acting on someone else's orders. One of my neighbors explained to a visitor what I was doing: "There are four of them, two north of the river and two south of it. When they have collected all this information they will report back to their chief."

12 "A second national characteristic is a mental refusal to accept established authority" (Kanza, 1968, p. 59).

The mayor is probably as well qualified for his job as anyone in Manteke, although he sometimes has difficulty withstanding the ruthless and subtle opposition of those past masters of the political arts, the village elders. Whenever he attempts a positive approach to a local problem he does so as a private citizen, as when he joined with other relatively prosperous men in contributing money for a schoolhouse. Although personal abilities are certainly of some consequence, a comparison between Manteke and other communes indicates the overriding importance of closeness to government headquarters at a higher level and to urban markets. Territorial staffs, in law, are civil servants with exclusively administrative responsibilities, but in fact they function as the political agents of the provincial government in its dealings with the rural population. The mayor of Manteke, which is only a short distance from the territorial offices in Songololo, owes his position to the support of Songololo against the council; in a difficult situation, such as the strike of the judges for higher pay, the necessary decisions are made by territorial headquarters, not by the council or even by the mayor. During the election campaign of 1965 the mayor acted as the chief propagandist, under territorial supervision, for Abako. The list of Abako candidates and their relationship to the political interests of the different communes in the territory were controlled from Songololo.

When territorial headquarters is farther away and access is more difficult, the commune operates with a measure of independence. The mayor can represent the people rather than "the government," and they are likely to credit him with traditional chiefly attributes as a sign of their identification with him. On the other hand, when the provincial government was located at Binza, between Kinshasa and Kasangulu, patronage was dispensed in Kasangulu Territory directly by the ministers and other members of the higher staff; territorial headquarters was thus bypassed and its political role was reduced.

Commercial opposition to government is strongest in communes closest to the major markets, which are the urban centers. It frequently expresses itself through traders' associations and cooperatives, many of which have their effective headquarters in Kinshasa. During the election campaign of 1965 the "progressive" party, Mwinda, which challenged the "conservative old men" of Abako for control of the provincial government, drew much of its support from commercial organizations. They put up opposition candidates and sent propagandists into the villages. In Manteke this predominantly urban, commercial hostility to the provincial government intensified local attacks on the mayor, who became for the duration of the campaign the focus of a variety of resentments he did not really deserve.[13]

In more remote areas mayors are likely to cooperate with traders (though there may be only a few), particularly in raising funds for road mending and bridging. These cooperative efforts for local improvements are jealously watched by territorial authorities; several times in 1965, according to newspapers reports, the authorities forbade such efforts as an infringement of government prerogatives. The officers of one cooperative, after publicly criticizing the condition of the roads, were forbidden to hold any more meetings on the ground that they had threatened public order. A village headman was fined by the commune for sponsoring an independent market.

The 1965 campaign was not simply a matter of traders versus the government. Many civil servants were also strong Mwinda supporters. Commerce and government are the two chief means of making money, but they are complementary and depend on each other. Politicians invest their salaries in bars, stores, and trucks, founding businesses for which, while they are in office, they obtain quotas and other privileges distributed by patronage; out of office, the politician becomes a full-time trader until he is reappointed or reelected to public office. Because political parties thus represent essentially the same elements of the population, they take shape only at the time of elections.

THE COMMUNAL COURT

The *chefs médaillés,* and later the *chefs de secteur,* were made presidents of government-instituted courts administering customary law on the assumption that this practice gave official sanction to an indigenous institution; the assumption was part of the accepted view of the chief, who was supposed to arbitrate disputes among his followers. In modern times, according to law, the mayor is president of the communal court, but his other tasks are so burdensome that, at least in Manteke, he has been allowed to appoint someone else to preside as his deputy. For any case the bench is composed of five judges, four of whom are nominally advisers to the judge-president. The five are chosen from a staff of nine, three of whom the mayor appoints from each *groupement* after consulting local opinion. To be considered, a man must have shown his ability in village affairs, and he must be physically vigorous to do the necessary traveling. The court is itinerant, visiting each *groupement* in turn.

13 *Etudes Congolaises,* 8(6):16–56.

About half of the court's time is taken up with land cases, which often last for days or weeks. The court meets in the village of the parties or of one of them; in intervals between hearings on a land case the court may judge marital disputes, which take up most of the rest of its time. The third important category of cases includes breaches of the peace: quarrels, insults, witchcraft, debt, and violations of the regulations of the commune.

Cases are judged by customary law, the law that applies to similar matters when they are regulated by committees of elders. Statute law modifies customary law with respect to the maximum penalties the court can inflict and gives jurisdiction in serious cases, such as assault, to the Parquet (i.e., the magistrature), which applies the written law. Statute law also requires the court to sanction communal regulations, applying prescribed penalties for offenses that do not exist in customary law. Judgments may be appealed to the territorial court, which is the highest customary court, and thence to the Parquet if it is alleged that due process has not been observed. The communal court's decisions and its tendencies in the administration of customary law are subject to review by judicial officers of the territorial administration, who sometimes send instructions to the clerk of the court. According to rule, the judicial officers should also inspect the court's records, but no such inspection had taken place in Manteke since 1960.

The judges in Manteke are usually related in some way to the disputants, and it is recognized that such relationships influence individual judges. The fact that at least two of the judges hearing a case must come from another *groupement* provides a safeguard against bias. The theory of justice is that the court seeks out the truth and that the truth is absolute; questioning proceeds until all the judges are satisfied that the truth has been discovered. It is not necessary that both disputants accept the judgment. The best testimony to the judges' honesty, amounting almost to proof, is that I never heard it impugned except by an occasional loser. The people complained only of the severity of the fines, which follow rates set in accordance with government policy.

The character and the reputation of the communal court in Kasangulu are rather different. The judges are appointed in the same way from among local worthies, but the parties who appear before them are drawn from a heterogeneous population. Kasangulu is a growing town whose people have come from every part of Kongo Central, and even the rural population of the commune, as of the territory as a whole, is very mixed. The judges are therefore often unrelated to, even unacquainted with, the people whose cases they hear.[14] As a result they are much less conscientious than the Manteke judges, who are also elders of the community; in Kasangulu the judges are not elders because the population does not form a community.

In Manteke the court as an institution may be considered a success; the people readily resort to it and have integrated it with the local political system. Yet, if asked, the people of Manteke would not rate the court as highly as I do, for it does not hand down the kind of decisions they think they want. If it did, revolution or emigration would ensue, and a modification of the social structure as radical as those of 1700 and 1885.

Government authorities at higher levels have usually expressed dissatisfaction with the communal courts. The colonial administrators who inspected the Manteke court from time to time commented adversely on the abilities and attitudes of the judges. In the official view the court was an educational device, like compulsory labor, intended not simply to administer customary law but to improve it so that society should progressively conform to European ideals. Accordingly, judgments regulating quarrels between partners in concubinage were criticized for "condoning immorality." At present the court is free of this kind of harassment, and it probably functions much more effectively.[15]

The colonial authorities discovered that the customary courts, besides bridging the gap between the bureaucratic and customary domains, tended also to preserve the autonomy of custom. As long as customary law remained particularistic and uncodified it could be effectively administered only by local elders and could be modified or controlled only to a limited extent. The modern provincial government, according to its published statements, experiences a similar dissatisfaction with the customary courts:

L'examen sur les juridictions anciennement appelées indigènes révèle que la legislation actuelle reconnaît un pouvoir judiciaire aux chefs et sous-chefs traditionnels. Il résulte que la coutume seule attribue des compétences aux juges et soustrait ceux-ci à l'influence progressive du droit écrit. Le maintien de cette situation risquerait de stagner l'appareil judiciaire du fait que le législateur a laissé inorganisée l'institution coutumière et ne s'est attaquée [sic] sporadiquement qu'aux tribunaux de secteur.[16]

14 The customary law the judges are to apply is that of Kasangulu, which may differ from that of Manteke or Manianga and which in any event is not standard throughout the commune. This problem dates back to the beginnings of the colony and to the growth of extracustomary centers.

15 The principal area of uncertainty is that of witchcraft accusations; the subject is too complex for treatment here.

16 Arrêté gouvernemental 5/64 (31 March 1964), relatif à la remuneration des

The document continues with a description of the structure of customary adjudication, which is represented as hierarchical. An essential element in the hierarchy is the village headman, who is described as president of a family council. The trouble, the analysis concludes, is that the lower levels of the hierarchy have been left unregulated, with the result that anarchy has afflicted the social structure. Like most other public announcements of the provincial government, the proclamation to which the above excerpt is the preamble had no practical consequences. Its significance lies in its expression of opinion, in which are mingled Kongo dissatisfaction and colonial ideology.

CUSTOM IN KONGO CENTRAL [17]

The version of *la politique indigène*, now called *politique coutumière*, discussed in this section was upheld by the group that governed the province from 1962 to 1965, a group derived from the revolutionary Abako of 1960. Empirically, the policy of this group was to maintain and expand its own privileges, and much of the apparatus of government — provincial ministries and the like — was devoted solely to this end. The government's ostensible functions — public works, conservation, education, and the like — were carried over, in large measure, from the preceding colonial regime. The ideology accompanying them and supporting the government's avowed policy was also, and to a greater degree, a carry-over in its assumptions, vocabulary, political content, and use of ethnographic authorities.

The ideology is expressed in public statements and government documents, including edicts. It has little to do with the government's real activities and procedures; almost all the edicts issued remained null and of no effect from the moment of issue, and some were never even published. In general, the province operated on the assumption that prevails at the communal level: government is the business of those in office. From the beginning the assembly had great difficulty and little success in inducing the government to present a legislative program or to answer questions on its policies (Monnier, 1964, pp. 246–250). On the other hand, as members of the government, the deputies were eager to allocate to themselves appropriate perquisites, including salaries, medical benefits, insurance, and the like. One proposed form of insurance with wide appeal would have guaranteed administration jobs to deputies unsuccessful in subsequent elections.

juges de carrière (coutumier) dans la province du Kongo Central: Exposé des motifs (in Assemblée provinciale, "Bulletin Officiel," 2° anneé, no. 4).

[17] Provincial administration has been radically reorganized since mid-1966 (see *Etudes Congolaises*, 10(2):92–106).

The budget, or the lack of one, was the great mystery of the government's operations. It was recognized, however, that the principal item of expenditure was salaries. Between 1960 and 1964 the number of administrative officials in Kongo tripled,[18] and even the published salary rates showed a rapid increase. The regime owed such stability as it had to its capacity for absorbing the ambitious and the influential by continually creating new cabinet posts, directorates, committees, and secretaryships, and by raising salaries. According to an informed estimate, 80 to 85 percent of the provincial revenue was paid to a staff that could accomplish very little because of the shortage of funds; yet it was politically impossible to reduce the payroll substantially. In addition to salaries there was a variety of fringe benefits, negatively catalogued in the administration's resolutions for the future: "Tous les véhicules doivent obligatoirement rentrer aux garage après les heures de service . . . dépolitiser les garages," for example, or "La sûreté doit être uniquement au service de l'autorité établie et non au service des individus."[19] The instances of corruption, especially embezzlement, which came to public notice from time to time were a less important feature of the system than the technically legal drain on the treasury occasioned by high salaries.

The domain of customary law was the society of those who were excluded from the system of patronage briefly outlined above.[20] The cleavage between the governors and the governed was expressed in law and in judicial practice. Government officials were exempt from the jurisdiction of customary courts; together with the government's commercial clients, officials formed the majority of the class of wealthy people operating normally in the urban rather than in the rural economy, who were fined at double the usual or peasant rate after being convicted in courts applying statute law.[21]

The provincial government, seeking to demonstrate its concern for the popular will, paid lip service to the importance of custom and tradition: "La politique coutumière va être renforcée grâce à la restauration de l'autorité coutumière, que d'aucuns ignorent qu'elle assure toujours l'harmonie et l'armature sociale de nos populations. Des contacts fructueux avec les Chefs Coutumiers seront multipliés à cet effet."[22] So from time to time the government convoked meetings, at the territorial or provincial level, of *chefs coutumiers* and *notables*.

18 Introductory speech by Governor Moanda at the Conférence économique et financière du Kongo Central (*Etudes Congolaises*, 7(9):46).

19 *Ibid.*, pp. 51, 52.

20 Cf. *Etudes Congolaises*, 7(8):46.

21 This policy obtained in Songololo Territory, at least.

22 Déclaration gouvernementale, 8 novembre 1962 (in Monnier, 1964, p. 258).

These are conventional terms. A "customary chief," actually a non-customary official exercising noncustomary responsibilities in a noncustomary area, was defined either as a *chef médaillé* of the colonial era or as the successor of such a chief, normally his uterine nephew. A "notable" was the head of a *groupement* included in the domain of the *chef médaillé*.[23]

In Mbanza Manteke both terms (*chef coutumier* and *notable*) applied to NSAKA. At a territorial conference of customary authorities he would be one of three notables representing the *groupements* of Mbanza Manteke, Mbanza Nkazi, and Ngombe. Only the customary chiefs attended a provincial conference, and NSAKA would be one of them; he represented all of Mbanza Manteke, which was formerly a sector and is now a commune. NSAKA is the "nephew" of Manyonza. He supplanted his elder brother, a man of less ability and political acumen, in the succession. The brother seems not to resent his replacement, but many other people do. NSAKA, in conversation with strangers such as Angolan refugees and American anthropologists, describes himself as *mfumu a nsi* and takes some trouble to give the impression that he occupies a traditional, and territorial, chiefship. Nobody else refers to him by this title, and most people strongly resent any suggestion that he has some sort of responsibility for them. Those who wish to be polite may on occasion address him by the title *mfumu a ngalu-pama*, which is a KiKongolization of *chef de groupement*.

Despite all the resentment he has aroused, NSAKA is an able and conscientious man, as good a representative of the elders as could be found; he takes seriously the common interests of his "chiefdom." In setting up councils of such people, however, the government revealed the ambivalence of its policies; as a means of communication between the governor and the population the councils of chiefs and notables bypassed the elected communal officials and made the ostensibly democratic functions of the commune derisory.

The nominal purpose of the councils was to advise the government on customary affairs, such as marriage payments, codification of customary laws and proverbs, creation of a museum, encouragement of folk music, publication of oral tradition, and the study of traditional science (Monnier, 1964, p. 258). Not even a beginning was made toward realization of these aims. A permanent council created by a law prescribing that it meet at least once every three months [24] apparently

[23] Province du Kongo Central, décret-loi du 6 octobre 1964, Chapitre XII, Art. 99 (published in *Moniteur Congolais*, no. 20 [15 Oct. 1964] p. 583; cited in Monnier, 1965, p. 21).

[24] Arrêté gouvernemental 0018/63, "Création d'un conseil coutumier" (in "Bulletin officiel du Kongo Central," no. 6 [July 1963], pp. 4–6).

never met. Nevertheless, the terms of eligibility to membership made
the council a convenient patronage device whereby clients not otherwise provided for could be appointed to it and draw a stipend of
4,000 francs a month, plus family allowances and expenses. One of the
recommendations of the financial conference of 1964 was that the
permanent council be abolished, but a new law reinstated it, endowed
it for the first time with an organization, and set out nomination
procedures for the membership.[25] These procedures, in practice, allowed Abako candidates unsuccessful in the preceding elections to be
appointed to the council at a stipend now raised to 10,000 francs a
month, plus allowances and expenses.

In spite of the nominal existence of the permanent council, a provincial conference of "customary chiefs" held in Matadi in March
1966, accompanied by a barrage of publicity, comprised an entirely
new group of people, among whom the chiefs were outnumbered by
administrative officials. No customary chief was appointed to the chair-
manship of any of the study committees. None of the topics to be
discussed by the committees — respect for authority, payment of
honorariums to customary chiefs, imposed agricultural programs, road
maintenance by village labor, prohibition of political activity — can
reasonably be regarded as customary. The governor's opening speech
at the conference clearly equated "respect for traditional authority"
with abstention from politics, that is, from any challenge to the
government.[26]

It is well known that customary authorities exist only as a figment of
government policy. The extraordinary equivocations detailed in the
preceding paragraphs, selected from a considerable collection of official documents in the same vein, show that official interest in
custom springs from its authoritarian possibilities. It is accordingly the royalist model of traditional society which the government favors, although under the preceding regime, at least in the
Lower Congo, this model lost ground to a pragmatic one. In the protracted debate carried on by Belgian scholars and officials concerning
the nature of custom, the view that the customary implied the popular
rather than the traditional gradually gained favor. This view carried
with it recognition of the legislative capacity of custom, the capacity
to produce new rules suited to new conditions, and also a certain
autonomy of the rural population in the conduct of customary affairs
(A. Sohier, 1944).

25 Arrêté 11/041/A.1/030/K.C./65 (in "Bulletin officiel," no. 9 [3 March 1965]);
Arrêté 32/65 (18 Oct. 1965), relatif á la réorganisation et au bon fonctionnement du
Conseil Coutumier; Cabinet du Gouverneur (unpublished).
26 Official publicity releases dated 24 and 29 March 1966.

The trend has now been reversed. Rural Kongo society is officially described as hierarchical, in so thoroughgoing a fashion that the provincial government appears as the apex of a chain of command extending down to the last individual villager.

The urbanized Congolese elite, like urban elites elsewhere, find this image appealing. Products of mission education, they have been cut off since boyhood from profound participation in village life. Nothing in their training enables them to distinguish between the myth of *la coutume* and a reality they scarcely know. As politicians, whether in government or outside it, they reveal two concerns in their approach to the customary domain. First, they seek to control it; they are distressed that customary law should remain uncodified and customary courts should escape central supervision, which they consider necessary to progress. Second, in planning for the future they propose to overcome rural stagnation by telling the peasants what to do: for example, to regroup into larger villages. This policy, as in colonial times, is accompanied by denials that rural initiative exists and by active measures to frustrate it when it does appear.

GOVERNMENT AND LAND

Since litigation concerning land constitutes the political arena par excellence of rural society, government policy in regard to land, as carried out publicly through the courts or privately as patronage, is critical for the total relationship of government to custom and hence for the social structure as a whole. This policy encapsulates most of the ambiguities and politically useful ambivalences mentioned in the preceding section. Only a brief discussion of some of its aspects is possible here.

According to customary law in the Manteke area, land transfers fall into two categories: transfers that create status inequality between the parties, which may be loans or gifts, and transfers that leave the relative status of the parties unaffected, which take the form of pawns or sales. There is no direct material return, in the first category, for a temporary loan or for a permanent gift. In the second category, however, a pawn, which is a temporary transfer, and a sale, which is permanent, require an equivalent material return.

In the first category of transfers, the donor is of higher rank than the recipient; by the very fact of the transfer, the latter may be incorporated into the donor's *kinkazi* ("authority"). If the incorporation is permanent, a stranger or a slave recipient is assimilated into the kinship category *mwana* ("child"). Indirect material returns take the form of prestations due from client to patron, from *mwana* to *se*. Gifts are revocable, and thus in theory the client's continued enjoyment of them depends on his continued respect for the relationship. The proverb, *Kyasumbwa ka kivakululwanga ko; kyankayilu vakulwa kwandi*, means "A thing bought is not taken back; a thing given may be."

In the second category, the object transferred is incorporated in the *kinkazi* of the recipient, whose status relative to the donor remains unchanged. The objects exchanged are land, persons, and goods [27] — persons or land against each other or against goods. Only land and persons however, are objects of *kinkazi*; by mediating between the social and economic systems, goods provide convertibility. This ambiguity (noted in chap. 6) marks the relation between the two categories of transfer, gift and sale. For example, in different versions of the story, the two lengths of cloth Nsiku Nsesi gave to NGOMA LUBOTA were either payment for land in the forest Mfula or prestations due from him as Child on the occasion of a feast.

We may assume that wherever and whenever a powerful chief established himself in precolonial times, gift rather than sale prevailed in land transactions; the conventions for this structure already existed, and their application can be observed today among the minutiae of village politics. In such instances the entire local economy would be adapted to the redistributive pattern; examples occur in missionary accounts, and the pattern is explicit in Manteke accounts of "the old chiefs."

Nevertheless, Manteke probably never had any chiefs of importance, at least not after the eighteenth century. Throughout the region land was regularly sold in precolonial times. *Bisi Manteke* do not now sell land, although they look forward to the day when commercial development connected with the hydroelectric potential of the Congo River will enable them to profit by leasing it. In the past, according to tradition, groups abandoned their land completely, but none sold an entire estate, nor was land offered for sale as chickens might be. There is no doubt, however, that marginal parcels of land were sold to immigrants and to neighbors. Traditions recited in court show that this practice also prevailed in the Ndibu and Yombe regions.

It has become something of a public dogma, however, that selling land is contrary to Kongo custom, that it was never done and would be contrary to the principles of traditional society. This view is based partly on the work of Van Wing, who is often quoted (1959, pp. 85, 94):

27 The objects exchanged also include "money," i.e., conventional exchange units such as shells (*nzimbu*) and trade goods (guns, beads, cloth) which have acquired monetary value, but do not include animals and other foodstuffs, which have a communicatory rather than a commercial significance.

Le clan est la collectivité de tous les descendants, par filiation utérine, d'une aieule commune. . . . Il comprend tous les individus des deux sexes . . . les défunts et les vivants.

Le clan et la terre qu'il occupe, constituent une chose indivise; et l'ensemble est sous la domination des Bakulu [ancestors]. Il s'en suit que l'aliénation absolue du sol ou d'une de ses parcelles est une chose contraire à la mentalité des Bampangu.

These statements applying to the BaMpangu (BaNtandu) were generalized and incorporated in quasi-official policy. Malengreau challenged the argument, pointing out its mysticism and circularity, and asserted that in native eyes "cette conception désincarnée de la propriété n'a aucun sens" (1939, p. 12). The dogma as it related to the BaKongo, however, was only one aspect of the more general one that individualism and landed property, which explained the economic dynamism of Europe, were lacking in Africa. Colonial law relating to native rights in land centered on the notion of rights sui generis, a fundamental ambiguity that has been the subject of an extensive literature (Boelaert, 1957; Dufour, 1963).

The net result of the official doctrine was to give the government control over all important transfers of land from customary to commercial use. In colonial times this control was an essential part of the dominion exercised jointly by the government and European concessionary enterprises. The beneficial result claimed for it is that peasants were protected from pauperism, large landowners, and moneylenders. The same body of law, with all its obscurities, is still in effect; since independence it has enabled the government of Kongo Central to profit considerably from negotiated concessions. On a smaller scale, the transfer of lands near towns and commercial centers has been incorporated into the patronage structure of the local and provincial political systems. The present state of affairs is perhaps best summarized in the words of a minor official who presided over a territorial court: "It depends on which rule you are following. Under the written law no native can own land; but in customary law of course he can." The justification, now as formerly, for this provision of the written law is said to be *la coutume*.

The persistence at the government level of the dogma that selling land is contrary to custom, in spite of the evidence, is at least partly explained by its congruence with authoritarian policies. The same view is also widely entertained, however, by the educated elite, no matter what their home regions. The Abbé Ferdinand Ngoma, for example, who is from Manianga, states it as a universal Kongo custom that land is inalienable (1963, p. 30). Territorial officials say the same thing, after handing me records in their custody which amply demonstrate the contrary. The individual's point of view is largely a matter of education. I found it possible to tell whether a man's schooling had been Protestant or Catholic by asking him a few questions about land tenure and chiefship; Catholics usually refer to the royalist model.

Quite apart from dogmas and models, the inalienability of land may be the custom of eastern Kongo, and thus a regional peculiarity, but the truth of this hypothesis has not been fully established. Further research will have to distinguish carefully between hierarchical models incorporating a dogma of inalienability and the actual existence of hierarchical groups. A survey of Lemfu land cases heard by the Kasangulu territorial court since 1940 yielded two traditions describing sale of land. In one instance testimony referring to a sale was not essential to the issue and passed without comment; in the other, the Belgian president of the court said that the alleged sale was contrary to Kongo custom and could not have happened, and that therefore the witness' testimony as a whole was untrustworthy.

The difficulties that beset the investigator in this field may be illustrated by the following incident. Among Lemfu and Ngombe (Ndibu) informants the principle of inalienability was widely upheld, but one well-known authority on custom, to my surprise, flatly asserted that the ancestors had sold land, and even gave me a formula for negotiating such sales. The formula would apparently have been appropriate to any kind of sale, but we were talking only about land. There could have been no mistake; I explained at length exactly what I was interested in, and why, and went over the entire subject with him in French as well as in KiKongo. A couple of months later the same informant, after a virtuoso display of the forensic art, won an important land case; when the verdict was announced he and his followers triumphed in an extravagant display of customary rituals and insignia. The following day, when I repeated my question about land, he said that land sales were inconceivable. This man well knew that cases are won as much by strategy as by divine right and prayers to the ancestors, although he was careful not to omit the prayers. His advice on how to win arguments about land included such remarks as this: "Too many people nowadays want to be *fondateurs*; they won't rest content with being a *mwana* although that's a position much easier to defend in court because you're not answerable for the whole tradition right back to Mbanza Kongo. Take me, for example . . ."

Quite apart from its role in *la politique coutumière*, the royalist model of land tenure played a part in what might be called the foreign policy of the province. This policy was centered, from 1962 to the end of 1965, on control of the *zones annexes*, areas earmarked for the future expansion of the city and now definitively incorporated in Kinshasa. The provincial government laid claim to these areas, and beyond them to the city itself, which has now been declared a national territory like the District of Columbia. The reasons for the province's eagerness in the matter were baldly stated in the newspaper *Kongo dia Wene* (18 March 1961, p. 7): "Since we [the BaKongo] have the majority of the votes, there is room for hope that we would get all the jobs." Kinshasa, with a population of probably more than 2 million, is the political and economic hub of the nation. Control of the city would not only, as the newspaper noted, give the province special access to the central government; it would enormously enlarge the empire of patronage under the control of the governor and his party.

From time to time it was suggested that the hereditary owners of the land on which Kinshasa is built should be given a special political role in the city. In practice, since the city's population consists mostly of immigrants, it was only with regard to the *zones annexes* that the argument can be advanced with any hope of success. The province's claims, expressed in traditionalistic form, prompted unsympathetic journalists in Kinshasa to refer to Kongo Central as "l'ancien royaume Abako":

Plusieurs tentatives de division du terrain ancestral ont été entamées ce dernier temps par certains irresponsables avides du pouvoir. On a même voulu méconnaître le droit à la propriété des chefs de terres prônant ainsi un régime foncier contraire à la coutume sacrée de nos ancêtres. Certains sont allés jusqu'à vouloir méconnaître l'autorité des chefs traditionnels. . . .

La Ville de Léopoldville n'est pas et ne sera jamais neutralisée. C'est une partie du terrain ancestral.[28]

The importance of the *zones annexes* in the political economy of Kongo Central gave the politicians who represented them a powerful role in the province. Since the inhabitants were mostly not BaKongo but BaHumbu, their representatives were in a position to withhold their allegiance (G.M., 1963); on the other hand, alliance with the dominant group in the provincial government was an important asset in the internal politics of the *zones annexes*. In practice, the province's main interest in this area was the patronage possibilities of land tenure, sale, and lease; land was much in demand for housing and industry, and its value rose rapidly. Commercial land concessions depended on the recognition of customary rights, which could be challenged and

28 From a speech by Governor Moanda, printed in Assemblé Provinciale, C.R.A., Procès-Verbal (Sept. 1962), no. 3 (cf. Monnier, 1964, p. 261).

defended in the customary courts. These courts, in turn, were supervised by the Bureau of Customary Affairs in the provincial Ministry of the Interior. In the cabinets of 1962 and 1965, the ministry was given to the leader of first one and then the other of the two factions in the *zones annexes*. When political pressures of this order were brought to bear upon them, customary society and customary law in the *zones annexes* crumbled into corruption and anarchy.

IMAGES OF CUSTOM

An old man, when asked why land is no longer sold, gave two reasons: the arrival of the Word of God and the abolition of slavery. The coming of the missionaries, and behind them the colonial government, led to a new political constitution, not simply a modification of the old by the suppression of warfare and witch-hunts. It introduced a new kind of chief, the government chief, and in response to the innovation new competitive techniques and new mythologies were invented. Eventually there resulted a synthesis of new and old which is now called "custom." The main features of customary society, responding to the conditions that developed between 1908 and 1921, assumed their present form during the 1920's. Two of those conditions, the abolition of slavery and the interdiction of witchcraft trials, served to deprive village society of any means of dealing with matters on which political interest had formerly focused. On the other hand, the missions, the government, and the labor market provided new if limited resources around which political activity could be reconstituted; the government courts became the new political arena, and the developing cities provided an escape for at least some of those who lost out in local politics. Some aspects of modern customary society may be regarded as more or less consciously protective devices adopted to preserve rural autonomy; one example is the mystification of chiefship, tradition, and land tenure.

When I arrived in Kongo I avoided saying that I wanted to study rural government; I said I wanted to study custom. My remark regularly raised a smile; custom is taken seriously, but it is not usually thought of as a subject to be studied. It is as though a foreigner came to the United States to study democracy. In fact, custom and democracy are very similar. Each is nothing less than a way of life, or "the foundation of our society." Ordinary people, asked to describe this foundation, talk about a defunct or obsolescent institution such as chiefship or the New England town meeting. When it is pointed out that such an example is hardly central to modern life, they attempt a general definition that is plainly inconsistent with a great deal of what actually happens in their society. In spite of such inconsistencies, Kongo is in fact a customary or tradition-oriented society, just as the United States is a democratic one. "Tradition-oriented" means that people think and argue about their society and their own role in it in terms of an idiom that refers to precedents supposedly established in earlier generations. The usual European view, still current in the work of social scientists, is that tradition is an autonomous constraining force, and that traditional societies — their cultures, structures, mores, the mental attitudes of their members — are in some way anachronistic survivals from the past, out of date and due to pass away as soon as the people open their eyes to the modern way of doing things. Rural Kongo is clearly no more traditional, in this sense, than Kinshasa or New York.

Custom as a way of life means different things to different people. Custom summarized as chiefship is, in a way, a projection of the illusion of solitary grandeur, or of a deep-seated desire for a secure independence. All over Kongo there are little settlements of a few houses, a few years old, founded by men who have gathered their dependents, shaken off the dust of their villages from their feet, and built anew on land of their own, behind signs proclaiming Mbanza Such-and-such. In the words of André Ryckmans, "De nombreux proverbes illustrent ce caractère égalitaire et cette idée maîtresse de la mentalité Kongo: tout homme est libre, chacun mérite consideration, personne n'est méprisable" (in Kestergat, 1961, pp. 171–172).

The individualism that prompts the building of new settlements is born of insecurity. Those who feel themselves the losers in local politics, and who are not strong enough to found a new *mbanza*, tend to join prophetic churches in which discipline and rules are emphasized. Those who are relatively secure, and those who deplore the abuse of power, present custom in terms of *kinkazi* and committee government, rather than *kimfumu*. The views of all concerned should be duly consulted, they say; nothing should be secret or arbitrary. Custom, in this view, is symbolized by the rituals of etiquette, not by the sword (*mbeele*) or the snail shell (*kodya*). For such people the chief, as Ryckmans described him, is "médiateur plus que gendarme, arbitre plus que juge, guide beaucoup plus que législateur" (in Kestergat, 1961, p. 171).

As a model for the organization of society at large, chiefship is upheld by those who feel that they are themselves chiefs by right. They might be saying, "All the world are slaves, except you and me, and even you . . ." That is in fact a just paraphrase of the views of DISA and NKUTI in Manteke. To the governor of the province and his associates, custom means the obligation of the people to obey the established authority without question. The same authoritarian view is upheld by most individuals when they discuss what is wrong with their society: "Somebody should order that it be straightened out." According to one of its original members, a main purpose of the provincial council on customary affairs was to straighten out, once and for all, "the roads from Kongo" and to show who was a slave and who was not by definitely establishing the true traditions for the whole province. At about the same time (i.e., just after the constitution of the province) the new government tried to impose a moratorium on all land cases in the customary courts, pending a survey and registration of landholdings. The basic assumption was that the truth, though concealed, is there, and that an act of chiefship will discover it. The attempt was never seriously pursued, and its failure coincided with the onset of cynical disillusionment which is now the prevailing mood. The cynicism finds expression: "You know why those people [Abako] are making such a mess of the government? Because they are all slaves; not one of them knows how he came from Mbanza Kongo."

These contrasting and yet complementary interpretations of custom came out clearly in separate interviews I had with two Kongo politicians, one in and one out, to whom I said that I was studying the meaning of custom. Each spontaneously embarked on a long discourse concerning the 1960 Round Table conference in Brussels which prepared the way for national independence, and which both politicians had attended as representatives of Abako. At the conference a division in the Abako delegation foreshadowed the present division of the political leadership between the group in power and the outs, who form a loosely coordinated opposition. The in spokesman believed the delegation's sole responsibility was to follow the leadership of Kasa-Vubu; the out spokesman regarded the delegation as a committee of which Kasa-Vubu was simply the chairman. The political situation in 1966 was similarly interpreted from the two points of view. The out said, "We should discuss differences in a reasonable way"; the in could scarcely find terms strong enough to condemn the disloyalty of the opposition, and when he referred to the leader of Mwinda the word *ndoki* ("witch") was obviously on the tip of his tongue. The chief is right, and to oppose what is right is witchcraft.

Thus the BaKongo employ traditional models in evaluating present politics, at the provincial and village levels alike. A somewhat different point of view is that of the elite reflecting on customary society, the rural enclave, the setting from which they themselves, or their parents, escaped. Two kinds of concern are dominant. The urban elite, as Congolese, need a sense of cultural heritage, even though the symbols and organizational forms of customary society are no longer relevant to their lives. Second, customary society presents itself as a political problem.

The elite are the educated, those who have passed through a school system that even after independence remains ideologically European. Secondary school textbooks on world civilization begin with Etruscans and end with modern France. A history book recently prepared for younger children in Congo centers the reader in Africa but then invites him, in his mind's eye, to look out across the Atlantic to St. Helena, prison of Napoleon. Schoolboys learn a good deal about the Romans. Meanwhile, all discussions of African sociology are conducted in a vocabulary built on evolutionary assumptions; African culture is reduced to an assemblage of barbarisms: chiefs, witch doctors, fetishism, sorcery, poison ordeals. Small wonder that the author of a manuscript on marriage, unable to describe custom as he knows it in the terms available to him, gives up the attempt:

> Le système clanique du mariage embrasse toute une série de complexités qui échappent très souvent à la connaissance de l'Européen. Pour bien comprendre il faut être de la race noire. Je parle des arcanes de la coutume indigène, propres aux moeurs des congolais tout comme les coutumes occidentales dont nous sommes l'objet des continuels reproches de la part des Européens.

The elite, owing their success and prosperity to their participation in urban, European institutions, are driven to accept the European evaluation of their way of life as resulting from evolutionary progress away from the rural way of life. This evaluation confuses situational with historical change (Mitchell, 1966); it is not rural Kongo society that has adapted to urban conditions, but individual BaKongo who have moved into, and adjusted to, a social matrix structured by very different economic and political forces. A correlated European assumption prevalent among the elite is that evolutionary progress from rural to urban is dependent on the evolving mentality of individuals.

Colonial literature is replete with discussions about evolution: Can it be accomplished by education? If so, can it be accomplished in one generation? The evolutionary assumption was justification for colonial tutelage; it persisted in Congo in 1966 because the characteristic colonial structures had not fundamentally changed. The elite both in and out of government advocated policies of rural reform predicated on the tradition-bound inertia of the peasant mind. Their condescension toward rural folk was expressed in various ways. A territorial administrator attending an Ndibu wedding in my company shattered my enjoyment of the occasion by asking whether I could see any signs that "these simple people" were making progress toward civilization; on hearing his question I recalled the missionary who asked me, on hearing that I lived in a village, if I did not find the people's mentality primitive. Again, a correspondent of the newspaper *L'Etoile du Congo*, making a tour of the towns in Kongo Central in February 1965 in order to report on Mwinda's prospects in the forthcoming elections, dismissed the rural population in a single sentence: "A côté de ces 'progressistes' . . . il reste la grosse masse d'électeurs, composée en grande partie de paysans attachés à la tradition. Pour ceux-ci, l'Abako doit rester immuable et ne peut connaître aucune modification de doctrine." Yet, in fact, the commune of the BaMboma voted overwhelmingly for Mwinda because they were led to believe by a critical examination of the alternatives that Abako headquarters in Songololo was attempting to bamboozle them.

The elite attitude, reinforced by colonial education and present self-interest, leads to the formulation of exclusively authoritarian policies (e.g., regrouping the villages into model communities equipped with services of all kinds but devoid of realistic political institutions) which are no more likely to succeed than those of the past. Meanwhile, the actual demands issuing from the villages either are ignored or are treated as challenges to established authority; villagers ask for roads and medical services and are told to obey their customary chiefs and work harder at cultivating their land.

One of the possibilities for the future is that rural autonomy will be destroyed by subjecting the administration of customary law to bureaucratic control. In at least those areas where land is commercially valuable, especially near the towns, some system of sharecropping and intermittent wage labor would probably arise, as in similar situations in southern Europe and Latin America. If, on the other hand, communal government is genuinely based on popular participation, and if opportunities for rural economic initiative are presented, few will regret the passing of ancestral custom; *fu kya nsi* will take on new meaning.

12

CONCLUSION:
AN ANTHROPOLOGICAL PERSPECTIVE

Mbanza Manteke, both village and region, has some special features, but they do not suffice to set it apart in the Lower Congo. It is economically unattractive and its population density is low, but the region is only moderately isolated from the main commercial routes and centers. It is heavily Protestant, but not unique in this regard. In 1921 and 1959, largely because of Mabwaka Mpaka the prophet (MacGaffey, 1966b), it was an important center of Kimbanguist enthusiasm, which has since declined markedly. The village of Manteke was created by Henry Richards, but most Kongo settlements, even those that still occupy traditional sites, are artificial and synthetic creations; characteristically the influence of the missions, whether Protestant or Catholic, is strong in them. The impact of the urban, industrial world is made apparent, even in the remotest villages, by the sight of a brick house being built for the future retirement of a city bureaucrat, or of a sailor on leave, carousing with his friends, who hastens to assure the visitor of his familiarity with New York and Philadelphia.

Environmental factors, both local and distant, as well as cultural trends that might not lend themselves to deterministic analysis, lead to regional variations in culture and social structure which cannot be measured directly by resources ordinarily available to the fieldworker. Yet, after extensive traveling and close reading of court records and other documents from three different territorial headquarters, I have endeavored to compare Mbanza Manteke with other parts of Kongo. Some of the relevant data are mentioned in this book. The differences do not seem profound; one immediately recognizes familiar processes and structures in descriptions of Ntandu, Manianga, and Yombe.

The social structure everywhere is a compromise between what people would like and what they can achieve. Whatever may have been true in the past (and it is doubtful that what appear as the inherent contradictions of Kongo society could ever be resolved), the people are now, on the whole, dissatisfied with their social condition. From a utilitarian or materialist point of view their dissatisfaction is not easily explained. They would all like to have more money, to be able to eat more meat, wear better clothes, and build brick houses with iron roofs, but neither their opinions nor their behavior suggests that their poverty is the main source of their discontent. They could be better off, in material terms, if every man were content to work in his forests, drink his palm wine, and live at peace with his neighbors. Instead the villagers invest relatively large amounts of their time and money in litigation and in funeral proceedings, from which no substantial material benefit is gained. No group, having added to its landholdings by successful litigation, begins immediately to cultivate more land than before. Land as a material resource is readily available; the best evidence of its availability is that in 1964–65 hundreds of Angolans settled in the Manteke region, and a total of perhaps a quarter of a million (more, by some estimates) in Kongo Central, nearly all of them south of the Congo River. As long as these refugees are ready to admit their clientship — that is, their jural dependence on the owners of the land — the only difficulty likely to result is a quarrel between *bankazi* jealous of each other's right to settle clients. Landownership is not so much the object as the idiom of dispute. The resource being competed for in terms of kinship, descent, and tradition is concrete but immaterial: status definition, conferring security.

On the other hand, environmental factors limit economic resources at a more general level. Productivity generates political power only through the medium of trade. Changes in the pattern of trade are clearly related to the transition in about 1700 from the first to the second phase of Kongo social history. Intensive penetration by Europeans interested in direct control of production and marketing introduced a new phase in 1885. The isolation of customary society within the colonial regime, effected politically by indirect rule, was effected economically through the doctrine that because the native was not an economic man economic opportunities need not be set before him. Only in the 1950's did a small, much-touted middle class emerge under strict European supervision; the initiatives thus permitted were credited to European training and example. At present a similar policy is followed, public funds (derived from foreign aid) being invested in the rural economy mainly in development projects controlled by the government. Most people expect to make money by commerce rather than by production; since exchange rates, import quotas, and, to some extent, prices and wages are determined by government officials, commercial profits are affected more by political than by economic (market) factors.

The new class of politicians who are also traders maintains itself by controlling institutions of European origin associated with the regime of statute law; the regime of customary law segregates the peasantry and the urban poor, whose destinies are controlled by the new class. Entry into the new class depends on education, but since 1960 schooling has become increasingly difficult to obtain in the rural areas, and in both town and country it has become expensive. The cleavage between the privileged elements of the population and the rest is widely recognized. Government spokesmen speak of the national and local elections and the councils of customary chiefs as serving to bridge the gap; intellectuals in the commercial sector speculate enthusiastically on the role of peasant cooperatives. In practice, the peasants have been repeatedly cheated of what they were promised in return for their participation in elections and cooperatives, and this too is well known and explicitly discussed.

The regime of customary law, which isolates the rural population and much of the urban population, also creates and safeguards a measure of local autonomy because the source of legitimacy incorporated in the law is tradition, not a code drawn up by a legislature or bureaucracy. The principal terms of tradition are descent, pedigree, and patrifilial relations. In form, the terms are carried over from precolonial times, but the functional burden of status definition they support is largely a colonial innovation; under indirect rule, the indigenous code of symbolism, rhetoric, and magic was made to serve as an administrative code subject to judicial enforcement. From a rational-legal point of view, however, tradition is intrinsically ambiguous: it purports to record history, but in fact it denies history. The contradiction is resolved by continuous but illegitimate political processes.

For individuals, the pervasive politization of public life is the chief source of insecurity. The sense of insecurity does not affect everyone equally; five or six elderly men and a much larger number of women in Mbanza Manteke are uninterested in tradition and its conflicts, and have virtually withdrawn from public affairs. But most human beings need to know who they are, and react in specific ways to identify conflicts in the social order, that is, to contradictory assessments of their status. In Kongo the primary field of status ambiguity is slavery. There is probably no one who is not tacitly considered to be a slave by a fair number of his neighbors. Slaves, for BaKongo as for Tallensi, are kinless persons, almost nonpersons, analogous to witches and ghosts (*min'kuyu*) roaming the trackless waste beyond the boundaries of society. On the other hand, hardly anyone accepts this evaluation of his status; instead, the individual sees himself as a freeman (*mfumu*) able to identify the four corners of his social identity: Father, Mother, and two Grandfathers. The contrast between these two evaluations parallels the contrast between history and tradition; tradition and pedigree socially identify each individual to his own satisfaction, but history indicates that most people are slaves (i.e., immigrants who have been assimilated into the local structure of estates) and, in any event, provides no means of vindicating anyone's pedigree unambiguously. Those who are relatively unsuccessful in mustering support for their traditions face a constant challenge to their legitimacy.[1] It is an obvious fact of everyday life that this consideration generates enormous amounts of social energy.

The reactions of those facing the stigma of slavery include flight to a New Jerusalem, whether another village or, nowadays, a town. Some, passionately persuaded of the justice of their cause, stay to fight, investing all available resources in litigation. Kimbanguism, which appeals especially to the socially marginal, exhibits both reactions: as a millenarian movement it looks to the creation of a new regime in which new sources of legitimacy will vindicate the faithful; as a sect it permits withdrawal into little enclaves of righteousness partly dissociated from the secular world. Both programs are favored by a private code whereby the ordinary significance of social events is reinterpreted in such a way as to overcome contradictions. The code also justifies (or is fulfilled by) shamanistic behavior which is more or less characteristic of the various Kimbanguist movements. Schizoid symptoms, institutionalized among Kimbanguists, are characteristic of Kongo society as a whole; they appear again in the insistence on "reading between the lines" (see chap. 9, n. 14) and in the witchcraft complex. Witches look like friends but are really enemies; they cause misfortunes that look natural, and they can be unmasked only by supernatural means.

The sources of this insecurity can be discovered only by actor-centered inquiry. It is for this reason that my book begins with tradition. Tradition describes a structure of corporate groups presumed (by the actor) to be perpetual. Filiation unambiguously locates individuals in this structure, or at least, so people say, it did until recently, when antisocial people began to obscure the true lines of filiation. To the actor, the system ought to be in equilibrium and would be if the rules were obeyed. From this point of view descent is the basis of corporate grouping, as the myth says: "In Mbanza Kongo the King divided his Children into twelve clans." An objective account of Kongo social

---

[1] The KiKongo word for "slave," as status designation or insult, is comparable to "bastard" in English.

structure is, however, a catalogue of controversies. Fundamental rights over land and persons are always uncertain in some degree. The identity and the position of corporate units at any organizational level are in doubt, such units emerging and dissolving with some rapidity. Uncertainty is the primary characteristic of what we would like to call the structure, and not a marginal phenomenon attributable to the accidents of process, the stresses of change, or the imperfections of humanity. Moreover, it cannot be argued that whatever the arguments concerning the application of the principles (who is and who is not a slave) the principles themselves must be accepted by everyone, since it turns out that contradictory rules are upheld by different people and, on occasion, by the same people.

Yet daily life is far from disorderly; in spite of structural ambiguities, individuals do manage to get married, to cultivate land, to be decently buried. Process itself is highly ordered, partly because the rules of etiquette and of public debate are formal and strict. The roles they prescribe — who is to say what, and when he is to say it, at a funeral, for example — constitute a structure much better defined than that of matrilineal descent. It is from the basis of this processual structure that the BaKongo conduct their violent and inconclusive arguments about corporate rights. The quantitative structure characteristic of the society in a particular historical phase emerges from process, although from the actor's viewpoint process presupposes corporate actors. From the historical point of view, locality is the basis of corporate grouping, descent a way of describing it. The clan sections, supposedly segments of an original clan (*mvila*), are in fact built up locally by political means.[2]

Although economic circumstances affect the distribution of power in each historical phase and thus limit the kinds of corporate structure which can emerge in each, such structures are obviously not simple functions of economic relations. Using the resources available, people strive to realize an ideally desirable state of affairs, which is called "Mbanza Kongo."[3] *Mbanza* means a densely populated, prosperous

[2] From the actor's viewpoint the primary factors in status discrimination, in order of logical priority, are sex, seniority, descent, and locality. The first two of these establish the matrix, male/female, elder/cadet (*bataata ye bamaama, bambuta ye baleeke*), which provides the structure of a number of origin myths (e.g., Van Wing, 1959, p. 419) and the ordinary type of clan tradition (*kinkulu*) in which Na Nkala Nene appears on the scene with his sister (*busi*) and his cadet (*nleeke*). From the historical point of view the order of priority is reversed. (For order of priority in status discrimination, see Smith, 1960, pp. 297–304.)

[3] There is some evidence of a tendency toward more strongly hierarchical structures in the parts of Kongo Central where rainfall is higher, forest cover heavier, prosperity greater, and population denser.

community in which a strong chief, supernaturally inspired, assures every honest citizen his due. The idea of a social unit complete in four parts, bounded and oriented, applies to spaces (including villages, other habitations, graves, and funeral enclosures), processes (including human life, KiNkimba, and other rituals), persons, and regulatory committees. Social organization, patterned in this way, takes the form of a network linking statuses (*fulu*, "status"). Statuses are occupied by persons, individual and corporate; the distinction between status and the occupant of a status is quite explicit in phrases such as "We agreed to put Kingani into that place" and "The man alive now in that place [*mu fulu kyokyo*] is Kingani." The rightful occupant of a status knows its charter (traditions, pedigree) and exercises the rights attached to it. A man who has no such rights has no social personality.

In addition to its sociological aspect, Kongo ideology incorporates metaphysical notions relating to the nature and origins of power and of evil and to the contrast between life and death; in other words, it embodies a conception of the universe. In these notions the same patterns appear, achieving physical expression in color symbolism, witchcraft beliefs, chiefly insignia, and the contents of charms. The universal application of similar patterns unifies culture and social structure, neither serving as the original source of order. Moreover, as far as the evidence goes, it appears that the essential processes of Kongo social life, and the symbols associated with them, have remained much the same through the recorded phases of Kongo history.

The methods and conclusions of this study are commonplace enough today. "Structure and process" is as much a cliché now as "structure and function" was twenty years ago. Anthropologists are no longer likely to treat order and authority as synonymous; correspondingly, corporate structure as such, though it remains a fundamental topic, is a beginning rather than an end.

INOKENE, IKYELE

BIBLIOGRAPHY

ABBREVIATIONS

ARSC Académie Royale des Sciences Coloniales. A later designation of the IRCB.

ARSOM Académie Royale des Sciences d'Outre-Mer. The present designation of the IRCB.

Cah. Econ. et Soc. Cahiers Economiques et Sociaux. Published by IRES.

CRISP Centre de Recherches et d'Informations Socio-Politiques, Brussels.

IRCB Institut Royal Colonial Belge. In book citations, the reference is to the Section des Sciences Morales et Politiques.

IRES Institut de Recherches Economiques et Sociales, Université Lovanium, Kinshasa.

COURT RECORDS AND MANUSCRIPTS

The records of communal courts and of the earlier sector and chiefdom courts are kept by the commune of Mbanza Manteke. Until 1961 the records were written in KiLeta, the government's simplified form of KiKongo, a crude and ambiguous language. Court records are now written in KiKongo.

In the 1940's the records were legible but brief, often amounting to no more than "Kingani did so-and-so. According to custom, and in the eyes of the government, this is a bad thing. Kingani is fined so much." With the evolution of the new "custom," the clerks, under prodding by the administration, began to record arguments in more detail. From 1960 onward, however, record keeping grew more slipshod, and the records of many court cases are voluminous but illegible. Moreover, a clerk would often scribble down a wealth of irrelevant minutiae but fail to record the essentials of the argument. Extracting pertinent information from records so carelessly kept is an extremely laborious task.

Territorial court records, written almost entirely in French, are usually legible. Yet they, too, present a difficulty: The meaning of key terms is often obscured in translation from KiKongo, the language spoken by the witnesses. Copies of some territorial (appeal) decisions are inserted in communal records, but the main source is the file of original records at territorial headquarters.

To refer to court records, I give first a place-name, then a case number and a year, and in some instances a volume number. The courts' numbering systems are not always consistent. The place-names used in citations are as follows:

Mbanza Manteke   Records of the court of the Commune des Bamboma and its predecessors.

     Matadi   Records of the court to which cases were appealed from Mbanza Manteke. In 1958 the court was moved to Songololo, and the records from that date onward are located there.

   Kasangulu   Records of the Kasangulu Communal Court.

     Pool   Records of the court of appeal for Kasangulu Territory, located at territorial headquarters in Kasangulu.

Also in manuscript form is the correspondence of Henry Richards, covering the period 1884–1919. These manuscripts are in the possession of the American Foreign Baptist Missionary Society, Valley Forge, Pennsylvania.

GOVERNMENT PUBLICATIONS AND PERIODICALS

The publications of the Assemblée Provinciale of Kongo Central used in this study are the "Bulletin Officiel" and the "Comptes Rendues Analytiques," both in mimeograph form.

Four journals, published irregularly in the years just before and after independence, were useful to me. Most of the articles are in KiKongo, but some are written in French. They are:

Kongo dia Ngunga. Abako newspaper. Kinshasa: 1954–1962.

Kongo dia Ntotila. Kinshasa: 1960–1962.

Kongo dia Wene. Kinshasa. First issue dated 19 January 1961.

Kongo Dieto. Kinshasa.

I have also consulted the *Etudes Congolaises*, published at Kinshasa by the Institut National d'Etudes Politiques, and *"Ngonge:* Carnets d'Histoire et de Littérature Kongo," ed. Paul Raymaekers et al., published irregularly in mimeograph form at Kinshasa.

BOOKS AND ARTICLES

Andersson, E.
   1958 *Messianic Popular Movements in the Lower Congo.* Studia Ethnographica Upsaliensia, XIV. Uppsala.
Bentley, W. Holman
   1887 *Dictionary and Grammar of the Kongo Language.* London: Baptist Missionary Society.
   1900 *Pioneering on the Congo.* London: Religious Tract Society. 2 vols.
Bittremieux, Léo
   1920 "Mayombsche Reisboek," *Congo 1920,* II (2):247–259.
   1922–1927 *Mayombsche Idioticon.* Ghent: Erasmus.

1923 "Van een ouden blinden hoofdman," *Congo 1923*, II(4):531–552.

1924 "De geschiedenis van Kangu," *Congo 1924*, I (1):71–79.

1934 *Mayombsche Namen*. Louvain.

1936 *La Société Secrète des Bakhimba au Mayombe*. Mémoires, Vol. V. Brussels: IRCB.

Boelaert, E.

1957 "Les Trois Fictions du droit foncier congolais," *Zaïre*, XI (4):399–427.

Bohannan, L.

1949 "Dahomean Marriage," *Africa*, XIX (3):273–287.

1952 "A Genealogical Charter," *Africa*, XXII (4):301–315.

Bohannan, Paul

1955 "Some Principles of Exchange and Investment among the Tiv," *American Anthropologist*, LVII:60–70.

1963 " 'Land,' 'Tenure' and Land-Tenure." In *African Agrarian Systems*, ed. D. Biebuyck. London: Oxford University Press.

Brásio, Antonio Duarte

1961 *D. António Barroso, Missionário, Cientista, Missiólogo*. Lisbon: Centro de Estudos Históricos Ultramarinos.

Claridge, G. Cyril

1922 *Wild Bush Tribes of Tropical Africa*. London: Seeley Service.

CRISP

1960 *Congo 1959: Documents belges et africains*. 2d ed. Brussels: CRISP. 1962.

1961 *Congo 1960*. Brussels: CRISP. 2 vols.

1962 *Abako 1950–1960: Documents*. Brussels: CRISP.

Cuvelier, J.

1930–31 "Traditions congolaises," *Congo 1930*, I(4):469–487; *Congo 1931*, II(2):193–208.

1934 *Nkutama a mvila za makanda*. Imprimerie de la Mission Catholique de Tumba.

1946 *L'Ancien Royaume de Congo*. Bruges: Desclée de Brouwer.

De Bouveignes, O., and J. Cuvelier

1951 *Jérôme de Montesarchio*. Namur: Grands Lacs.

Decapmaker, J.

1943 "Le Lévirat chez les Kongo," *Aequatoria*, VI(2):54–55.

1949 "La Famille dans le matriarcat," *Aequatoria*, XII(9):95–102.

1951 "Les Funérailles chez les Bakongo," *Aequatoria*, XIV(3):81–84; (4):125–128.

1959 "Le Matriarcat en face de l'évolution," *Aequatoria*, XXII(3):98–100.

De Cleene, N.

1935 "Les Chefs indigènes au Mayombe," *Africa*, VIII(1):63–75.

1936 "L'Elément religieux dans l'organisation sociale des Bayombe," *Congo 1936*, I(5):706–711.

1937a "La famille dans l'organisation sociale du Mayombe," *Africa*, X(1):1–15.

1937*b* "La Structure de la société Yombe et un aspect de notre politique indigène, *Bulletin*, IRCB, VIII(1):44–51.

1946 *Le clan matrilinéal dans la société indigène, hier, aujourd'hui, demain.* Mémoires, Vol. XIV. Brussels: IRCB.

De Hemptinne, J.

1928 "La Politique indigène du gouvernement belge," *Congo* 1928, II:1–16.

De Munck, J.

1956 *Kinkulu kia nsi eto.* Imprimerie de la Mission Catholique de Tumba.

Dennett, R.

1887 *Seven Years among the Fjort.* London: Sampson Low.

1898 *Notes on the Folklore of the Fjort.* London: The Folklore Society.

1905 "Bavili Notes," *Folk-Lore* (London), XVI:371–406.

1906 *At the Back of the Black Man's Mind.* London: Macmillan.

De Roeck, H.

1958 "Classification des Clans de la Region de Matadi." Mimeo.

De Rouvre, Charles

1880 "La Guinée méridionale indépendante, Congo, Kakongo, N'Goyo, Loango, 1870–1877," *Bulletin de la Société de Géographie* (Paris), 6th ser., XX:289–327, 401–434.

De Smet, R. E.

1966 *Cartes de la densité et de la localisation de la population de l'ancienne province de Léopoldville (République démocratique du Congo).* Brussels: CEMUBAC.

De Sousberghe, L.

1963 "Les Pende: Aspects des structures sociales et politiques." *Miscellanea Ethnographica.* Annales, Sciences humaines, no. 46. Tervuren: Musée Royal de l'Afrique Centrale.

1965 "Cousins croisés et descendants: Les systèmes du Ruanda et du Burundi comparés à ceux du Bas-Congo," *Africa*, XXXV(4):396–421.

1966 "L'Immutabilité des relations de parenté par alliance dans les sociétés matrilinéaires du Congo," *Bulletin des Séances*, ARSOM, no. 3, pp. 377–397.

1967*a* "Enfance hors-lignage et solidarité clanique dans les sociétés congolaises," *Africa-Tervuren*, XIII(1):10–14.

1967*b* "Le mariage chez les Bakongo d'après leurs proverbes," *Paideuma*, XIII:190–197.

Devroey, E., and R. Vanderlinden

1938 *Le Bas-Congo: Artère Vitale de Notre Colonie.* Brussels: Goemaere.

D'Hanis

1890 "Organisation politique, civile et pénale de la tribu des Mousseronghes," *Bulletin de la Société Royale Belge de Géographie*, XIV:137–153.

Domont, J. M.

1957 *La Prise de conscience de l'individu au milieu rural Kongo.* Mémoires, section des sciences politiques, XIII, 1. Brussels: ARSC.

Douglas, Mary

1955 "Social and Religious Symbolism of the Lele of the Kasai," *Zaïre*, IX(4):385–402.

1963 *The Lele of the Kasai*. London: Oxford University Press.

Doutreloux, Albert

1959 "Note sur le domaine foncier au Mayumbe," *Zaïre*, XIII(5):499–508.

1965 "Prophétisme et culture." In *African Systems of Thought*, ed. M. Fortes and G. Dieterlen. London: Oxford University Press.

1967 *L'Ombre des Fétiches: Société et Culture Yombe*. Publications de l'Université Lovanium de Léopoldville. Louvain: Editions Nauwelaerts.

Dufour, Jean P.

1963 "Quelques Aspects juridiques du problème foncier au Congo." In *African Agrarian Systems*, ed. D. Biebuyck. London: Oxford University Press.

Durkheim, Emile

1961 *The Elementary Forms of the Religious Life*. Trans. J. W. Swain. New York: Collier.

Fortes, Meyer

1949 "Time and Social Structure: An Ashanti Case Study." In *Social Structure: Studies Presented to A. R. Radcliffe-Brown*, ed. M. Fortes. Oxford: Clarendon Press.

1967 "Totem and Taboo." In *Proceedings of the Royal Anthropological Institute* (1966). London: Royal Anthropological Institute.

Franck, Louis

1921 "La Politique indigène, le service territorial et les chefferies," *Congo* 1921, I(2):189–201.

Fukiau, André

1967 "La Mommification Kongo." Kivunda: Académie Congolaise.* Mimeo, in KiKongo.

Gelders, V.

1943 *Le Clan dans la Société Indigène*. Mémoires, Vol. XI. Brussels: IRCB.

Goodenough, Ward H.

1951 *Property, Kin, and Community on Truk*. Yale University Publications in Anthropology, no. 46.

Gray, Robert F.

1953 "Positional Succession among the Wambugwe," *Africa*, XXIII(3):233–243.

Guinness, Mrs. H. M.

1882(?) *The First Christian Mission on the Congo*. London: Hodder & Stoughton.

Hocart, A. M.

1952 "Kinship Systems." In *The Life-Giving Myth*. London: Methuen.

*The mimeographed publications of L'Académie Congolaise are obtainable from André Fukiau. See note by J. M. Janzen in *Africa*, XXXVII, no. 7 (Jan. 1967), p. 92.

Hulstaert, G.
1938 *Le Mariage des Nkundo*. Mémoires, Vol. VIII. Brussels: IRCB.
Jadin, L.
1957 "Relation sur le royaume du Congo du P. Raimondo da Dicomano, missionaire de 1791–1795." *Bulletin des Séances*, ARSC, XXVII(2): 307–337.
Janzen, John M.
1967 "A Lower Congo Example of the Regional Council as a Micropolity." Paper read at tenth annual meeting of African Studies Association, New York, November 1967.
Johnston, H. H.
1884 *The River Congo*. London.
Kalenda, M.
1958 "Considérations sur les droits du père de famille en régime matri-linéal," *Bulletin des Juridictions Indigènes et du Droit Coutumier Congolais* (Elisabethville), XXVI(12):359–362.
Kamuna, Joseph
1966 "Sadila Nsi." Kivunda: Académie Congolaise. Mimeo.
Kanza, T. R.
1968 "The Problems of the Congo," *African Affairs*, LXVII(266):55–62.
Kestergat, Jean
1961 *André Ryckmans*. Brussels: Charles Dessart.
Kroeber, A. L.
1948 *Anthropology*. New York: Harcourt, Brace.
Laman, Karl E.
1936 *Dictionnaire Kongo-Français*. Brussels: IRCB.
1953 *The Kongo I*. Studia Ethnographica Upsaliensia, IV. Uppsala.
1957 *The Kongo II*. Studia Ethnographica Upsaliensia, VIII. Uppsala.
1962 *The Kongo III*. Studia Ethnographica Upsaliensia, XII. Uppsala.
Lemarchand, René
1961 "The Bases of Nationalism among the BaKongo," *Africa*, XXXI(4): 344–354.
Lévi-Strauss, Claude
1958 *Anthropologie Structurale*. Paris: Plon.
M., G.
1963 "Le Problème du statut du district de Léopoldville," *Etudes Congo-laises*, IV(5):25–31.
Mabie, Catharine L.
1952 *Congo Cameos*. Philadelphia: Judson.
MacGaffey, Wyatt
1966a "Field Research in Kongo Central," *Cah. Econ. et Soc.*, IV(2):211–216.
1966b "Autobiography of a Prophet," *Cah. Econ. et Soc.*, IV(2):231–235.
1966c "Concepts of Race in the Historiography of Northeast Africa," *Journal of African History*, VII(1):1–17.
1968 "Kongo and the King of the Americans," *Journal of Modern African Studies*, VI(2):171–181.

1969 "The Beloved City: Commentary on a Kimbanguist Text," *Journal of Religion in Africa*, II(2):129–147.

Malengreau, Guy

1939 "Le Régime foncier dans la société indigène: Le Bas-Congo," *Congo* 1939, II(1):1–46.

1947 *Les Droits fonciers coutumiers chez les indigènes du Congo belge.* Mémoires, Vol. XV. Brussels: IRCB.

Malinowski, B.

1935 *Coral Gardens and Their Magic.* London: Allen and Unwin. 2 vols.

Manker, E.

1932 "Niombo: Die Totenbestattung der Babwende," *Zeitschrift für Ethnologie*, LXIV(2):159–172.

Marchal, Gilles

1947 "Origem de raça Solongo (Zaïre) segundo a lenda," *Portugal em Africa*, IV(20):78–86.

Mayer, A.

1966 "The Significance of Quasi-Groups in the Study of Complex Societies." In *The Social Anthropology of Complex Societies.* London: Tavistock.

Mayer, Iona

1965 *The Nature of Kinship Relations.* Rhodes-Livingstone Papers, 37. Manchester: Manchester University Press.

Meillassoux, C.

1960 "Essai d'interpretation du phénomène économique dans les sociétés traditionelles d'auto-subsistance," *Cahiers d'Etudes Africaines*, I(4): 38–67.

Mertens, J.

1942 *Les Chefs couronnés chez les BaKongo orientaux.* Mémoires. Vol. XI, fasc. 1. Brussels: IRCB.

1944–1952 "La Juridiction indigène chez les Bakongo orientaux," *Kongo-Overzee*, Vols. X–XVIII *passim*. Final installment, in XVIII (1952), 4, has an index to the whole series.

Mertens, Victor

1948 "Le Mariage chez les Bambata (Bakongo) et ses implications sociales," *Zaïre*, II(10):1099–1126.

Milheiros, Mario

1954 "Registro etnográfico e social sobre a tribo dos Sòlongos," *Mensario Administrativo*, no. 83–84, pp. 3–89; no. 85–86, pp. 3–51.

Mitchell, J. G.

1966 "Theoretical Orientations in African Urban Studies." In *The Social Anthropology of Complex Societies.* London: Tavistock.

Monnier, Laurent

1964 "Province du Kongo Central." In *Collection d'Etudes Politiques*, no. 2. Léopoldville: IRES.

1965 "Le Kongo Central et la seconde législature," *Etudes Congolaises*, VIII(6):16–56.

Munzele, Jacob
   1966 "Bakulu Beto ye Diela Diau." Kivunda: Académie Congolaise. Mimeo.
Murdock, G. P.
   1949 *Social Structure*. New York: Macmillan.
Nauvelaert, N.
   1938 "Note sur la société Yombe," *Congo* 1938, I(4):405–415.
Ndongala, E.
   1966 "Mutations structurelles de l'économie traditionelle dans le Bas-Congo sous l'impact de la colonisation et de la décolonisation," *Cah. Econ. et Soc.*, IV(1):3–32.
Ngoma, Ferdinand
   1963 "L'Initiation Ba-Kongo et sa Signification." Thèse préparée a l'Ecole Pratique des Hautes Etudes (VI Sect.), Sorbonne.
Paine, Robert
   1967 "What Is Gossip About? An Alternative Hypothesis," *Man*, n.s., II(2):278–285.
Pauwels, Johan M.
   1965 "La Garde d'enfants de divorces en coutume Solongo: Un aspect d'une coutume Kongo patrilinéaire," *Revue Juridique du Congo*, XLI(1):1–8.
Peigneux, F.-J.-A.
   1934 "Le Droit coutumier du groupe Gombe-Matadi," *Bulletin des Juridictions Indigènes et du Droit Coutumier*, I(6):111–116, 132–145.
Phillips, R. C.
   1888 "The Lower Congo: A Sociological Study," *Journal of the Anthropological Institute*, XVII(17):214–237.
Powdermaker, Hortense
   1967 *Stranger and Friend: The Way of an Anthropologist*. New York: W. W. Norton.
Powell, H. A.
   1960 "Competitive Leadership in Trobriand Political Organisation," *Journal of the Royal Anthropological Institute*, XC(1):118–145.
Radcliffe-Brown, A. R.
   1950 "Introduction." In *African Systems of Kinship and Marriage*, ed. A. R. Radcliffe-Brown and Daryll Forde. London: Oxford University Press.
Raymaekers, Paul
   1959 "L'Eglise de Jésus-Christ sur la Terre par le prophète Simon Kimbangu: Contribution a l'étude des mouvements messianiques dans le Bas-Congo," *Zaïre*, XIII(7):677–756.
   1960 "Matériaux pour une étude sociologique de la jeunesse africaine du milieu extra-coutumier de Léopoldville." Kinshasa: IRES. Mimeo.
Richards, A. I.
   1950 "Some Types of Family Structure amongst the Central Bantu." In *African Systems of Kinship and Marriage*, ed. A. R. Radcliffe-Brown and Daryll Forde. London: Oxford University Press.

Sahlins, M. D.

1963 "Poor Man, Rich Man, Big-Man, Chief: Political Types in Melanesia and Polynesia," *Comparative Studies in Society and History*, V (3): 285–303.

Slade, Ruth

1962 *King Leopold's Congo*. London: Oxford University Press.

Smith, M. G.

1956 "On Segmentary Lineage Systems," *Journal of the Royal Anthropological Institute*, LXXXVI(2):39–80.

1960 *Government in Zazzau, 1800–1950*. London: Oxford University Press.

1966 "A Structural Approach to Comparative Politics." In *Varieties of Political Theory*, ed. David Easton. Englewood Cliffs, N.J.: Prentice-Hall.

Sohier, Antoine

1943 *Le Mariage en droit coutumier congolais*. Mémoires, Vol. XI. Brussels: IRCB.

1944 "Note sur la notion de 'coutume' et de 'droit coutumier congolais,' " *Bulletin des Séances*, IRCB, XV(1):34–41.

1954 *Traité elémentaire de droit coutumier du Congo belge*. 2d ed. Brussels: F. Larcier.

Sohier, Jean

1966 "Du Dynamisme léopoldien à l'immobilisme belge," *Problèmes Sociaux Congolais*, no. 73, pp. 41–71.

Soret, Marcel

1959 *Les Kongo nord-occidentaux*. Paris: Institut International Africain.

1963 "La Propriété foncière chez les Kongo du Nord-Ouest." In *African Agrarian Systems*, ed. D. Biebuyck. London: Oxford University Press.

Stanley, H. M.

1879 *Through the Dark Continent*. New York: Harper. 2 vols.

1885 *The Congo and the Founding of Its Free State*. London: Sampson Low. 2 vols.

Swartz, Marc J.

1960 "Situational Determinants of Kinship Terminology," *Southwestern Journal of Anthropology*, XVI(4):393–397.

Torday, Emil

1925 *Causeries congolaises*. Brussels: Dewit.

Troesch, Joseph

1953 "Historia politica de Maiombe," *Portugal em Africa*, no. 55, pp. 18–25; no. 57, pp. 187–197.

Tshinkela, Germain

1965 *Le Miroir Mukongo*. Léopoldville: Procure des Frères.

Van der Kerken, Georges

1919 *Les Sociétés bantoues du Congo belge et les problèmes de la politique indigène*. Brussels: Bruylant.

Van de Velde, Liévin

1886 "La Région du Bas-Congo et du Kwilou-Niadi: Usages et coutumes des indigènes," *Bulletin de la Société Royale Belge de Géographie*, 10th year, pp. 347–412.

Van Reeth, E. P.
1935 *De Rol van den Moederlijken Oom in de Inlandsche Familie*. Mémoires, Vol. V. Brussels: IRCB.

Van Roy, H., and J. Daeleman
1963 *Proverbes Kongo*. Tervuren: Musée Royale de l'Afrique Centrale.

Vansina, Jan
1964 "Noms personnels et structure sociale chez les Tyo (Teke)," *Bulletin des Séances*, ARSOM, no. 4, pp. 794–804.
1966 *Kingdoms of the Savanna*. Madison: University of Wisconsin Press.

Van Wing, J.
1959 *Etudes Bakongo*. 2d ed. Brussels: Desclée de Brouwer. 1st ed., 1922 and 1938.

Ward, Herbert
1895 "Ethnographical Notes Relative to the Congo Tribes," *Journal of the Royal Anthropological Institute*, XXIV:293–599.

Weeks, John H.
1908 "Notes on Some Customs of the Lower Congo People," *Folklore*, XIX(4):409–437.
1914 *Among the Primitive Bakongo*. London: Seeley Service.

INDEX

Abako (political party), 84n, 283, 290, 295, 298, 300; symbols of, 257 and n; local leaders of, 277

Affinity, 31, 50, 54, 81, 84, 236n; egalitarian significance of, 34, 99; and divorce, 138–139

American Baptist Foreign Missionary Society, 1, 5, 10n, 12

Ancestors, 202, 293; cult of, 157–158, 235–236

Andersson, E., 250, 260

Angolans, 1, 8 and n, 115, 164, 173, 289, 302; sponsors of, 221–222

Bangu region, 12, 25

Baptist Missionary Society, 12, 255

Bentley, W. Holman, 29, 240, 248

Bikadyo, Na, 57, 59, 203, 244–245, 237n

bisi ("inhabitants or members of"), 10n; *Manianga*, viii; *Manteke*, 10, 13; *Kongo*, 11n; *Luozi*, 13

Bittremieux L., 11 and n, 17, 18n, 25, 112, 204, 216, 218, 247, 234n, 247n, 259; on KiNkimba, 248–250

Bracelets, 33, 201, 231; names of, 52

Cadet. See *nleeke*

Cão, Diogo, 3, 206

Charms, 226, 230, 237, 252; ingredients for, 224, 246

Chiefdoms, 6–7, 253, 265, 266, 270–273

Chiefs, the four, 118–147 *passim*, 150, 196, 222, 304

Chiefs and chiefship, ix, 50–51, 53, 153, 191, 193, 211–257 *passim*; in government, 6–7, 71–72, 252, 277, 289–291, 296; insignia of, 19, 31, 191, 197, 244–248, 256–257, 335–336; authoritarian ideal of, 207, 259–264, 270–271, 297–298; decrees concerning, 253–254; appointment of, 263–273

Children and Grandchildren, 28, 31, 32, 77, 148–208 *passim*; political role of, 63, 70, 92, 236, 266

Clans, 36–55 *passim*, 304; tradition and, 17–18, 34; categorical function of, 32, 164–165, 172; exogamy and, 121–122; governmental function of, 240, 244; in colonial science, 260–262; and land tenure, 293

Clan sections, 17–18, 244; and land tenure, 55, 212; and exogamy, 70; structure of, 193, 197, 211

Clients and clientage, 34, 47 and n, 49, 294, 302; entry into, 221–222, 290–291

Committees, governing, 70, 143; at funerals, 150; descent groups and, 172, 213; in litigation, 196; and chiefship, 230, 235–240; and markets, 243

Commune of the BaMboma, 1, 6, 227, 263, 300; origin and characteristics of, 7–8; history of, 276–278; operation of, 278–284

Congo River, 3; in tradition, 19, 23n

Corporations: and kinship terminology, 92–93; in colonial science, 260–262; actor's view of, 304. *See also* Descent groups; *fulu*

Court, communal, 7; and land tenure, 47, 196–197; testimony in, 80–81; and paternity, 124; and divorce, 134–136; records of, 205, 307; and village headman, 274; operation of, 284–287

Court, territorial, 7, 208; appeals to, 197, 206, 285; records of, 307

Cultivation, 173–179

Culture-historical school, 260

Custom, viii, 263, 294; and etiquette, 108–110; and social structure, 117, 207, 296; European idea of, 184, 207, 254, 255, 266, 276; and chiefship, 191, 273, 297; in modern politics, 256–257, 287–291, 298; and village headman, 273–276; in education, 294, 299